Parties, Politics, and
Public Policy in America

Parties, Politics, and Public Policy in America
Eighth Edition

William J. Keefe
University of Pittsburgh

A Division of Congressional Quarterly Inc.

Printed in the United States of America

Cover: Paula Anderson
Book design: G & S Typesetters, Inc.

Library of Congress Cataloging-in-Publication Data

Keefe, William J.
    Parties, politics, and public policy in America / William J.
Keefe. — 8th ed.
      p. cm.
    Includes bibliographical references and index.
    ISBN 1-56802-352-9
    1. Political parties—United States. I. Title.
JK2265.K44 1997   97-37702
324.273—dc21

For Martha, Kathy, Nancy, Jodi, and John

Table of Contents

Chapter Seven
The American Party System:
Problems and Perspectives   262

Index

Tables and Figures

Tables

Figures

Preface

The American party system is not in the best of health. Apart from a scattering of politicians and academicians, few people take political parties seriously. Voters generally ignore the parties, politicians often dismiss them, activists typically bypass them, and the media usually slight them. Almost everyone, it seems, distrusts them—if they think about them at all. The weakness of the parties shows up in both the government and the electorate. Key outsiders—interest groups, political action committees, the media, campaign management firms, political consultants, and direct-mail fund raisers—often play a more important role in campaigns than do parties. The blunt truth is that party organizations often find themselves in the role of bystander. As candidates struggle to win office, they use party money and intelligence, if available, and advertise the party label, if appropriate, but count on victory through use of techniques validated in mass merchandising. In major races sound bites count for more than organization, endorsements, and face-to-face electioneering. Even the most ingenuous candidates know that "the image" is more important than "the party." In this highly individualistic, entrepreneurial system of electing public officials, sometimes the decisive fact about candidates is whether they are incumbents, not whether they are Democrats or Republicans.

The weakness of the parties is pronounced in the presidential election process. Ironically, reforms have contributed to this condition. The reforms introduced in the presidential nominating process have diminished the independent role of the national convention. All recent experience shows that the convention meets chiefly to ratify the results of the preconvention struggles in primary and caucus-convention states. Convention proceedings are dominated by candidate organizations, not state party delegations. Party spending in presidential campaigns has been subordinated to public financing, as provided by the Federal Election Campaign Act. In the process of nominating presidential candidates in the new participatory system, the preferences of party leaders count for less and less, the preferences of amateur activists and assorted enthusiasts for more and more. The presidential campaign itself has become a major media event. In shaping presidential elections, the media are the closest thing the nation has to parties. For candidates and public officials alike, more often than not, it is the party label that matters, not the party mission.

In the electorate, where the parties are in serious trouble, independence and split-ticket voting flourish and strong partisanship and straight-ticket voting decline. If party depended mainly on widespread popular support, the days would be numbered for both major parties. But happily for party advocates, including myself, this is not the case. Inertia, the lack of alternatives, traditional infrastructure, and public law support and protect the two-party system about as well as possible. The major parties are thus not about to fade away.

Here and there one finds some evidence of party vitality. Party cohesiveness in the U.S. House of Representatives is somewhat greater today than a decade or two ago. And some party leaders now exhibit a greater concern with party-building activities designed to strengthen their organizations. Probably of most importance, the national parties have increased their capacity to raise campaign funds, particularly soft money, thus permitting them to offer better services to candidates and state party organizations. Nonetheless, the long-run impact of these changes on the party role in recruitment, nominations, campaigns, voter mobilization, and governing remains to be seen. It stretches the facts to suggest that the parties currently are doing well, playing a dominant role in any of these activities. Hanging on is more like it, particularly in the electorate's domain.

The parties have suffered from prolonged neglect by the public and from overattention by the reformers. Scholars, meanwhile, continue to be intrigued by them. Numerous books, monographs, and articles have been published on American parties in recent years. I have drawn extensively on this interesting literature. The scholarship tracks that I followed are amply reflected in the notes.

The American party system and its environment are not static. Many changes have taken place in recent years, and this eighth edition examines these changes carefully. Among the topics that receive new or expanded analysis are the following: changing party electoral alignments, policy and ideological differences between the parties, party performance in Congress, presidential nominating politics, voter participation and nonvoting, change and continuity in voting behavior, campaign finance scandals and campaign finance legislation, soft money excesses, political action committees, public-party linkages, and public skepticism concerning government and politics.

The American party system may need to be rescued from its detractors, but that is not the main purpose of this book. Nor is the purpose to sketch a blueprint showing where the best opportunities lie for making further changes. The central purpose is one of exegesis: to bring into focus the major features of the parties, to account for party form and functions, and to examine and interpret the parties' present condition.

For their help on all of the editions of this book, I want to thank good friends Holbert N. Carroll and Morris S. Ogul of the University of Pittsburgh. Neither one realizes how much he has taught me over the years. I also owe a debt to a number of other persons who provided ideas, data, and thoughtful critiques on one or more editions: Herbert E. Alexander, Paul A. Beck, Keith Burris, Edward F. Cooke, Stephen Craig, William J. Crotty, Robert L. Donaldson, David Fitz, John Havick, Brooke Harlow, Jon Hurwitz, Charles O. Jones, Jodi Keefe-McCurdy, Dan McCurdy, David C. Kozak, Paul Lopatto, Thomas E. Mann, Leslie McAneny, Roger McGill, Colleen McGuiness, James M. Malloy, Michael Margolis, Russell Moses, Scott Moxley, David M. Olson, Raymond E. Owen, Guy Peters, Josie Raleigh, Bert A. Rockman, Phil Sidel, Roopa Singh, Robert S. Walters, Myra E. Weinberg, Donna Woodward, and Sidney Wise. Paul Mullen, Andrew Konitzer, David Jones, and Stephanie Muraca provided indispensable research assistance for this eighth edition. I am indebted to Eugene J. Gabler of Congressional Quarterly and Sharon Snyder of the Federal Election Commission for their valuable assistance in assembling data for me. Everyone mentioned in this paragraph should know how much I appreciate their advice and friendship. Nonetheless, they are not perfect. Despite their assistance and good intentions, errors of fact and interpretation may have crept into a page here and there. If this turns out to be the case, I hope they will step forward immediately and acknowledge their culpability. I also thank David R. Tarr and Brenda Carter of CQ for their support and encouragement. Debbie Hardin provided excellent editorial assistance.

Finally, I want to acknowledge the assistance of my wife, Martha, who helped in so many ways to prepare this edition as well as the earlier ones.

Chapter One

Political Parties and
the Political System

The American political party system is not an insoluble puzzle. But it does have more than its share of mysteries. The main one, arguably, is how it has survived for so long or, perhaps, how it survived at all, in a difficult and complicated environment. The broad explanation, arguably as well, is that the party system survives because parties are an inevitable outgrowth of civil society ("factions . . . sown in the nature of man," thought James Madison[1]); because parties perform functions important to democratic polities ("democracy is unthinkable save in terms of parties," wrote E. E. Schattschneider[2]); and because the American public has never held particularly high expectations of parties or made particularly rigorous demands on them—thus in truth their survival has not been contingent on performance.

A logical starting point for understanding the political party system, an enduring institution of American society, is to recognize that parties are less what they make of themselves than what their environment makes of them.[3] Put another way, in language social scientists sometimes invoke, parties typically are the dependent variable. That is, to a marked extent the party owes its character and form to the impact of four external elements: the legal–political system, the election system, the political culture, and the heterogeneous quality of American life. Singly and in combination, these elements contribute in significant and indelible ways to the organizational characteristics of the parties, to the manner in which they carry on their activities, to their internal discipline, to the behavior of both their elite and rank-and-file members, and to their capacity to control the political system and to perform as policy-making agencies.

The Parties and Their Environment

The Legal–Political System

The Constitution of the United States was written by men who were apprehensive of the power of popular majorities and who had scant sympathy for the existence of party. Their basic intent, evident in the broad thrust of the Constitution and in line after line of its text, was to establish a government that could not easily be brought under the control of any one element, whatever its size, that might be present in the country. The underlying theory of the Founders was both simple and pervasive: power was to check power, and the ambitions of some men were to check the ambitions of other men.* The two main features in this design were federalism and the separation of powers—the first to distribute power among different levels of government; the second to distribute power among the legislative, executive, and judicial branches. Division of the legislature into two houses, with their memberships elected for different terms and by differing methods, was thought to reduce further the risk that a single faction (or party) might gain ascendancy. Schattschneider developed the argument in this way:

> The theory of the Constitution, inherited from the time of the Glorious Revolution in England, was legalistic and preparty in its assumptions. Great reliance was placed in a system of separation of powers, a legalistic concept of government incompatible with a satisfactory system of party government. No place was made for the parties in the system, party government was not clearly foreseen or well understood, government by parties was thought to be impossible or impracticable and was feared and regarded as something to be avoided. . . . The Convention at Philadelphia produced a constitution with a dual attitude: it was proparty in one sense and antiparty in another. The authors of the Constitution refused to suppress the parties by destroying the fundamental liberties in which parties originate. They or their immediate successors accepted amendments that guaranteed civil rights and thus established a system of party tolerance, *i.e.*, the right to agitate and to organize. This is the proparty aspect of the system. On the other hand, the authors of the Constitution set up an elaborate division and balance of powers within an intricate governmental structure designed to make parties ineffective. It was hoped that the parties would lose and exhaust themselves in futile attempts to fight their way through the labyrinthine framework of the government, much as an attacking army is

---

*In addition to using terms such as "candidate," "legislator," "member," and "representative" to apply to men and women in politics, I have referred to them occasionally in the masculine gender—"he," "him," "his." This is simply a matter of style. These pronouns are employed generically.

expected to spend itself against the defensive works of a fortress. This is the antiparty part of the constitutional scheme. To quote Madison, the "great object" of the Constitution was "to preserve the public good and private rights against the danger of such a faction [party] and at the same time to preserve the spirit and form of popular government."[4]

Federalism is inimical to the development of centralized parties. In the United States, federalism guarantees that not only will there be fifty state governmental systems but also fifty state party systems. No two states are exactly alike. No two state party systems are exactly alike. The ideology of one state party may be sharply different from that of another. Contrast, for example, the state Democratic party of Mississippi with its counterpart in New York or the state Republican party of Utah with its counterpart in Connecticut.[5] And within each state all manner of local party organizations exist, sometimes functioning in harmony with state and national party elements and sometimes not. There are states (and localities) where the party organizations are active and well financed and those where they are not, those where factions compete persistently within a party and those where factional organization is nonexistent, those where ideology and issues are important and those where they are not, those where the parties seem to consist mainly of the personal followings of individual politicians and those where party leaders exercise significant influence.[6] Parties differ from state to state and from community to community, and the laws that govern their activities and shape their influence also differ. A great variety of state laws, for example, govern nominating procedures, ballot form, access to the ballot, campaign finance, and elections. On the whole, northeastern states are most likely to have statutes that foster stronger parties, whereas southern states tend to have statutes that weaken them.[7] Similarly, strong ("monopolistic") local party organizations have been more prominent and durable in the East than anywhere else.[8] The broad point is that the thrust of federalism is toward fragmentation and parochialism, permitting numerous forms of political organization to thrive and inhibiting the emergence of cohesive and disciplined national parties.

The Election System

The election system is another element in the environment of political parties. So closely linked are parties and elections that it is difficult to understand much about one without understanding a great deal about the other. Parties are in business to win elections. Election systems shape the way the parties compete for power and the success with which they do it. Several examples will help to illustrate this point.

A state's election calendar may have a substantial impact on party for-

What Is a Political Party?

"A political party is first of all an organized attempt to get power."

—E. E. Schattschneider

"[A party is] any group, however loosely organized, seeking to elect governmental office-holders under a given label."

—Leon Epstein

"Party is a body of men united, for promulgating by their joint endeavors the national interest, upon some particular principle in which they are all agreed."

—Edmund Burke

"A party isn't a fraternity. It isn't something that you join because you like the old school tie they wear. It is a gathering together of people who basically share the same political philosophy."

—Ronald Reagan

"We Democrats are all under one tent. In any other country we'd be five splinter parties."

—Thomas P. ("Tip") O'Neill, Jr.

"A party is not . . . a group of men who intend to promote public welfare 'upon some principle in which they are all agreed. . . .' A party is a group whose members propose to act in concert in the competitive struggle for political power."

—Joseph A. Schumpeter

SOURCES: E. E. Schattschneider, *Party Government* (New York: Holt, Rinehart and Winston, 1942), 37; Leon Epstein, *Political Parties in Western Democracies* (New York: Praeger, 1967), 9; Edmund Burke, *Works*, vol. I (London: G. Bell and Sons, 1897), 375; *Pittsburgh Post Gazette,* March 20, 1980, 9; *Washington Post,* June 17, 1975, 12; and Joseph A. Schumpeter, *Capitalism, Socialism and Democracy* (New York: Harper and Row, 1942), 283.

tunes. Many state constitutions establish election calendars that separate state elections from national elections—for example, gubernatorial from presidential elections. The singular effect of this arrangement is to insulate state politics from national politics. Similarly, the behavior of voters may also weaken linkages between these levels. Even in those states in which governors are elected at the same time as the president, the chances are better than three in ten that the party that carries the state in the presidential contest will lose at the gubernatorial level. (The outcomes in presidential-gubernatorial voting from 1964 to 1996 are indicated in Table 1-1.) What is more, the national tides that sweep one party into the presidency may be no more than ripples by the time a state election is held two years later. Although the Democratic party won presidential election after presidential election during the 1930s and 1940s, a great many governorships and state legislatures remained safely Republican. Recent Republican success in presidential elections (1968, 1972, 1980, 1984, 1988) was not accompanied by significant gains for the party at the state level. Throughout this period—from the 1960s to 1994—the Democratic party held many more governorships and legislative chambers than the Republican party. Party fortunes in the states were sharply reversed in 1994 when Republicans captured not only both houses of Congress but also a majority of governorships and state legislative chambers.

The use of staggered terms for executive and legislative offices diminishes the probability that one party will control both branches of government at any given time. When the governor is elected for four years and the lower house is elected for two years—the common pattern—chances are that the governor's party will lose legislative seats, and sometimes its majority, in the off-year election. The same is true for the president and Congress. Whatever the virtues of staggered terms and off-year elections, they increase the likelihood of divided control of government.

The use of single-member districts with plurality elections for the election of legislators carries important ramifications for the parties. When an election is held within a single-member district, only one party can win; the winning candidate need receive only one more vote than the second-place candidate, and all votes for candidates other than the victor are lost. Although the single-member district system discriminates against the second-place party in each district, its principal impact is virtually to rule out the possibility that a minor party can win legislative representation. Indeed, only a handful of minor party candidates have ever held seats either in Congress or in the state legislatures. The device of single-member districts with plurality elections has long been a major bulwark of the two-party system.[9]

Single-member districts distort the relationship between the overall vote for legislative candidates within a state and the number of seats won by each party. The discrepancy may be sizable. The majority party in the state legislature nearly always profits from its ingenuity in drawing district lines. Gerrymandering, in other words, can be effective. Consider the 1992 congressional elections in Texas, under a district map fashioned by Democratic

TABLE 1-1   Split Outcomes in Presidential–Gubernatorial Voting:
            States Carried by Presidential Candidate of One Major Party
            and by Gubernatorial Candidate of Other Major Party:
            1964 to 1996

Year	Gubernatorial elections	Split outcomes	Percentage
1964	25	9	36
1968	21	8	38
1972	18	10	56
1976	14	5	36
1980	13	4	31
1984	13	5	38
1988	12	4	33
1992	12	4	33
1996	11	3	27

SOURCE: Various issues of *Congressional Quarterly Weekly Report.*

legislators. Although Republican House candidates received 48 percent of
the statewide vote, they won a mere 30 percent of the seats (nine out of
thirty).[10] Nevertheless, extreme partisan gerrymandering may be on the way
out. In 1986 the Supreme Court refused to invalidate an Indiana reapportionment act that favored the Republican party, stating that this particular
gerrymander of state legislative districts was not sufficiently offensive to warrant judicial intervention. At the same time, the Court warned that gerrymanders would be held unconstitutional "when the electoral system is
arranged in a manner that will consistently degrade a voter's or a group of
voters' influence on the political process as a whole."[11] Thus, solutions to
the problem of gerrymandering may be found in the courts. The lasting
impact of the Supreme Court's opinion should become apparent in the coming years. State legislators have been served notice that egregious gerrymandering, which entrenches the dominant party, will not pass constitutional muster.

Few, if any, electoral arrangements have had a greater impact on political parties than the direct primary, an innovation of the reform era of the
early twentieth century. The primary was introduced to combat the power of
party oligarchs who, insulated from popular influences, dominated the selection of nominees in state and local party conventions. The primary was
designed to democratize the nominating process by empowering the voters
to choose the party's nominees. Today, all states employ some form of pri-

mary system, although mixed convention-primary arrangements are used in a handful of states. In New York, for example, a candidate for a statewide office must receive at least 25 percent of the party convention vote to win a place on the primary ballot. Access to the primary ballot in Colorado requires a candidate to obtain 20 percent of the convention vote, whereas a 15 percent vote is required by the Massachusetts Democratic party.[12]

The convention method survives for the nomination of presidential and vice-presidential candidates. But the reality is that the preconvention struggle has become so decisive that it now governs the presidential selection process. The conventions simply ratify the voters' choices in caucus and primary states, and primaries have become particularly important. In 1996 about three fourths of the states, including all the largest ones, selected their delegates in presidential primaries.

The precise impact of the primary on the parties is difficult to establish. Its effects nevertheless appear to be substantial. First, by transferring the choice of nominees from party assemblies to the voters, the primary has increased the probability that candidates with different views on public policy will be brought together in the same party. Whatever their policy orientations, the victors in primary elections become the party's nominees, perhaps to the embarrassment of other party candidates.

Second, observers contend that primaries have contributed to a decline in party responsibility. Candidates who win office largely on their own and who have their own distinctive followings within local electorates have less reason to defer to party leaders or to adhere to traditional party positions. Their party membership is simply what they choose to make it. Third, the primary has contributed to numerous intraparty clashes; particularly bitter primary fights sometimes render the party incapable of generating a united campaign in the general election.[13] Finally, primaries apparently contribute to the consolidation of one-party politics. In an area where one party ordinarily dominates, its primaries tend to become the arena for political battles. The growth of the second party is inhibited not only by the lack of voter interest in its primaries but also by its inability to attract strong candidates to its colors. One-party domination reveals little about the party's organizational strength—indeed, one-party political systems likely will be characterized more by factionalism and internecine warfare than by unity, harmony, and ideological agreement.

"The cumulative effect of the direct primary," in the view of David B. Truman,

> is in the direction of organizational atrophy. The direct primary has been the most potent in a complex of forces pushing toward the disintegration of the party. . . . Even in those states using a closed primary and some reason-

ably restrictive form of enrollment to qualify as a voter in the primary, the thrust of the direct primary is disintegrative. In states that have embraced the full spirit of the direct primary by providing for an open system in one or another of its forms, where in effect anyone can wander in off the street to vote in the primary election of any party or where any organized interest group can colonize any party, the likelihood of any organization controlling nominations on a continuing basis is small.[14]

Such are the arguments developed against the primary. Of course, others can be made on its behalf.[15] In some jurisdictions, moreover, the dominant party organization is sufficiently strong that nonendorsed candidates have little or no chance of upsetting the organization's slate. Potential challengers may abandon their campaigns once the party leaders or the organization have made known their choices. Other candidacies may not materialize because the prospects for getting the nod from party leaders appear unpromising. Taking the country as a whole, nevertheless, the evidence is persuasive that the primary weakens party organization. Unable to control its nominations, a party forfeits some portion of its claim to be known as a party, some portion of its raison d'être. The loose, freewheeling character of American parties owes much to the advent, consolidation, and extension of the direct primary.

For an additional illustration of the relationship between the election system and the party system, consider the use and impact of nonpartisan elections. While searching for a formula to improve city government early in the twentieth century, reformers hit on the idea of the nonpartisan ballot— one in which party labels would not be present. The purpose of the plan was to free local government from the issues and divisiveness of national and state party politics and from the grip of local party bosses, which in turn, it was thought, would contribute to the effectiveness of local units. The nonpartisan ballot immediately gained favor and, once established, has been hard to dislodge; indeed, the plan has grown in popularity over the years. Today, substantially more than half of the American cities with populations of more than 5 thousand have nonpartisan elections.[16]

A large variety of political patterns are found in nonpartisan election systems. In some cities with nonpartisan ballots, the party presence is nonetheless quite visible, and there is no doubt which candidates are affiliated with which parties. Elections in these cities are partisan in everything but label. In other cities, local party organizations compete against slates of candidates sponsored by various nonparty groups. In still other cities, the local parties are virtually without power, having lost it to interest groups that recruit, sponsor, and finance candidates for office. Finally, in some nonpartisan elections neither party nor nonparty groups slate candidates, thus leaving individual candidates to their own devices. This type is particularly prevalent in small cities.

It is difficult to say how much nonpartisan elections have diminished the vitality of local party organizations. Here and there the answer is plainly, "very little if at all"; elsewhere, the impact appears to have been substantial. Whatever the case, where parties are shut out of the local election process, other kinds of politics enter—possibly centered on interest groups (including the press), celebrity or name politics (the latter favoring incumbents), or the idiosyncratic appeals of individual office seekers. Where party labels are absent, power is up for grabs. Whether the voters in any real sense can hold their representatives accountable, lacking the guidance that party labels furnish, is problematic at best.

Myths to the contrary, election systems are never designed to be neutral and never are neutral. Some election laws and constitutional provisions, such as the single-member district system or the rigorous requirements that minor parties must meet to gain a place on the ballot, provide general support for the two-party system. Of the nineteen minor party candidates for the presidency in 1996, for example, only the Reform and Libertarian parties managed to get their candidates on the ballots of all fifty states. The Reform party's candidate, Ross Perot, received 8 million popular votes (8.4 percent), and the other eighteen candidates shared 1.5 million votes.

Other laws and constitutional provisions make party government difficult and sometimes impossible. Included here are such system features as staggered terms of office, off-year elections, direct primaries, and nonpartisan ballots. The major parties are not always passive witnesses to existing electoral arrangements. At times they simply endure them because it is easier to live with conventional arrangements than to try to change them or because they recognize their benefits. At other times major parties seek new arrangements because the prospects for party advantage are sufficiently promising to warrant the effort. It is a good bet that no one understands or appreciates American election systems better than those party leaders responsible for defending party interests and winning elections.

The Political Culture and the Parties

A third important element in the environment of American political parties is the political culture—"the system of empirical beliefs, expressive symbols, and values which defines the situation in which political action takes place."[17] As commonly represented, the political culture of a nation is the amalgam of public attitudes toward the political system, its subunits, and the role of the individual within the system. It includes the knowledge and

TABLE 1-2   Trends in Popular Support in Wisconsin for the Party System: 1964 to 1984 (Shown as Percentage Supportive of Parties)

	1964	1966	1970	1972	1974	1976	1984
Diffuse support							
The parties do more to confuse the issues than to provide a clear choice on issues. (disagree)	21	19	21	28	24	19	29
The political parties more often than not create conflicts where none really exists. (disagree)	15	14	19	18	18	17	29
It would be better if, in all elections, we put no party labels on the ballot. (disagree)	67	56	44	42	38	36	45
Support for responsible party government							
A senator or representative should follow his or her party leaders even if he or she doesn't want to.	23					10	19
Contributor support							
People who work for political parties during political campaigns do our nation a great service.	68					53	77
The best rule in voting is to pick the best candidate, regardless of party label. (disagree)	10				5	6	6
Cleavage function support							
Democracy works best where competition between political parties is strong.	74				73	66	73

SOURCE: Jack Dennis, "Public Support for the Party System, 1964–1984" (Paper delivered at the annual meeting of the American Political Science Association, Washington, D.C., August 28–31, 1986), 19. Also see his earlier study, "Support for the Party System by the Mass Public," *American Political Science Review* 60 (September 1966): 600–615.

TABLE 1-3   Ticket-Splitting: Percentage
of Voters Casting Votes for
President of One Party and for
House Member of Other Party

Election year	Voters splitting ticket
1960	14%
1964	15
1968	18
1972	30
1976	25
1980	28
1984	26
1988	31
1992	27
1996	22

SOURCES: Center for Political Studies, University of Michigan; for 1988, ABC News/ *Washington Post,* as reported in *Public Opinion,* January–February 1989, 27; and, for 1992 and 1996, Voter News Service national exit polls.

beliefs people have about the political system, their feelings toward it, their identification with it, and their evaluations of it.

Although there is little comprehensive information on the public's political orientations toward the party system, scattered evidence indicates that large segments of the public do not evaluate parties or party functions in a favorable light. Studies of the Wisconsin electorate between 1964 and 1984 by Jack Dennis bear on this point.[18] The range of public attitudes on a series of propositions about American parties, including those that reveal diffuse or generalized support for the party system as a whole and for the norm of partisanship and those that reveal acceptance of the ideas or practices congruent with a system of responsible parties, is presented in Table 1-2.

The principal conclusion to be drawn from the data provided in the table is that the public is highly skeptical of the parties and their activities. In 1964, 90 percent of the Wisconsin electorate endorsed the idea that "the best rule in voting is to pick the best candidate, regardless of party label." By 1984, 94 percent accepted this idea. An overwhelming majority of the public believes that the parties do more to confuse issues than to clarify them and that they often provoke unnecessary conflict. Less than half of the electorate sees any merit to even having party labels on the ballot.

FIGURE 1-1   The Public's Perception of the Party Best Able to Handle the Most Important Problem Facing the Nation: 1945 to 1996

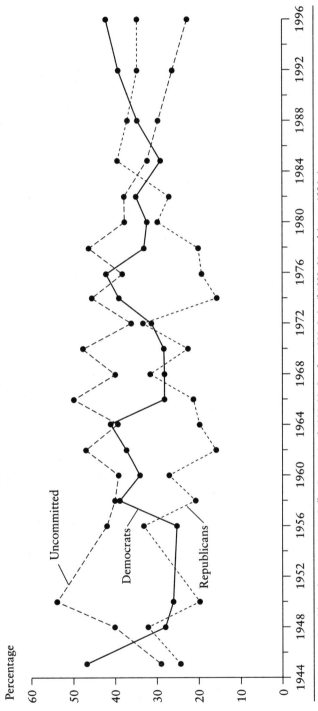

SOURCE: Developed from data appearing in *Gallup Report*, April 1985, 23; October 1988, 8; April 1992, 31; and August 1996, 4.

The Wisconsin data also reveal that support for cohesive and disciplined parties is extremely limited. Only about one out of five persons believes that a legislator "should follow his or her party leaders even if he or she doesn't want to." Overall, little in this profile of popular attitudes suggests that the public understands or accepts the tenets of a responsible party system.[19]

Whether the orientations of the Wisconsin voters to the parties are representative of popular attitudes is hard to say. But it seems likely that this is the case. In nationwide surveys of voter attitudes toward control of the presidency and Congress by the same party, typically less than half of the voters believe that the country is better off when the same party controls both branches.[20] The public prefers divided control of government.

Virtually all surveys that tap popular understanding and appreciation of the parties indicate that the public has little confidence in the parties. A nationwide survey by the *Washington Post* in 1992, for example, found that 82 percent of the public agreed with the proposition that "both parties are pretty much out of touch with the American people." Additionally, two out of three voters said it would be good for the country "if there were a new major political party to compete with the Democrats and Republicans."[21]

Popular dissatisfaction with the party system is also reflected in the trends concerning party identification. In 1937, 84 percent of all people identified themselves as Democrats or Republicans. But by the 1970s and 1980s, partisans averaged only about 70 percent. Since 1990, the typical Gallup survey has shown partisans to make up less than 70 percent of the electorate. Put another way, self-professed independents now compose about one third of the voters, as contrasted with one sixth half a century earlier.

Trends in split-ticket voting (voting for candidates of more than one party in the same election) show a similar erosion of citizen linkage to the parties. Consider the voting behavior of the public for the offices of president and member of the U.S. House of Representatives (see Table 1-3). In the 1960 Kennedy-Nixon race, only 14 percent of all voters split their tickets to vote for a presidential candidate of one party and for a House candidate of the other. In 1988 an extraordinary 31 percent of the voters split their tickets between these offices. In a three-way race in 1996, 22 percent of the voters who voted for Bill Clinton or Bob Dole split their tickets at the congressional level. (Additionally, of course, voters for Ross Perot, who received 8.4 percent of the national vote, had essentially no alternative but to vote for a Democratic or Republican House candidate.)

Ticket-splitting is a major explanation for the frequent appearance of a truncated political system, with one party winning the presidency and the other party winning one or both houses of Congress. Bill Clinton's relatively easy victory over Bob Dole in 1996 (49.2 percent to 40.7 percent), for

Parties and . . .

Political systems and political parties come and go. The American two-party system, however, is a survivor. It has been around, in more or less its present form, for well over a century. How does the public view it? Data from national surveys by the *Los Angeles Times Mirror,* presented below, suggest these conclusions: First, a significant majority of the public believes that the two parties are not as alike as "two peas in a pod"—one out of four voters perceives "a great deal" of difference between the parties. Second, much of the public correctly perceives the parties' ideological thrusts: a conservative, business-oriented Republican party versus a liberal, working-class, labor-oriented Democratic party.

Thinking of the Democratic and Republican parties, would you say there is a great difference in what they stand for, a fair amount of difference, or hardly any difference at all?

	1987
A great deal	25%
A fair amount	45
Hardly at all	25
No opinion/don't know	5

SOURCE: *The People, the Press, and Politics* (Los Angeles: Times Mirror, 1987), 125; and *The People, the Press, and Politics* (Washington, D.C.: Times Mirror Center for the People and the Press, 1990), 50.

example, did little to reshape the Congress. The Democrats picked up only ten seats in the House and lost two in the Senate. Republicans continued to control both houses.

Adding to the party problem, many voters see little or no difference in the effectiveness of the parties in governing. Surveys by the Gallup Poll, starting as long ago as the 1940s, have asked voters to identify the most important problem facing the nation and to select the party best able to handle it. The results are instructive (see Figure 1-1). Over most of the period from 1945 to 1985, the Democratic party received much higher marks than the Republican party. But beginning with Ronald Reagan's second term, the public came to view the Republican party as best able to deal with public problems. In the late 1980s and early 1990s, the advantage shifted back to the Democratic side. Perhaps the most important fact revealed by the data,

... *the Public*

What does it mean to you when someone says he or she is a Republican?

	1987	1990
Conservative	21%	22%
Rich, powerful, monied interest	18	21
Business-oriented	13	10
Not for the people	5	4
Against government spending	5	6

What does it mean to you when someone says he or she is a Democrat?

	1987	1990
For working people	21%	18%
Liberal	18	18
Too much government spending	7	3
Cares for poor, disadvantaged	7	7
For social programs	7	9

NOTE: For the second and third questions, only the leading answers are listed. Also, the replies were unprompted, with some respondents offering more than one answer. About half of the sample consists of "other" and "don't know" responses.

however, is that voters who cannot distinguish between the parties' capacity to handle major problems (or who have no opinion) sometimes outnumber those who select either party. In most surveys, one fourth to one third of all voters take a neutral stance when asked to judge the two parties as agencies for solving major public problems.[22]

The evidence thus indicates that American political parties rest on a relatively narrow and uncertain base of popular support. Scarcely anyone can fail to notice the widespread skepticism of politics and politicians that pervades popular thought. Few vocations stir so little interest as that of the politician. The language of American politics is itself laced with suspicion and hostility. In the argot of popular appraisal, political organizations turn into "machines," party workers emerge as "hacks," political leaders become "bosses," and campaign appeals degenerate into "empty promises" or

FIGURE 1-2   The Voting Behavior of Groups in the 1996 Presidential Election (Shown as Percentage of Two-Party Vote)

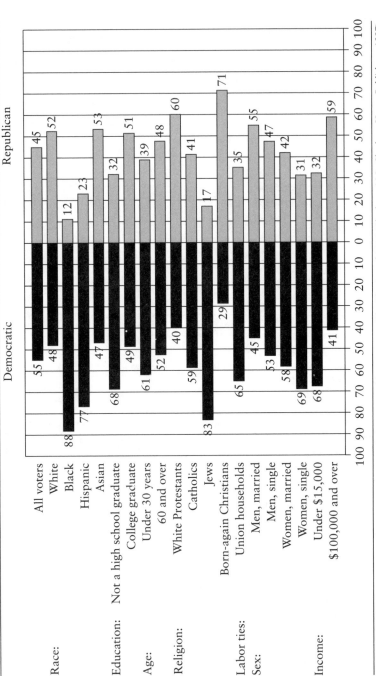

SOURCES: Developed from Voter News Service exit poll data in Gerald M. Pomper, *The Election of 1996* (Chatham, N.J.: Chatham House Publishers, 1997), 179–181, and *New York Times*, November 10, 1996.

NOTE: The Ross Perot vote is not shown. His vote among various social groups was similar to his national vote, except among blacks and Jews, who gave him much less support than the average voter. His strongest supporters were young white men, independents, midwesterners, first-time voters, and voters who were unhappy over their financial situation.

"sheer demagoguery." That some politicians have contributed to this state of affairs by debasing the language of political discourse or by their behavior, as in the Watergate affair, is perhaps beside the point. The critical fact is that the American political culture contains a strong suspicion of the political process and the agencies that try to dominate it, the political parties.

A Heterogeneous Nation

To complete the analysis of the environment of American parties, it is necessary to say something about the characteristics of the nation as a whole. No array of statistics is required to make the point that the United States is a nation of extraordinary diversity. The American community is composed of a great variety of economic and social interests; class configurations; ethnic and religious groups; occupations; regional and subregional interests; and loyalties, values, and beliefs. There are citizens who are deeply attached to inherited patterns and those who are impatient advocates of change, those who care intensely about politics and those who can take it or leave it, and those who elude labeling—those who are active on one occasion and passive on another. There are citizens who think mainly in terms of farm policy, some who seek advantage for urban elements, others whose lives and political interests revolve around business or professions. Diversity abounds. Sometimes deep, sometimes shallow, the differences that separate one group from another and one region from another make the formation of public policy that suits everyone all but impossible.

The major parties must accommodate themselves to the vast diversity of the nation. And they have done this remarkably well. Each party attracts and depends on a wide range of interests. Voting behavior in the 1996 presidential election (Clinton vs. Dole) illustrates this point (see Figure 1-2). In 1996, the Democratic party did particularly well among African Americans, Jews, Hispanics, Catholics, women, persons with lower incomes and limited education, union members, and younger persons. For the Republicans, the most distinctive supporters were born-again Christians, white Protestants, married men, and persons with incomes of more than $100,000. An important point to recognize is that neither party excludes any group from its calculations for winning elections. On the contrary, each party expects to do reasonably well among nearly all groups.

The heterogeneity of the nation is one explanation for the enduring parochial cast of American politics. As Herbert Agar has explained,

> Most politics will be parochial, most politicians will have small horizons, seeking the good of the state or the district rather than of the Union; yet by diplomacy and compromise, never by force, the government must water

down the selfish demands of regions, races, classes, business associations, into a national policy which will alienate no major groups and which will contain at least a plum for everybody. This is the price of unity in a continentwide federation.[23]

Party Organization

Party organization has two common features in all parts of the United States. First, parties are organized in a series of committees, reaching from the precinct level to the national committee. Second, party committee organization parallels the arrangement of electoral districts. With the exception of heavily one-party areas, party committees will be found in virtually all jurisdictions within which important government officials are elected. The presence of party committees, however, reveals little about their activities or their vitality in campaigns.

A familiar description of American parties begins by likening their organizational structure to that of a pyramid. At the top of the pyramid rests the national committee, at the bottom the precinct organizations, with various ward, city, county, and state committees lodged in between. Although it is convenient to view party organization within this pattern, it is misleading if it suggests that power flows steadily from top to bottom, from major national leaders to local leaders and local rank and file. Subnational committees actually have substantial autonomy, particularly in the crucial matters of selecting and slating candidates for public office (including federal office), raising and spending money, and conducting campaigns. (See a sketch of party organization in Figure 1-3.)

The National Committee

The most prestigious and visible of all party committees is the national committee.[24] The people who serve on the national committee of each party are prominent state politicians, chosen in a variety of ways and under a number of constraints. Their official tenure begins when they are accepted by the national convention of each party.

The selection of national committee members is not a simple matter. The Democratic party, operating under its 1974 charter, has elaborate provisions governing the composition of its national committee. Among its membership are the chair and the highest ranking official of the opposite gender of each recognized state party, two hundred additional members allotted to the

FIGURE 1-3   Party Organization in the United States: Layers of Committees and
Their Chairs

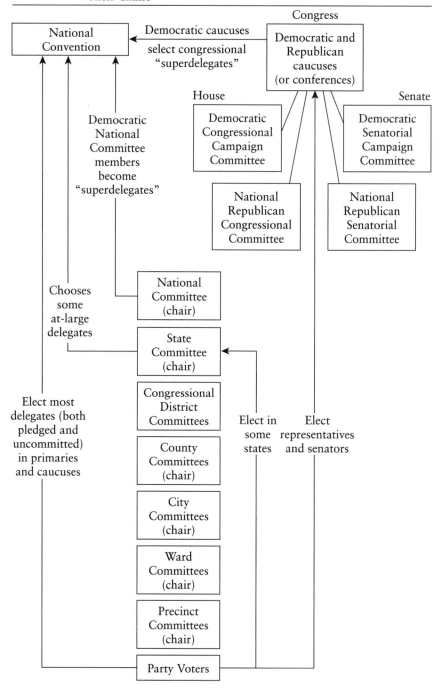

states on the same basis as delegates are apportioned to the national convention, and a number of delegates representing such organizations as the Democratic Governors' Conference, the U.S. Congress, the National Finance Council, the Conference of Democratic Mayors, the National Federation of Democratic Women, the Democratic County Officials Conference, the State Legislative Leaders Caucus, and the Young Democrats of America. As in the case of delegates to the party's national convention, members of the national committee must be selected "through processes which assure full, timely, and equal opportunity to participate" and with due attention to affirmative action standards.

To know what the national committee is, it is necessary to look at what it does.[25] One of its principal responsibilities is to make arrangements for the national convention every four years. In this capacity it chooses the convention site, prepares a temporary roster of convention delegates, and selects convention speakers and temporary officers who will manage the assembly in its opening phase. The committee is especially active during presidential campaigns in coordinating campaign efforts, publicizing the party and its candidates, and raising money. Following the election, the committee often faces the task of raising the necessary funds to pay off campaign debts.

The influence of the president on his party's national committee is substantial. "I don't think the Republican National Committee [RNC] can ever really be independent," a committee staff member said. "[The committee has] a responsibility to the leader. Policy is always made at the White House, not here. We accept it and support it."[26] The same is true for the Democratic National Committee (DNC). "The president likes a party that serves as a supportive tool for the president," observed a state party chair during the Carter administration. "An independent organization is looked upon as a nuisance. That is inevitable." Or, as a White House aide remarked, President Carter "is turned on to the DNC as a service institution."[27]

Strains between the national committee and the White House nevertheless are not much below the surface. Tension sometimes stems from a perception that the White House is too demanding—in particular, that the administration expects the national committee to center its efforts on the president's reelection, even at the expense of other offices. Thus, for example, the general chair of the DNC, Gov. Roy Romer (Colo.) complained that the national party had not paid sufficient attention to the election of its congressional and gubernatorial candidates in 1996. "You've got to have a very close working relationship with the president and vice president because they help you raise the money," he remarked. "But don't think that the DNC ought simply to be the campaign finance arm of the executive branch."[28]

The national committees come to life during presidential election years. During nonpresidential years most of the national committee's work is carried on by committees or the national chair. Study groups occasionally are created by the committee (perhaps under instructions from the national convention) to examine certain problems, such as party organization, party policy, or convention management. In 1969, for example, the DNC created the Commission on Party Structure and Delegate Selection, known as the McGovern–Fraser Commission, to hold hearings and to suggest proposals for changes in party procedures. Included in its wide-ranging report were recommendations urging state parties (and, in certain cases, state legislatures) to eliminate discrimination of all kinds in party rules; to open party meetings and processes to participation by all members of the party; to remove or moderate restrictive voter registration laws or practices; and to provide for the fair representation of blacks, women, and young persons in state delegations to the national convention.

Four subsequent reform commissions—the Mikulski Commission (1972–1973), the Winograd Commission (1975–1978), the Hunt Commission (1981–1982), and the Fairness Commission (1984–1985)—further refined party rules. The broad thrust of the 1969 to 1978 reforms was to increase popular participation in the presidential nominating process while at the same time diluting the power of party professionals. In counterpoise, the recommendations of the Hunt Commission were directed toward restoring the influence of party regulars and officeholders in the presidential nominating process and relaxing certain other party rules introduced in the 1970s.

For some time, the RNC has been more effective than its Democratic counterpart in raising campaign funds (especially through direct-mail methods) and in providing services for its party's candidates. Focusing on party-building activities, the RNC beat the DNC to the punch in making a variety of technical services available to party candidates at both the national and state levels; these services include fund-raising assistance, consultant advice, candidate training, public opinion surveys, and computer analyses of voting behavior. The money gap between the parties is substantial. During the 1995–1996 election cycle, for example, the Republican party's three national-level committees (national committee, senatorial committee, and congressional committee) raised $416.5 million in hard money (a 62-percent increase over 1991–1992), and the three Democratic committees raised $221 million (a 36-percent increase over 1991–1992). When "soft" money is added (that is, money raised outside the limitations of the Federal Election Campaign Act and that is prohibited from being used in federal elections), Republican party committees raised $555 million to the Democrats' $345 million.[29] The reality is that national Democratic committees are no match for the Republican committees in assisting their candidates and their state and local affiliates.[30]

The National Chair

The head of the national party is the national chair.[31] Although the chair is officially selected by the members of the national committee, in practice he or she is chosen by the party's presidential candidate shortly after the national convention has adjourned. Very few leaders in either party have held the position for an extended period—the chair of the party winning the presidency usually receives a major appointment in the new administration, and the chair of the losing party is replaced by a new face. When the chair of the out party becomes vacant, the national committee selects the new leader. Factional conflicts may come to the surface when the committee is faced with the responsibility of finding a replacement, because the leading candidates will usually be identified with certain wings of the party.

The central problem with which the national chair must come to terms in presidential election years is the direction and coordination of the national campaign. The Republican national organization has far outstripped its Democratic rival in the task. One major reason is that such national chairs as Ray C. Bliss (1965–1969) and Bill Brock (1977–1981) concentrated their efforts on organizational reform, seeking in particular to strengthen state and local Republican organizations by providing them with all kinds of "electioneering" assistance.[32] A successful fund-raising program, based on more than two million small contributors, makes these efforts possible.[33]

An absence of adequate financial resources has been particularly burdensome for the Democratic party's national chair. Kenneth M. Curtis, who resigned the chair in 1978 after only one year in office, described what his job was like:

> Have you ever tried to meet the payroll every two weeks of a bankrupt organization and deal with 363 bosses [national committee members] and 50 state chairs? . . . I tried it for a year and simply decided I'd like to do something else with my life. It's not the sort of job that you lay down in the street and bleed to keep.[34]

But the party's situation is changing. Under recent DNC chairs, the party has expanded its contributor base, become more competitive in raising funds, strengthened itself organizationally, and increased its support of candidates, state party organizations, and party-building activities. From an organizational standpoint, the national Democratic party is now better poised to challenge its Republican counterpart in election campaigns.

Congressional and Senatorial Campaign Committees

The other principal units of the national party organization are the congressional and senatorial campaign committees, one committee for each party in each house. These committees, composed of members of Congress, are independent of the national committees. The campaign committees are an outgrowth of the need of members of Congress to have organizations concerned exclusively with their political welfare. As such, the committees raise campaign funds for members, help to develop campaign strategies, conduct research, and otherwise provide assistance to members running for reelection.[35] In addition, the committees may make funds available for party candidates in states or districts where the party has no incumbent. A certain degree of informal cooperation occurs between the party committees of Congress and the national committees, but for the most part they go their separate ways: the former bent on securing reelection of incumbent legislators and on improving the party's prospects for winning or retaining control of Congress; the latter preoccupied with the presidential race.

The Republican campaign committees are the most active and best financed. In 1996 the National Republican Senatorial Committee spent twice as much money on Republican senatorial candidates as the Democratic Senatorial Campaign Committee did on its candidates—$66 million to $31 million. On the House side, the National Republican Congressional Committee (NRCC) disbursed $74 million to the Democrats' $26 million.[36] Nevertheless, the spending gap between the parties is not as large today as it was in the 1970s and 1980s. Occasionally, the NRCC enters congressional primary fights, supporting one Republican over another. Overall, the influence of the national Republican party committees on House and Senate elections has grown substantially over the years. Democrats still have something to learn from the Republicans about party building.[37]

State Committees

Midway between the national party apparatus and local party organizations are the state party committees, often called state central committees.[38] So great are the differences between these committees from state to state—in membership selection, size, and function—that it is difficult to generalize about them. In some states the membership is made up of county chairs; more commonly, state committee members are chosen in primaries or by local party conventions. Their numbers range from fewer than a hundred members to several hundred. In some states the state central committee is a genuinely powerful party unit and is charged by custom with drafting the party platform, slating statewide candidates, and waging an intensive fundraising campaign. In other states the committee's impact on state politics is scarcely perceptible. In a fashion similar to that found at the national level, the state chair is ordinarily selected by the party's gubernatorial candidate. And like the national chair, the state leader is usually a key adviser to the governor on party affairs, particularly on matters involving the distribution of patronage.[39]

Local Party Organization

Below the state committee of the party is the county committee, ordinarily a very large organization composed of all the precinct officials within the county. At the head of this committee is the county chair, who is usually elected by the members of the county committee. Often a key figure in local party organization, the county chair is active in the campaign planning, in the recruitment and slating of party candidates, in the supervision of campaign financing, and in the allocation of patronage to the party faithful. In many counties, the leader's power is enhanced by his active recruitment of candidates for precinct committee members—the very people who in turn elect him to office. Some states have congressional district party organizations, developed around the office of U.S. representative. Where these committees exist, they function essentially as the member's personal organization, set off from the rest of the party and preoccupied with errand running for constituents and the election of the member. Although local party officials, such as the county chair, may be instrumental in controlling the original congressional nomination, their influence on the representative's policy orientations is virtually nil. Indeed, one of the dominant characteristics of congressional district organization is its autonomy. Further down the line are the city and ward committees, which vary in size and importance throughout the country. Their activities, like those of other committees, are centered on campaigns and elections.

The cornerstone of American party organization is the precinct committee, organized within the tens of thousands of election or voting districts of the nation. In metropolitan areas a precinct is likely to number one thousand or two thousand voters; in open-country areas, perhaps only a dozen. The complexity of party organization at the precinct level is mainly a function of precinct size. The precinct committee member is chosen in one of two ways: by the voters in a primary election or by the vote of party members attending a precinct caucus.

In the lore of American politics, elections are won or lost at the precinct level. A strong precinct organization, the argument runs, is essential to party victory, and the key to a strong organization is a precinct leader bent on carrying his precinct. In attempting to advance their party's fortunes, the committee members engage in four main activities: those associated with the campaign itself, party organizational work (for example, recruitment and organization of workers), promulgation of political information, and identification and recruitment of candidates for local office. For most jurisdictions, it appears, the most important activities are those related to the campaign, such as inducing and helping people to register, contacting voters, raising money, campaigning for votes, and transporting voters to the polls. Undoubtedly differences exist in the role perceptions of party officials. A study of precinct leaders in Massachusetts and North Carolina, for example, found that about 60 percent saw their principal task as that of mobilizing voters.[40] In Connecticut and Michigan the leading activities of precinct officials are fund raising, canvassing, and distributing literature.[41] And in Pittsburgh, about two thirds of the committee members describe their most important task as electoral—but here they tend to be indifferent to organizational goals and more supportive of particular candidates than of the party slate as a whole.[42] One study has shown that the organizational vitality of local parties (as measured by such things as the presence of officials, allocation of time to party business, regular meetings, the existence of a budget, and participation in various kinds of campaign activities) is highest in the East (for example, New Jersey, New York, Pennsylvania, and Delaware) and Midwest (for example, Indiana, Ohio, and Illinois) and lowest in the South (for example, Louisiana, Georgia, Florida, Kentucky, and Texas).[43]

Does the strength of local party organizations make a difference in electoral politics? A study by John P. Frendreis, James L. Gibson, and Laura L. Vertz provides a two-part answer. First, the presence of well-organized and active local party organizations does not have a significant direct effect on the persuasion of voters and thus on election results. That appears to be the domain of candidate organizations. But second, and of overlooked importance, in jurisdictions where a party organization is active, the party more likely will be involved in recruitment and therefore able to field a full slate of candidates. Party building, in other words, comes a step at a time. The structural strength of the party, this study suggests, provides a base for the eventual development of competitive party politics.[44]

The Changing Parties: "Old Style" and "New Style" Politics

In the late nineteenth and early twentieth centuries the best examples of strong party organization could be found in the large cities of the Northeast and Midwest—New York City, Boston, Philadelphia, Jersey City, Kansas City, and Chicago. Well-organized and strongly disciplined, the urban machine during this era was virtually invincible. Precinct and ward officials maintained steady contacts with their party constituencies—finding jobs for people out of work; helping those who were in trouble with the law; aiding others to secure government benefits such as welfare payments; assisting neighborhoods to secure government services; helping immigrants to cope with a new society; and helping merchants and tradespeople in their efforts to obtain contracts, licenses, and the like. The party organization was at the center of community life, an effective mediator between the people and their government. Party officials were "brokers," exchanging information, access, and influence for loyalty and support at the polls.

Today the picture is much different. Although the party organizations continue to provide social services in certain large cities, the volume of such exchanges has declined sharply. Numerous factors have contributed to this loss of function, including (1) the growth of civil service systems and the corresponding decline in patronage, (2) the relative decline in the value of patronage jobs, (3) the arrival of the welfare state with its various benefits for low-income groups, (4) the steady assimilation of immigrants, (5) the growing disillusionment among better educated voters over many features of machine politics, and (6) the coming of age of the mass media with its potential for contacts between candidates and their publics. Many disadvantaged citizens remain, particularly in large cities, who continue to rely on local party leaders for assistance in solving the problems in their lives. But most Americans scarcely give a thought to using party officials in this way. Where the parties have suffered a loss of functions, it is reasonable to assume that they have also suffered a loss of vitality. The result has been a decline in their ability to deliver the vote on election day.

Except for certain local offices here and there, party organizations have much less influence on election outcomes now than in the past. Relatively few voters rely on the parties for information on campaigns or for voting cues. "Controlling" votes, except perhaps in a few big city wards, is a lost art. Today the most important players are the media, and what counts in campaigns is the candidate's image. As Peter Hart, a well-known poll taker observed, "A campaign is not played out anymore so much for people or voters; it's played out for the media." [45] Assisted by their advisers, candidates plan steadily for ways to gain media attention, to establish good relationships with print and broadcast media, and to generate favorable newspaper stories or acquire a few seconds of exposure on television. An "old style" party leader of the 1930s or 1940s would be left incredulous at the scope of today's campaign activities that fall outside the purview of the party organization.

Television is central to major campaigns because "retail" politics has given way to "wholesale" politics. [46] Candidates no longer rely as much on precinct organization, and they have less time to stand at mill gates, march in parades, or visit an array of plants, businesses, farms, or halls. Another city or state (or airport) is on the day's agenda. As opportunities for personal visits with voters (including party, civic, labor, and business leaders) have diminished, emphasis has shifted to the wholesale politics of the television commercial, the 15- or 30-second political spot. The mediating function of local leaders, reflected in their assessments of candidates and their interpretations of issues for rank-and-file voters, has atrophied in the face of television dominance.

The key feature of this new style of politics is the growth of *candidate-centered* campaigns. Nowhere is the campaign apparatus of the parties as important as the personal organizations of individual candidates. Candidates—for minor offices and major ones, incumbents and challengers—all have their own organizations for managing the activities of campaigns. Within these units the key decisions are made on campaign strategies, issues, worker recruitment, voter mobilization, and the raising and spending of funds. Candidates often hire campaign management firms, public relations specialists, and political consultants to assist them. These professionals conduct public opinion surveys; prepare films and advertising; raise money; buy radio and television time; write speeches; provide computer analyses of voting behavior; and develop strategies, issues, and images. Less and less of campaign management is left to chance, hunch, or the party organizations.

Candidate-centered campaigns revolve around candidate-centered fund raising. Although the national parties supply funds to candidates and spend money on their behalf, their financial role in national campaigns is not as decisive as that of individual contributors or of political interest groups. Typically, House candidates obtain about half of their funds from individual contributors, whereas Senate candidates receive almost two thirds of their funds from this source. Political action committees (PACs) rank next in importance. House incumbents in 1996 received 41 percent of all their campaign funds from PACs; Senate incumbents, 23 percent.[47] Interest groups clearly have outpaced the parties in funding campaigns for Congress. Their prominence contributes to the candidate-centeredness of contemporary American politics and also to the demands for campaign finance reform.

The role of independent expenditures in campaigns also needs to be understood. Under the Federal Election Campaign Act (FECA) passed in 1971 and amended several times since, limits are placed on the amount of money an individual or PAC can give to a federal candidate. In addition, a presidential candidate who accepts federal funds for the general election campaign cannot accept private contributions. But no limit exists on the amount of money that supporters of federal candidates can spend to aid their campaigns as long as the funds are spent *independently*—that is, without contact with the candidates or their campaign organizations. As a result, groups of all kinds spend heavily, especially in media advertising, opposing as well as supporting presidential and congressional candidates. In the 1996 general election, independent expenditures by PACs exceeded $10 million, about 85 percent of which was allocated to congressional races.[48] The intense involvement of groups in campaigns has changed the nation's political ambiance and its political structures, serving to promote the independence of candidates and officeholders from party controls, while making them more reliant on interest groups and, presumably, more sensitive to their claims.

The Activities of Parties

A principal thesis in the scholarship on political parties is that they are indispensable to the functioning of democratic political systems. Scholars have differed sharply in their approaches to the study of parties and in their appraisals of the functions or activities of parties, but they are in striking agreement on the linkage between parties and democracy. Representative of a wide band of analysis, the following statements by V. O. Key Jr. and E. E. Schattschneider, respectively, sketch the broad outlines of the argument:

> Governments operated, of course, long before political parties in the modern sense came into existence. . . . The proclamation of the right of men to have a hand in their own governing did not create institutions by which they might exercise that right. Nor did the machinery of popular government come into existence overnight. By a tortuous process party systems came into being to implement democratic ideas. As democratic ideas corroded the old foundations of authority, members of the old governing elite reached out to legitimize their positions under the new notions by appealing for popular support. That appeal compelled deference to popular views, but it also required the development of organization to communicate with and to manage the electorate. . . . In a sense, government, left suspended in mid-air by the erosion of the old justifications for its authority, had to build new foundations in the new environment of a democratic ideology. In short, it had to have machinery to win votes.[49]

> The rise of political parties is indubitably one of the principal distinguishing marks of modern government. The parties, in fact, have played a major role as *makers* of governments, more especially they have been the makers of democratic government. . . . [Political] parties created democracy and . . . modern democracy is unthinkable save in terms of the parties. . . . The parties are not . . . merely appendages of modern government; they are in the center of it and play a determinative and creative role in it.[50]

The contributions of political parties to the maintenance of democratic politics can be judged in a rough way by examining the principal activities in which they engage. Of particular importance are those activities associated with the recruitment and selection of leadership, the representation and integration of interests, and the control and direction of government.

PAC Contributions to Congressional Candidates: 1978 to 1996

Under the terms of the Federal Election Campaign Act adopted in 1971, corporations and unions are permitted to use funds from their treasuries to establish and administer political action committees (PACs) and to solicit financial contributions to them. Amendments to the act in 1974 further encouraged the development of PACs and their financial participation in partisan campaigns. In 1974 there were about six hundred PACs; in 1997 they numbered more than four thousand. Their contributions to House and Senate candidates have grown apace:

Year	Total contributions to congressional candidates (in millions)	Percentage of total contributions given to incumbents
1978	$ 34.1	57
1980	55.2	61
1982	83.6	66
1984	105.3	73
1986	132.7	68
1988	147.9	74
1992	179.2	72
1996	201.4	66

SOURCE: Assorted press releases, Federal Election Commission.

Recruitment and Selection of Leaders

The processes by which political leaders are recruited, elected, and appointed to office form the central core of party activity.[51] The party interest, moreover, extends to the appointment of administrative and judicial officers—for example, cabinet members and judges—once the party has captured the executive branch of government.[52] As observed earlier, the party organizations do not necessarily dominate the process by which candidates are recruited or nominated. Increasingly, candidates are self-starters, choosing to enter primaries without waiting for approval from party leaders. With their own personal followings and sources of campaign money, they often

pay scant heed to party leaders or party politics. Some candidates are recruited and groomed by political interest groups. Many candidates find interest groups a particularly lucrative source of campaign funds. The loose-
ness of the American party system creates conditions under which party
control over many of the candidates who run under its banner is thin or
nonexistent.

What do the candidates say about the importance of parties in their decision to run for office? A study by Thomas A. Kazee and Mary C. Thornberry of thirty-six candidates who ran for Congress in competitive districts
found that twenty-two (61 percent) were self-starters, six (17 percent) were
party-recruited, and eight (22 percent) were of a "mixed" variety (self-
starters encouraged to some extent by party activists). Many self-starters
had participated in party affairs prior to their decision to run, which suggests that the party role in the recruitment of members of Congress is more
important than the above percentages suggest.[53] And other studies have
found that county party chairs often report that they participate in the recruitment of congressional candidates.[54]

Although no longer a dominant force in electoral politics, the parties
still play an important role in finding candidates and in electing them to
office. It is difficult to see how hundreds of thousands of elective offices could
be filled in the absence of parties without turning each election into a free-
for-all, conspicuous by the presence of numerous candidates holding all va-
rieties of set, shifting, and undisclosed views. Composing a government out
of an odd mélange of officials, especially at the national level, would be very
difficult. Any form of collective accountability to the voters would vanish.
Hence, whatever their shortcomings, by proposing alternative lists of candidates and campaigning on their behalf, the parties bring certain measures of
order, routine, and predictability to the electoral process.

The constant factors in party politics are the pursuit of power, office,
and advantage. Yet, in serving their own interest in winning office, parties
make other contributions to the public at large and to the political system.
For example, they help to educate the voters concerning issues and mobilize
them for political action, provide a linkage between the people and the government, and simplify the choices to be made in elections. The parties do
what voters cannot do by themselves: From the totality of interests and issues in politics, they choose those that will become "the agenda of formal
public discourse."[55] In the process of shaping the agenda, they provide a
mechanism by which voters not only can make sense out of what government does but can also relate to the government itself. The role of the parties in educating voters and in structuring opinion has been described by
Robert MacIver in this way:

Public opinion is too variant and dispersive to be effective unless it is organized. It must be canalized on the broad lines of some major division of opinion. Party focuses the issues, sharpens the differences between contending sides, eliminates confusing crosscurrents of opinion. . . . The party educates the public while seeking merely to influence it, for it must appeal on grounds of policy. For the same reason it helps to remove the inertia of the public and thus to broaden the range of public opinion. In short the party, in its endeavors to win the public to its side, however unscrupulous it may be in its modes of appeal, is making the democratic system workable. It is the agency by which public opinion is translated into public policy.[56]

Representation and Integration of Group Interests

The United States is a complex and heterogeneous nation. An extraordinary variety of political interest groups, organized around particularistic objectives, exists within it. Conflicts between one group and another, between coalitions of groups, and between various groups and the government are inevitable. Because one of the major functions of government is to take sides in private disputes, what it decides and does is of high importance to groups. When at their creative best, parties and their leaders help to keep group conflicts within tolerable limits. Viewed from a wider perspective, the relationship between parties and private organizations is one of bargaining and accommodation—groups need the parties as much as the parties need them. No group can expect to move far toward the attainment of its objectives without coming to terms with the realities of party power; the parties, through their public officeholders, can advance or obstruct the policy objectives of any group. At the same time, no party can expect to achieve widespread electoral success without significant group support. Quid pro quo, Latin's most useful political expression, explains this nexus.

Bargaining and compromise are key elements in the strategy of American parties. The doctrinal flexibility of the parties means that almost everything is up for grabs—each party can make at least some effort to satisfy virtually any group's demands. Through their public officials, the parties serve as brokers among the organized interests of American society, weighing the claims of one group against those of another, accepting some programs and modifying or rejecting others.[57] The steady bargaining that takes place between interest groups and key party leaders (in the executive and legislative branches) tends to produce settlements the participants can live with for a time, even though these compromises may not be wholly satisfactory to anyone. In addition, of deeper significance, the legitimacy of government itself depends in part on the capacity of the parties to represent diverse interests and to integrate the claims of competing groups in a broad program of public policy. Their ability to do this is certain to bear on their electoral success.

The thesis that the major parties are unusually sensitive to the representation of group interests cannot be advanced without a caveat or two. Parties are far more solicitous toward the claims of organized interests than toward those of unorganized interests. The groups that regularly engage the attention of parties and their representatives in government are those whose support (or opposition) can make a difference at the polls. Organized labor, organized business, organized agriculture, organized medicine—all have multiple channels for gaining access to decision makers. Indeed, party politicians are about as likely to search out the views of these interests as to wait to hear from them. In recent years, special cause groups—those passionate and uncompromising lobbies concerned with single issues such as gun control, abortion, tax rollbacks, equal rights, nuclear power, and the environment—have kept legislators' feet to the fire, exerting extraordinary influence as they judge members on the "correctness" of their positions. By contrast, many millions of Americans are all but shut out of the political system. The political power of such groups as agricultural workers, sharecroppers, migrants, and unorganized labor has never been commensurate with their numbers or, for that matter, with their contribution to society. With low participation in elections, weak organizations, low status, and poor access to political communications, their voices are often drowned out in the din produced by organized interests.[58]

No problem of representation in America is more important than that of finding ways to move the claims of the unorganized public onto the agenda of politics. But the task is formidable: "All power is organization and all organization is power. . . . A man who has no share in any form of organized power is not independent of organized power. He is at the mercy of it."[59]

Control and Direction of Government

A third major activity of the parties involves the control and direction of government. Parties recruit candidates and organize campaigns to win political power, gain public office, and take control of government. Given the character of the political system and the parties themselves, it is unrealistic to suppose that party management of government will be altogether successful. In the first place, the separate branches of government may not be captured by the same party. In more than two thirds of the elections from 1950 to 1996, the party that won the presidency was unable to win control of both houses of Congress. Every Republican president since Dwight D. Eisenhower has faced this problem. Division of party control complicates the process of governing, forcing the president to work not only with his own party in Congress but also with elements of the other party. The legislative success of Republican presidents usually depends on gaining the support of conservative Democrats, mainly from the South. The result is that party achievements in majority building tend to be blurred in the mix of coalition votes, and party accountability to the voters suffers. In the second place, even though one party may control both the legislative and executive branches, its margin of seats in the legislature may be too thin to permit it to govern effectively. Disagreement within the majority party, moreover, may be so great on certain issues that the party finds it virtually impossible to pull its ranks together to develop coherent positions. When majority party lines are shattered, opportunities arise for the minority party to assert itself in the policy-making process. In the third place, midterm (or off-year) elections invariably complicate the plans of the administration party. The president's party almost always loses seats in both houses. In 1994 the Democratic party lost a whopping fifty-two seats in the House and eight in the Senate. Since 1946 the administration party at midterm has suffered an average loss of twenty-eight seats in the House and four in the Senate (see Table 1-4). Very few events are as predictable in American elections or as dispiriting for administrations as the chilly midterm verdict of the voters. And finally, the problems the majority party has in managing the federal government are often replicated at the state level.

The upshot is that although the parties organize governments, they do not wholly control decision-making activities. In some measure they compete with political interest groups bent on securing public policies advantageous to their clienteles, and sometimes certain groups have fully as much influence on the behavior of legislators and bureaucrats as legislative party leaders, national and subnational party leaders, or the president. Yet, to identify the difficulties that confront the parties in seeking to manage the government is not to suggest that the parties' impact on public policy is insubstantial. Not even a casual examination of party platforms, candidates' and officeholders' speeches, or legislative voting can fail to detect the contributions of the parties to shaping the direction of government or can ignore the differences that separate the parties on public policy matters.

An understanding of American parties begins with recognizing that party politicians set greater store in the notion of winning elections than in using election outcomes to achieve a broad range of policy goals. Candidates have interests and commitments in policy questions, but rarely do they rule out bargaining and compromise in order to achieve half a "party loaf." Politicians tend to be intensely pragmatic and adaptable persons. For the most part, they are attracted to a particular party more because of its promise as a mechanism for moving into government than as a mechanism

TABLE 1-4   Off-year Gains and Losses in
Congress by the President's
Party: 1946 to 1994

Year	House		Senate	
1946	D	−55	D	−12
1950	D	−29	D	−6
1954	R	−18	R	−1
1958	R	−47	R	−13
1962	D	−4	D	+4
1966	D	−47	D	−3
1970	R	−12	R	+2
1974	R	−48	R	−5
1978	D	−15	D	−3
1982	R	−26	R	0
1986	R	−5	R	−8
1990	R	−8	R	−1
1994	D	−52	D	−8

NOTE: R = Republican; D = Democrat.

for governing itself. Party is a way of organizing activists and supporters to make a bid for office.[60] This is the elemental truth of party politics. That the election of one aggregation of politicians as against another has policy significance, as indeed it does, comes closer to representing an unanticipated dividend than a triumph for the idea of responsible party government.

Notes

1. Alexander Hamilton, John Jay, and James Madison, *The Federalist* (New York: Modern Library, 1937), 55.
2. E. E. Schattschneider, *Party Government* (New York: Holt, Rinehart and Winston, 1942), 1.
3. This proposition is debatable. For the counterposition—one that stresses the capacity of parties to shape themselves—see Austin Ranney, *Curing the Mischiefs of Faction: Party Reform in America* (Berkeley: University of California Press, 1975), especially Chapter 1; and Jeane Jordan Kirkpatrick, *Dismantling the Parties: Reflections on Party Reform and Party Decomposition* (Washington, D.C.: American Enterprise Institute for Public Policy Research, 1978). For a wide-ranging analysis of the proposition presented in the text, see Robert Harmel and Kenneth Janda, *Parties and Their Environments* (New York: Longmans, 1982).
4. Schattschneider, *Party Government,* 6–7.

5. See a study of ideological polarization in state party systems by Robert D. Brown and Gerald C. Wright, "Elections and State Party Polarization," *American Politics Quarterly 20* (October 1992): 411–426. Some states, such as Utah and California, are highly polarized (liberal Democrats vs. conservative Republicans), whereas in other states, such as Louisiana and Arizona, there is little difference in the ideology of the party coalitions (both are conservative). In states in which the parties are ideologically polarized, there is less split-ticket voting, fewer party defections, less vote swing, and less volatility in election results.

6. David R. Mayhew, *Placing Parties in American Politics* (Princeton, N.J.: Princeton University Press, 1986).

7. David E. Price, *Bringing Back the Parties* (Washington, D.C.: CQ Press, 1984), particularly Chapter 5.

8. Mayhew, *Placing Parties in American Politics,* particularly Chapters 2 and 7.

9. For a careful exposition of this argument, see Schattschneider, *Party Government,* 67–84.

10. *Congressional Quarterly Weekly Report,* April 17, 1993, 966. Taking the country as a whole, Republican candidates received 45.6 percent of the House vote in 1992 but only 40.5 percent of the House seats. Gerrymandering is a significant explanation for the disparity between votes and seats in some states. But a more important explanation is that the parties represent different types of districts. Many Democratic representatives are elected from inner-city districts where turnout is low. Republicans, by contrast, typically do well in upscale suburban constituencies where turnout is higher than average.

11. *Davis v. Bandemer,* 106 S. Ct. 2810 (1986). For a comprehensive examination of legislative reapportionment, see Bernard Grofman, "Criteria for Districting: A Social Science Perspective," *UCLA Law Review 33* (October 1985): 77–184. The political considerations in reapportionment are explored in Q. Whitfield Ayres and David Whiteman, "Congressional Reapportionment in the 1980s: Types and Determinants of Policy Outcomes," *Political Science Quarterly 99* (Summer 1984): 303–314.

12. Price, *Bringing Back the Parties,* 126.

13. For studies of the effects of divisive primaries on party unity and election outcomes, see Donald B. Johnson and James R. Gibson, "The Divisive Primary Revisited: Party Activists in Iowa," *American Political Science Review 68* (March 1974): 67–77; Patrick J. Kenney and Tom W. Rice, "The Relationship between Divisive Primaries and General Election Outcomes," *American Journal of Political Science 31* (February 1987): 31–44; Patrick J. Kenney, "Sorting Out the Effects of Primary Divisiveness in Congressional and Senatorial Elections," *Western Political Quarterly 41* (September 1988): 765–777; James I. Lengle, Diane Owen, and Molly W. Sonner, "Divisive Nominating Mechanisms and Democratic Party Electoral Prospects," *Journal of Politics 57* (May 1995): 370–383; and Paul S. Herrnson and James G. Gimpel, "District Conditions and Primary Divisiveness in Congressional Elections," *Political Research Quarterly 48* (March 1995): 117–150.

14. David B. Truman, "Party Reform, Party Atrophy, and Constitutional Change: Some Reflections," *Political Science Quarterly 99* (Winter 1984–1985): 649–650.

15. For a more extensive analysis of the primary, see Chapter 3.

16. The introduction of partisan information in nonpartisan elections has the effect of turning them into partisan contests. See a study by Peverill Squire and Eric

R. A. N. Smith, "The Effect of Partisan Information on Voters in Nonpartisan Elections," *Journal of Politics 50* (February 1988): 169–179.

17. Lucian W. Pye and Sidney Verba, eds., *Political Culture and Political Development* (Princeton, N.J.: Princeton University Press, 1965), 513.

18. The data and general line of argument developed in these paragraphs are derived from Jack Dennis, "Support for the Party System by the Mass Public," *American Political Science Review 60* (September 1966): 600–615; Dennis, "Changing Support for the American Party System," in *Paths to Political Reform*, ed. William J. Crotty (Lexington, Mass.: Heath, 1980), 35–66; and Dennis, "Public Support for the Party System, 1964–1984" (Paper delivered at the annual meeting of the American Political Science Association, Washington, D.C., August 28–31, 1986), 19. Also see Thomas M. Konda and Lee Sigelman, "Public Evaluations of the American Parties, 1952–1984," *Journal of Politics 49* (August 1987): 814–829.

19. A system of "responsible parties" would be characterized by centralized, unified, and disciplined parties committed to the execution of programs and promises offered at elections and held accountable by the voters for their performance. For an analysis of this model, see Chapter 7.

20. See *The American Enterprise* (January/February 1993): 107–108.

21. *Washington Post*, July 8, 1992.

22. For a careful analysis of the meaning of data such as presented here, see Martin P. Wattenberg, *The Decline of American Political Parties, 1952–1984* (Cambridge, Mass.: Harvard University Press, 1986), especially Chapter 4, and his earlier study, "The Decline of Political Partisanship in the United States: Negativity or Neutrality?" *American Political Science Review 75* (December 1981): 941–950. Wattenberg finds that negative attitudes toward the parties have not increased significantly since the 1950s. Instead, the public has become more neutral in its evaluation of them. For a challenge to the "neutrality hypothesis," see Stephen C. Craig, "The Decline of Partisanship in the United States: A Reexamination of the Neutrality Hypothesis," *Political Behavior 7* (1985): 57–78.

23. Herbert Agar, *The Price of Union* (Boston: Houghton Mifflin, 1950), xiv.

24. For an instructive study of the national committee and the national chair, see Cornelius P. Cotter and Bernard C. Hennessy, *Politics without Power: The National Party Committees* (New York: Atherton Press, 1964).

25. Two studies that trace the growing importance of the national party are Charles H. Longley, "National Party Renewal," and John F. Bibby, "Party Renewal in the National Republican Party," in *Party Renewal in America: Theory and Practice*, ed. Gerald M. Pomper (New York: Praeger Special Studies, 1980), 69–86 and 102–115.

26. *Congressional Quarterly Weekly Report*, February 16, 1974, 352.

27. *Congressional Quarterly Weekly Report*, January 14, 1978, 61.

28. *New York Times*, March 27, 1997.

29. Press release, Federal Election Commission, March 19, 1997.

30. See Paul S. Herrnson, *Party Campaigning in the 1980s* (Cambridge, Mass.: Harvard University Press, 1988), especially Chapter 2.

31. See Cotter and Hennessy, *Politics without Power*, 67–80. They see the roles of the national chair as "image-maker, hell-raiser, fund-raiser, campaign manager, and administrator."

32. Robert J. Huckshorn and John F. Bibby, "State Parties in an Era of Political

Change," in *The Future of American Political Parties,* ed. Joel L. Fleishman (Englewood Cliffs, N.J.: Prentice Hall, 1982), 82.

33. F. Christopher Arterton, "Political Money and Party Strength," in *The Future of American Political Parties,* ed. Joel L. Fleishman, 105.

34. *Congressional Quarterly Weekly Report,* January 14, 1978, 58.

35. The chair of a congressional campaign committee is a major political plum. The chair has numerous opportunities to help party candidates be elected and, more important, to help incumbents be reelected. The chair concentrates on fund raising, "signs the checks" for the party's candidates, and inevitably gains the gratitude of winners.

36. Press release, Federal Election Commission, March 19, 1997.

37. See an instructive study of the expanded role of the national parties in congressional elections by Herrnson, *Party Campaigning.* Along the same lines, see Paul S. Herrnson, "Reemergent National Party Organizations," in *The Parties Respond,* ed. L. Sandy Maisel (Boulder, Colo.: Westview Press, 1990), 41–66.

38. See a study of the growing importance of state legislative campaign committees in New York by Diana Dwyer and Jeffrey M. Stonecash, "Where's the Party?: Changing State Party Organizations," *American Politics Quarterly 20* (July 1992): 326–344.

39. For an examination of the strength of party organizations at the state level, see John F. Bibby, Cornelius P. Cotter, James L. Gibson, and Robert J. Huckshorn, "Trends in Party Organizational Strength, 1960–1980," *International Political Science Review 4* (January 1983): 21–27; and "Assessing Party Organizational Strength," *American Journal of Political Science 27* (May 1983): 193–222.

40. Lewis Bowman and G. R. Boynton, "Activities and Role Definitions of Grassroots Party Officials," *Journal of Politics 28* (February 1966): 121–143. Also see Lee S. Weinberg, "Stability and Change among Pittsburgh Precinct Politicians," *Social Science* (Winter 1975): 10–16.

41. Barbara C. Burrell, "Local Political Party Committees, Task Performance and Organizational Vitality," *Western Political Quarterly 39* (March 1986): 48–66.

42. Michael Margolis and Raymond E. Owen, "From Organization to Personalism: A Note on the Transmogrification of the Local Political Party," *Polity 18* (Winter 1985): 313–328.

43. James L. Gibson, Cornelius P. Cotter, John F. Bibby, and Robert J. Huckshorn, "Whither the Local Parties?: A Cross-Sectional and Longitudinal Analysis of the Strength of Party Organizations," *American Journal of Political Science 29* (February 1985): 139–160.

44. John P. Frendreis, James L. Gibson, and Laura L. Vertz, "The Electoral Relevance of Local Party Organizations," *American Political Science Review 84* (March 1990): 225–235. Indicators of the structural strength of a party organization include the presence of a constitution and bylaws, a complete set of officers, an active chair, bimonthly meetings, a year-round office, staff, and a budget.

45. Quoted in Albert R. Hunt, "The Media and Presidential Campaigns," in *Elections American Style,* ed. A. James Reichley (Washington, D.C.: Brookings Institution, 1987), 53.

46. See a column by R. W. Apple, Jr., in the *New York Times,* February 11, 1988.

47. Press release, Federal Election Commission, December 31, 1996.

48. Press release, Federal Election Commission, April 22, 1997.

49. V. O. Key, Jr., *Politics, Parties, and Pressure Groups* (New York: Crowell, 1964), 200–201.
50. Schattschneider, *Party Government*, 1.
51. Agreement among students of political parties on the nature of party functions, their relative significance, and the consequences of functional performance for the political system is far from complete. Frank J. Sorauf points out that among the functions attributed to American parties have been simplifying political issues and alternatives, producing automatic majorities, recruiting political leadership and personnel, organizing minorities and opposition, moderating and compromising political conflict, organizing the machinery of government, promoting political consensus and legitimacy, and bridging the separation of powers. The principal difficulty with listings of this sort, according to Sorauf, is that "it involves making functional statements about party activity without necessarily relating them to functional requisites or needs of the system." He suggests that, at this stage of research on parties, emphasis should be given to the activities performed by parties, thus avoiding the confusion arising from the lack of clarity about the meaning of function, the absence of consensus on functional categories, and the problem of measuring the performance of functions. See his instructive essay, "Political Parties and Political Analysis," in *The American Party Systems: Stages of Political Development*, ed. William Nisbet Chambers and Walter Dean Burnham (New York: Oxford, 1967), 33–53.
52. In about four fifths of the states, judges are chosen in some form of partisan or nonpartisan election. In the remaining states they come to office through appointment. A few states employ the so-called Missouri Plan of judge selection, under which the governor makes judicial appointments from a list of names supplied by a nonpartisan judicial commission composed of judges, lawyers, and laypeople. Under this plan, designed to take judges out of politics, each judge, after a trial period, runs for reelection without opposition; voters may vote either to retain or to remove the judge from office. If a majority of voters cast affirmative ballots, the judge is continued in office for a full term; if the vote is negative, the judge loses office and the governor makes another appointment in the same manner. But even under this plan, the governor may give preference to aspirants of his own party. Irrespective of the system used to choose judges, party leaders and party interest will nearly always be involved.
53. Thomas A. Kazee and Mary C. Thornberry, "Where's the Party? Congressional Candidate Recruitment and American Party Organizations," *Western Political Quarterly* 43 (March 1990): 61–80. For a discussion of the role of the national parties in recruiting candidates for Congress, see Herrnson, *Party Campaigning in the 1980s*, 48–56.
54. See Cornelius P. Cotter, James L. Gibson, John F. Bibby, and Robert J. Huckshorn, *Party Organization in American Politics* (New York: Praeger, 1984); and Gibson, Cotter, Bibby, and Huckshorn, "Whither the Local Parties?" 139–160. And for additional evidence on the vitality of local parties, see Kay Lawson, Gerald Pomper, and Maureen Moakley, "Local Party Activists and Electoral Linkage," *American Politics Quarterly* 14 (October 1986): 345–375.
55. Theodore J. Lowi, "Party, Policy, and Constitution in America," in *The American Party Systems*, ed. William Nisbet Chambers and Walter Dean Burnham, 263.
56. Robert MacIver, *The Web of Government* (New York: Macmillan, 1947), 213.
57. See a discussion of the party role in "the aggregation of interests" in Gerald M.

Pomper, "The Contributions of Political Parties to American Democracy," in *Party Renewal in America,* ed. Gerald M. Pomper, 5–7.

58. Few facts about the political participation of Americans are of greater significance than those that reveal its social class bias. A disproportionate number of the people who are highly active in politics are drawn from the upper reaches of the social order, from among those who hold higher status occupations, are more affluent, and are better educated. Citizens from lower socioeconomic levels constitute only about 10 percent of the participants who are highly active in politics. See Sidney Verba and Norman H. Nie, *Participation in America: Political Democracy and Social Equality* (New York: Harper and Row, 1972), especially Chapter 20.

59. Harvey Fergusson, *People and Power* (New York: Morrow, 1947), 101–102.

60. Consider the development and components of a party model based on the idea that the only standard useful in evaluating the vitality of American parties is simply the ability of the party to win office. Using this standard, Joseph Schlesinger argues that the major parties are healthier now than ever in the past. See his "On the Theory of Party Organization," *Journal of Politics 46* (May 1984): 369–400.

Chapter Two

The Characteristics
of American Parties

The major parties are firm landmarks on the American political scene. In existence for more than a century, the parties have made important contributions to the development and maintenance of a democratic political culture and to democratic institutions and practices. In essence, the parties form the principal institution for popular control of government, and this achievement is remarkable given the limitations under which they function. This chapter examines the chief characteristics of the American party system.

The Primary Characteristic: Dispersed Power

Viewed at some distance, the party organizations may appear to be neatly ordered and hierarchical—committees are piled, one atop another, from the precinct to the national level, conveying the impression that power flows from the top to the bottom. In reality, however, the American party is not nearly so hierarchical. State and local organizations have substantial independence in most party matters. The practices that state and local parties follow, the candidates they recruit or help to recruit, the campaign money they raise, the auxiliary groups they form and re-form, the innovations they introduce, the organized interests to which they respond, the campaign strategies and issues they create, and, most important, the policy orientations of the candidates who run under their label—all bear the distinctive imprints of local and state political cultures, leaders, traditions, and interests.[1]

Although there is no mistaking the overall decentralization of American parties, the power of the national party to control the presidential nominating process has grown immensely—particularly for the Democratic party. The Democratic reform movement, begun in the late 1960s, drastically altered the rules and practices of state parties in matters related to the selection of national convention delegates. In 1974 the Democratic party held a midterm convention to draft a charter—the first in the history of either major party—to provide for the governance of the party. The charter formally establishes the Democratic national convention as the highest authority of the party and requires state parties to observe numerous standards in the selection of convention delegates. Moreover, as a result of a 1975 Supreme Court decision, national party rules must govern if a conflict arises between national and state party rules concerning the selection of delegates. "The convention serves the pervasive national interest in the selection of candidates for national office," the Supreme Court ruled, "and this national interest is greater than any interest of an individual state." [2]

The centralizing reforms of the Democratic party, however, need to be kept in perspective. On the whole, they have contributed more to the devitalization of the national party organizations than to their strengthening. The reforms have not increased the probability that candidates who are nominated will win the election. Furthermore, the spread of presidential primaries and the opening up of party caucuses have transformed the national convention, diminishing its independent role in choosing the presidential nominee. In recent conventions the delegates have done little more than ratify the choices made earlier in party primaries and caucuses. In effect, the average party voter, joined by candidate enthusiasts, not the convention, picks the nominee. And in reality the choice may be limited simply to the candidates who have somehow survived the Iowa caucuses and the New Hampshire primary. The party conventions themselves are less and less party gatherings. Rather, they are assemblies dominated by the leading candidate, his organization, his entourage of advisers, and the activists drawn to his preconvention campaign. Public officials and party leaders draw power from their relationship to the candidate whose nomination the convention will confirm. Those aligned with candidates rejected in the preconvention period are of minimal interest, even to television reporters in search of an angle that can be parlayed into a story. All recent conventions have been dominated by the leading candidate and his organization. The same can be said for state delegations—where all the action takes place in candidate caucuses. When the preconvention struggle produces a nominee, the party presence in the convention is scarcely more than a backdrop.

In the Democratic party, the impact of national party agencies on state and local organizations is felt in both the presidential nominating process and in the distribution of campaign funds.[3] National rules thoroughly regulate the processes by which Democratic national convention delegates are chosen (see Chapter 3). The impact of Republican national party agencies on subnational parties shows up most clearly in matters of campaign finance. In the 1995–1996 election cycle, national Republican party committees' contributions to House and Senate candidates and expenditures on their behalf totaled about $35 million, whereas Democratic committees' contributions and expenditures came to $25 million; more than 90 percent of these funds were spent on behalf of candidates. In addition, Republican national-level committees spent $150 million in so-called soft money (funds raised outside the limits of federal law and used to finance state and local election activities and to strengthen the parties as institutions), as contrasted with the Democrats' $122 million. (Soft money collected by the Democrats was up 242 percent from 1992, and that collected by the Republicans was up 178 percent.)[4] As recently as the 1989–1990 election cycle, the fund-raising gap between the national parties was on the order of four-to-one in favor of the Republicans. Today it is less than two-to-one.[5]

National party leaders do not have a great impact on the nomination of candidates for Congress. Ordinarily, these nominations are treated as local matters, even though members of Congress are national officials. Furthermore, congressional party leaders rarely attempt to discipline fellow party members who stray from the reservation—who vote with the other party on key legislative issues or otherwise fail to come to the aid of their party. (In an unusual action in 1983, the House Democratic Caucus removed a Texas representative, Phil Gramm, from the Budget Committee because he had played a major role in shaping President Reagan's budget strategy in the previous Congress. In response, Gramm resigned his seat, switched parties, and was reelected as a Republican. Other conservative "Boll Weevil" Democrats who had supported Reagan's economic program suffered no penalties, however.) Members who ignore their party typically escape sanctions and, by dramatizing their capacity to resist party claims, sometimes improve their standing with the voters.

The position of the national party apparatus is also revealed in the character and activities of the national committee. For the party in power, the national committee is predominantly an arm of the president. Neither national committee has significant influence on fellow party members in Congress, on the party's governors, or on the party's public officials further down the line. The shaping of party positions on major questions of public policy is thus well beyond the capacity of the committee.

Factors Contributing to the Dispersal of Party Power

The position of the national party is strongly affected by the legal and constitutional characteristics of the American political system. American parties must find their place within a federal system where powers and responsibilities lie with fifty states as well as with the national government. The basic responsibility for the design of the electoral system in which the parties compete is given to the states, not to the nation. Not surprisingly, party organizations have been molded by the electoral laws under which they contest for power. State and local power centers have naturally developed around the thousands of governmental units and elective offices found in the states and the localities. With his distinctive constituency (frequently a safe district), his own coterie of supporters, and his own channels to campaign money, the typical officeholder has a remarkable amount of freedom in defining his relationship to his party. His well-being and the organization's well-being are not identical. To press this point, it is not too much to say that officeholders are continuously evaluating party claims and objectives in the light of their own career aspirations. When the party's claims and the officeholder's aspirations diverge, the party ordinarily loses out. A federal system, with numerous elective offices, opens up an extraordinary range of political choices to subnational parties and, especially, to individual candidates.

For all of its significance for the party system and the distinctiveness of American politics, however, federalism is but one of several explanations for the fragmentation of party power. Another constitutional provision, separation of powers, also contributes to this condition. A frequent by-product of separation of powers is a truncated party majority—when one party controls one or both houses of the legislature and the other party controls the executive. At worst, the result is a dreary succession of narrow partisan clashes between the branches; at best, a clarification of differences between the parties occasionally may come about. At no time, however, does a truncated majority help in the development and maintenance of party responsibility for a program of public policy. The dimensions of this party problem in the states are revealed by the data provided in Table 2-1. Currently, well over half of all gubernatorial-legislative elections lead to divided party control of the branches. Republican governors in particular are likely to confront this situation. The pattern at the national level is just about the same.

A third factor helping to disperse party power is the method used to make nominations. It was noted earlier that nominations for national office are sorted out and settled at the local level, ordinarily without interference from national party functionaries. One of the principal supports of local control over nominations is the direct primary. Its use virtually guarantees that candidates for national office will be tailored to the measure of local specifications. Consider this analysis by Austin Ranney and Willmoore Kendall:

TABLE 2-1   Incidence of Party Division (Governor vs. Legislature)
Following 1988, 1992, and 1996 Elections

Relation between governor and legislature	Following 1988 Election		Following 1992 Election		Following 1996 Election	
	Number	Percentage	Number	Percentage	Number	Percentage
Governor opposed[a]	31	63	29	59	31	63
Governor unopposed	18	37	20	41	18	37

SOURCE: Various issues of the *Congressional Quarterly Weekly Report*.

[a]At least one house controlled by a majority of the other party.

A party's *national* leaders can affect the kind of representatives and senators who come to Washington bearing the party's label only by enlisting the support of the state and local party organizations concerned; and they cannot be sure of doing so even then. Assume, for example, that the local leaders have decided to support the national leaders in an attempt to block the renomination of a maverick congressman, and are doing all they can. There is still nothing to prevent the rank and file, who may admire the incumbent's "independence," from ignoring the leaders' wishes and renominating him. The direct primary, in other words, is *par excellence* a system for maintaining *local* control of nominations; and as long as American localities continue to be so different from one another in economic interests, culture, and political attitudes, the national parties are likely to retain their present ideological heterogeneity and their tendency to show differing degrees of cohesion from issue to issue.[6]

Fourth, the distribution of power within the parties is affected by patterns of campaign finance. Few, if any, campaign resources are more important than money. A large proportion of the political money donated in any year is given directly to the campaign organizations of individual candidates instead of to the party organizations. Candidates with access to campaign money are automatically in a strong position vis-à-vis the party organization. Not having to rely heavily on the party for campaign funds, candidates can stake out their independence from it. Whether candidates can remain independent from the interest groups that pour money into their campaigns is another question.

Fifth, a pervasive spirit of localism dominates American politics and adds to the decentralization of political power. Local interests find expression in national politics in countless ways. Even the presidential nominating process may become critical for the settlement of local and state political struggles. A prominent political leader who aligns with the candidate who eventually wins the presidential nomination, particularly if his support comes early in the race, can put new life into his own career. He gains access to the nominee and increased visibility. If his party wins the presidency, an appointment in the new administration may be offered to him. Or if he chooses to run for a major public office, he is likely to secure the support of the president. National conventions settle more than national matters.

Congress has always shown a remarkable hospitality to the idea that governmental power should be decentralized. A great deal of the major legislation that has been passed in recent decades, for example, has been designed to make state and local governments participants in the development and implementation of public policies. Locally based political organizations profit from these arrangements. A basic explanation for Congress's defense of state and local governments lies in the backgrounds of the members themselves. Many of them were elected to state or local office prior to their election to Congress. They are steeped in local lore, think in local terms, meet frequently with local representatives, and work for local advantage. Their steady attention to the local dimensions of national policy helps to safeguard their own careers and to promote the interests of those local politicians who look to Washington for assistance in solving community problems. The former Speaker of the House, Thomas P. ("Tip") O'Neill Jr. (D-Mass.), had it right when he said, "All politics is local." [7]

Finally, the fragmentation of party power owes much to the growing importance of outsiders in the political process. Chief among them are the media, campaign management firms, and political interest groups. Today, virtually all candidates for important offices hire expert consultants to organize their campaigns, to shape their strategies, and to mold their images. And they strain for media coverage that presents them in a favorable light— what counts, candidates know, is how they are perceived by the voters. As for political interest groups, their role in campaigns, particularly in their financing, has become much more important than in the past. In 1996 PACs contributed about $201 million to the campaigns of candidates for Congress—$24 million more than in 1992 and six times as much as they gave in 1978. Interest group money has become a major force in American politics, particularly in congressional elections. And in all likelihood, interest group influence on officeholders has increased. [8] As PAC money and interest group influence have become major campaign issues, the prospects have increased that tighter restrictions on PAC campaign gifts will be enacted.

The Power of Officeholders

Writing in the 1960s, James M. Burns sketched the organizational strength of state parties:

> At no level, except in a handful of industrial states, do state parties have the attributes of organization. They lack extensive dues-paying memberships; hence they number many captains and sergeants but few foot soldiers. They do a poor job of raising money for themselves as organizations, or even for their candidates. They lack strong and imaginative leadership of their own. They cannot control their most vital function—the nomination of their candidates. Except in a few states, such as Ohio, Connecticut, and Michigan, our parties are essentially collections of small cliques and they are often shunted aside by the politicians who understand political power. Most of the state parties are at best mere jousting grounds for embattled politicians; at worst they simply do not exist, as in the case of Republicans in the rural South or Democrats in the rural Midwest.[9]

Is the situation different today? Yes, in some respects. Recent research has shown that the parties are stronger organizationally than they were in the 1960s. At the state level, for example, most parties now maintain a permanent state headquarters in the state capital with a professional staff. State party budgets have grown in size, and systematic fund raising has become a more important activity. Party organizations are better equipped to provide candidates with services, including research assistance and campaign money. They are also more effective in recruiting candidates for public office in many jurisdictions. Organizational vitality is particularly evident in the Republican party. About three fourths of all Republican state parties and one fourth of all Democratic state parties can be classified as "strong" or "moderately strong" from an organizational standpoint.[10] But this still leaves a number of states where at least one party is weak and inconspicuous.

Strong everywhere, however, are independent candidate and officeholder organizations. They dominate the campaign and election process. Candidates and officeholders—aided by hired consultants and assorted handlers—at all levels develop strategies and issues, raise funds, recruit workers, interact with interest groups, assemble coalitions, cultivate the media, make news, and mobilize voters. The party organization may provide useful services to the candidates, facilitating their campaigns, but that is about it. Candidates shape their own campaigns and win largely on their own efforts and on their own terms. The perspective of Barbara G. Salmore and Stephen A. Salmore is instructive:

> Technology is the development most responsible for ending party primacy in campaigns. . . . What made the advent of television and the computer

unique was that they provided candidates everywhere with an effective alternative means of getting information about themselves to the voters. Newspapers, magazines, and radio paled in comparison with what television offered—a powerful combination of visual and aural messages. Candidates could enter voters' homes and give party organizations competition they had never had before. . . . Once candidates learned that they could independently compete with party organizations and that they had the direct primary as the vehicle to do it, why should they give up their independence and control of their messages to the party organizations?[11]

In the candidate- and media-centered politics of the late twentieth century, the party may be only an afterthought in the career calculation of members. Consider these observations about contemporary members of Congress—the first by a political scientist, Burdett A. Loomis; the second by former Speaker Thomas S. Foley (D-Wash.):

Policy entrepreneurs. Free-lance artists. Independent operators. Idea merchants. Central to almost all characterizations of a new political style is a sense of independence. Congressmen and senators can depend on their own enterprises for reelection, for legislative initiatives, for publicity, for a sense of certainty in their uncertain lives.[12]

Nobody in the United States Congress ever talks about the Democratic or Republican party. . . . I have never heard a member of the Congress refer to a colleague and urge a vote for him because he was in the same party. Most Democrats and Republicans could not recall three items in the platform of their party. . . . We have 435 parties in the House.[13]

Law and the Parties

One of the major features of American parties is that their organization and activities are extensively regulated by law—state law in particular. David E. Price has distinguished two general bodies of state law: statutes that relate to *nominations and elections* and statutes that affect *party cohesion in government*.[14]

Laws affecting nominations and elections differ from state to state. A few examples will help to illustrate their diversity. Although the direct primary system is used everywhere, some states still permit party conventions to participate in the choice of nominees. For example, state law or party rules may stipulate that a candidate for a statewide office must receive a certain percentage of the party's state convention vote to qualify for a place on the primary ballot. In some states, law or practice encourages the parties to make preprimary endorsements; in other states such gatekeeping action is

TABLE 2-2   Party Capacity for Influencing Nominations, as Reflected in State Laws and Practices

Region	Number of states in region	Number of states in which party conventions help choose major state-level nominees	Number of states in which parties regularly make pre-primary endorsements	Number of states in which primary voting is limited to persons pre-registered by party	Total	Index of party strength (total/number of states in region)
Northeast	10	3	6	8	17	1.7
Border	4	0	0	4	4	1.0
South	11	0	0	2	2	0.2
Midwest	12	1	7	4	12	1.0
West	13	3	3	7	13	1.0
Regular party organization states	8	2	6	5	13	1.6

SOURCES: Developed from data in David E. Price, *Bringing Back the Parties* (Washington, D.C.: CQ Press, 1984), 128–129 (as adapted). Price examines eleven party-strengthening laws and practices in the states, three of which, referred to here, are central to party influence on nominations. The table also reflects the presence of party-strengthening laws and practices in states where local parties traditionally have been strongest. As identified by David R. Mayhew, who examined the structure of American parties at the local level, these "regular party organization states" are Connecticut, Delaware, Illinois, New Jersey, New York, Ohio, Pennsylvania, and Rhode Island. Local party organizations in these states have been distinguished by hierarchy, substantial autonomy, lasting power, an active role in the nominating process, significant patronage, and an absence of factional conflict. See Mayhew, *Placing Parties in American Politics* (Princeton, N.J.: Princeton University Press, 1986), Chapter 2.

prohibited. States vary sharply in the extent to which they seek to protect the integrity of the parties by limiting primary voting to persons preregistered by party. The best (or at least most benign) arrangement, from the standpoint of the parties, is the closed primary. (See Table 2-2 for data on regional differences in party influence on nominations as promoted by state laws or practices.) States also differ significantly in how their laws protect the parties from independent candidates and "sore losers" (candidates who lose their party's nomination and then run under another banner in the general election). As a final example, law in eight states helps to promote the parties through public funding of campaigns, channeled through the parties.

The impact of state law on party cohesion in government is sizable. Laws may make it easy for the parties to function as collectivities or they may make it difficult. Where ballots facilitate straight-ticket voting, for example, as they do in twenty-one states, the probability increases for gubernatorial-legislative coattailing and thus for the election of candidates who share the same party label. The election calendar may also affect party control of government. Election of the governor and the legislature at the same time promotes party control, whereas elections held at different times encourage divided control of government. Finally, states differ in the degree to which they consolidate executive power. Short terms for the governor, prohibition against reelection, and provision for a multiplicity of statewide elective offices all contribute to the weakness of executive authority and, ultimately, to the fragmentation of party power.

State laws can be either a boon or a barrier to strong parties. Party-strengthening laws are most likely to be found in the northeastern states. Southern states are least likely to have laws favorable to the parties, their leaders, and their organizations. Intraregional variation is particularly noticeable in the Midwest and West. In the Midwest, Kansas and Nebraska do not have nearly as many pro-party laws as Michigan and North Dakota. In the West, California is largely antiparty in its statutes, and Utah is considerably more pro-party. On the whole, state law is more likely to have a negative than positive impact on the strength of the parties. Can the parties be trusted? Are they worth preserving? In most states the law seems to say no, probably not, or, at best, perhaps.

Variations in Party Competition from State to State and from Office to Office

Familiar and conventional interpretations in American politics are never easy to abandon. Old labels persist even though their descriptive power has been sharply eroded. Such is the case in the designation of the American two-party system. Vigorous two-party competition in all jurisdictions is clearly unattainable. Surprisingly little two-party competition is found, however, in certain electoral districts of the nation. The American party system is in some places and at some times strongly two-party, and in other places and at other times, dominantly one-party. In some states and localities factional politics within one or both major parties is so pervasive and persistent as to suggest the presence of a multiple-party system. Competition between the parties is a condition not to be taken for granted, despite the popular tendency to bestow the two-party label on American politics.

Competitiveness in Presidential and Congressional Elections

Although in many states and localities little more than a veneer of competitiveness exists between the parties, this is not the case in presidential elections. Contests for the presidency provide the best single example of authentic two-party competition, particularly in recent decades.[15] With but three exceptions in all *two-party* presidential contests since 1940, the losing presidential candidate has received at least 45 percent of the popular vote; the exceptions occurred in 1964 (Barry Goldwater received 39 percent of the vote), 1972 (George McGovern, 38 percent), and 1984 (Walter F. Mondale, 41 percent). Several elections in the modern era have been extraordinarily close: in 1960 John F. Kennedy received 49.7 percent of the popular vote to Richard Nixon's 49.5 percent, and in 1968 Nixon obtained 43.4 percent to Hubert H. Humphrey's 42.7 percent (with George C. Wallace receiving 13.5 percent). In another extremely close race in 1976, Jimmy Carter received 50.1 percent of the vote, and Gerald R. Ford received 48.0 percent.

A view of presidential elections from the states is worth examining. In the past two decades the number of one-party states and regions in presidential elections has declined precipitously. The tempo of Republican growth in the once-solid Democratic South has quickened (see Figure 2-1). The watershed in southern political history appears to have been 1952. Dwight D. Eisenhower carried four southern states (Florida, Tennessee, Texas, and Virginia), narrowly missing victories in several others, and received more than 48 percent of the popular vote throughout the South. Nixon's victory in 1968 was similarly impressive. In the District of Columbia and in thirty-nine states outside the South, Humphrey led Nixon by about 30,000 votes; in the eleven southern states Nixon led Humphrey by more than 500,000 votes. The high point of Republican appeal was reached in 1972, when Nixon received 70 percent of the southern vote, a much larger proportion than he received in 1968. One result of the 1976 nomination by the Democrats of Jimmy Carter, a native of Georgia, was that the Republican surge in the South was arrested; although Gerald Ford ran well in nearly all states of the Confederacy, he carried only Virginia. In 1980 the Republicans again did well in the South. Reagan received 53.6 percent of the major party vote in the South, winning all of this region's states except Georgia. In 1984 his percentage jumped to 62.6, a level well above his national average of 58.8. In 1988 George Bush also substantially exceeded his national showing in winning 58.8 percent of the southern vote. With a southern governor

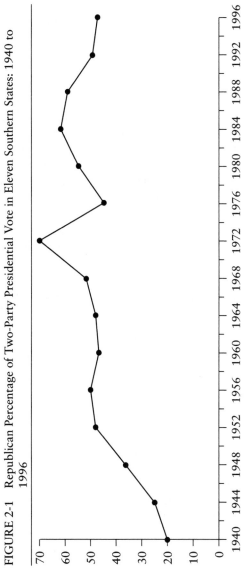

FIGURE 2-1 Republican Percentage of Two-Party Presidential Vote in Eleven Southern States: 1940 to 1996

at the head of the Democratic ticket in 1992, the Republican advantage narrowed; in the two-party vote, George Bush led Bill Clinton in the states of the Confederacy by only 50.9 percent to 49.1 percent. In 1996 Bill Clinton edged Bob Dole 50.05 percent to 49.95 percent in these states.

At the other end of the scale, certain traditionally Republican strongholds have become more competitive. At one time immoderately Republican, Maine, New Hampshire, and Vermont are no longer in the bag. Each election puts a further strain on old party loyalties. Landslide elections occur from time to time, as in 1964 (Johnson over Goldwater), 1972 (Nixon over McGovern), and 1984 (Reagan over Mondale), but they are often followed by cliffhangers, as in 1968 (Nixon over Humphrey) and 1976 (Carter over Ford). What is more, some presidential elections are much closer than they appear at first glance. In 1988, for example, a switch of fewer than 600,000 votes from Bush to Dukakis (out of 91.5 million cast) in eleven states would have led to the election of Dukakis. (Bush narrowly carried such big states as Illinois, Pennsylvania, and California.) Clinton's margin over Bush in 1992 was more comfortable (43.0 percent to 37.4 percent, with Perot garnering 18.9 percent). Clinton won reelection in 1996 by a comfortable margin of 49.2 percent to Dole's 40.7 percent. It is a good guess that most future presidential elections will be closely competitive—decided by thin margins in a handful of states—especially when no incumbent is in the race.

Congressional elections are another story. Many congressional districts have a long history of one-party or incumbent domination. The diversion of House and Senate elections from the mainstream of competitive politics is obvious (see Table 2-3). In the typical election during the 1990s, about 20 percent to 25 percent of the House elections were marginal—that is, elections in which the winning candidate received less than 55 percent of the vote. Though more competitive than those of the House, Senate elections usually result in control by the same party.[16] Incumbency is the key factor in limiting turnover of congressional seats. As would be expected, party control is most likely to shift when a seat is open—when no incumbent is running.

House elections have become so one-sided that the 55–45 division may no longer constitute a good measure of marginality. If a marginal district is defined as one won by less than 60 percent of the vote, the results are somewhat different. Even so, in 1996, when Republican House candidates nationwide narrowly edged Democratic House candidates (48.9 percent to 48.6 percent), about 60 percent of the districts were won by a margin of 60 to 40 or greater. Both parties thrive on safe-district politics, and in most elections fewer than a dozen House seats switch party hands.

Filling out this account of limited competitiveness at the congressional

TABLE 2-3 Marginal, Safer, and Uncontested Seats in House and Senate
Elections: 1990 to 1996 (by Percentage of Total Seats)

	House				Senate			
Election margin	1990	1992	1994	1996	1990	1992	1994	1996
Seats won by Democrats by less than 55 percent of the vote ⎤	7.0	14.1	11.0	10.9	11.4	28.6	18.2	23.5
Seats won by Republicans by less than 55 percent of the vote ⎦ (Marginal)	5.8	11.3	11.9	11.6	14.3	25.7	21.2	35.3
Seats won by Democrats by 55 percent or more of the vote ⎤	43.5	41.1	34.1	35.5	31.4	28.6	18.2	14.7
Seats won by Republicans by 55 percent or more of the vote ⎦ (Safer)	25.3	26.6	35.7	38.1	28.6	14.3	42.4	26.5
Uncontested seats	18.4	6.9	7.3	3.9	14.3	2.8	0.0	0.0

SOURCE: Data drawn from various issues of *Congressional Quarterly Weekly Report.*

level is evidence on the advantage of incumbency (see Table 2-4). In the usual election, more than 90 percent of the House incumbents on the ballot are returned to Washington. A record for House incumbents was established in 1988, when more than 98.5 percent were reelected. In 1992 and 1994, 93 percent and 90 percent, respectively, were returned to Washington—but some by closer margins than usual in these elections marked by substantial antiincumbent sentiment. Senate incumbents face stiffer opposition, but they ordinarily do well. In 1996 only one incumbent lost in the general election. Few incumbents ordinarily fall by the wayside in the primaries, though in 1992 nineteen House members were denied renomination. Most of these members lost because of unfavorable redistricting plans or because they had received damaging publicity for their involvement in the House banking scandal. Notwithstanding recent experience, the blunt truth is that Congress is an arena for two-party politics not because its members are produced by competitive environments but because both parties have managed to develop and protect large blocs of noncompetitive seats. Incumbency is a major factor in each party's success in reducing competition.[17]

TABLE 2-4   The Advantage of Incumbency in House and Senate
Elections: 1974 to 1996

| Year | | Total number of incumbents | | | | Percentage of incumbents running in general election elected |
		Defeated in primary	Running in general election	Elected in general election	Defeated in general election	
1974	House	8	383	343	40	89.56
	Senate	2	25	23	2	92.00
1976	House	3	381	368	13	96.59
	Senate	0	25	16	9	64.00
1978	House	5	377	358	19	94.96
	Senate	3	22	15	7	68.18
1980	House	6	392	361	31	92.09
	Senate	4	25	16	9	64.00
1982	House	4	383	354	29	92.42
	Senate	0	30	28	2	93.33
1984	House	3	408	392	16	96.07
	Senate	0	29	26	3	89.65
1986	House	2	391	385	6	98.46
	Senate	0	28	21	7	75.00
1988	House	1	408	402	6	98.53
	Senate	0	27	23	4	85.18
1990	House	1	406	391	15	96.31
	Senate	0	32	31	1	96.88
1992	House	19	351	327	24	93.16
	Senate	1	27	23	4	85.18
1994	House	4	382	345	37	90.31
	Senate	0	26	24	2	92.31
1996	House	2	381	360	21	94.49
	Senate	1	19	18	1	94.74

SOURCES: *Congressional Quarterly Weekly Report,* March 25, 1978, 755; November 15, 1986, 2891; November 12, 1988, 3267; November 10, 1990, 3797; and November 7, 1992, 3557. The data for 1994 and 1996 were provided by Eugene J. Gabler of Congressional Quarterly.

Competitiveness at the State Level

A wide range of competitiveness exists in the fifty states, as shown by the data of Figure 2-2. In devising this figure, the degree of interparty competition was calculated for each state by blending four separate state scores: the

FIGURE 2-2   The Fifty States Classified According to Degree of Interparty
Competition, 1989–1994

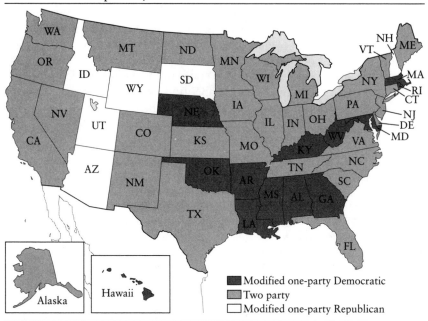

Modified one-party Democratic
Two party
Modified one-party Republican

SOURCE: Based on the classification of John F. Bibby and Thomas M. Holbrook, "Parties in State Politics,"
in *Politics in the American States: A Comparative Analysis,* ed. Virginia Gray and Herbert Jacob (Washington, D.C.: CQ Press, 1996), 105. The classification scheme was originally developed by Austin Ranney.

average percentage of the popular vote received by Democratic gubernatorial candidates; the average percentage of Democratic seats in the state senate; the average percentage of Democratic seats in the state house of representatives; and the percentage of all terms for governor, senate, and house in which the Democrats were in control. Taken together, these percentages constitute an "index of competitiveness" for each state.

In about 40 percent of the states, party competition for state offices lacks an authentic ring. Over the period of this study, 1989 to 1994, thirteen states were classified as modified one-party Democratic and six states as modified one-party Republican. Thirty-one states met the test of two-party competition—a larger number than at any time in the past several decades.[18] No state emerges as a one-party state, though these states were commonly found in the past, particularly in the once solidly Democratic South.

Competitiveness is associated with several factors. The Democratic party is strongest in the Deep South and in certain border and New England states; the Republican party dominates in certain western and mountain states, such as Utah, Idaho, and Wyoming. Two-party states are found throughout the country, and include such southern states as Texas, Florida, South Carolina, and North Carolina. Virtually all of the most populous and industrialized states are competitive in elections for state offices.

Interparty competitiveness cannot be measured simply in terms of the struggle to capture state offices. Some states in the modified one-party categories exhibit vigorous two-party competition in national elections. Mississippi and Alabama, for example, classified as one-party Democratic states, voted Republican in all five presidential elections between 1980 and 1996. Competitiveness must therefore be explored along several dimensions.

Competitiveness at the Office Level

Party competition differs greatly not only between states but also between offices in the same state. The complexity inherent in the concept of competitiveness is revealed in Figure 2-3. To unravel the figure, examine the location of each state office on the horizontal and vertical axes. The horizontal axis shows the extent to which the parties have controlled each office over the period of the study; the vertical axis shows the rate of turnover in control of the office between the parties. Some offices are steadfastly held by one party, and other offices are genuinely competitive. Wide variations exist within each state. Taking the northern states as a group, there is less competition for seats in the House than for any other office. By contrast, the offices of governor and senator are the most competitive—even these offices, however, are not significantly competitive.

Overall, the pattern of competition depicted by the data in Figure 2-3 testifies to the inability of state parties to compete for and to control a range of offices. To emphasize a point made earlier, the figure suggests, albeit subtly, that the successful officeholder is one who develops and maintains his own campaign resources, knowing that the party organization is about as likely to be a spectator to his career as a guardian of it.[19]

The Persistent Two-Party System in America

Despite the existence of one-party systems here and there, political competition in the United States usually comes down to competition between the two major parties, Democratic and Republican. The reason American politics has been receptive to a two-party rather than a multiple-party system, as in many European democracies, is not plain. What follows is a summary of the principal hypotheses, less than laws but more than hunches, that have been offered as explanations.

FIGURE 2-3   Party Competition for Individual Offices (Selected States)

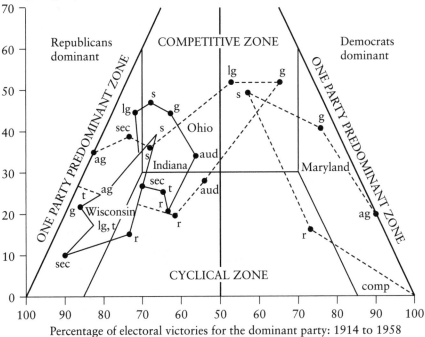

Percentage of elections
in which there was a
change of party: 1914 to 1958

SOURCE: Joseph A. Schlesinger, "The Structure of Competition for Office in the American States," *Behavioral Science 5* (July 1960): 203. "The more centrally located on the horizontal axis the more competitive an office was in overall terms; the higher on the diagram the more rapid the rate of turnover; and correspondingly, the lower on the diagram an office falls, the longer the cycles of one-party control, regardless of the degree of overall competition."

NOTE: g = governor; s = U.S. senator; r = U.S. representative; lg = lieutenant governor; sec = secretary of state; ag = attorney general; aud = auditor; t = treasurer; comp = comptroller.

A familiar explanation is that electing House members from single-member districts by plurality vote helps to support the two-party pattern. Under this arrangement a single candidate is elected in each district, and he or she needs to receive only a plurality of the vote. Third party candidates have slight inducement to run, because the prospects are poor that they could defeat the candidates of the two major parties. On the other hand, if members of Congress were elected under a proportional representation scheme, with several members chosen in each district, third party candidates would undoubtedly have a better chance of winning some seats.[20] Third parties face the same obstacle in presidential elections as they do in congressional races: Only one party can win. For the office of the presidency, the entire nation takes on the cast of a single-member district. Each state's electoral votes are awarded as a unit to the candidate receiving a plurality of the popular vote; all other popular votes are in effect wasted. In 1968, for example, George Wallace, candidate of the American Independent party, received about five million popular votes in states outside the South but won electoral votes only in the five southern states he carried. Running as an independent in 1980, John B. Anderson received nearly six million popular votes (6.6 percent of the total vote) but no electoral votes. And in 1992, Ross Perot received nearly twenty million popular votes (winning more than 27 percent of the vote in Maine, Alaska, Idaho, Utah, and Kansas), only to be skunked in the electoral college. Doing much worse in 1996 (eight million popular votes, or 8.4 percent), Perot was again shut out in the electoral college. If electoral votes were divided in proportion to popular votes in each state, third party and independent candidates would make a bigger dent in the electoral vote totals of the major parties. Electoral practices in the United States are hard on third parties—so successful in limiting competition that they force outsiders to think about running for the nomination of a major party.

The diversity and flexibility that characterize the two major parties also contribute to the preservation of the two-party system. The policy orientations of the parties are rarely so firmly fixed as to preclude a shift in emphasis or direction to attract emerging interests within the electorate. Moreover, each party is made up of officeholders with different views. Almost any political group, as a result, can discover some officials who share its values and predilections and who are willing to represent its point of view. The adaptability of the parties and the officeholders not only permits them to siphon off support that otherwise might contribute to the development of third parties but also creates a great deal of slack in the political system. Groups pressing for change know that there is always some chance that they can win acceptance for their positions within the existing party framework.

Another central explanation for the durability of the two-party system in America is found in a tradition of dualism.[21] Early political conflict occurred between those who favored adoption of the Constitution and those who opposed it. Subsequently, dualism was reflected in struggles between Federalists and Anti-Federalists and, later still, between Democrats and Whigs. Since the Civil War, the main party battle has been fought between Democrats and Republicans. In sum, the main elements of conflict within the American political system have ordinarily found expression in competition between two dominant groups of politicians and their followings. This, in a nutshell, is the essence of American party history. Third parties have cropped up to challenge the major ones, but their lives ordinarily

Single-Member Districts and Party Representation, 105th Congress (1997–1998)

Members of the U.S. House of Representatives (and of most state legislatures) are elected from single-member districts. (For the small states of Alaska, Delaware, North Dakota, South Dakota, Vermont, and Wyoming—each of which elects one U.S. representative—the entire state is a single-member district.) The single-member district system is a distorting mirror for popular preferences. It inflates the number of seats won by the majority party while reducing the number won by the minority party. Because only one candidate can win in each district, all votes for the losing candidate are wasted. The relationship between votes (statewide congressional vote for each party) and seats won in a variety of states in 1996 is reflected in the table.

State	Democratic		Republican	
	Statewide congressional vote	Seats won	Statewide congressional vote	Seats won
Utah (3)	41%	0%	59%	100%
Oklahoma (6)	37	0	63	100
Massachusetts (10)	64	100	36	0
Iowa (5)	45	20	55	80
Kentucky (6)	45	20	55	80
Oregon (5)	58	80	42	20
Arizona (6)	40	20	60	80
Minnesota (8)	57	75	43	25
Alabama (7)	46	29	54	71
Connecticut (6)	57	67	43	33
Tennessee (9)	49	44	51	56
Michigan (18)	54	56	46	44

SOURCE: *Congressional Quarterly Weekly Report*, November 9, 1996, 3250–3257.

NOTE: The number of House members for each state is shown in parentheses.

TABLE 2-5   Third Party and Independent Presidential Candidates
Receiving 5 Percent or More of Popular Vote

Candidate (party)	Year	Percentage of popular vote	Electoral votes
Theodore Roosevelt (Progressive)	1912	27.4	88
Millard Fillmore (Whig-American)	1856	21.5	8
Ross Perot (Independent)	1992	18.9	0
John C. Breckinridge (Southern Democrat)	1860	18.1	72
Robert M. LaFollette (Progressive)	1924	16.6	13
George C. Wallace (American Independent)	1968	13.5	46
John Bell (Constitutional Union)	1860	12.6	39
Martin Van Buren (Free Soil)	1848	10.1	0
James B. Weaver (Populist)	1892	8.5	22
Ross Perot (Reform)	1996	8.4	0
William Wirt (Anti-Masonic)	1832	7.8	7
John B. Anderson (Independent)	1980	6.6	0
Eugene V. Debs (Socialist)	1912	6.0	0

SOURCE: *Congressional Quarterly Weekly Report,* October 18, 1980, 3147 (as adapted and updated).

have been short and uneventful—so wary are many voters about new political movements and untested or less predictable politicians. Third parties or independent candidates rarely receive as much as 5 percent of the popular vote; this has occurred only thirteen times since 1832 (see Table 2-5).

A profusion of other themes might be explored in seeking to account for the two-party character of American politics. Election law, for example, makes it difficult for all but the most well-organized and well-financed third parties to gain a place on the ballot. In presidential elections they must struggle in state after state to recruit campaign workers and funds and to collect signatures for their nominating petitions.[22] Even audiences may be hard to come by. In addition, because the risk of failure looms so large, new political organizations must strain to find acceptable candidates to run under their banner. Aspiring politicians are not notable for their willingness to take quixotic risks for the sake of ideology or principle, particularly if there is some chance that a career in one of the major parties is available. The extraordinary costs of organizing and conducting major campaigns, the difficulties that attend the search for men and women to assume party outposts, and the frustrations that plague efforts to cut the cords that bind American voters to the traditional parties all serve to inhibit the formation and maintenance of third parties. It also appears that the restless impulse for new alternatives that often dominates other nations, thus leading to the formation of new political parties, is found less commonly in the United States.

Finally, strange as it may seem, one-partyism enhances the two-party system. Each party has a number of areas (states or districts) that vote consistently and heavily for its candidates, irrespective of the intensity of forces that play on voters there and elsewhere. Even when one of the major parties has a particularly bad election year, it is never threatened with extinction. Republicans may clean up in outstate and downstate Illinois, but Chicago will remain safely Democratic. Most of the rural, less-populous counties of Pennsylvania will vote Republican " 'til the cows come home," but Pittsburgh, Philadelphia, and other industrial areas will vote to elect Democratic candidates. Year in and year out, for most offices, Maryland and Rhode Island turn to the Democrats, while Utah and South Dakota faithfully vote Republican. One-party areas remove some of the mystery that surrounds American elections. Each major party owes something to them, counts on them, and is not often disappointed.

Parties as Coalitions

Viewed from afar, the American major party is likely to appear as a miscellaneous collection of individual activists and voters, banded together in some fashion to attempt to gain control of government. But there is more shadow than substance in that view; when the party is brought into focus, its basic coalitional character is revealed. The point is simple but important: The party is much less a collection of individuals than it is a collection of social interests and groups. In the words of Maurice Duverger, "A party is not a community but a collection of communities, a union of small groups dispersed throughout the country." [23]

Functioning within a vastly heterogeneous society, the major parties have naturally assumed a coalitional form. Groups of all kinds—social, economic, religious, and ethnic—are organized to press demands on the political order. In the course of defending or advancing their interests, they contribute substantial energy to the political process—by generating innovations, posing alternative policies, recruiting and endorsing candidates, conducting campaigns, and so on. No party seriously contesting for office could ignore the constellation of groups in American political life.

Traditionally, each party has had relatively distinct followings in the electorate. The urban working classes, union families, Blacks, Catholics,

The Voting Behavior of Southern Whites . . .

	1980		1984		1988		1992		1996	
	D	R	D	R	D	R	D	R	D	R
Vote for president	35%	62%	28%	72%	33%	67%	41%	59%	39%	61%

SOURCES: Developed from data in *Public Opinion*, December/January 1985, 4; *The '88 Vote* (New York: Capital Cities/ABC Inc., 1989), 55; and Gerald M. Pomper, "The Presidential Election," in *The Election of 1992*, ed. Gerald M. Pomper (Chatham, N.J.: Chatham House Publishers, Inc., 1993), 139.

From shortly after the Civil War to mid-twentieth century, the Democratic party maintained a virtual monopoly of power in the states of the Confederacy. In party language, the confederate states were the "Solid South," because in election after election citizens voted overwhelmingly for Democratic candidates. The cohesion of the South stemmed from the experience of secession and the collective bitterness over the loss of the war, from the durable economic interests of an agricultural society, and, most important, from a widespread desire to maintain segregation and White supremacy by excluding Blacks from the political system.

But historical cohesion has its limits. The Solid South was destined for destruction when the national Democratic party became active in the 1940s in promoting policies, economic as well as racial, that were anathema to the party's conservative southern wing. In 1948 southern Democrats rebelled and created a "bolter" party, the Dixiecrats. Although this

Jews, persons at the lower end of the educational scale, and the poor have been mainstays of the Democratic party since the New Deal. Southerners and various nationality groups have also played major roles in the Democratic party. In counterpoise, the Republican coalition has had a disproportionate number of supporters from such groups as big business, industry, farmers, small-town and rural dwellers, Whites, Protestants, upper-income and better-educated persons, nonunion families, and "old stock" Americans. Coalition politics has been a major feature of successful election campaigns.

. . . in Presidential and Congressional Elections

insurgent party failed—the Dixiecratic candidates carried only four states—it served as an instrument of transition for many southern Whites disillusioned with the liberal thrust of the national Democratic party. Thus southern Whites who had voted for the Dixiecrats in 1948 found it possible in 1952 to do the unthinkable, to vote for a Republican, Dwight D. Eisenhower. And as a result of the support of these "Presidential Republicans," Eisenhower carried four southern states and only narrowly lost several others. Republican strength continued to grow, and by the mid-1980s at least two out of three southern White voters were supporting Republican presidential candidates. In 1996 Bob Dole received 61 percent of the southern White vote to Bill Clinton's 39 percent. (In the three-way race, the percentages were Dole 56, Clinton 36, and Perot 8.)

Throughout the 1950s and 1960s, Republican strength in the South was largely confined to presidential elections. Republican congressional candidates generally fared poorly. The pattern of southern politics is sharply different today. Southern Whites are as likely to vote for Republican congressional candidates as they are for Republican presidential candidates. So substantial has the shift been that it is now common for the Republicans to elect nearly two thirds of all southern members of Congress.

The South has become a genuine two-party system for national offices. State and local offices continue to be dominated by the Democratic party. The South's first fling with a minor party candidate was in 1968, when Alabama's George C. Wallace ran for the presidency. Today's two-party competition in the South is the natural extension of a secular trend begun some four decades ago.

Today, these coalitions are clearly in flux, particularly on the Democratic side. For example, although the vast majority of state and local offices in the South continue to be controlled by the Democratic party, the Republicans have made major gains at the national level and especially in presidential elections. Consider recent history. Disillusioned over the liberal thrust of the party, many lifelong southern Democrats bolted in 1964 to support Barry Goldwater, the Republican nominee. In even greater number they moved

The Most Loyal Groups
in the Party Coalitions

| | Presidential election year | | | |
Groups	1984	1988	1992	1996
Percentage points more Democratic than the nation as a whole				
African Americans	50	41	40	35
Jews	27	19	37	29
Hispanics	22	24	18	23
Unmarried women	10	12	10	13
Union households	13	12	12	10
Percentage points more Republican than the nation as a whole				
White fundamentalist or evangelical Christians	19	27	23	24
Southern Whites	12	14	11	15
High income	10	8	10	10
Asians	—	—	17	7
Whites	5	6	2	5

SOURCE: Developed from data in Voter News Service national exit polls, as reported in *New York Times*, November 10, 1996.

NOTE: Low income in 1996 is defined as less than $15,000 annually, high income as $75,000 and over. Of the total vote in 1996, African Americans made up 10 percent; Hispanics, 5 percent; Jews, 3 percent; unmarried women, 20 percent; and union households, 23 percent. Whites cast 83 percent of the total vote.

into the ranks of the American Independent party in 1968, voting for George Wallace in preference to the Democratic and Republican nominees, Hubert Humphrey and Richard Nixon, respectively. In 1972 southern voters switched to Nixon. With a Georgian, Jimmy Carter, at the head of the Democratic ticket in 1976, they abandoned their newly found Republicanism and returned to the Democratic fold. But their stay was brief. In 1980 and 1984 they voted decisively for Ronald Reagan, and he swept the region (losing

TABLE 2-6   Intraparty Conflict in Senate Roll-Call Voting,
104th Congress, Second Session

| Region | Percentage of northern and southern Democrats voting with a majority of their own party | | | | |
	90% or more	80–89.9%	70–79.9%	60–69.9%	50–59.9%
Northern Democrats	43	43	14	0	0
Southern Democrats	0	40	20	20	20

SOURCE: Developed from party unity data compiled in *Congressional Quarterly Weekly Report,* December 21, 1996, 3463.

NOTE: Failures to vote, in this analysis, do not lower party unity scores. The table shows that 43 percent of northern Democrats voted with their party at least 90 percent of the time; by contrast, no southern Democrats scored this high in party unity.

only Georgia in his first election). And in 1988 and 1992 George Bush ran 5 to 6 percentage points stronger in this region than he did nationally. He carried every southern state in 1988 and seven of thirteen in 1992. In 1996 Bob Dole carried eight of thirteen southern states, winning Texas with its 32 electoral votes but losing Florida with its 25 electoral votes.

Some loss in the distinctiveness of religious groups' voting behavior has occurred in recent years. In 1960 Catholics voted 28 percentage points more Democratic than the electorate as a whole (78 percent to 50 percent). Protestants, by contrast, voted 12 percentage points more Republican than the national average (62 percent to 50 percent). And in 1964 Catholics voted strongly for Lyndon Johnson (76 percent as contrasted with his national average of 61 percent). Since then, Catholic support for Democratic presidential candidates has declined. In 1984, according to most surveys, the Catholic vote mirrored the national vote—59 percent Republican, 41 percent Democratic.[24] In 1996, 53 percent of Catholics voted for Bill Clinton as compared with his national average of 49 percent. Although the overall Protestant vote has become somewhat less Republican over the years, the vote of *White* Protestants has been strongly Republican. In recent presidential elections, about two out of three White Protestants have voted for the GOP candidate. Interestingly, evangelical Christians now vote overwhelmingly Republican; although Bush received only 37 percent of the national vote in 1992, he received 61 percent of the fundamentalist vote. In 1996 Bob Dole received 41 percent of the national vote but 65 percent of the vote of born-again Christians. It remains to be noted that the most distinctive vote of all religious groups today is the Jewish vote; in 1992 and 1996 about eight out of ten Jews voted for Clinton.

Union members have become a less predictable element in the Democratic coalition than they were in the past, particularly during the Kennedy and Johnson years. In 1984 union families favored Walter Mondale over Ronald Reagan by a margin of only 52 percent to 48 percent. In 1988 they preferred Michael Dukakis to George Bush by a hefty margin of 63 percent to 37 percent—a party division about the same as in the 1976 race between Jimmy Carter and Gerald Ford. In 1992 voters in union households gave Clinton a narrow majority—55 percent to Bush's 24 percent and Perot's 21 percent. Clinton did better in 1996, winning 59 percent of the vote of union families to Dole's 30 percent and Perot's 9 percent. Overall, the voting behavior of group members is more volatile today than in the past— as would be expected in a period of *dealignment* in which group attachments to the parties become weaker.

American parties are fragile because they are coalitions. At times they seem to be held together by nothing more than generality, personality, and promise. Perhaps what is surprising, all things considered, is that they hold together as well as they do.

The chief threat to party cohesion develops once the election is over and the party is placed in government. It is at this point that coalitions sometimes split apart. The party unity data in Table 2-6 show how often northern and southern Senate Democrats voted in agreement with a majority of their party in the second session of the 104th Congress (1996). For northern Democrats, party positions were obviously important. More than three fourths of this group voted with their party 80 percent or more of the time. Southern Democrats were much less likely to vote with a majority of their party. Nonetheless, although intraparty conflict is fairly common in both houses, there is less of it today than a decade or two ago. The main reason for this is that the constituencies of southern Democrats have become more similar to those of northern Democrats, and hence there are fewer conflicts between them over the thrust of public policy.

The voting behavior reflected in Table 2-6 makes it clear that significant disagreement hides behind the party label, especially in the case of congressional Democrats. When party coalitions come apart in Congress, biparty coalitions often form. The most enduring and successful biparty coalition in the history of Congress has been the conservative coalition formed by a majority of southern Democrats and a majority of Republicans. In existence in one form or another since the late 1930s, this coalition comes together on essentially the same policy issues that divide northern from southern Democrats. During the early 1980s, the conservative coalition played a key role in the adoption of the Reagan administration's legislative program. Since then, the coalition's influence has declined. Currently it comes together on about 12 percent of all recorded votes (as contrasted with more than 20 percent in the 1970s). When it does form, however, it usually wins. In 1995 the coalition appeared on 11 percent of the recorded votes of both chambers and won 98 percent of the time. In 1996 it appeared on 12 percent of the recorded votes and won 99 percent of the time.[25]

Parties of Ideological Heterogeneity

To win elections and gain power is the unabashedly practical aim of the major party. As suggested previously, this calls for a strategy of coalition building in which the policy goals of the groups and candidates brought under the party umbrella are subordinated to their capacity to contribute to party victory. The key to party success is its adaptability, its willingness to do business with groups and individuals holding all manner of views on public policy questions. The natural outcome of a campaign strategy designed to attract all groups (and to repel none) is that the party's ideology is not easily brought into sharp focus. It is, in a sense, up for grabs, to be interpreted as individual party members and officeholders see fit.

The data in Figure 2-4 illuminate the ideological distance that separates members of the same party (and also the differences between the parties) on proposals of key interest to the Americans for Democratic Action (ADA)—a group well known for its identification with liberal causes and policies. Those senators voting in harmony with ADA objectives in the 104th Congress supported such positions and policies as an increase in federal spending on education by closing certain corporate tax loopholes, low-income home energy assistance, a raise in the minimum wage, an increase in funds available for job training and job placement, an increase in funds for legal assistance service for the poor, federal standards for nursing homes, drug discounts in state Medicaid programs, student loans through the government, maintenance of the entitlement status of welfare benefits, and legal protection for doctors who perform late-term abortions. In addition, members voting in agreement with the ADA opposed various reductions in Medicare, deployment of antimissile systems, lobby bans on nonprofit organizations, limits on punitive damage awards, an easing of occupational safety and health regulations, and the relaxation of antitrust rules for medical provider service networks. An examination of this sketch of ideological

FIGURE 2-4 Democratic and Republican Support of Americans for Democratic Action (ADA) Positions, by Region and Certain Individual Senate Members, 104th Congress, First Session

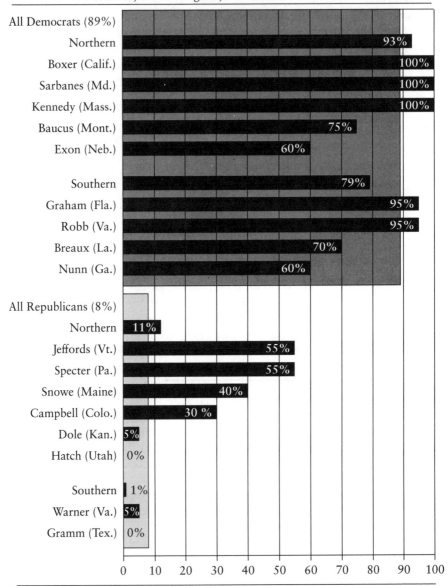

SOURCE: Developed from data appearing in *ADA Today*, March 1996 (Washington, D.C.)

NOTE: The eleven states of the Confederacy plus Kentucky and Oklahoma are classified as southern; all others are classified as northern. Eleven Democrats had ratings of 100 percent pro-ADA; twenty-eight Republicans had ratings of 0 percent.

conflict in the Senate makes it clear that serious differences are found within each party as well as between them.

The divisions within each major party are easy to identify. Historically, southern Democrats have not viewed the world (and policy questions) in the same light as northern Democrats. Similarly, some eastern and western Republicans have been out of step with fellow party members from the South or the Midwest. Yet it is easy to exaggerate intraparty conflict. In the 104th Congress (following the Republicans' capture of both houses in 1994), for example, both parties were unusually cohesive and frequently in opposition with each other. The truth of the matter is that both parties now have more unity than in recent decades and more than is commonly supposed.

Ideological coherence within each party varies over time. Nevertheless, important and continuing policy differences between the parties are clearly apparent. Democratic members of Congress and Democratic congressional candidates are much more likely to support social welfare legislation and an expanded role for the federal government, for example, than are Republican officeholders and Republican candidates. Programs to advance minority rights, to make available federal funds for public education, to improve the lot of low-income individuals and families, to support family planning programs (including abortion counseling at federally funded clinics), to provide medical care for the elderly, to curtail different forms of defense spending, to regulate business, and to promote the interests of labor typically produce substantial disagreement between the parties, with most Democrats aligned on the liberal side and most Republicans aligned on the conservative side. The congressional parties do differ. Hence, even though some party members may be marching to different drums some of the time, most of them are usually playing the same tune.

Parties of Moderation and Inclusivity

Another way to view American parties emphasizes their moderation and inclusivity. They are, in fact, "catchall" parties in which all but the most extreme and intractable elements in society can find a place and, in the process, stake a claim to a piece of the action.

The American party is anything but clannish. It will lend a friendly ear to just about any request. All groups are invited to support the party, and in some measure all do. Almost everything about the major party at election time represents a triumph for those who press for accommodation in American politics. Platforms and candidate speeches, offering something to virtually everyone, provide the hard evidence that the parties attempt to be inclusive rather than exclusive in their appeals and to draw in a wide rather than a narrow band of voters. "No matter how devoted a party leadership may be to its bedrock elements," V. O. Key Jr., observed, "it attempts to picture itself as a gifted synthesizer of concord among the elements of society. A party must act as if it were all the people rather than some of them; it must fiercely deny that it speaks for a single interest."[26]

The inclusivity of the major American parties means that they occupy virtually all of the political space in the political system. Minor parties are forced to search for distinctiveness. Some fashion narrow appeals. Others press bizarre or hopeless causes. Still others maneuver only at the ideological fringes, seeking to address extreme left wing or right wing audiences. Their dilemma is that only a relative handful of voters are at each ideological pole and only a few will be attracted to a narrow or single-issue appeal. The net result is that most minor parties struggle to secure candidates, financing, media attention, and credibility. The bottom line is that they struggle simply to stay in business.

The Founders established an intricate system of divided powers, checks and balances, and auxiliary precautions to reduce the government's vulnerability to factions. The "Madisonian system"—separation of powers, staggered terms of office, bicameralism, federalism, life appointments for federal judges, fixed terms of office for the president and members of Congress, among other things—makes it difficult for any group (faction or party) to gain firm control of the political system. Today's parties qualify as Madison's factions, but with an unexpected twist. They are in no way a factional threat. Their inclusivity and moderation represent at least as great an obstacle to factional domination of government as do formal constitutional arrangements. Because the major parties include all kinds of interests, they are not free to favor a single interest or a small cluster of interests to the exclusion of others. Standing party policies are an expression of earlier settlements among divergent interests. Virtually every new policy can be contested by interested party elements. Every affected interest expects a hearing, bargaining occurs as a matter of course, and accommodation typically takes place. The broad consequences, ordinarily, are first that policy making is a slow process and second that policy changes are introduced incrementally. The parties' moderation ordinarily means that no one wins completely and no one loses completely. (One consequence of this is that the public often has difficulty in deciding which party to single out for credit and which party to blame.) This argument is sketched in Figure 2-5.

FIGURE 2-5   Moderate Parties and Policy Making

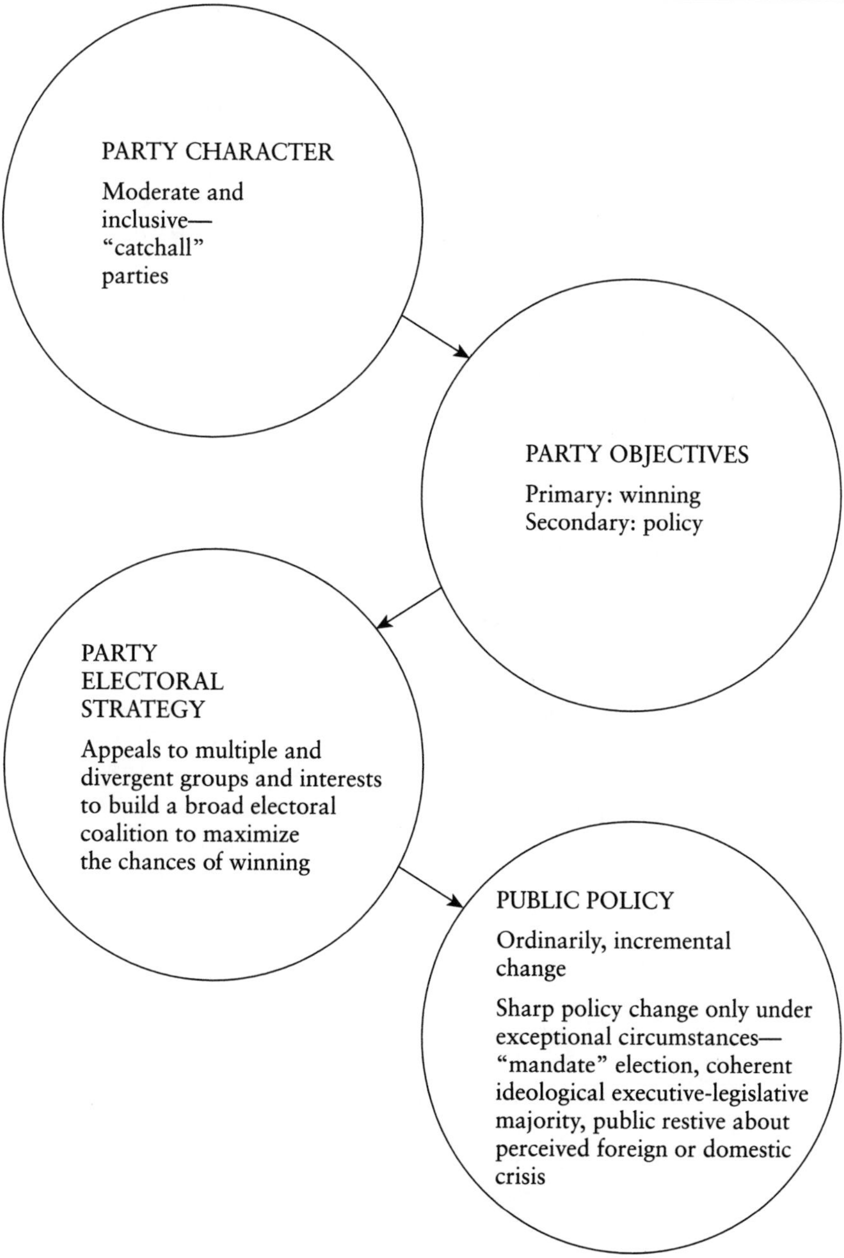

PARTY CHARACTER

Moderate and
inclusive—
"catchall"
parties

PARTY OBJECTIVES

Primary: winning
Secondary: policy

**PARTY
ELECTORAL
STRATEGY**

Appeals to multiple and
divergent groups and interests
to build a broad electoral
coalition to maximize
the chances of winning

PUBLIC POLICY

Ordinarily, incremental
change

Sharp policy change only under
exceptional circumstances—
"mandate" election, coherent
ideological executive-legislative
majority, public restive about
perceived foreign or domestic
crisis

The Party as an Interest Group

Although American parties are sometimes criticized for their cool detachment from important social and economic issues, the same cannot be said for their attitude toward a band of issues having high relevance for the party, *qua* party. Certain kinds of issues, or policy questions, that come before legislatures present the party with an opportunity to advance its interests as an organization—in much the same fashion as political interest groups attempt to secure or block legislation that would improve or impair their fortunes. As E. E. Schattschneider wrote some years ago, within each party is both a "public" and a "private" personality.[27] The public dimension of the party is on display when larger questions of public policy are brought before the legislature. As often occurs on these questions, party lines fail to hold; factions ease away from the party; and biparty coalitions are born, empowered for the moment as the majority. The party's public appearance, in the judgment of many critics, leaves much to be desired. The fundamental flaw is that the party nominally in control of government, but rent by factionalism and fragmentation, cannot be held responsible by the public for its decisions. The problem is not that party unity collapses on all issues but that it collapses with sufficient frequency to make it less than a dependable agent for carrying out commitments presumably made to the electorate.

In sharp contrast is the private personality of the party. Though it would be an exaggeration to argue that the party is engaged in steady introspection, it is surely true, as Schattschneider has observed, that "the party knows its private mind better than it knows its public mind." [28] It has a sharp sense of where the best opportunities lie for partisan advantage and of the perils and pitfalls that can threaten or damage party interests. Numerous occasions arise for transmitting benefits to the party organization and its members. Patronage can be extracted from government at all levels. In some jurisdictions literally hundreds or thousands of jobs are available for distribution to party stalwarts. At the national level, the custom of "senatorial courtesy" guarantees that senators will have the dominant voice in the selection of candidates to fill various positions, such as district court judges and U.S. marshals. This custom calls on the president, before nominating a person for a position in a state, to consult with the senators of that state (if they belong to the same party as he does) to learn their preference for the position. If he should nominate someone objectionable to the senators of that state, the prospects are strong that the full Senate will reject the nominee, irrespective of his qualifications. On questions of this sort—those that touch the careers and political fortunes of members—party unity is both high and predictable.

Legislators have never won reputations for queuing up behind proposals that might limit maneuvering in the interest of their careers or their party's welfare. With only a few exceptions, for example, they have opposed plans to extend the merit system, to take judges out of politics, and to empower independent boards or commissions to assume responsibility for reapportionment and redistricting. There is a private side to such public questions—to extend the merit system is to cut back party patronage, to remove judges from the election process is to cut off a career avenue for legislators with their sights on the court, and to give a nonlegislative commission control over redistricting is to run the risk of a major rearrangement of legislative districts and a resultant loss of offices. Legislators and the parties they represent take seriously their role as guardians of the welfare of the organization and the personal interests of its members. As a collectivity, the American party is most resourceful and cohesive when it is monitoring party business. And party business is about as likely to intrude on the great public questions as it is on those of narrow or parochial concern. Opportunities to advance the party cause—through debate, legislation, or investigations— are limited only by a failure of imagination.

The Ambiguity of Party Membership

For those people who set great store by neat and orderly arrangements, the American major party is vastly disappointing. There are numerous examples of the party in disarray. A particularly good one, in the judgment of some students of American politics, involves the concept of party membership.

Who is a party member in the United States? The answer is not clear, though a stab at the question can be made by considering the legal aspects of party membership. Closed primary states have tests of membership. Legal party membership in these states is determined by self-classification at the stage of registration. The significance of establishing membership is that each party's primary is open only to members registered in that party.[29] About one half of the states have authentic closed primary systems. By contrast, open primary states have no test of party affiliation. Gaining membership consists merely of the voter's request for the ballot of the party in whose primary he wishes to participate. In certain open primary states the voter is automatically given the ballots of all the parties, with instructions to mark one and discard the rest.

Apart from primary voting in closed primary states, membership in a major party is of slight moment. In effect, anyone who considers himself a Democrat is a Democrat; anyone who considers himself a Republican is a Republican. A citizen may register one way and vote another or not vote at all. No obligations intrude on the party member. He can be a member without applying for admission, a beneficiary without paying dues or contributing to campaigns, a critic without attending meetings, an interpreter without knowing party vocabulary, an apostate without fearing discipline. To the citizen who takes politics casually, it may be the best of all worlds. The typical American is insensitive to the claims, problems, and doctrine of his party. His principal participation in party life is through the act of voting—sometimes for his party and sometimes not.

The Indomitable Party?

The party in America is at the center of the political process. Nonetheless, its grip on political power is far from secure. To be sure, the people who are recruited for party and public offices, the issues that they bring before the electorate, the campaigns in which they participate, and the government that they help to organize and direct—all are influenced by party. The basic problem remains, however, that the party is unable to control all the routes to political power. In some jurisdictions, nonpartisan election systems have been developed to try to remove parties from politics, and to a degree they have succeeded. Moreover, so thoroughly are some states and localities dominated by one party that party itself has come to have little relevance for the kinds of men and women recruited for office or for the voters in need of cues for casting their votes. Devices such as the direct primary have also cut into the power of the party organization, serving in particular to discourage national party agencies from attempting to influence nominations, including those for national office, and to open up the nominating process to all kinds of candidates. In addition, divided party control of government has become a chronic problem of both state and national governments. Typically one party winds up controlling the executive branch and the other party one or both houses of the legislative branch. Determining which party is the majority party has become increasingly difficult.

The party-in-the-electorate—voters who regard themselves as party members—probably has never been weaker than it is right now. Almost one third of all voters profess to be independents. Strong partisans are less numerous than in the past. Split-ticket voting is common everywhere. Most voters do not view parties in a favorable light and many believe that party control over government is undesirable. Skepticism about the parties is endemic. On the whole, the nation's political culture is a hostile environment for parties. The absence of citizen interest in elections also takes a toll on party vitality. It is a spectacular fact that almost 100 million citizens who might have voted in the 1996 presidential election chose to ignore it. In the midst of the signs of party deterioration, it is not surprising that the influence of the mass media, public relations experts, campaign management firms, spin doctors, and political action committees has grown markedly in virtually all phases of campaigns and elections.

Perhaps the wonder of American politics is that the party system functions as well as it does. From the perspective of party leaders, the Constitution is a vast wasteland, scarcely capable of supporting vigorous parties; federalism, separation of powers, checks and balances, and staggered elections all have proved inimical to the organization of strong parties. National and state constitutions apparently were drafted by those who were suspicious of the concentration of power in any hands; their designs have served to fracture or immobilize party power. The party itself is an uneasy coalition of individuals and groups brought together for limited purposes. Within government, power is about as likely to be lodged in nooks and crannies as it is in central party agencies. Conflict within the parties is sometimes as intense as it is between the parties. As for the individual party member, he has a great many rights but virtually no responsibilities for the well-being of the party.

Public disillusionment over the parties places a further strain on their capacities. Many voters believe that the parties have not posed imaginative solutions for such nagging issues as racial injustice, urban decay, inflation, unemployment, and poverty. Similarly, citizens are concerned about the "old" politics that seems to dominate the parties, manifested in a preoccupation with patronage, perquisites, and the welfare of the organization instead of public policy. The parties are also subject to harsh criticism for their apparent willingness to yield to the blandishments of pressure groups and local interests while too frequently ignoring broad national interests and problems. For many citizens, parties appear as starkly conservative institutions, fearful of innovation and unable to shape intelligent responses to contemporary dilemmas.

Negative attitudes toward government, politics, and parties undoubtedly have increased in recent years. An opinion survey by the Times Mirror Center for the People and the Press several years ago concluded that "cynicism toward the political system in general is growing as the public in unprecedented numbers associates Republicans with wealth and greed, Democrats with fecklessness and incompetence." [30]

The party reforms of the modern period have done more to weaken the parties than to strengthen them. The spread of presidential primaries, the opening up of caucuses, the emergence and consolidation of participatory politics at the expense of elites, and the institutionalization of federal campaign finance law (and Supreme Court rulings concerning it) have diminished the role of parties and party leaders in presidential elections. All too often, parties are scarcely more than spectators to the campaign clashes of candidate organizations. As for the members of Congress, party is as much or as little as they choose to make of it. In the current state of free-floating politics, interest groups have gained increasing influence over election outcomes and, arguably, over public policies. Their role in financing congressional campaigns is one of the main reasons that campaign expenditures have grown rapidly, increasing at a rate that far outstrips inflation. In sum, in important respects, the politics of the late 1990s looks much different from the politics of the 1960s.

For those citizens who believe that democratic politics depends on the presence of viable parties, conditions must surely appear grim. Even so, it is by no means clear that the major parties are in the process of withering away, to be replaced by government without parties or government by multiple-party coalitions. Survival in this weakened state seems much more likely. And finally, it is useful to remember that, whatever else may be said of American parties, they have never been particularly strong.

Notes

1. On the decentralization of American parties, see Robert Harmel and Kenneth Janda, *Parties and Their Environment* (New York: Longmans, 1982), especially Chapter 5.
2. *Cousins v. Wigoda*, 419 U.S. 477 (1975). This case involved the seating of the Illinois delegation to the 1972 Democratic National Convention. The Court upheld the right of the Democratic convention to refuse to seat the Illinois delegation, which, according to findings of the credentials committee, had violated national party rules concerning the selection process for delegates and whose makeup inadequately represented youth, women, and minorities. The right of the national party to establish rules concerning delegate selection was further strengthened by the Court in a case involving Wisconsin's open presidential primary: *Democratic Party of the U.S. v. LaFollette*, 101 S. Ct. 1010 (1981).
3. The centralizing reforms in the delegate selection process of the Democratic party have not altered the basic decentralization of the party. See William J. Crotty, "The Philosophies of Party Reform," in *Party Renewal in America: Theory and Practice*, ed. Gerald M. Pomper (New York: Praeger Special Studies, 1980), especially 45–48.
4. Press release, Federal Election Commission, March 19, 1997.
5. See Paul S. Herrnson's analysis of the growing role of national party committees in providing services, such as fund raising and advertising, for House candidates. The Republican party has been much more active in this respect. "Do Parties Make a Difference?: The Role of Party Organizations in Congressional Elections," *Journal of Politics* 48 (August 1986): 589–615; and *Party Campaigning in the 1980s* (Cambridge, Mass.: Harvard University Press, 1988). And see an

earlier article by Elizabeth Drew, "Politics and Money," *New Yorker,* December 6, 1982, 64.

6. Austin Ranney and Willmoore Kendall, *Democracy and the American Party System* (New York: Harcourt, 1956), 497.

7. Thomas P. O'Neill with William Novak, *Man of the House: The Life and Political Memoirs of Speaker Tip O'Neill* (New York: Random House, 1987), 26.

8. See the interesting evidence of the influence of moneyed interests on congressional decision making marshalled by Richard L. Hall and Frank M. Wayman, "Buying Time: Moneyed Interests and the Mobilization of Bias in Congressional Committees," *American Political Science Review 84* (September 1990): 797–820.

9. James M. Burns, *The Deadlock of Democracy: Four Party Politics in America* (Englewood Cliffs, N.J.: Prentice Hall, 1963), 236–237. For an instructive study of state party organizations and leaders, see Robert J. Huckshorn, *Party Leadership in the States* (Amherst: University of Massachusetts Press, 1976).

10. See Cornelius P. Cotter, James L. Gibson, John F. Bibby, and Robert J. Huckshorn, *Party Organizations in American Politics* (New York: Praeger, 1984); and Bibby, Cotter, Gibson, and Huckshorn, "Parties in State Politics," in *Politics in the American States: A Comparative Analysis*, ed. Virginia Gray, Herbert Jacob, and Kenneth Vines (Boston: Little, Brown, 1983).

11. Barbara G. Salmore and Stephen A. Salmore, *Candidates, Parties, and Campaigns: Electoral Politics in America,* 2d ed. (Washington, D.C.: CQ Press, 1989), 255–256.

12. Burdett Loomis, *The New American Politician: Ambition, Entrepreneurship, and the Changing Face of Political Life* (New York: Basic Books, 1988), 244.

13. Representative Foley made this statement prior to becoming Speaker; he is quoted in Austin Ranney, *The Referendum Device* (Washington, D.C.: American Enterprise Institute for Public Policy Research, 1981), 70. Ranney is cited in Salmore and Salmore, *Candidates, Parties, and Campaigns,* 248.

14. This section on law and the parties is based primarily on the findings of David E. Price, *Bringing Back the Parties* (Washington, D.C.: CQ Press, 1984), especially Chapter 5. Contrast the heavily regulated parties of today with those of half a century ago described by E. E. Schattschneider in *Party Government* (New York: Holt, Rinehart and Winston, 1942), 11: "The extralegal character of political parties is one of their most notable qualities."

15. The competitiveness of presidential elections also can be examined from the perspective of the electoral college. Of the forty-six presidential elections held between 1876 and 1968, twenty-one can be classified as "hairbreadth elections"— those in which a slight shift in popular votes in a few states would have changed the outcome in the electoral college. See Lawrence D. Longley and Alan G. Braun, *The Politics of Electoral College Reform* (New Haven, Conn.: Yale University Press, 1972), especially 37–41.

16. Although Senate elections are more competitive than those of the House, the trend since 1970 has been toward less competitive nonsouthern Senate races. See Donald Gross and David Breaux, "Historical Trends in U.S. Senate Elections, 1912–1988," *American Politics Quarterly 19* (July 1991): 284–309. *Congressional Quarterly Weekly Report,* May 6, 1989, 1060–1065.

17. The literature on legislative-constituency relations, which includes examination of the incumbency factor in elections, is impressive. Anyone who takes the time to read the following studies on the subject will know vastly more than any nor-

mal person should know: David R. Mayhew, "Congressional Elections: The Case of the Vanishing Marginals," *Polity* 6 (Spring 1974): 295–317; Gary C. Jacobson, "The Effects of Campaign Spending in Congressional Elections," *American Political Science Review* 72 (June 1978): 469–491; Jon R. Bond, Gary Covington, and Richard Fleisher, "Explaining Challenger Quality in Congressional Elections," *Journal of Politics* 47 (May 1985): 510–529; Donald A. Gross and James C. Garrand, "The Vanishing Marginals, 1824–1980," *Journal of Politics* 46 (February 1984): 224–237; Robert S. Erikson and Gerald C. Wright, "Voters, Candidates, and Issues in Congressional Elections," in *Congress Reconsidered*, 3d ed., ed. Lawrence C. Dodd and Bruce I. Oppenheimer (Washington, D.C.: CQ Press, 1985), 87–108; John C. McAdams and John R. Johannes, "Constituency Attentiveness in the House: 1977–1982," *Journal of Politics* 47 (November 1985): 1108–1139; Glenn R. Parker and Suzanne L. Parker, "Correlates and Effects of Attention to District by U.S. House Members," *Legislative Studies Quarterly* 10 (May 1985): 223–242; Melissa P. Collie, "Incumbency, Electoral Safety, and Turnover in the House of Representatives, 1952–1976," *American Political Science Review* 75 (March 1981): 119–131; John R. Alford and John R. Hibbing, "Increased Incumbency Advantage in the House," *Journal of Politics* 43 (November 1981): 1042–1061; James E. Campbell, "The Return of the Incumbents: The Nature of the Incumbency Advantage," *Western Political Quarterly* 36 (September 1983): 434–444; Diana Evans Yiannakis, "The Grateful Electorate: Casework and Congressional Elections," *American Journal of Political Science* 25 (August 1981): 568–580; Richard Born, "Generational Replacement and the Growth of Incumbent Reelection Margins in the U.S. House," *American Political Science Review* 73 (September 1979): 811–817; Candice J. Nelson, "The Effect of Incumbency on Voting in Congressional Elections, 1964–1974," *Political Science Quarterly* 93 (Winter 1978–1979): 665–678; John R. Johannes and John C. McAdams, "The Congressional Incumbency Effect: Is It Casework, Policy Compatibility, or Something Else?" *American Journal of Political Science* 25 (August 1981): 512–542; Warren Lee Kostroski, "Party and Constituency in Postwar Senate Elections," *American Political Science Review* 67 (December 1973): 1213–1234; and Lyn Ragsdale, "Incumbent Popularity, Challenger Invisibility, and Congressional Voters," *Legislative Studies Quarterly* 6 (May 1981): 201–218. And see these books: David R. Mayhew, *Congress: The Electoral Connection* (New Haven, Conn.: Yale University Press, 1974); Richard F. Fenno, *Home Style: House Members in Their Districts* (Boston: Little, Brown, 1978); Gary C. Jacobson and Samuel Kernell, *Strategy and Choice in Congressional Elections* (New Haven, Conn.: Yale University Press, 1981); and Gary C. Jacobson, *The Politics of Congressional Elections* (Boston: Little, Brown, 1987), especially Chapter 3.

18. See John F. Bibby and Thomas M. Holbrook, "Parties in State Politics," in *Politics in the American States: A Comparative Analysis*, ed. Virginia Gray and Herbert Jacob (Washington, D.C.: CQ Press, 1996), 103–109. Also see the early study by Austin Ranney, "Parties in State Politics," in *Politics in the American States: A Comparative Analysis*, ed. Herbert Jacob and Kenneth Vines (Boston: Little, Brown, 1976), 63–65.

19. See a study by Thomas H. Little that finds that in states where legislative minority parties hold sufficient seats to be competitive, they develop intricate organizations, are active in election politics, and vote cohesively in the legislature. Noncompetitive minority parties have minimal organizational vitality, are little

involved in campaigns, and are engaged less frequently in partisan voting. "Electoral Competition and Legislative Minority Parties: Schlesinger's Parties in a Legislative Setting," *American Review of Politics* 16 (Fall 1995): 299–316.

20. Single-member districts clearly play a significant role in protecting the American major parties from the incursions of minor parties. What would happen if American states and communities were to adopt proportional representation (PR) elections, which require the use of multimember districts? See an enlightening essay by Douglas J. Amy on how the introduction of PR might affect the two-party system. "Proportional Representation and the Future of the American Party System," *American Review of Politics* 16 (Fall–Winter 1995): 371–383.

21. For analysis of the dualism theme, see V. O. Key Jr., *Politics, Parties, and Pressure Groups* (New York: Crowell, 1964), 207–208.

22. Major party nominees are automatically given access to the general election ballot. Minor, new party, and independent candidates have to qualify for the ballot by establishing a certain level of support, which is set by state law. For an analysis of ballot access laws, see Bruce W. Robeck and James A. Dyer, "Ballot Access Requirements in Congressional Elections," *American Politics Quarterly* 10 (January 1982): 31–45. Also see Richard Winger, "How Ballot Access Laws Affect the U. S. Party System," *American Review of Politics* 16 (Winter 1995): 321–350.

23. Maurice Duverger, *Political Parties* (New York: Wiley, 1965), 17.

24. *Gallup Report,* November 1988, 6–7.

25. *Congressional Quarterly Weekly Report,* December 21, 1996, 3466.

26. Key, *Politics, Parties, and Pressure Groups,* 221.

27. Schattschneider, *Party Government,* 133–137.

28. Schattschneider, *Party Government,* 134.

29. In 1973 the U. S. Supreme Court upheld, in a 5–4 decision, a New York state law that requires a voter to register his party affiliation thirty days in advance of a general election to be eligible to vote in that party's next primary election. Had the Court not upheld this "closed" provision, nothing would prevent voters from switching parties as often as they like, permitting Democrats to vote in Republican primaries and Republicans to vote in Democratic primaries. *Rosario v. Rockefeller,* 410 U.S. 752 (1973).

30. *The People, the Press, and Politics, 1990* (Washington, D.C.: Times Mirror Center for the People and the Press, 1990), 32, 2.

Chapter Three

Political Parties and the Electoral Process: Nominations

It is probable that no nation has ever experimented as fully or as fitfully with mechanisms for making nominations as has the United States. The principal sponsor of this experimentation is the federal system itself. Under it, responsibility for the development of election law lies with the states. Their ingenuity, given free rein, has often been remarkable. A wide variety of caucuses, conventions, and primaries—the three principal methods of making nominations—has been tried out in the states. The devices that have lasted owe their survival not so much to a widespread agreement on their merits as to the inability of opponents to settle on alternative arrangements and to the general indifference of the public at large to major institutional change.

Nominating Methods

Caucus

The oldest device for making nominations in the United States is the caucus. In use prior to the adoption of the Constitution, the caucus is an informal meeting of political leaders held to decide questions concerning candidates, strategies, and policies. The essence of the caucus idea, when applied to nominations, is that by sifting, sorting, and weeding out candidates before the election, leaders can assemble substantial support behind a single candidate, thus decreasing the prospect that the votes of like-minded citizens will be split among several candidates. Historically, the most important form of caucus was the legislative caucus, which, until 1824, was used successfully for the nomination of candidates for state and national offices, including the presidency. The major drawback to the legislative caucus was that membership was limited to the party members in the legislature, thereby exposing the caucus to the charge that it was unrepresentative and undemocratic. A modest reform in the legislative caucus occurred when provisions were made for seating delegates from districts held by the opposition party. Nevertheless, when the (Jeffersonian) Republican caucus failed to nominate Andrew Jackson for the presidency in 1824, it came under severe criticism from many quarters and shortly thereafter was abandoned for the selection of presidential nominees. (But another form of caucus survives in the presidential nominating process. See the subsequent analysis of the caucus-convention system for choosing delegates to the parties' national nominating conventions.)

Party Conventions

Advocates of reform in the nominating process turned to the party convention, already in use in some localities, as a substitute for the legislative caucus. The great merit of the convention system, it was argued, was that it could provide for representation, on a geographical basis, of all elements within the party. The secrecy of the caucus was displaced in favor of a more public arena, with nominations made by conventions composed of delegates drawn from various levels of the party organizations. As the convention method gained in prominence, so did the party organizations; state and local party leaders came to play a dominant role in the selection of candidates.

The convention system, however, failed to live up to its early promise. Although it has been used for the nomination of presidential candidates from the 1830s to the present, it has given way to the direct primary for most other offices. Critics found that it suffered from essentially the same disabling properties as the caucus. In their view, it was sheer pretense to contend that the conventions were representative of the parties as a whole; instead, they were run by party bosses without regard either for the views of the delegates or for the rules of fair play. A great many charges involving corruption in voting practices and procedures were made, and there was much truth in them. Growing regulation of conventions by the legislatures failed to assuage the doubts of the public. The direct primary came into favor as reformers came to understand its potential as a device for dismantling the structure of boss and machine influence and for introducing popular control over nominations.

Direct Primary

Popular control of the political process has always been an important issue in the dogma of reformers. The direct primary, with its emphasis on voters instead of on party organization, was hard to resist. Once Wisconsin adopted it for nomination of candidates for state elective offices in 1903, its use spread steadily throughout the country. Connecticut became the last state to adopt it, in 1955, but only after much tampering with the idea. The Connecticut model (the challenge primary) combines convention and primary under an arrangement in which the party convention continues to make nominations, but with this proviso: if the party nominee at the convention is challenged by another candidate who receives as much as 20 percent of the convention votes, a primary must be held later. Otherwise, no primary is required, and the name of the convention nominee is automatically certified for the general election.

Part of the attractiveness of the primary is its apparent simplicity. From one perspective, it is a device for transferring control of nominations from the party leadership to the rank-and-file voters; from another, it shifts this control from the party organization to the state. The primary rests on state law: It is an official election held at public expense on a date set by the legislature and is supervised by public officials. It has often been interpreted as an attempt to institutionalize intraparty democracy.

It is not surprising that the direct primary has had a better reception in reformist circles than anywhere else. For the party organization, it poses problems, not opportunities. If the organization becomes involved in a contested primary for a major office, it probably will have to raise large sums of money for the campaign of its candidate. If it remains neutral, it may wind up with a candidate who either is hostile to the organization or is unsympathetic toward its programs and policies. Even if it abandons neutrality, there is no guarantee that its candidate will win; indeed, a good many political careers have been launched in primaries in which the nonendorsed candidate has convinced the voters that a vote for him is a vote to crush the machine. Finally, the primary often works at cross purposes with the basic party objective of harmonizing its diverse elements by creating a balanced ticket for the general election. The voters are much less likely to nominate a representative slate of candidates, one that recognizes all major groups within the party, than is the party leadership. Moreover, if the primary battle turns out to be bitter, the winner may enter the general election campaign with a sharply divided party behind him.[1] It is no wonder that some political leaders have viewed the primary as a systematically conceived effort to bring down the party itself.

Types of Primaries

Four basic types of state primaries are in use: *closed, open, blanket,* and *nonpartisan.* Two special forms of primaries are also used: *runoff* and *presidential.* (The latter is analyzed in the section on the presidential nominating process.)

Closed Primary

Twenty-six states use a closed primary to make nominations.[2] The key feature of this primary is that the voter can participate in the nomination of candidates only in the party to which he or she belongs—and this is established through registration as a party member.[3] State laws vary substantially in the ease with which voters can switch back and forth between the parties. Voters in the closed primary states of Iowa, Ohio, and Wyoming, for example, can change their party registration on election day—a provision that makes their systems palpably open. Other closed primary states establish a deadline for changing parties sometime prior to primary election day. South Dakota sets this deadline at a mere fifteen days and Oregon at twenty days, whereas New York and Kentucky set it at about eleven months. The mean requirement is roughly two months. Some closed primary states prohibit voters from switching parties once the candidates have filed declarations of candidacies, and other less restrictive states encourage "voter floating" by permitting changes in party registration after candidates have declared themselves. Sharp differences exist among closed primary states in how they foster or protect party efficacy and integrity.[4]

Other differences in closed primary systems may result from the 1986 Supreme Court ruling in *Tashjian v. Republican Party of Connecticut.* The case arose from the efforts of the Connecticut state Republican party to attract independents by permitting them to vote in its primary elections. Unable to change the state's closed primary law in the legislature, the party successfully challenged it in court. By a 5–4 vote, the Supreme Court ruled that states may not require political parties to hold closed primaries that permit only voters previously enrolled in a party to vote. This ruling leaves the choice of primary system to the parties instead of to state legislatures. Hence, a state party may choose to open its primary to unaffiliated (or independent) voters or it may choose to bar their participation. Within a year of the Court's decision, seven other states enacted enabling legislation under which a party could permit unaffiliated voters to vote in its primary. The trend is clearly toward openness. In 1996, for example, nearly two thirds of the Republican *presidential* primaries and caucuses were open to any registered voter. The *Tashjian* decision does not outlaw closed primaries, and presumably many state parties will continue to permit only registered party members to vote in their primaries.[5]

Open Primary

From the point of view of the party organization, the open primary is less desirable than the closed primary. Twenty-one states (not counting states that use blanket or nonpartisan primaries) have some form of open primary— defined as one in which the voter is not required to register as a party member to vote in a party primary. Provisions for open primaries differ from state to state. In nine states the voter is given the ballots of all parties, with instructions to vote for the candidates of only one party and to discard the other ballots.[6] Nothing can prevent Democrats from voting to nominate Republican candidates or Republicans from voting to nominate Democratic candidates. The strongest appeal of this form of open primary is that it preserves the secrecy of the voter's affiliation or preference.

In the other twelve open primary states, voters are required to declare a party preference at the polls to obtain a ballot. In some states the declaration is recorded by election officials and in other states it is not. A voter's right to participate in a particular primary may be challenged. Interestingly, switching parties from one primary to the next in certain open primary states, such as Rhode Island, is more difficult than switching in certain closed primary states, such as Iowa.

Party leaders suffer from a special anxiety in open primary states: the possibility that voters of the competing party will raid their primary, hoping to nominate a weak candidate who would be easy to defeat in the general election.[7] Whether raiding occurs with any frequency is difficult to say, but in some states large numbers of voters do cross over to vote in the other party's primary when an exciting contest is present. One of the central arguments used by the state of Connecticut in the *Tashjian* case was the party's need to protect itself from raiding by members of the other party. The Supreme Court found this defense of the closed primary "insubstantial."

The use of open (crossover) primaries in the presidential nominating process has been a continuing source of aggravation for some party leaders, because these primaries permit nonparty members to influence the choice of a party's nominee. In Wisconsin, one study has shown, roughly 8 to 11 percent of all voters in presidential primaries are partisan crossovers—that is, Democrats voting in the Republican primary or Republicans voting in the Democratic primary. And a surprising one third of each party's primary participants are self-styled independents. In a close race, the presence of these outsiders can make a difference in the outcome.[8]

To combat crossover voting, the charter of the Democratic party, adopted in 1974, specified that delegates to the party's national convention be chosen through procedures that limit participation to Democratic voters. Despite this provision, Wisconsin continued to permit voters to participate in the state's Democratic presidential primary without regard to party affiliation. When delegates were later chosen in the Democratic caucus system, they were obligated to vote in accordance with the voters' presidential preferences as revealed in the open primary. In a decision designed to protect party processes, the Supreme Court ruled in 1981 that states could continue to hold open presidential primaries, but that the results did not have to be recognized in selecting state party delegates to the convention.[9] The effect of this decision was to require Wisconsin in 1984 to select its delegates in closed caucuses—that is, caucuses limited to Democrats only. This restriction did not last long. In the belief that the "Democrats only" provision had produced considerable ill will and had narrowed the party's base, the Democratic National Committee (DNC) voted in 1986 to permit Wisconsin Democrats to return to their traditional open primary, in which independents and Republicans can participate. This new rule thus accepts the open-primary heritage of states such as Wisconsin and Montana, but it does not permit other states to change their systems by opening their delegate selection processes to members of other parties.

Blanket Primary

The states of Alaska, Washington, and California complete the circle of open primary systems with what is known as a "blanket" or "jungle" primary. No other primary is as open. Nor does any other type offer voters a greater range of choice. Under its provisions the voter is given a ballot listing all candidates of all parties under each office. Voters may vote for a Democrat for one office and for a Republican for another office. Or they may vote for a candidate of a third party. They cannot vote for more than one candidate per office. Independents can of course participate. The blanket primary is an invitation to ticket-splitting. This system, which is consistent with the emergence and consolidation of candidate-centered politics, is anathema to anyone who believes parties stand for something and that they should be held accountable for the performance of government. California adopted its "jungle" primary in 1996, via an initiative supported by six out of ten voters.[10]

Nonpartisan Primary

In a number of states, judges, school board members, and other local government officials are selected in nonpartisan primaries. State legislators in

Nebraska are also selected on this basis. The scheme itself is simple: The two candidates receiving the greatest number of votes are nominated; in turn, they oppose each other in the general election. No party labels appear on the ballot in either election. The nonpartisan primary is defended on the grounds that partisanship should not be permitted to intrude on the selection of certain officials, such as judges. By eliminating the party label, runs the assumption, the issues and divisiveness that dominate national and state party politics can be kept out of local elections and local offices. Although nonpartisan primaries muffle the sounds of party, they do not eliminate them. It is not uncommon for the party organizations to slip quietly into the political process and to recruit and support candidates in these primaries; in such cases, about all that is missing is the party label on the ballot.

Since 1975 Louisiana has had an "open elections" law that renders its primaries nonpartisan. Under this system, all candidates for an office are grouped together in a primary election. A candidate who receives a majority of the primary vote is elected, thus eliminating the need for a general election. If no candidate obtains a majority of the votes cast, the top two, irrespective of party affiliation, face each other in a runoff general election. Among the apparent effects of the open elections law have been a pronounced advantage for incumbents, a growing number of candidates who have no party affiliation, costlier campaigns, and, perhaps most important, the development of institutionalized multifactionalism—marked by intensified campaigning at the primary stage with numerous candidates competing for the same office. Party obviously counts for little in the Louisiana setting. Even the ballot has been modified, changing from party column to office block as a means of inhibiting straight party voting.[11]

Runoff Primary

The runoff or second primary is a by-product of a one-party political environment. As used in southern states, this primary provides that if no candidate obtains a majority of the votes cast for an office, a runoff is held between the two leading candidates. The runoff primary is an attempt to come to terms with a chronic problem of a one-party system—essentially all competition is jammed into the primary of the dominant party. With numerous candidates seeking the nomination for the same office, the vote is likely to be sharply split, with no candidate receiving a majority. A runoff between the top two candidates in the first primary provides a guarantee, if only statistical, that one candidate will emerge as the choice of a majority of voters. This is no small consideration in those southern states where the Democratic primary has long been the real election and where factionalism within the party has been so intense that no candidate would stand much of a chance of consolidating his party position without two primaries—the first to weed out the losers and the second to endow the winner with the legitimacy a majority can offer.

An Overview of the Primary

The great virtue of the direct primary, from the perspective of its early Progressive sponsors, was its democratic component, its promise for changing the accent and scope of popular participation in the political system. Its immediate effect, it was hoped, would be to diminish the influence of political organization on political life. What is the evidence that the primary has accomplished its mission? What impact has it had on political party organization?

An important outcome of having the primary system is that party leaders have been sensitized to the interests and feelings of the most active rank-and-file members. Fewer nominations are cut and dried. Even though candidates who secure the organization's endorsement win more frequently than they lose, their prospects often are uncertain.[12] The possibility of a revolt against the organization, carried out in the primary, forces party leaders to take account of the elements that make up the party and to pay attention to the claims of potential candidates. There is always a chance—in some jurisdictions, a strong possibility—that an aspirant overlooked by the leadership will decide to challenge the party's choice in the primary. The primary thus induces caution among party leaders. A hands-off policy—one in which the party makes no endorsement—is sometimes the party's only response. If it has no candidate, it cannot lose; some party leaders have been able to stay in business by avoiding the embarrassment that comes from primary defeats. In some jurisdictions, party intervention in the primary is never even considered, so accustomed is the electorate to party-free contests. For the public at large, the main contribution of the primary is that it opens up the political process.[13]

The significance of party endorsements in primary elections varies from state to state, as shown by the research of Malcolm E. Jewell and David M. Olson. Party endorsements are usually decisive (and rarely even challenged) in both parties in Connecticut and Delaware; in the Democratic party in Colorado, North Dakota, and Rhode Island; and in the Republican party in New York. Endorsements are sometimes challenged in one or both parties in such states as Utah, Illinois, New Mexico, and Wisconsin, but the endorsed candidates are rarely upset. On the other hand, endorsed candidates are usually challenged, and occasionally upset, in the Democratic primaries of New York and Minnesota and the Republican primaries of Utah and Massachusetts. Where endorsements are most effective, the party organizations often provide their endorsees with organizational assistance, financing, and personnel.[14]

The primary has not immobilized party organizations, but it has caused a number of problems for them. Party leaders' lack of enthusiasm for primaries is not hard to understand knowing that, among other things, the primary (1) greatly increases party campaign costs (if the party backs a candidate in a contested primary); (2) diminishes the capacity of the organization to reward its supporters through nominations; (3) makes it difficult for the party to influence nominees who establish their own power bases in the primary electorate; (4) creates opportunities for people hostile to party leadership and party policies to capture nominations; (5) permits anyone to wear the party label and opens the possibility that the party will have to repudiate a candidate who has been thrust on it; and (6) increases intraparty strife and factionalism.[15] It seems no institution is better designed than the primary to stultify party organization and party processes.

On the whole, the primary has not fulfilled the expectations of its sponsors. Several things have gone awry. To begin with, competitiveness has been absent in primaries. The surprising number of nominations won by default has several causes. First, uncontested primaries may be evidence of party strength—that is, potential candidates stop short of entering the primary because their prospects appear slim for defeating the organization's choice. Second, the deserted primary simply may demonstrate the pragmatism of politicians: They do not struggle to win nominations that are unlikely to lead anywhere. As V. O. Key and others have shown, primaries are most likely to be contested when the chances are strong that the winner will be elected to office in the general election and will be least likely to be contested when the nomination appears to have little value.[16] Thus, the tendency is for electoral battles to occur in competitive districts or in the primary of the dominant party. Third, the presence of an incumbent reduces competition for a nomination. In House elections between 1956 and 1974, Harvey L. Schantz has shown, 55 percent of all Democratic primaries were contested when no incumbent was running and only 37 percent when an incumbent was in the race; for Republican primaries, the percentages were 44 and 20, respectively.[17] A study of gubernatorial primaries by Jewell and Olson, covering the years 1960–1986, found that Democratic primaries were contested 65 percent of the time when incumbents were seeking reelection and 86 percent of the time when they were not; for Republicans the comparable figures were 56 percent and 74 percent. Competitive primaries are also less likely to occur in states in which party endorsements are standard practice.[18] Overall, the prospects for a primary contest are greatest in districts where the party has a chance to win in November and where no incumbent is in the race.

Experience with the primary has also shown that it is one thing to shape an institution so as to induce popular participation and quite another to realize such participation. No fact about primaries is more familiar than that large numbers of voters assiduously ignore them. A majority of voters usually stays away from the polls on primary day, even when major statewide races are to be settled. A turnout of 25 to 30 percent of the eligible electorate is the norm in many jurisdictions. The promise of the primary is thus only partially fulfilled. The reality is that the public is not keenly interested in the nominating process.

The National Convention

The American national convention is surely one of the most remarkable institutions in the world for making nominations. In use since the Jacksonian Era, it is the official agency for the selection of each party's candidates for president and vice president and for the ratification of each party's platform. At the same time, it is the party's supreme policy-making authority, empowered to make the rules that govern party affairs.

The national convention historically has served another function of prime importance to the parties. It has been a meeting ground for the party itself, one in which leaders could tap rank-and-file sentiments and in which the divergent interests that make up each party could, at least in some fashion, be accommodated. In its classic role, the national convention presents an opportunity for the national party—the fifty state parties assembled—to come to terms with itself, permitting leading politicians to strike the necessary balances and to settle temporarily the continuing questions of leadership and policy. Under the press of other changes in the presidential nominating process, however, the party role in conventions has recently been diminished.

Until the 1970s, national convention decisions could best be explained by examining the central role of national, state, and local party leaders and the behavior of state delegations. These were the "power points" in the classic model of convention politics, aptly described by the authors of *Explorations in Convention Decision Making*:

> Historically, state delegations have been thought to be the key units for bargaining in conventions; operating under the unit rule, they bargain with

each other and with candidate organizations. The rank-and-file delegates are manipulated by hierarchical leaders holding important positions in national, state, and local party organizations. In order to enhance their bargaining position, these leaders often try to stay uncommitted to any candidate until the moment that their endorsement is crucial to victory for the ultimate nominee. After the presidential balloting is over, the vice presidential nomination is awarded to a person whose selection will mollify those elements of the party who did not support the presidential choice. At the end of the convention, all groups rally around the ticket and the party receives a boost in starting the fall campaign.[19]

The classic model of convention decision making bears only modest resemblance to the patterns of influence at play in the most recent party conventions. In broad terms, decentralization of power is now the chief characteristic of the struggle for the presidential nomination. State delegations have given way to candidate blocs in importance, and party leaders have been displaced by the leaders of candidate organizations. Party leaders have few resources with which to bargain in those state delegations that are split among candidates. The governor who heads a state delegation may be nothing more than a figurehead; meetings of many state delegations are concerned more with announcements (for example, bus departures for the convention site) and ceremonies than with strategy. In contrast, the action is found in the candidate caucuses, where the strategy sessions on candidates, rules, and platform planks occur. Uncommitted delegates have become less numerous than in the past. (But see the subsequent discussion of a change that increases the number of uncommitted delegates at the Democratic convention.) Today's party conventions are dominated by candidates and their organizations. Accordingly, the influence that party and elected officials wield in conventions is largely a product of their affiliation with one of the candidate organizations.

The decline of the party presence in national conventions results from a confluence of forces: the delegate selection rules that opened up the parties to amateur activists and contributed to the spread of presidential primaries, the capacity of candidates to dominate campaign fund raising (using government subsidies under a matching system since 1976), and the general weakness of state and local party organizations.[20] The reliance of candidates on party leaders in the preconvention period has never been less—in most states, party leaders cannot do much either to help or to hurt a candidate's chances to win delegates. What matters to the candidate is winning the immediate primary or placing well (as judged by the mass media) to attract new funds and to build momentum for the next contest. In the modern scheme of campaigning, expert consultants, an active personal organization spread out around the state, and the mass media loom much more important to the candidates than do party structures and party leaders.

Selection of Delegates

National convention delegates are chosen by two methods: presidential primaries and caucus-conventions. Each state chooses its own system, and it is not unusual for a state to switch from one method to another between elections in response to criticisms by the press, the public, and politicians unhappy about recent outcomes.

Loosely managed by the parties, the caucus-convention system provides for the election of delegates by rank-and-file members (mixed with candidate enthusiasts) from one level of the party to the next—ordinarily from precinct caucuses to county conventions to the state convention and from there to the national convention. The first-tier caucuses (mass meetings at the precinct level) are crucial, because they establish the delegate strength of each candidate in the subsequent conventions, including the national. Candidates and their organizations must turn out their supporters for these initial party meetings; a loss at this stage cannot be reversed.

At one time the chief criticism of the caucus-convention system was that it was essentially closed, dominated by a few party leaders who selected themselves, key public officials, "fat cats" (major financial contributors), and lesser party officials as delegates. The democratizing reforms of the 1970s changed all this, opening up the caucuses to participation by average party members and short-term activists willing to spend an afternoon or evening in discussion and voting. Today, the delegate-selection caucuses are dominated by competing candidate organizations and their enthusiasts, and prominent party officials may or may not be found in their ranks. Preoccupied with the struggle for delegates, the media pay scant attention to the caucus as a party event.

Delegate selection systems vary from state to state and from party to party. On the Democratic side, slightly more than one third of the states have open presidential primaries (where any registered voter may participate), nearly one third have closed primaries (where only registered Democrats may participate), and about one third have caucuses (both open and closed, with open the most common). Some states use both primaries and caucuses; typically, in this arrangement, the caucus is expected to select the delegates to reflect the primary results.

For the Republicans, the most common method for selecting delegates is the open primary; it is used in one half of the states, including populous California, Illinois, Ohio, and Texas. Another one quarter of the states use closed primaries, including Florida, New York, and Pennsylvania. And about one quarter of the states use caucuses, all but a few of which are open. As in the case of the Democrats, Republican caucus states tend to be rural, less populous, and midwestern (e.g., Iowa, Minnesota) or western (e.g., Montanta, Utah, Alaska, Nevada, and Wyoming).

Popular participation is much lower in caucus states than in primary states. In 1996 fewer than 100,000 voters (about 17 percent) took part in the key Iowa Republican caucuses, whereas more than 200,000 voted in the Republican primary in tiny New Hampshire. In Louisiana, in 1996, less than 5 percent of the state's half-million Republicans took part in the caucuses in which columnist Pat Buchanan defeated Sen. Phil Gramm, severely damaging Gramm's prospects.

The caucus-convention system poses major problems for party leaders.[21] In most caucus states party regulars have been reduced to bystanders as candidate organizations, bolstered by amateur enthusiasts, vie with one another for votes and delegates. Intraparty conflict also appears to occur more frequently in caucus states than in primary states. Finally, party leaders have become sensitive to the charge that caucus results may not be representative of voter sentiment generally. For these reasons, particularly the latter one, states that change their nominating systems in the future are more likely to switch to primaries than caucuses.[22]

Used by all of the most populous states, presidential primaries are easier for the public to understand. A large majority of each state's delegates is chosen on primary day by the direct vote of the people; the remaining delegates are chosen through party processes following the primary. Like the direct primary used to nominate national, state, and local officials, the presidential primary was designed to wrest control of nominations from the bosses (the party professionals) and to place it in the hands of the people by permitting them to choose the delegates to the nominating conventions in a public election. In 1904 Florida became the first state to adopt a presidential primary law. In little more than a decade, about half of the states had adopted some version of it. Its use since then has fluctuated. Only sixteen states and the District of Columbia held presidential primaries in 1968. The popularity of presidential primaries grew in the 1970s and 1980s. In 1996 presidential primaries were held in one or both parties in forty-two states, with Republicans using this method somewhat more than Democrats. Altogether, Democrats chose about 75 percent of their delegates in primaries, Republicans about 85 percent.

The broad objective of presidential primaries is to encourage popular participation in the selection of presidents. In 1996 about fourteen million people voted in the Republican primaries and about eight-and-a-half million in the Democratic primaries—about 10 percent of the voting-age population. Several hundred thousand voters took part in caucuses. Perhaps twenty-three million voters participated in choosing the nominees in 1996, as contrasted with ninety-six million who voted in the general election. Obviously, many voters do not attach importance to the nominating process, even when the presidency is at stake.[23]

Prior to the 1970s, the manner in which national convention delegates were selected was left to the states. Today, the Democratic party in particular tightly regulates the methods of delegate selection. The dimensions of national party control can best be appreciated by examining Table 3–1, which includes certain major rules in effect for the 1996 Democratic National Convention. In the selection of delegates, the rules make clear, not much is left to chance or to the discretion of individual state parties.

An amalgam of recommendations by five party study commissions, stretching from 1969 to 1985, the rules were designed to serve several major objectives: (1) to stimulate the participation of rank-and-file Democratic voters in the presidential nominating process; (2) to increase the representation of certain demographic groups (particularly women, Blacks, and young people) in the convention through the use of guidelines on delegate selection; (3) to eliminate procedures held to be undemocratic (such as the unit rule, under which a majority of a state delegation could cast the state's total vote for a single candidate); (4) to enhance the local character of delegate elections (by requiring 75 percent of the delegates in each state to be elected at the congressional district level or lower); and (5) to provide through proportional representation that elected delegates fairly reflect the presidential candidate preferences of Democratic voters in primary states and Democratic participants in caucus-convention states. (The proportional representation rule was relaxed in the 1980s but is mandatory today.)

For many members of the first commission, the McGovern–Fraser Commission, the underlying objective was to diminish the power of party professionals in the convention, while at the same time increasing that of party members and activists at the local level. They succeeded in extraordinary degree. A new type of participant, to whom candidates and issues were central, came to predominate in the Democratic convention. Party leaders and public officials, thoroughly overshadowed in the 1972 and 1976 conventions, gradually have been readmitted since then. Following a recommendation of the Winograd Commission, the DNC adopted a provision to expand each 1980 state delegation by 10 percent to include prominent party and elected officials. Since then, the number of these officials, who gain their seats automatically (that is, without facing the voters) has grown. "Superdelegates," as they are called, made up nearly 20 percent of the 1996 Democratic convention. In this group were Democratic members of Congress, the party's governors, the members of the Democratic National Committee, and various prominent state party officials.

TABLE 3-1   Principal Delegate Selection Rules for the 1996 Democratic
National Convention

Rule 1A:	State parties shall adopt affirmative action and delegate selection plans which contain explicit rules and procedures governing all aspects of the delegate selection process. . . .
1D:	State delegate selection and affirmative action plans shall be submitted to the DNC [Democratic National Committee] Rules and Bylaws Committee for approval. . . .
2A:	Participation in the delegate selection process shall be open to all voters who wish to participate as Democrats.
2C:	Nothing in these rules shall be interpreted to encourage or permit states with party registration and enrollment, or states that limit participation to Democrats only, to amend their systems to open participation to members of other parties.
3A:	All official party meetings and events related to the national convention delegate selection process . . . shall be scheduled for dates, times, and public places which would be most likely to encourage the participation of all Democrats, and must begin and end at reasonable hours.
5C:	In order to achieve full participation by groups that are significantly underrepresented in our party's affairs, each state party shall develop and submit party outreach programs, including recruitment, education and training, in order to achieve full participation by such groups in the delegate selection process and at all levels of party affairs.
6A:	In order to encourage full participation by all Democrats in the delegate selection process and in all party affairs, the national and state Democratic parties shall adopt and implement affirmative action programs with specific goals and timetables for African Americans, Hispanics, Native Americans, Asian/Pacific Americans, and women.
6C:	State delegate selection plans shall provide for equal division between delegate men and delegate women. . . .
6G:	Each state affirmative action program shall include outreach provisions to encourage the participation and representation of persons of low and moderate income. . . .
7C:	Seventy-five percent of each state's base delegation shall be elected at the congressional district level or lower. Twenty-five percent of each state's base delegation shall be elected at large.
7D:	In those states with more than one congressional district, after the election of district-level delegates and prior to the selection of at-large delegates, each state Democratic Chair shall certify pledged party leader and elected official delegates equal to 15 percent of the state's base delegation. . . .
8A:	[Unpledged party leader and elected official delegates shall include] members of the DNC . . . the Democratic president and vice president . . . all Democratic members of the U.S. House and Senate . . . Democratic governors . . .

and all former Democratic presidents, vice presidents, House and Senate majority leaders, House speakers, and chairs of the DNC.

9A: The selection of at-large delegates shall be used, if necessary, to achieve the equal division of positions between men and women and the representation goals established in the state party's affirmative action plan.

10A: No meetings, caucuses, conventions or primaries which constitute the first determining stage in the presidential nomination process . . . may be held prior to the first Tuesday in March or after the second Tuesday in June in the calendar year of the national convention. Provided, however, that the Iowa precinct caucuses may be held no earlier than fifteen days before the first Tuesday in March; that the New Hampshire primary may be held no earlier than seven days before the first Tuesday in March; that the Maine first-tier caucuses may be held no earlier than two days before the first Tuesday in March.

11A: All candidates for delegate in caucuses, conventions, committees and on primary ballots shall be identified as to presidential preference, uncommitted or unpledged status at all levels of a process which determines presidential preference.

11J: Delegates elected to the national convention pledged to a presidential candidate shall in all good conscience reflect the sentiments of those who elected them.

12A: Delegates shall be allocated in a fashion that fairly reflects the expressed presidential preference or uncommitted status of the primary voters or, if there is no binding primary, the convention and caucus participants. States shall allocate district level delegates and alternates in proportion to the percentage of the primary or caucus vote won in that district by each preference, except that preferences falling below a 15 percent threshold shall not be awarded any delegates.

12G: Under no circumstance shall the use of single-delegate districts be permitted.

16A: The unit rule, or any rule or practice whereby all members of a party unit or delegation may be required to cast their votes in accordance with the will of a majority of the body, shall not be used at any stage of the delegate selection process.

19C: In the event the delegate selection plan of a state party provides or permits a meeting, caucus, convention or primary which constitutes the first determining stage . . . to be held prior to or after the dates for the state as provided in Rule 10 . . . [the number of the state's delegates] shall be reduced by 25 percent. In addition, none of the members of the DNC from that state shall be permitted to vote as members of the state's delegation. . . . [If a state violates proportional representation as provided in Rule 12] the delegation of the state shall be reduced [by 25 percent]. . . . [If a state permits a threshold other than 15 percent] the delegation of the state shall be reduced [by 25 percent].

SOURCE: *Delegate Selection Rules for the 1996 Democratic National Convention* (Washington, D.C.: Democratic National Committee, 1995).

Democratic Party's Delegate Selection Rules . . .

In the Democratic party, national rules prescribe in detail how delegates to the national nominating convention are to be chosen. Initially, the reformers focused on means to make the party more open, the delegate selection process more democratic, and the delegates themselves more representative of major demographic groups. The recent commissions, by contrast, have sought chiefly to restore the influence of professional politicians in the convention and to give state parties somewhat wider latitude to formulate methods for selecting delegates.

For party officials, rule making is no day at the beach. Candidates, interests, party blocs, and state politicians must be accommodated. New rules, moreover, produce unanticipated consequences as well as winners and losers.

The one constant in Democratic presidential selection politics is change.

Intraparty Democracy

McGovern–Fraser Commission (1969–1972)

Developed rules to permit all Democratic voters a "full, meaningful, and timely" opportunity to take part in the presidential nominating process.

Required each state party to include in its delegation Blacks, women, and young people in numbers roughly proportionate to their presence in the state population.

Required at least 75 percent of each state delegation to be selected at a level no higher than the congressional district.

Eliminated practices held to be undemocratic, such as the unit rule.

Mikulski Commission (1972–1973)

Reaffirmed many McGovern–Fraser guidelines.

Dropped "quotas" but required states to establish affirmative action plans to encourage full participation by all Democrats, with special efforts required to include minority groups, Native Americans, women, and youth.

Required a fair reflection of voters' presidential preferences (thus proportional representation) at all levels of the delegate selection process, with a few exceptions.

Created a national party compliance review commission to monitor implementation of state affirmative action and delegate selection programs.

. . . *Key Provisions of Reform Commissions*

Intraparty Democracy and Party Renewal

Winograd Commission (1975–1978)

Specifically identified women, Blacks, Hispanics, and Native Americans as the objects of "remedial action to overcome the effects of past discrimination."
Shortened the period for delegate selection from six to three months.
Eliminated last vestiges of winner-take-all systems.
Outlawed "crossover" primaries.
Increased the size of state delegations by 10 percent to augment representation of top party leaders and elected officials.
Required delegates to vote on the first ballot for the presidential candidate they were elected to support.
Voted not to require each state to have an equal number of men and women in its delegation, but the Democratic National Committee later adopted equal-division rule.

Party Renewal

Hunt Commission (1981–1982)

Retreated from proportional representation by permitting state parties to adopt winner-take-all or winner-take-more systems.
Provided that 14 percent of the delegates to the 1984 convention be chosen on the basis of their public office or party status ("superdelegates").
Tightened the primary-caucus "window" by reducing the period between the Iowa caucuses and the New Hampshire primary from thirty-six days to eight.
Eliminated binding first ballot for delegates.

Fairness Commission (1984–1985)

Increased number of superdelegates from 568 to about 650 for the 1988 convention.
Lowered threshold from 20 to 15 percent, thus making it easier for trailing candidates to share in the distribution of delegates.
Permitted Wisconsin and Montana to conduct open (or crossover) primaries, banned earlier by the Winograd Commission.

Superdelegates were introduced to the delegate-selection process to pro-vide for peer review of candidates by professional politicians and, at the same time, to diminish the influence of amateur activists and interest groups. They were to be the new power brokers of the convention. But it has not worked out that way. Because the candidates campaign for superdelegates' votes in the same way as they campaign for popular support, the vast ma-jority of the superdelegates arrive at the convention not as free agents but as delegates fully committed to individual candidates. Like other politicians in search of influence, superdelegates want to endorse the ultimate winner and to do so as early as possible, when endorsements count the most.

The way in which delegates are allocated to candidates has been a per-sistent problem for the Democrats. Tinkering and temporizing, the party has vacillated between winner-take-all and proportional representation since the 1970s. In 1988, for example, the national Democratic rules permitted state parties to choose from among three broad plans. First, states could select the *proportional representation* method, under which any Democratic candi-date who reached the 15-percent threshold of the primary or caucus vote was entitled to a proportionate share of the delegates; candidates who failed to reach the threshold did not qualify for any delegates. Second, states could adopt what amounts to a *winner-take-all* system. In this direct-election form, voters cast ballots for individual delegates who were pledged to can-didates or uncommitted. The candidate who came in first in a district could win all or most of the delegates instead of sharing them with the trailing can-didates. Third, states could choose a *winner-take-more* plan. Here, the win-ning candidate in each district was given a bonus delegate before the rest were divided proportionally.

For the 1992 and 1996 conventions, Democratic party rules required all states to allocate their publicly elected delegates on a proportionate basis, giving each candidate who reached the 15-percent threshold the appropriate share of delegates.

Proportional representation has several side effects. First, it permits the candidate who builds an early lead (the front-runner) to continue to pile up delegates even in states won by another candidate. Even so, it still takes a long time for the leading candidate to assemble a majority of delegates, as other candidates reach the threshold and share in the distribution of dele-gates. Second, proportional representation prevents a trailing candidate from winning big—capturing a large share of the delegates in a populous state, as could occur under a winner-take-all arrangement. And third, as Priscilla Southwell pointed out, proportional representation may prove ad-vantageous for some lesser-known, outsider candidates because their sec-ond- and third-place finishes in the early caucuses and primaries will entitle them to delegates and perhaps keep their candidacies alive.[24]

The Republican party was considerably less active than the Democratic party in the 1970s and 1980s in restructuring its delegate selection rules, but it did make a few changes. Its current rules require open meetings for delegate selection; ban automatic (ex officio) delegates; and provide for the election, not the selection, of congressional district and at-large delegates (unless otherwise provided by state law). State Republican parties are urged to develop plans for increasing the participation of women, young people, minorities, and other groups in the presidential nominating process, but they are not required to do so. The push to nationalize party rules, pronounced among Democratic reformers for the past two decades, finds only limited support among Republicans. Rather, Republicans continue to stress the federal character of their party. The basic authority to reshape delegate selection rules remains with state parties.[25]

Republican delegate selection practices differ in several major respects from those of the Democrats. First, Republicans have resisted the allure of proportionality in delegate allocation, placing much more emphasis on some version of winner-take-all. In 1996, for example, well over one half of the Republican state parties used winner-take-all or direct election and only about one fourth used proportional representation. A few Republican state parties use winner-take-all but provide for proportional representation if no candidate receives a majority of the vote. Second, the Republican party has no provision for the automatic selection of party or public officials—superdelegates, in Democratic nomenclature. Third, the party has no requirement that state delegations be evenly divided between men and women, a rule imposed on state Democratic parties beginning in 1980. (The numbers of women delegates has increased nonetheless in Republican conventions—about one third of the total in 1996.) Fourth, each state Republican party is free to schedule its primary or caucus as it sees fit. On the Democratic side, the primary-caucus calendar is tightly regulated by national party rules. Party differences in delegate selection reflect basic party differences in philosophy and organization that can be summed up in the appellations "federal" Republicans and "national" Democrats.

Evaluating Presidential Primary and Caucus-Convention Systems

Sometimes it appears as though the only persons who are satisfied with the presidential nominating process are the winners—the nominees and their supporters. Everyone else, it seems, can find reasons to be unhappy or frustrated about the process.

To the initiated and uninitiated voter alike, the primaries and caucuses are a mass of oppositions and paradoxes. Unpredictability reigns. Victory in a single state can be the key to the nomination. And victories in the early primaries and caucuses are usually crucial. Consider recent outcomes. In the judgment of many observers, on the day that John F. Kennedy defeated Hubert H. Humphrey in the West Virginia primary in 1960—a Catholic winning in an overwhelmingly Protestant state—he sewed up the nomination. In 1964 the critical Republican primary took place in California, where Barry Goldwater narrowly defeated Nelson Rockefeller. In 1972 George McGovern's nomination seemed to be guaranteed by his win in California. Jimmy Carter's string of early primary victories in 1976, beginning with his narrow win in New Hampshire, gave him a commanding lead. His weakness in late primaries, marked by several losses to California governor Jerry Brown, had no effect on the nomination. Challenged by Edward M. Kennedy and Jerry Brown in 1980, Carter again won the New Hampshire primary and five of the next six primaries, forcing Brown out of the race. Kennedy won ten of thirty-four primaries, but half of those victories came on the last day of the primary season, too late to matter. Although the Democratic struggle in 1984 was much different, a case can be made that Walter F. Mondale's successes in Alabama and Georgia on "Super Tuesday," the second Tuesday in March, were indispensable, serving to keep him from elimination after a series of media and real victories by Gary Hart. In 1988 Michael Dukakis's victory in New Hampshire was critical, following his third-place finish in Iowa. His clear-cut victory over Jesse Jackson in Wisconsin seven weeks later, following many inconclusive primaries in a multicandidate field, appeared to seal the nomination for him. On the Republican side, George Bush's victory over Kansas senator Bob Dole in New Hampshire and his sweep of the South on "Super Tuesday" three weeks later settled the nomination for all intents and purposes.

In 1992 Bill Clinton's sweep of the southern primaries in the second week of March, followed by major victories in Illinois and Michigan the next week, all but sewed up the nomination. Former senator Paul E. Tsongas promptly suspended his campaign. Only Jerry Brown actively challenged Clinton in the remaining 30 primaries and caucuses. When it was all over, Clinton had won 52 percent of the primary vote to Brown's 20 percent and Tsongas's 18 percent (with the remainder allocated to others or uncommitted).[26] In the Republican contest, George Bush won handily, capturing every state and a total of 73 percent of the primary vote. Pat Buchanan received 22 percent and David Duke 1 percent of the vote (with the remainder going to others or uncommitted).[27]

In 1996 Bob Dole survived a rocky start, narrowly defeating Pat Buchanan in Iowa (26 percent to 23 percent, with Lamar Alexander receiving

18 percent and Steve Forbes 10 percent), and losing to him in unpredictable New Hampshire (Buchanan, 27 percent; Dole, 26 percent; Alexander, 23 percent; Forbes, 12 percent). And Dole's campaign was in serious trouble after a late February loss to Forbes in Arizona. But crucial wins in the South's first primary in South Carolina in early March and in Georgia several days later changed things dramatically. When Dole swept the South on so-called Super Tuesday a week later, his nomination was all but inevitable. The truth is that southern states were as decisive in Dole's nomination victory in 1996 as they had been in Clinton's in 1992 and Bush's in 1988. New Hampshire's main contribution in 1996, by way of contrast, was to create confusion and uncertainty, doing more to undermine campaigns than to provide momentum for any one of them.

The site of state victories makes a difference. When a major state emerges as the focus of the preconvention struggle, no one questions it, but when Iowa and New Hampshire vault a dark horse into prominence or otherwise dominate the selection process it is another matter. Both George McGovern in 1972 and Jimmy Carter in 1976 owed their nominations to their strong showings in these states. And Gary Hart, another outsider, almost parlayed a better-than-anticipated vote in the Iowa caucuses in 1984 (15 percent to Mondale's 45 percent) and a victory in New Hampshire into the nomination. For Bush and Dukakis in 1988, New Hampshire's results obliterated their poor showings in Iowa and, most important, made them the clear-cut front-runners. Bill Clinton's impressive second-place finish in New Hampshire in 1992 (after neighboring-state candidate Tsongas) put him in a strong position for the approaching southern primaries, which he won decisively.[28] The most important result of an early victory or unanticipated good showing is the free media time it produces. For anyone except their natives, it is simply mind-boggling to learn that Iowa and New Hampshire, with about 3 percent of the nation's population, receive about 30 percent of the media coverage given the entire campaign for the presidential nomination.[29]

At bottom, the issue is the representativeness of Iowa and New Hampshire, particularly in the Democratic electorate. Neither state has a major metropolitan area, a large urban (unionized) workforce, or a sizable minority population. The voters in these states are patently not a cross section of the majorities[30] that elect Democratic presidents, and they are more likely to vote Republican than Democratic in November. Their occasional prominence in controlling the route to the nomination leaves attentive Democrats in the other forty-eight states and the District of Columbia baffled, if not wholly incredulous.

Regional variation in candidate strength also can be decisive. If, in 1976, the western primaries and caucuses had been held at the beginning of the nominating season instead of near the end, both Jimmy Carter and Ronald Reagan might have fared differently.[31] In 1980 both Carter and Reagan gained critical momentum by winning a string of early southern primaries. In 1984 Walter Mondale's virtual sweep of the industrial Northeast gave him a lead that Gary Hart's later victories in western states could not overcome. Southern primaries and caucuses were crucial for Bush in 1988, Clinton in 1992, and Dole in 1996. Sequence makes a difference.

The electoral results in the early caucus-convention and primary states are the peculiar dynamic of the presidential nominating process. And overemphasis of the results by the media is the norm. Often speaking with greater finality than the voters themselves, the media create winners and losers, front-runners and also-rans, candidates who should "bail out" and candidates who have earned "another shot." Voters learn who did better than expected and who did worse than expected. Winning or placing well is translated into a major political resource, with the psychological impact greater than the number of delegates won. The rewards for capturing the media's attention are heightened visibility, an expanded and more attentive journalistic corps, television news time, interest group cynosure, endorsements, campaign funds,[32] and a leg up on the next contest.

In the nominating process the media have become the new parties:

> The television news organizations in this country are an enormously dominant force in primary elections. They're every Tuesday night, not only counting the votes, but, in some cases, setting the tone. (A member of the Jimmy Carter organization)

> . . . [if] you're short of delegates, the real determining factor's going to be the psychological momentum the press creates. Is he a winner? Can he get the nomination? (A member of the Fred Harris organization)

> You go into a place like New Hampshire and you've got two things in mind. Primarily is winning New Hampshire. Secondly is getting out the stories about your candidate and where he stands and all that to the rest of the country. (A member of the Ronald Reagan organization)

> Everywhere we go, we're on a media trip; I mean we're attempting to generate as much free television and print, as much free radio, as we can get. Any angle can play. (A member of the Morris Udall organization)[33]

> If you're not first or second in New Hampshire, you might as well pack your bags. (John Sears, Republican political consultant)[34]

> The task of a presidential hopeful, threading a path through the minefield of successive primary elections, is not to win a majority but rather to survive. Survival means gaining as high as possible a rank among the candidates running for election. Coming in first in early primaries means achiev-

ing the visibility that ensures that a candidate will be taken seriously by the news media. (Nelson W. Polsby, *Consequences of Party Reform*)[35]

Were it not for the media, the Iowa caucuses and the New Hampshire primary results would be about as relevant to the presidential nomination as opening-day baseball scores are to a pennant race. (David L. Paletz and Robert M. Entman, *Media Power Politics*)[36]

You've got to love it, huh? The winnowing process has begun, and we've been winnowed in. (A Dukakis adviser, following the media's favorable interpretation of Dukakis's third-place finish in the Iowa caucuses)[37]

What really matters is the interpretation of election results by the print and broadcast media. Christopher Arterton wrote:

> Those who manage presidential campaigns uniformly believe that interpretations placed upon campaign events are frequently more important than the events themselves. In other words, the political contest is shaped primarily by the perceptual environment within which campaigns compete. *Particularly in the early nomination stages, perceptions outweigh reality in terms of their political impact.* Since journalists communicate these perceptions to voters and party activists and since part of the reporter's job is creating these interpretations, campaigners believe that journalists can and do affect whether their campaign is viewed as succeeding or failing, and that this perception in turn will determine their ability to mobilize political resources in the future: endorsements, volunteers, money, and hence, votes.[38]

The opening weeks of the nominating process are critical, because more and more states have shifted their primaries and caucuses to the early part of the season—"front loading," in the argot of analysts and political junkies. For the 1996 season, California moved its presidential primary date from June to the fourth Tuesday in March, ostensibly to increase its influence in the process. Another populous state, Ohio, advanced its primary to mid-March, linking up with three other midwestern states (Illinois, Michigan, and Wisconsin). Opening with a number of southern primaries, March is now the key month.

One of the major effects of front loading is that candidates must get out of the blocks fast. Slow starters usually find themselves out of the race in a matter of weeks. Bill Clinton had the 1992 Democratic nomination nailed down before half of the states, including many big ones, had even voted. In 1996 Phil Gramm was first to abandon the Republican race—following opening losses in the Alaska, Louisiana, and Iowa caucuses—and Lamar Alexander, Richard G. Lugar, and Steve Forbes withdrew a few weeks later following poor showings in the southern primaries.

Inconclusive results in the early caucuses and primaries mean that the struggle for the nomination may continue to the end of the season (the second Tuesday in June) and perhaps beyond, to the convention itself. Trying to predict how the calendar will affect individual candidacies, state or regional influence, or voting patterns is impossible, however. Too many imponderables, including the peculiar mix of candidacies, are present. And what serves certain interests in one election may not in the next.

The Democratic party has sought to diminish the significance of the early phase of the presidential nominating process by adopting a rule to restrict the nominating season (the caucus-primary "window") to the period of early March to early June, with a few exceptions, such as Iowa and New Hampshire. Narrowing the window gives an advantage to well-known candidates with campaign organizations in place and to those with significant national followings. But not too much should be made of that. The major development is front loading.[39] For most candidates, who do poorly and run out of funds, the end of the race comes early. If a clear-cut front-runner has emerged by mid-March, the last three months of the season may be nothing more than the mop-up stage. But if two or more strong candidates survive after the southern primaries, as happened in 1988 on the Democratic side, the race has just begun (and the front-loading states have miscalculated).

The Republican party has also become sensitive to the scheduling of nominating events. In an effort to combat front loading and to stretch out the nominating process, the 1996 Republican convention approved changes in party rules that give states a bonus in delegates if they move back their caucus or primary to a later date in 2000; any state that votes after May 15, for example, will receive 10 percent more delegates, whereas those that vote in the last half of April or the first half of May get only a 7.5 percent increase. The convention also restricted the nominating season by barring delegate-selection events in January of 2000.[40]

A realistic campaign for the presidential nomination is expensive. Money separates the serious candidate from the dilettante or the rank outsider. Of course there is never enough of it, and the law does not make it easy to raise. Under the Federal Election Campaign Act, no individual can contribute more than $1,000 to any campaign. Moreover, candidates can qualify for matching federal funds only after they have raised $100,000 in small sums ($250 or less, $5,000 per state) in each of twenty states. Political action committees may contribute up to $5,000 to a candidate, but their gifts are not eligible for matching public money. Candidates are thus compelled to develop a large network of small contributors, spread around the country— making fund raising a chore for all candidates and a major obstacle for some. Plans and activities to raise money must be launched long in advance of the election year. It is thus easy to mark the opening of a new campaign. It begins with the creation of fund-raising committees and the scramble for money. The money hustle is aptly described by the press secretary to Fred Harris, who sought the Democratic nomination in 1976:

> You're caught in a kind of vicious circle. In order to raise money, especially money from more than twenty states, then you have to have national media attention, not just good local media that Fred has been able to generate. . . . But in order to raise that kind of money dispersed among twenty states then you need national media exposure. You need it because people do judge by national media exposure as to whether the campaign is serious or not and, believe me, they hesitate before they give money. . . . They're going to wait until they see Fred's smiling face on national television.[41]

The system of caucus-conventions and presidential primaries is a crazy quilt of activity. Candidates fly from one end of the country to the other, then back again, emphasizing certain states, de-emphasizing others, and doing their best to impose their interpretations on the most recent results. Candidates are never wholly confident about how or where they should spend their time or money; voters are not quite sure what is going on. Yet there is more to the system than its awkwardness, complexity, and unpredictability.

Popular participation in the presidential nominating process generally was not of much consequence prior to the reforms of the 1970s. Candidates, following their instincts and the advice of assorted national and state politicians, chose to enter primaries, to avoid them, or to participate in certain ones while skipping others. As recently as 1968, only sixteen states even held primaries. And Hubert Humphrey captured the Democratic nomination that year even though he did not contest any primaries (which were dominated by Eugene McCarthy and Robert F. Kennedy). In states using the caucus-convention system, the chief method of nomination, one or a few leaders typically controlled the selection of delegates and thus the outcome. To win the nomination, candidates spent much of their time cultivating key state party leaders. Only a few candidates at any time, moreover, were thought to be "available" for the office—that is, possessed of attributes that would prompt party leaders around the country and the media to take them seriously. Presidential nominees were chosen in a relatively closed system from among a very select group.

That ambiance and the rules and practices that fostered it have disappeared. Today the system is remarkably open. The impact of party leaders and organizations is minimal in the process. No leader can "deliver" a state. Candidates rarely write off a primary or caucus, though they often downplay the significance of certain ones. And most important, the rank-and-file voters now play a central role in the presidential nominating process.[42] In 1976 nearly twenty-nine million voters cast ballots in both parties' primaries. The number rose to about thirty-two million in 1980 and, with fewer primaries and no contest on the Republican side, declined to about twenty-four million in 1984. A record was established when thirty-five million voters took part in the 1988 presidential primaries. Participation dropped to about thirty-three million in 1992, and in 1996, with Clinton unchallenged, to a total of about twenty-three million. Ordinarily, between one-half million and one million voters turn out for the first-tier caucuses in the caucus-convention states.[43] The presidential nominating process is much more under the control of the voters than ever in the past.[44] In this new participatory system even an incumbent president may have reason to fear a challenge to renomination, as Carter faced Kennedy in 1980 and Bush faced Buchanan in 1992. Whether the new system produces better presidential candidates (or better presidents) than those previously chosen in smoke-filled rooms is another matter.

Presidential primaries, because they tap voters' preferences in a more direct fashion than caucuses and involve a much larger sector of the electorate, present a particularly good opportunity for testing candidates, policies, and issues in a variety of states.[45] Consider evidence of recent decades. The Vietnam War was the pivotal issue in both the 1968 and 1972 Democratic primaries. It contributed to President Johnson's decision not to seek reelection in 1968 and, four years later, was central to George McGovern's nomination. When an outsider, Jimmy Carter, won a large majority of the Democratic primaries in 1976, the intensity of voters' resentment toward the "Washington establishment" was revealed. Voter attitudes toward conservatism were brought to light in 1980. Ronald Reagan easily won the first primary in New Hampshire (following a narrow loss to George Bush in Iowa, the first caucus-convention state), lost narrowly to Bush in Massachusetts, and then won six primaries in a row—all by large margins. Most of the other contenders for the Republican nomination, faring poorly in the early primaries, soon withdrew. Reagan lost only four of the thirty-two primaries he entered. On the Democratic side in 1984, an intense struggle culminated in a close victory for Walter Mondale—one that he gained without a majority of the national primary (or caucus) vote and one that revealed both the party's contradictions and its bleak prospects in the November election. Much the same could be said for Michael Dukakis in 1988. In 1992 Clinton won as a centrist candidate over a relatively unknown field—one that quickly dwindled to Paul Tsongas (who stopped active campaigning in mid-March) and Jerry Brown; Clinton won more primaries (32) than any previous Democratic candidate. After foundering in Iowa and New Hampshire in 1996, Bob Dole recovered with key victories in the South. Numerous factors contributed to his resurgence, including a superior organization (especially important in a crowded March schedule of primaries and caucuses), heavy early spending, the support of the Republican establishment (plus key Christian conservative leaders), the collapse of his opposition, and the polarizing impact of Pat Buchanan's populist campaign.

Contested presidential primaries may take a toll on party unity. Enmities and resentment among party elites and voters are the by-products of contentious nominating campaigns and a significant influence on their behavior in general elections. An analysis of Democratic presidential primaries, caucuses, and general election outcomes over a sixty-year period by James Lengle, Diane Owen, and Molly Sonner found that divisiveness at the nominating stage hurts the party's prospects for winning the general election. From 1932 to 1992, Democratic presidential candidates lost more than three fourths of those states that experienced divisive primaries but only half of the states with nondivisive primaries or those with caucuses. "Political loyalties, attitudes, and perceptions of voters in nominating campaigns," the authors wrote, "are influenced enormously by the structure and intensity of the competition fostered by nominating mechanisms." The Republican party appears to be less affected by divisiveness at the nominating stage.[46]

What has been the overall impact of the preconvention struggle on the choice of nominees? The primary and convention-caucus process has become decisive, sharply constricting the significance of the national conventions in the selection of presidential nominees. John Kennedy owed his nomination in 1960, more than anything else, to his successes in primary states. Numerous state and local Democratic candidates would have preferred a safer candidate, but they found it impossible to withstand the surge of public support behind Kennedy. Democratic party professionals were again confounded in 1972 and 1976 when party outsiders, George McGovern and Jimmy Carter, respectively, won numerous primary victories and, aided by their successes in nonprimary states, captured the nominations. On the Republican side, despite the advantage of the presidency, Gerald R. Ford barely escaped with the nomination in 1976 after an extraordinary preconvention challenge by Ronald Reagan, who won ten primaries. (President Ford won seventeen.) After the first wave of primaries in 1980, there was not much doubt concerning the eventual winners. Carter won nine of the first thirteen Democratic primaries, and Reagan won ten of the first thirteen Republican primaries. In 1984, benefiting from delegate selection and delegate distribution rules that diminished the chances of outsiders and winning where it counted, Mondale had captured the nomination by the end of the primary and caucus season. Reagan had virtually no opposition. In 1988 Bush had the Republican nomination sewed up by early March, Dukakis the Democratic nomination by mid-April. In 1992 both Bush and Clinton spent most of the primary-caucus season mopping up in one state after another following a string of victories in the South and Midwest. Dole's victory in 1996 closely resembled Bush's in 1992; after Super Tuesday it was all over but the shouting.

The preconvention struggle, however, may not always settle the choice of the nominee. If it does not, the selection will turn on convention bargaining. A brokered convention, characterized by sparring between leading candidates (perhaps including some who avoided the primaries and caucuses) and by a more important role for party leaders and public officials, is thus still a possibility. Sooner or later, doubtlessly, there will be one.

Institutions usually change without much fanfare or public awareness. Such is the case of the presidential nominating process, in which several patterns have emerged. First, de facto regional primaries have quietly developed, beginning with New England (but not including New Hampshire, of course). Next come the southern states (with South Carolina and Georgia a bit ahead of the pack), then the heavy hitters of the Midwest (Illinois, Michigan, Ohio, and Wisconsin), and then the West (especially delegate-heavy California). Other states not in the informal regional system may find it tempting to link up with their neighbors.

Second, protracted struggle for the nomination is now more likely to be the exception than the rule. Front loading has led to a more compact process and to a strengthened opportunity for a quick knockout. In 1996 three fourths of all states held their caucuses and primaries before the end of March (twenty-seven in March alone—a development that clearly benefits front-runners).

Third, early money and standing organization are more important than ever. Once the campaign begins, in this tighter schedule of events, scant time is available to raise money, solicit endorsements, shape issues, or put an organization in place. In the 1996 Republican struggle, following New Hampshire, only Dole was sufficiently well-positioned, financially and organizationally, to compete effectively in any state. For serious contenders, the nominating campaign must begin far in advance of the presidential year. No one can wait around for lightning to strike.

The Convention Delegates

The ramifications of political reforms are often much larger than anticipated. The new emphasis on popular participation in the delegate selection process, coupled with the requirements for affirmative action plans to promote the representation of disadvantaged groups, has sharply changed the composition of Democratic national conventions. Prior to the 1970s, Democratic delegates were preponderantly male, middle-aged, and white. And they were usually party regulars—officials of the party, important contributors, and reliable rank-and-file members. Public officeholders were prominent in all state delegations. The selection process itself was dominated by state and local party leaders.

The reforms produced a new breed of delegate. As a result of the guidelines adopted by the McGovern–Fraser Commission, the representation of women, blacks, and young persons in the national convention increased dramatically. For example, the proportion of women delegates grew from 13 percent in 1968 to 40 percent in 1972, and that of Blacks from 5.5 to 15 percent. Under current rules, each Democratic state party is required to develop outreach programs to increase the number of delegates from groups that have been significantly underrepresented in the past, such as persons over sixty-five years old, physically handicapped individuals, and persons of low and moderate income. Another affirmative action rule specifies that in the selection of at-large delegates, preference shall be given to Blacks, Hispanics, Native Americans, Asian/Pacific Americans, and women. Moreover, all state delegation selection plans must provide for an equal division of delegates between men and women. These mandated changes have had a profound impact on the composition of state delegations.

The chief losers in the reordering of the 1970s were Democratic party professionals and public officeholders, as delegates animated by particular issues or candidates ("amateurs," in broad terms) replaced them in state after state. Recent changes in party rules—marked by adding superdelegates—have altered the composition of the convention. A survey of Democratic delegates in 1988 found that 43 percent held some party office and 26 percent held an elective (or public) office. Seventy-four percent of the delegates reported that they were engaged in party activities on a year-round basis. Twenty-two percent of the delegates, by contrast, said that they engage in party work only when the issues or candidates are important to them.[47] Clearly, professional politicians have reemerged after being sidelined by various party reform commissions. Whether their presence will make much difference remains to be seen. Recent conventions have been cut and dried, the presidential nominees having been chosen earlier by primary voters and caucus participants.

Changes in the composition of Republican convention delegations have come more gradually. Even so, a larger proportion of women, Blacks, and young people are being elected as Republican delegates than ever before. Amateur activists are also more numerous in Republican conventions, but not on the scale found on the Democratic side. Party leaders, longtime party members, and public officials have steadily played key roles in Republican conventions.

Convention delegates do not reflect a cross section of the population or a cross section of the party membership. Two characteristics in particular differentiate delegates from the wider public and rank-and-file party members: high income and substantial education. In 1996, 72 percent of the Democratic delegates and 73 percent of the Republican delegates had completed four years of college; 45 percent of the Democrats and 36 percent of the Republicans had undertaken graduate work. About one half of the delegates in each party had incomes in excess of $75,000 annually. Blacks made up 21 percent of the Democratic membership but only 3 percent of the Republican membership, and the percentages for Hispanics were 6 and 2, respectively. More than one third of the Democratic delegates were labor union members, as contrasted with less than 3 percent for the Republicans.[48]

Liberals are regularly overrepresented in the Democratic convention, conservatives in the Republican convention. Forty-three percent of the Democratic delegates described themselves as "very liberal" or "somewhat liberal," as contrasted with 27 percent for the Democratic membership as a whole. And whereas 53 percent of rank-and-file Republicans saw themselves as "very conservative" or "somewhat conservative," 66 percent of the Republican delegates described themselves in that fashion. More than one third of all Republican delegates, in fact, identified themselves as very conservative—a proportion twice as great as found among Republican voters. No Republican delegates identified themselves as liberals, as contrasted with 7 percent for GOP registered voters. Five percent of the Democratic delegates were somewhat or very conservative, as contrasted with 17 percent for rank-and-file party members.[49] Ideologically, these two party elites are quite different. What is more, ideological distinctiveness is much more characteristic of delegates than of average party voters.

The Politics of the Convention

Three practical aims dominate the proceedings of the national convention: to nominate presidential and vice-presidential candidates, to draft the party platform, and to lay the groundwork for party unity in the campaign. The way in which the party addresses itself to the tasks of nominating the candidates and drafting the platform is likely to determine how well it achieves its third objective, that of healing party rifts and forging a cohesive party. To put together a presidential ticket and a platform that satisfies the principal elements of the party is difficult. The task of reconciling divergent interests within the party occupies the convention from its earliest moments until the final gavel—at least in most conventions. By and large, convention leaders have been successful in shaping the compromises necessary to keep the national party, such as it is, from flying apart.

The Convention Committees

The initial business of the convention is handled mainly by four committees. The committee on credentials is given the responsibility for determining the permanent roll (official membership) of the convention. Its specific function is to ascertain the members' legal right to seats in the convention. In the absence of challenges to the right of certain delegates to be seated or of contests between two delegations from the same state, each trying to be seated, the review is handled routinely and with dispatch. Most state delegations are seated without difficulty. When disputes arise, the committee holds hearings and takes testimony; its recommendations for seating delegates are then reported to the convention, which ordinarily (but not invariably) sustains them. The committee on permanent organization is charged with selecting the permanent officers of the convention, including the permanent chair, the clerks, and the sergeant at arms. The committee on rules devises the rules under which the convention will operate and establishes the order of business.

Ordinarily the most important convention committee is the committee on resolutions, which is in charge of drafting the party platform. The actual work of this committee begins many weeks in advance of the convention, so that usually a draft of the document exists by the time the convention opens and the formal committee hearings begin. When a president seeks reelection, the platform is likely to be prepared under his direction and accepted by the committees (and later by the floor) without major changes.

A fight over the nomination may influence the drafting of the platform, because the leading candidates have an interest in securing planks that are compatible with their views. Indeed, the outcomes of clashes over planks may provide a good indication of which candidate will capture the nomination. In the 1968 Democratic convention, for example, it was all but certain that Hubert Humphrey would win the nomination when the convention, after a lengthy and emotional floor debate, adopted by a comfortable margin a plank that reflected the Johnson administration's position on the Vietnam War. Humphrey's two principal opponents, senators Eugene McCarthy and George McGovern, were the most prominent supporters of the losing minority plank, which called for an unconditional halt to the bombing of North Vietnam. In the 1976 Republican convention, intense struggles occurred in the platform committee between the forces of President Ford and those of Ronald Reagan. Almost all the planks adopted represented victories for the supporters of Ford, thus auguring well for his nomination.

The 1980 Republican and Democratic platforms were fashioned in sharply different ways. Harmony prevailed at the Republican convention, and the members quickly approved a platform with planks that meshed comfortably with the views of its nominee, Ronald Reagan. The document of the platform committee was adopted without change. Debate over the Democratic platform, by contrast, was acrimonious and protracted. Numerous minority reports were adopted on the floor. In the end, the delegates adopted a platform that in major respects (particularly in its economic and human needs planks) was more in line with the liberal views of Senator Kennedy and his partisans than with those of President Carter. The high level of conflict over the platform was surprising given that an incumbent president, the certain nominee, was seeking reelection. No one expects the president's forces to lose on key convention votes. In 1984 scarcely a discordant note was struck at the Republican convention as it renominated President Reagan and approved the platform without debate. On the Democratic side, compromises on the platform among the Walter Mondale, Jesse Jackson, and Gary Hart forces were sufficient to avert divisive floor fights, and the party, eschewing tradition, chose Geraldine A. Ferraro as its vice-presidential nominee.[50]

In 1988 Jesse Jackson won numerous platform concessions from Dukakis as party leaders worked hard to unify the party for the campaign. On the few planks that were controversial—for example, the Jackson-inspired planks on tax increases for the wealthy and Palestinian self-determination—Dukakis's forces prevailed. Adopted with a minimum of controversy, the 1988 Republican platform followed the conservative doctrines set down in the Reagan platforms of 1980 and 1984.

Winning a decisive majority of the Democratic delegates in 1992, Gov. Bill Clinton thoroughly controlled the platform-writing process and the convention. The forces of Paul Tsongas were permitted to bring up several minority planks for a floor vote, but they were easily defeated. The delegates of former California governor Jerry Brown were largely ignored by the Clinton majority, which was bent on fashioning a centrist platform. Several weeks later, the Republican convention adopted, without debate, a strongly conservative platform. Abortion-rights activists were unable to get six state delegations to support a motion for a floor debate on the subject. Many delegates who favored abortion rights attached higher priority to party harmony.[51]

The most remarkable feature of the 1996 Republican convention, arguably, was its preoccupation with conformity and unity. The discussion of contentious issues, such as abortion and affirmative action, was suppressed; platform fights never materialized; public displays of differences and discord were avoided; and speakers who might rock the boat, such as Pat Buchanan and several prochoice governors, were kept away from the podium. Although party moderates, such as Colin Powell, were the featured speakers at the convention, the platform that was adopted was ultraconservative. The party's presidential nominee, Bob Dole, said that he had not read it and, moreover, did not feel bound by it.

Selecting the Presidential Ticket

To some party leaders, the best convention is the one that opens with significant uncertainties and imponderables—a good, though not surefire, prescription for generating public interest in the convention, the party, and its nominees.[52] In the usual convention, however, uncertainties are far from numerous. Doubts are much more likely to surround the choice of the vice-presidential nominee than the presidential nominee. So many presidential candidates are screened out during the primary-caucus season that by the time the convention opens the range of choice has become sharply narrowed, perhaps nonexistent.

The early stages of the nominating process are especially important for the selection of presidential candidates (see Table 3-2). Typically, the candidate leading the public opinion polls at the start of the year (before the first delegate has even been chosen) winds up with the nomination. New opportunities for challenging leading candidates in primaries and caucuses may alter this pattern. In 1972 and 1976 the Democratic nomination was won by an outsider whose poll standings were unimpressive at the start of the year. And in 1980 Ronald Reagan won the Republican nomination, although he trailed in the early polls. Walter Mondale had a wide lead in the initial polls in 1984 and, after an early scare, nailed down the nomination before the Democratic convention opened. In 1988 George Bush's nomination went according to form, as he led from the outset. On the Democratic side, the early polls had Michael Dukakis trailing Gary Hart, Jesse Jackson, and Paul Simon. He did not wrap up the nomination until well into the primary season. In 1992 Bill Clinton trailed Jerry Brown in the polls until early February, when he assumed a commanding lead over the field.[53] In 1996 Bob Dole led the polls at the start of the year and, after a shaky start, won the nomination without much difficulty. President Clinton had no serious opposition.

The experience of past conventions is worth noting. In the 1960, 1968, and 1972 Republican conventions, Richard Nixon's nomination occurred on the first ballot, without significant opposition. In 1964, in the judgment of most party professionals, Barry Goldwater's nomination was assured by his victory over Nelson Rockefeller in the California primary. The great bulk of the Goldwater delegates had been captured earlier in state conventions. The Democratic experience is about the same. Lyndon Johnson's nomination in 1964 was a foregone conclusion, following the custom (at that time) that incumbent presidents were entitled to another term if they chose to run. In 1968, with the forces opposed to the Johnson administration in disarray

TABLE 3-2   Continuity and Change in Presidential Nominating Politics: 1936 to 1996

Year	Leading candidate at beginning of election year	Nominee
Party in power		
1936 (D)	Roosevelt	Roosevelt
1940 (D)	Roosevelt	Roosevelt
1944 (D)	Roosevelt	Roosevelt
1948 (D)	Truman	Truman
1952 (D)	Truman	Stevenson
1956 (R)	Eisenhower	Eisenhower
1960 (R)	Nixon	Nixon
1964 (D)	Johnson	Johnson
1968 (D)	Johnson	Humphrey
1972 (R)	Nixon	Nixon
1976 (R)	Ford	Ford
1980 (D)	Carter	Carter
1984 (R)	Reagan	Reagan
1988 (R)	Bush	Bush
1992 (R)	Bush	Bush
1996 (D)	Clinton	Clinton
Party out of power		
1936 (R)	Landon	Landon
1940 (R)	?	Willkie
1944 (R)	Dewey	Dewey
1948 (R)	Dewey-Taft	Dewey
1952 (R)	Eisenhower-Taft	Eisenhower
1956 (D)	Stevenson	Stevenson
1960 (D)	Kennedy	Kennedy
1964 (R)	?	Goldwater
1968 (R)	Nixon	Nixon
1972 (D)	Muskie	McGovern
1976 (D)	Kennedy-Humphrey	Carter
1980 (R)	Ford	Reagan
1984 (D)	Mondale	Mondale
1988 (D)	Hart	Dukakis
1992 (D)	Brown	Clinton
1996 (R)	Dole	Dole

SOURCE: Donald R. Matthews, "Presidential Nominations: Process and Outcome," in *Choosing the President*, ed. James David Barber (Englewood Cliffs, N.J.: Prentice Hall, 1974), 54 (as updated).

NOTE: D = Democrat; R = Republican.

following the assassination of Robert F. Kennedy, scarcely any doubt existed that Vice President Hubert Humphrey would become the party standard-bearer. In 1972 George McGovern arrived at the Democratic convention with more than twice as many delegate votes as any other candidate, and his nomination on the first ballot, though it could not have been predicted a few months earlier, was anything but a surprise at the convention. In 1976 Jimmy Carter came to the Democratic convention in Madison Square Garden with the nomination locked up. Some months earlier, that feat could not have been predicted either. First-ballot nominations occurred at both conventions from 1980 through 1996.

In only a few conventions in the past four decades has there been substantial doubt about the ultimate winner: Both conventions in 1952 (Dwight D. Eisenhower versus Robert A. Taft in the Republican convention and a wide-open contest in the Democratic convention), the Democratic convention in 1960 (John F. Kennedy, who won the presidential primaries, versus the field), and the 1976 Republican convention (Gerald R. Ford versus Ronald Reagan). It is unusual for a front-runner—the candidate holding the most delegate votes prior to the convention—to lose out at the convention. Often the front-runner is nominated on the first ballot.

The final major item of convention business is the selection of the party's vice-presidential nominee. Here the task of the party is to come up with the right political formula—the candidate who can add the most to the ticket and detract the least. The presidential nominee most often makes the choice, following rounds of consultation with various party and candidate organization leaders.[54] Although a great deal of suspense is usually created over the vice-presidential nomination, convention ratification comes easily once the presidential nominee has decided and cleared the selection with key leaders. Unless the presidential nominee is inclined to take a major risk to serve the interest of his own faction or ideology (as Barry Goldwater did in choosing Republican national chair William E. Miller in 1964), he selects a candidate who can help to balance the ticket and unify the party.[55] Jimmy Carter's choice of Walter Mondale in 1976 fits neatly into this category, as does Ronald Reagan's choice of George Bush in 1980. Mondale's selection of Geraldine A. Ferraro in 1984 broke with major party tradition in more ways than one: Representative Ferraro was the first woman to be nominated for the vice presidency, the first Italian American to be nominated for national office, and the first nominee to be anointed prior to the opening of the convention.

The choice of Sen. Lloyd Bentsen, a conservative Texan, by Michael Dukakis in 1988 was designed to bring ideological balance to the ticket and to attract voters in the South (and particularly in Texas with its large block of 29 electoral votes). Dukakis's "mini" southern strategy, centered on

Bentsen, plainly failed, as he lost every southern state. George Bush's surprising selection of a younger, telegenic U.S. senator, Dan Quayle of Indiana, reflected his desire to merge conservative and generational appeals. He hoped to satisfy the party's powerful conservative wing, win the attention of the postwar "baby boomers," improve the party's lagging position with women voters, and strengthen its prospects in the Midwest. Many conservatives were pleased with Quayle's selection, but undoubtedly he hurt the ticket as a result of prolonged controversies involving his qualifications and National Guard Service during the Vietnam War. In seeking to give the Democratic party a moderate and youthful image in 1992, Bill Clinton ignored notions of ideological and regional balance and chose Sen. Al Gore of Tennessee as his running mate, creating the party's first all-southern ticket since 1928.[56] And the strategy proved successful: Stressing change, the "new Democrats" carried five southern states and received strong support from younger (and also older) voters throughout the country.

For almost everyone, including the pundits, Bob Dole's choice of Jack Kemp as his running mate in 1996 was a surprising pick, in part because of their strained personal relationship but also because of their perceived incompatibility on certain issues. Dole chose Kemp, various observers contended, because he hoped to get a lift in the polls (where he trailed by double-digit numbers at the time of the convention), to reenergize his campaign, to unify his party (bringing together the tax-cutting and deficit-reducing wings), and to make his economic plan (to cut taxes while also balancing the budget) the centerpiece of his campaign. The choice of Kemp, the party's most prominent advocate of deep tax cuts, was widely interpreted as Dole's conversion to supply-side economics—an economic model he had often ridiculed.

The broad point is that the presidential candidate has a great deal of leeway in choosing the vice-presidential nominee. The need to reward or placate a certain party element may of course reduce the list of possible choices. Except for the most doctrinaire presidential candidate, the prime consideration is to pick a running mate who strengthens the ticket in terms of the party's strategy for winning the election.

A National Primary? Regional Primaries?

Dissatisfaction with the current system has led some politicians and analysts to prefer a single, one-day national primary. Under a typical proposal, to win the nomination a candidate would be required to obtain a majority of the popular vote cast in his party primary; if no candidate received a majority, a runoff election would be held between the top two finishers. A separate vote would be held for vice-presidential candidates. The national convention would be retained for writing the platform and fashioning party rules.

Another plan calls for regional primaries—all those states holding primaries within a region would be required to hold them on the same day.[57] A total of perhaps five regional primaries would be conducted, one each month from March through July in the presidential year, their order to be determined by lot. The national convention would continue, at least formally, to select the presidential candidate. When the primaries failed to produce a clear-cut winner, the actual choice would be made by the convention. As noted previously, with southern states leading the way, informal regional primaries are emerging; many states nevertheless are not part of any regional group.

Still another proposal would require all states using primaries to choose one of four dates (in March, April, May, or June) on which to hold them— thus bringing a measure of order to the system and diminishing the significance of a single state's early primary. Left to the decision of each state, a caucus-convention system could be used in place of a primary. The national convention would continue in its present form.

The adoption of a national primary law would represent the sharpest departure from the current system. It would favor well-known, well-financed candidates and would hurt outsiders—those lesser-known candidates who gain visibility and momentum through a win or an impressive showing in an early primary or caucus state. Inevitably, a national primary would have a destructive impact on the political parties, eliminating them from any role in the selection of presidential candidates. Austin Ranney wrote,

> [The] clear gainers in influence from the dismantling of the party organizations would be the national news media—the national television and radio networks, the major newspapers, and the wire services. . . . [Their] interpretations of the state primaries and caucuses, especially the early ones, already have a powerful influence on who wins or who loses. . . . In a national primary . . . the only preelection facts relevant to who was winning would be public opinion polls and estimates of the sizes of crowds at candidate meetings. The former are scientifically more respectable than the latter, but neither constitutes hard data in the sense that election returns do. And hard data of that sort would be available only after national primary day. Thus, a one-day national direct primary would give the news media even more power than they now have to influence the outcomes of contests for nominations by shaping most people's perceptions of how these contests were proceeding.[58]

The Media, the Presidential Nominating Process, and the Parties

It would be hard to exaggerate the importance of the print and broadcast media in shaping the presidential nominating process. Not surprisingly, media influence is as controversial as it is pivotal.

Critics charge that the media are preoccupied with the competitiveness, or "horse race," aspects of the presidential campaign and give too little attention to the candidates' records and issue positions. Complicated policy questions tend to be ignored by television and even by much of the print media. By contrast, horse race stories are easy for journalists to write, easy for television reporters to portray, and easy for the public to understand. These stories have a standard format: They tell where the candidates have been and where they are going; how their strategies have emerged; how crowds and organized groups are responding to them; how politicians evaluate them and their campaigns; how they have dealt with events and mistakes; who has endorsed them; and most important, who is winning and who is losing. What the campaign is all about is ordinarily lost in horse race accounts.

Numerous studies have shown that more than half of all stories on presidential campaigns have a horse race theme.[59] During the crucial first half of the 1988 presidential nominating season, 80 percent of the network news airtime was devoted to horse race stories and 20 percent to substantive issues. One of the campaign's early casualties, Bob Dole, had these observations on campaign reporting:

> What I witnessed generally on my own campaign plane was an aircraft filled with reporters who became each other's best audience. It was an ultra-insider's game of gossip and nit-picking that turned presidential campaign coverage into trivial pursuits. It was a daily spin from the experts on the state of the campaign, whether it came from a reporter who had been on board for one month, or one stop. . . . Preconceived notions, prewritten stories and premeditated clichés were all confirmed regardless of the facts. And if there was a nice soap opera campaign story out there, it would be kept on the spin cycle for a good week or so. All the while, reporters' necks were craned in the rear of the plane scanning the campaign staff up front for smiles or frowns, or seating arrangements that would somehow reveal the inside story. Meanwhile, the issues disappeared somewhere over Iowa airspace. . . . I just wish I was hounded on the federal deficit as I was on my staff. I just wish I was interrogated about American agriculture as I was about fund-raising. I just wish my voting record was as thoroughly scrutinized as were my wife's personal finances.[60]

Another feature of media coverage of nominating campaigns singled out by critics is the practice of focusing on front-runners at the expense of providing information on other candidates' campaigns. The early public opinion polls provide the initial impetus to prepare press and television stories on the front-runners. Thin on evidence, these early and speculative stories nevertheless generate additional coverage of the leaders, even before the first caucus or primary is held. In natural progression, the candidates who win or place well in the Iowa precinct caucuses, the New Hampshire primary, or both become media darlings and gain even more coverage. The interpretation of the election by candidates, handlers, and the media—so-called "spin control"—is what really counts. A narrow win can sometimes be translated into a striking victory in the next day's news or treated as a virtual loss, because the winner's vote failed to meet expectations set by the media.[61]

The media's role is particularly important in the early phase of the presidential nominating process. Television and press journalists sort out the candidates (ranking them as "the hopeless, the plausible, and the likely, with substantial differences between the three in the amount and quality of coverage"[62]), establish performance expectations, boost some campaigns while writing off others, and launch the bandwagons. Their evaluations create winners and losers. Candidates who capture the media's attention are rewarded out of proportion to the significance of the contests and perhaps to their shares of the vote as well. Early winners and surprise candidates gain momentum in this system of "lotteries driven by media expectations and candidate name recognition."[63]

The media also play a critical role in publicizing the factional appeals of candidates in primaries and caucuses. Increasingly, presidential candidates have eschewed coalition building while seeking to mobilize narrow ideological, religious, ethnic, or sectional followings. The more crowded the field, the greater the probability that an active, passionate, well-organized faction can keep the candidate in contention from one Tuesday to the next in the crucial early weeks of the season. Through extensive coverage of the campaign, the media help the candidates to attract, instruct, and mobilize their distinctive factional followings.[64]

Campaign schedules, speeches, and statements all revolve around the media. Candidates fly from one airport tarmac to the next, from one television market to the next, in their quest for press attention and free media time on local television stations. Nothing may be more important than free media time. Brief stops are the order of the day. During the 1988 nominating campaign preceding "Super Tuesday"—when most of the action was concentrated in the South—some candidates visited five or six states (or more accurately, assorted airports in these states) in a single day, not to see crowds of voters but to secure a few seconds of exposure on the local evening news (and, with luck, a snippet on the network news).

The influence of the media on the presidential nominating process obviously is pervasive. But two broad effects stand out. The first is that the media have undercut the position of party elites. As almost every candidate could testify, free media time and paid advertising are a much more effective means for influencing mass electorates than working through party leaders and party organizations. The media also provide an excellent opportunity for candidates, tutored by media consultants, to raise campaign money by gaining public attention. Impressive televised speeches sometimes produce a flood of campaign contributions. It is not far from the truth to suggest that the media are now used to "deliver" votes and money in a way that state and local politicians did a generation ago. What is more, political consultants and handlers are at least as important as any party professional in shaping campaign decisions.

Second, the media have played a key role in the transformation of the national party convention. They did this by becoming the vehicle by which candidates and candidate organizations distanced themselves from the party organization. Today's conventions are run by candidates and their organizations; the influence that party and elected officials wield is a function of their affiliation with candidate organizations. The vast majority of the delegates arrive at the convention committed to a candidate, and the convention meets to ratify the voters' choice, expressed in primaries and caucuses, as the presidential nominee. Typically, the nominee is known long in advance of the convention. The old "deliberative" convention, marked by high-stakes bargaining among party leaders, with the nomination in suspense, is all but extinct.

In virtually every phase, the new party convention is a media event. Activities are scheduled at times that will produce maximum television audiences. Deals are struck to avoid controversy. Politics is sanitized. Celebrities are properly celebrated. Speeches are kept brief. Trivial events and "news" are magnified by television reporters scurrying around for interviews. Orchestration and entertainment pervade the convention agenda as leaders strive to showcase their candidates, enhance the party's image, and hold an audience notorious for its short attention span. Elaborate efforts are made to avoid boring the viewers.

In this new environment, the convention takes on the appearance of a prepackaged television show or a tightly scripted infomercial. The absence of genuine news and spontaneity—in the midst of patriotic bunting, stagecraft, films, tributes, inspirationalism, and the celebration of average citizens, their lives, and even their dogs—had led the major networks to cut back convention coverage to a minimum, often to only a single prime-time hour per day. As for television viewers of the convention, their numbers have declined precipitously.

National party conventions have turned into spectacles, or made-for-TV shows, because they no longer actually choose the candidate, because they are trying to stay in business in a mass-oriented political system, because they are driven by the entertainment imperative, because party leaders prefer choreography to controversy, and because the media control the interpretation (and thus shape the politics) of the preconvention season. Not a great deal—maybe nothing—is left for the convention to decide. That at least has been the experience of the past several decades.

Notes

1. Does a hard-fought, divisive primary hurt the party's chances in the general election? Politicians and political observers tend to believe that it does—that supporters of the candidate or candidates who lost in the primary will switch their allegiance or decline to vote in the general election. Although the question is not settled, the preponderance of evidence suggests that conflictual (or competitive) primaries do have an adverse impact on the parties' chances for victory in the general election. The candidate who survives a primary battle is not as likely to win in November as a candidate who had little or no primary opposition. Support for this interpretation appears in Patrick J. Kenney and Tom W. Rice, "The Effect of Primary Divisiveness in Gubernatorial and Senatorial Elections," *Journal of Politics* 46 (August 1984): 904–915; and Robert A. Bernstein, "Divisive Primaries Do Hurt: U.S. Senate Races, 1956–1972," *American Political Science Review* 71 (June 1977): 540–545. But for a study that finds the relationship weak, see Richard Born, "The Influence of House Primary Divisiveness on General Election Margins, 1962–76," *Journal of Politics* 43 (August 1981): 640–661. The "carryover effect" has also been studied in presidential elections by Walter J. Stone. He finds a strong carryover effect among partisan and committed activists; that is, activists who supported candidates who lost the nomination were less active in the general election. See his article, "The Carryover Effect in Presidential Elections," *American Political Science Review* 80 (March 1986): 271–279. For additional evidence on the importance of the carryover effect, see Kenney and Rice, "Presidential Prenomination Preferences and Candidate Evaluations," *American Political Science Review* 82 (December 1988): 1309–1319. For the most recent studies of the effects of divisive primaries, see Kenney and Rice, "The Relationship between Divisive Primaries and General Election Outcomes," *American Journal of Political Science* 31 (February 1987): 31–44; and Patrick J. Kenney, "Sorting Out the Effects of Primary Divisiveness in Congressional and Senatorial Elections," *Western Political Quarterly* 41 (September 1988): 765–777. Preoccupation with the effects of divisive primaries may lead researchers to ignore the positive, *mobilizing* effects of participation in nominating campaigns. See a new study by Walter J. Stone, Lonnie Rae Atkeson, and Ronald B. Rapoport, "Turning On or Turning Off?: Mobilization and Demobi-

lization Effects of Participation in Presidential Nominating Campaigns," *American Journal of Political Science 36* (August 1992): 665–691.

2. This discussion of closed and open primaries rests largely on an analysis by Craig L. Carr and Gary L. Scott, "The Logic of State Primary Classification Schemes," *American Politics Quarterly 12* (October 1984): 465–476. Also see Malcolm E. Jewell and David M. Olson, *American State Political Parties and Elections* (Homewood, Ill.: Dorsey Press, 1978), 127–131; and David E. Price, *Bringing Back the Parties* (Washington, D.C.: CQ Press, 1984), 127–131.

3. The closed primary states, listed from least to most restrictive in terms of the length of time necessary to change party affiliation, are Iowa, Ohio, Wyoming, South Dakota, Oregon, Kansas, North Carolina, Delaware, Massachusetts, West Virginia, Pennsylvania, Florida, Colorado, Arizona, New Jersey, Nevada, Oklahoma, Maine, Nebraska, New Hampshire, New Mexico, Maryland, Connecticut, Kentucky, New York, and California.

4. Do members of the U.S. House of Representatives have higher party support scores than members elected from states with less restrictive, or more open, systems? The answer is that closed primary states do tend to produce more partisan officeholders; their partisanship, however, appears to be a function of party strength and other attitudes toward parties present in the state rather than the result of a closed primary nominating system. See Steven H. Haeberle, "Closed Primaries and Party Support in Congress," *American Politics Quarterly 13* (July 1985): 341–352.

5. *Tashjian v. Republican Party of Connecticut,* 107 S. Ct. 544 (1986). See a comprehensive analysis of the *Tashjian* decision by Leon D. Epstein, "Will American Political Parties Be Privatized?" *Journal of Law and Politics 5* (Winter 1989): 239–274.

6. The states with the purest form of open primary are Hawaii, Idaho, Michigan, Minnesota, North Dakota, Utah, Vermont, and Wisconsin. See a comprehensive classification scheme for state primary systems in Malcolm E. Jewell and David M. Olson, *Political Parties and Elections in American States* (Chicago: Dorsey Press, 1988), 89–94.

7. A study of Arkansas voters by Gary D. Wekkin finds that most crossover voters are not mischievous; rather, they cross over to vote in the other party's primary because they view the party favorably. Crossover voters also tend to defect to support the other party in the general election. See Wekkin's article, "Why Crossover Voters Are Not 'Mischievous Voters': The Segmented Partisanship Hypothesis," *American Politics Quarterly 19* (April 1991): 229–257.

8. The "crossover" voting data are drawn from Ronald D. Hedlund and Meredith W. Watts, "The Wisconsin Open Primary, 1968 to 1984," *American Politics Quarterly 14* (January–April 1986): 55–73. Also see Ronald D. Hedlund, Meredith W. Watts, and David M. Hedge, "Voting in an Open Primary," *American Politics Quarterly 10* (April 1982): 197–218; David Adamany, "Communication: Cross-over Voting and the Democratic Party's Reform Rules," *American Political Science Review 70* (June 1976): 536–541; and James I. Lengle and Byron E. Shafer, "Primary Rules, Political Power, and Social Change," *American Political Science Review 70* (March 1976): 25–40.

9. *Democratic Party of the U.S. v. LaFollette,* 101 S. Ct. 1010 (1981).

10. *Congressional Quarterly Weekly Report,* March 30, 1996, 902.

11. The observations made in this paragraph are based mainly on an analysis by Charles D. Hadley, "The Impact of the Louisiana Open Elections System Re-

form," *State Government 58*, no. 4 (1986): 152–157. Also consult Thomas A. Kazee, "The Impact of Electoral Reform: 'Open Elections' and the Louisiana Party System," *Publius 13* (Winter 1983): 132–139; and, for a general analysis of factionalism, see Earl Black, "A Theory of Southern Factionalism," *Journal of Politics 45* (August 1983): 594–614.

12. Laws in a few states make provisions for the parties to hold preprimary conventions for the purpose of choosing the organization slate. The candidates selected by these conventions will usually appear on the ballot bearing the party endorsement. In the great majority of states, however, slating is an informal party process; the party depends on its organizational network and the communications media to inform the voters which candidates carry party support.

13. For an unorthodox argument that the intraparty competition afforded by primaries encourages the parties to be responsive to voters, see John G. Geer and Mark E. Shere, "Party Competition and the Prisoner's Dilemma: An Argument for the Direct Primary," *Journal of Politics 54* (August 1992), 741–761.

14. Jewell and Olson, *Political Parties and Elections in American States*, 94–104. See also a study of the various factors that influence the value of a political party's preprimary endorsement to the candidate who received it. Overall, the proportion of endorsed candidates who win contested primaries is declining. Malcolm E. Jewell and Sarah M. Morehouse, "What are Party Endorsements Worth: A Study of Preprimary Gubernatorial Endorsements," *American Politics Quarterly 24* (July 1996): 338–362.

15. These themes appear in Frank J. Sorauf, *Party Politics in America* (Boston: Little, Brown, 1980), 220–224.

16. V. O. Key Jr., *American State Politics: An Introduction* (New York: Knopf, 1956); William H. Standing and James A. Robinson, "Inter-Party Competition and Primary Contesting: The Case of Indiana," *American Political Science Review 52* (December 1958): 1066–1077; and Malcolm E. Jewell, "Party and Primary Competition in Kentucky State Legislative Races," *Kentucky Law Journal 48* (Summer 1960): 517–535.

17. See Harvey L. Schantz, "Contested and Uncontested Primaries for the U.S. House," *Legislative Studies Quarterly 5* (November 1980): 545–562.

18. Jewell and Olson, *Political Parties and Elections in American States*, 105–106.

19. Denis G. Sullivan, Jeffrey L. Pressman, and F. Christopher Arterton, *Explorations in Convention Decision Making* (San Francisco: Freeman, 1976), 17.

20. Sullivan, Pressman, and Arterton, *Explorations in Convention Decision Making*, 20–21.

21. Ideologically extreme candidates tend to run better in caucus states than in primary states. See Barbara Norrander, "Nomination Choices: Caucus and Primary Outcomes, 1976–88," *American Journal of Political Science 37* (May 1993): 343–364.

22. Changing from one system to another has unanticipated consequences. Richard W. Boyd has shown, for example, that frequent elections depress turnout. Thus, states that switch from caucus-convention systems to direct primaries to select candidates and convention delegates will have a lower general election turnout. See his article, "The Effects of Primaries and Statewide Races on Voter Turnout," *Journal of Politics 51* (August 1989): 730–739.

23. Turnout in presidential primaries tends to be highest in those states distinguished by high levels of education, facilitative legal provisions on voting, and competitive two-party elections. Interestingly, high turnout is not associated with high

levels of campaign spending. See Patrick J. Kenney and Tom W. Rice, "Voter Turnout in Presidential Primaries: A Cross-Sectional Examination," *Political Behavior 7*, no. 1 (1985): 101–112. In terms of participation in presidential primaries, there is little or no difference between Democrats and Republicans. See Jack Moran and Mark Fenster, "Voting Turnout in Presidential Primaries," *American Politics Quarterly 10* (October 1982): 453–476. Candidate strategy does influence turnout. See a study of how the number of candidates in the opposition party and the intensity of campaigning in the presidential party influence aggregate turnout levels: Barbara Norrander and Gregg W. Smith, "Type of Contest, Candidate Strategy, and Turnout in Presidential Primaries," *American Politics Quarterly 13* (January 1985): 28–50. Turnout for first-tier caucuses is heightened by the presence of significant ideological choice among candidates, although no relationship exists between ideological range and turnout in primary states. See Steven E. Schier, "Turnout Choice in Presidential Nominations," *American Politics Quarterly 10* (April 1982): 231–245. Also see a model by Patrick J. Kenney and Tom W. Rice of how individual voters decide which candidate they prefer during the presidential nomination campaign: "A Model of Nomination Preferences," *American Politics Quarterly 20* (July 1992): 267–286.

24. Priscilla L. Southwell, "Rules as 'Unseen Participants': The Democratic Presidential Nominating Process," *American Politics Quarterly 20* (January 1992): 64.

25. William J. Crotty, *Political Reform and the American Experiment* (New York: Crowell, 1977), 255–260.

26. *Congressional Quarterly Weekly Report,* July 4, 1992, 72.

27. *Congressional Quarterly Weekly Report,* August 8, 1992, 65.

28. Bill Clinton was the first presidential candidate of either party since 1952 to be elected who did not win the New Hampshire primary.

29. See William C. Adams, "As New Hampshire Goes. . . ," in *Media and Momentum: The New Hampshire Primary and Nomination Politics,* ed. Gary R. Orren and Nelson W. Polsby (Chatham, N.J.: Chatham House Publishers, Inc., 1987), 42–49.

30. Are the voters who take part in presidential primaries ideologically unrepresentative? Evidence offered by Barbara Norrander indicates that they are not. See her article "Ideological Representativeness of Presidential Primary Voters," *American Journal of Political Science 33* (August 1989): 570–587. Also see an article by John G. Geer, "Assessing the Representativeness of Electorates in Presidential Primaries," *American Journal of Political Science 32* (November 1988): 929–945.

31. William R. Keech and Donald R. Matthews, "Patterns in the Presidential Nominating Process, 1936–1976," in *Parties and Elections in an Anti-Party Age,* ed. Jeff Fishel (Bloomington: Indiana University Press, 1978), 216.

32. For evidence that candidate spending heavily influences the outcome of the presidential nominating process, see Audrey A. Haynes, Paul-Henri Gurian, and Stephen M. Nichols, "The Role of Candidate Spending in Presidential Nomination Campaigns," *Journal of Politics 59* (February 1997): 213–225.

33. This observation and the previous three are drawn from F. Christopher Arterton, "Campaign Organizations Confront the Media-Political Environment," in *Race for the Presidency: The Media and the Nominating Process,* ed. James David Barber (Englewood Cliffs, N.J.: Prentice Hall, 1978), 5.

34. *Congressional Quarterly Weekly Report,* August 23, 1986, 1999.
35. Nelson W. Polsby, *Consequences of Party Reform* (New York: Oxford University Press, 1983), 67.
36. David L. Paletz and Robert M. Entman, *Media Power Politics* (New York: Free Press, 1981), 36.
37. Quoted in Christine F. Ridout, "The Role of Media Coverage of Iowa and New Hampshire in the 1988 Democratic Nomination," *American Politics Quarterly* 19 (January 1991): 50.
38. Arterton, "Campaign Organizations Confront the Media-Political Environment," 10 (emphasis added).
39. For a study of how state party leaders seek to enhance media coverage of their state's primary or caucus, see David S. Castle, "Media Coverage of Presidential Primaries," *American Politics Quarterly 19* (January 1991): 33–42. Front loading has been a particularly effective device for drawing attention to the state's delegate selection process.
40. *Congressional Quarterly Weekly Report,* August 17, 1996, 2299.
41. Arterton, "Campaign Organizations Confront the Media-Political Environment," 9.
42. Voters in primary and caucus states do not respond to exactly the same forces. A study of the 1984 Democratic party primaries and caucuses found that sociodemographic groups (in particular, Blacks and labor) and general economic circumstances (levels of unemployment and income) were the major factors in influencing candidates' vote shares. Their vote shares in caucus states were heavily influenced by the sociodemographic makeup of the population and by levels of campaign spending. Candidates have very little control over the dominant factors in primary states, but they have considerable control over the major factor of campaign spending in caucus states. T. Wayne Parent, Calvin C. Jillson, and Ronald E. Weber, "Voting Outcomes in the 1984 Democratic Party Primaries and Caucuses," *American Political Science Review 81* (March 1987): 67–84.
43. These figures on participation are derived from several sources: Austin Ranney, *Participation in American Presidential Nominations, 1976* (Washington, D.C.: American Enterprise Institute for Public Policy Research, 1977), 15–20; *Congressional Quarterly Weekly Report,* July 5, 1980, 1869; June 2, 1984, 1315–1317; July 7, 1984, 1618–1620; July 9, 1988, 1892–1897; July 4, 1992, 69–70; August 8, 1992, 65–67; and June 15, 1996, 1701.
44. See an analysis of the factors that affect turnout in presidential primaries by Lawrence S. Rothenberg and Richard A. Brody, "Participation in Presidential Primaries," *Western Political Quarterly 41* (June 1988): 253–271. Short-term factors, such as the closeness of the election and the presence of a hot contest, are particularly important in fostering participation.
45. But see a study of the 1980 presidential primaries by Barbara Norrander that finds that voters made little use of candidates' issue positions in deciding how to vote. The most frequent correlates of vote choice are the qualities of the candidates. "Correlates of Vote Choice in the 1980 Presidential Primaries," *Journal of Politics 48* (February 1986): 156–166. Additionally, for a study of the characteristics of voters who participate in presidential primaries, see Barbara Norrander, "Explaining Individual Participation in Presidential Primaries," *Western Political Quarterly 44* (September 1991): 640–655.
46. James I. Lengle, Diane Owen, and Molly W. Sonner, "Divisive Nominating

Mechanisms and Democratic Party Electoral Prospects," *Journal of Politics 57* (May 1995): 370–383 (quotation on p. 381).

47. *New York Times,* July 17, 1988.

48. *Washington Post,* August 11 and August 25, 1996.

49. *New York Times,* August 26, 1996.

50. Few contributions of the major parties are more likely to be criticized or ridiculed than the party platforms. Commentators have found them meaningless, irrelevant, and nearly useless in charting the direction of the government by the winning candidate and party. The truth is something else. Platform pledges tend to be adopted by the parties once they take control of government. Recently, about two thirds of all platform promises have been fulfilled in some measure. See Gerald M. Pomper and Susan S. Lederman, *Elections in America* (New York: Longman, 1980), especially 161–167; and Alan D. Monroe, "American Party Platforms and Public Opinion," *American Journal of Political Science 27* (February 1983): 27–42. Also see the persuasive evidence of Ian Budge and Richard I. Hofferbert that the policy positions and platforms of the parties have a significant impact on policy adopted by the party that wins the presidency. They conclude that party government in the United States largely reflects mandate theory. "Mandates and Policy Outputs: U.S. Party Platforms and Federal Expenditures," *American Political Science Review 84* (March 1990): 111–131.

51. *Congressional Quarterly Weekly Report,* August 22, 1992, 2519–2520.

52. One of the most important functions of the convention is the "rally function"—bringing the party together and creating enthusiasm for the ticket. One manifestation of this is that candidates usually benefit from a "bump" of 5 to 7 percentage points in public opinion surveys. See James E. Campbell, Lynna L. Cherry, and Kenneth A. Wink, "The Convention Bump," *American Politics Quarterly 20* (July 1992): 287–307.

53. *Gallup Poll Monthly,* February 1992, 26.

54. An exception to this rule occurred in 1956 when Adlai Stevenson, the Democratic presidential nominee, created a stir by declining to express a preference for his vice-presidential running mate. Left to its own devices, the convention quickly settled on a choice between senators Estes Kefauver and John F. Kennedy. Kefauver, who had been an active candidate for the presidency, won a narrow victory. Kennedy came off even better—he launched his candidacy for the presidential nomination in 1960.

55. The preference of party professionals for a balanced ticket grows out of their instinct for the conservation of the party and their understanding of the electorate. In the view of party professionals, the ticket should be broadly appealing instead of narrowly ideological or sectional. The factors that ordinarily come under review in the consideration of balance are geography, political philosophy, religion, and factional recognition.

56. Does balancing a ticket geographically make a difference? Specifically, does it increase the vote for the ticket in the vice president's home state? The answer is that it makes some positive difference if the candidate is from a small state, but "it is the presidential candidates who dominate the nation's politics." See Robert L. Dudley and Ronald B. Rapoport, "Vice Presidential Candidates and the Home State Advantage: Playing Second Banana at Home and on the Road," *American Journal of Political Science 33* (May 1989): 537–540. Also see an earlier study by Michael S. Lewis-Beck and Tom W. Rice, "Localism in Presidential

Elections: The Home State Advantage," *American Journal of Political Science 27* (May 1983): 548–556.

57. A variation of this regional plan would require all states to hold a presidential primary.

58. Austin Ranney, *The Federalization of Presidential Primaries* (Washington, D.C.: American Enterprise Institute for Public Policy Research, 1978), 36–37. This monograph provides a comprehensive analysis of the proposals discussed in this section.

59. Doris A. Graber, *Mass Media and American Politics,* 4th ed. (Washington, D.C.: CQ Press, 1993), 273–275. The tendency to treat elections as horse races did not begin with television, but it is also true that horse race coverage increased dramatically in the television era. Although coverage of policy issues has declined somewhat in recent years, Lee Sigelman and David Bullock report, it is still greater than it was during the newspaper era. See their article, "Candidates, Issues, Horse Races, and Hoopla: Presidential Campaign Coverage, 1888–1988," *American Politics Quarterly 19* (January 1991): 5–32.

60. U.S. Congress, Senate, *Congressional Record,* daily ed., 100th Cong., 2d sess., April 26, 1988, S4734–4735. The data on horse race versus issue airtime are taken from a study commissioned by *USA Today,* as reported in the issue of April 22, 1988.

61. See Ridout, "The Role of Media Coverage of Iowa and New Hampshire in the 1988 Democratic Nomination," especially 48–53.

62. William G. Mayer, "The New Hampshire Primary: A Historical Overview," in *Media and Momentum,* 16.

63. Henry E. Brady and Richard Johnston, "What's the Primary Message: Horse Race or Issue Journalism?" in *Media and Momentum,* 128.

64. Polsby, *Consequences of Party Reform,* 67.

Chapter Four

Political Parties
and the Electoral Process:
Campaigns and Campaign Finance

Political campaigns are difficult to describe for one very good reason: They come in an extraordinary variety of shapes and sizes. Whether there is such a thing as a typical campaign is open to serious doubt. Campaigns will differ depending on the office sought (executive, legislative, or judicial), the level of government (national, state, or local), the legal and political environments (partisan or nonpartisan election, competitive or noncompetitive constituency), and the initial advantages or disadvantages of the candidates (incumbent or nonincumbent, well known or little known), among other things.

The standards by which to measure and evaluate the effectiveness of campaigns are not easy to discover because of the vast number of variables that intrude both on campaign decisions and on voter choice. Does the party that wins an election owe its victory to a superior campaign or would it have won in any case? Data needed to answer the question are elusive. What is evident is that strategies that are appropriate to one campaign may be less appropriate or even inappropriate to another. Tactics that work at one time or in one place may not work under other circumstances. Organizational arrangements that satisfy one party may not satisfy the other. Campaigns are loaded with imponderables. Neither the party organizations nor the candidates have any control over numerous factors in a campaign. Moreover, parties and candidates cannot develop an immunity against campaign mistakes. Even so, in most cases it is not immediately clear when a miscalculation has been made, how serious it may have been, or how best to repair the damage.

Despite the variability and uncertainty that characterize political campaigns, a few general requirements are imposed on all candidates and parties. The candidate making a serious bid for votes must acquire certain resources and meet certain problems. Whatever his perspective of the campaign, the candidate will have to deal with matters of organization, strategy, and finances.

Campaign Organization

Very likely the single most important fact to know about campaign organization is that the regular party organizations are ill equipped to organize and conduct campaigns by themselves. Of necessity, they look to outsiders for assistance in all kinds of party work and for the development and staffing of auxiliary campaign organizations. A multiplicity of organizational units is created in every major election for the promotion of particular candidacies. Some in business will organize to support the Republican nominee and others will organize to support the Democratic candidate. And the same will be true for educators, lawyers, physicians, advertising executives, and even political independents, to mention but a few. At times these groups work in impressive harmony with the regular party organizations (perhaps to the point of being wholly dominated by them), and at other times they function as virtually independent units, seemingly oblivious to the requirements for communication or for coordination of their activities with those of other party or auxiliary units.

The regular party organizations share influence not only with citizen groups but also with political action committees (PACs) of interest groups. Among the best known are the American Medical Association Political Action Committee, the Realtors Political Action Committee, The National Rifle Association Political Victory Fund, the AFL-CIO Committee on Political Education, and the National Congressional Club. Like other campaign groups, these committees raise funds, endorse candidates, make campaign contributions, and spend money on behalf of candidates. In 1996 PACs contributed $201 million to candidates for Congress, which came to about 25 percent of their total campaign receipts. In addition, several hundred PACs and other groups spent $11 million independently on presidential and congressional races.[1]

At the top of the heterogeneous cluster of party and auxiliary campaign committees are the campaign organizations created by the individual candidates. Virtually all candidates for important, competitive offices feel they must develop personal campaign organizations to counsel them on strategy and issues, to assist with travel arrangements and speeches, to raise money, to defend their interests in party circles, and to try to coordinate their activities with those of other candidates and campaign units. The size of a candidate's personal organization is likely to vary according to the significance of the office and the competitiveness of the constituency. The member from a safe district, for example, habituated to easy elections, has less need of an elaborate campaign organization than a candidate from a closely competitive district. Some congressional districts are so safe (at least for the candidate, if not the party) that were it not for having to attend certain district party and civic rites, the incumbent could easily skip campaigning and remain in Washington.

In some campaigns the regular party organization is reduced to being just another spectator. Candidates commonly employ professional management firms to direct their campaigns instead of relying on the party organizations.[2] Most facets of American politics today come under the influence of public relations specialists and advertising firms. Possessing resources that the party organizations cannot match, they raise funds; recruit campaign workers; develop issues; gain endorsements; write speeches; arrange campaign schedules; direct the candidate's television appearances; and prepare campaign literature, films, and advertising. Indeed, they sometimes create the overall campaign strategy and dominate day-to-day decision making. Their principal task is to build images of candidates by controlling the way they appear to the general public. An adviser to Richard Nixon's 1968 presidential election campaign made the point in this observation:

> [Nixon] has to come across as a person larger than life, the stuff of legend. People are stirred by legend, including the living legend, not by the man himself. It's the aura that surrounds the charismatic figure more than it is the figure itself that draws the followers. Our task is to build that aura.[3]

Few features of American politics have changed more dramatically than the way in which candidates contend for office. Barbara G. Salmore and Stephen A. Salmore wrote,

> The role of the party boss has been taken over by the political consultant, that of the volunteer party worker by the paid telephone bank caller. Most voters learn about candidates not at political rallies but from television advertising and computer-generated direct mail; candidates generally gather information about voters not from the ward leader but from the pollster. The money to fuel campaigns comes less from the party organizations and "fat cats" and more from direct mail solicitation of individuals and special-interest political action committees. In short, candidates have become individual entrepreneurs, largely set free from party control or discipline.[4]

Campaign Strategy

The paramount goal of all major party campaigns is to form a coalition of sufficient size to bring victory to the candidate or party. Ordinarily, the early days of the campaign are devoted to the development and testing of a broad campaign strategy designed to produce a winning coalition. In the most general sense, strategy should be seen as "an overall plan for acquiring and using the resources needed for a campaign." [5] In developing a broad strategy, candidates, their advisers, and party leaders must take into consideration a number of factors. These include (1) the principal themes to be developed during the campaign; (2) the issues to be emphasized and exploited; [6] (3) the candidate's personal qualities to be emphasized; (4) the specific groups and geographical areas to which appeals will be directed; (5) the acquisition of financial support and endorsements; (6) the timing of campaign activities; (7) the relationship of the candidate to the party organization and to factions within it; and (8) the uses to be made of the communications media, particularly television.

To the casual observer, there appear to be no limits to the number of major and minor strategies open to a resourceful candidate. However, important constraints serve to shape and define the candidate's options. For example, campaign strategy will be affected by the political, social, and economic environments. Among the factors that intrude on campaign strategy are the competitiveness of the district, the nature of the electorate, the quality and representativeness of the party ticket, the unity of the party, the presence of an incumbent, the election timetable (for example, presidential or off-year election), and the predispositions and commitments of political interest groups. Although difficult to weigh its significance, the temper of the times will also affect the candidate's overall plan of action. "In eras of general complacency and economic well-being," V. O. Key has written, "assaults against the interests and crusades against abuses by the privileged classes seem to pay small dividends. Periods of hardship and unrest move campaigners to contrive strategies to exploit the anxieties of people—or to insulate themselves from public wrath." [7] Whatever the impact of these constraints on campaign strategy, most of them are beyond the control of the candidate; they are simply conditions to which the candidate must adjust and adapt. The overall strategy that the candidate fashions or selects must be consonant with the givens of the campaign environment. [8]

Opportunities and constraints vary from campaign to campaign and from candidate to candidate. Although this results in great diversity, the three overarching strategies that serious candidates usually follow can be depicted. The most important is for the candidate to *get supporters out to vote.* A great many elections are won or lost depending on the turnout of the party faithful. Minority party candidates probably would win most elections if they could increase the rate of turnout of their own supporters (assuming turnout for the major party candidates remained the same). The second general strategy is to *activate latent support.* Successful campaigns often turn on the ability of the candidate to activate potential voters among the groups that ordinarily support his party. For the Democratic candidate, this means that special efforts must be directed to involve such segments of the population as Catholics, Jews, African Americans, Hispanics, blue-collar workers, union members, urban residents, women, and low-income households. For the Republican candidate, this rule prescribes a similar effort to activate Protestants (especially born-again Christians, the religious right), whites, Asian Americans, suburban or rural residents, and professional, business, and managerial elements. Efforts may be made to catalyze powerful single-issue groups, such as those in the prochoice and prolife movements. The third general strategy is to *change the opposition.*[9] In recent years this strategy has been spectacularly successful. A large number of Democrats, for example, voted for Dwight D. Eisenhower in the elections of 1952 and 1956, and a large number of Republicans bolted their party to vote for Lyndon B. Johnson in 1964. Similarly, in 1972 Democrats in great numbers abandoned their party's candidate, George McGovern, to vote for Richard Nixon (though it is probable that they were not so much attracted to Nixon as repelled by McGovern). In 1980 about one fourth of all Democrats voted for Ronald Reagan, and in 1984, about one fifth. Fifteen percent of all Democrats voted for George Bush in 1988, and in 1992 about one fourth of all party identifiers voted for the nominee of the opposing major party or for Ross Perot. In 1996 one third of the identifiers of the two major parties strayed from their affiliations. Party switchers often play a crucial role in presidential elections.

Myths and facts are mixed in about equal proportion in the lore of campaign strategy. Strategies are not easily devised, sorted out, or tested. Indeed, it is scarcely ever apparent in advance which strategies are likely to be most productive and which least productive or even counterproductive. However disciplined and well managed campaigns may appear to those who stand on the outskirts, they rarely are in reality. As Stimson Bullitt has observed,

> A politician, unlike a general or an athlete, never can be invincible, except within a constituency which constitutes a sinecure. Furthermore, a candidate cannot even be sure that his campaigning will change the election result. . . . [A] politician must act on his hypotheses, which are tested only by looking backward on his acts. A candidate cannot even experiment. Be-

cause no one knows what works in a campaign, money is spent beyond the point of diminishing returns. To meet similar efforts of the opposition all advertising and propaganda devices are used—billboards, radio, TV, sound trucks, newspaper ads, letter writing or telephone committee programs, handbills, bus cards. No one dares to omit any approach. Every cartridge must be fired because among the multitude of blanks one may be a bullet. . . .

A common mistake of post-mortems is to assert that a certain event or a stand or mannerism of a candidate caused him to win or lose. Often no one knows whether the election result was because of this factor or despite it. Spectacular events, whether a dramatic proposal, an attack, or something in the news outside the campaign, are like a revolving door. They win some votes and lose others.[10]

Campaign decisions may be shaped as much by chance and the ability of the candidate to seize on events as by the careful formulation of a broad and coherent plan of attack. Consider the decision of John F. Kennedy in the 1960 presidential campaign to telephone Coretta Scott King to express his concern over the welfare of her husband, the Rev. Dr. Martin Luther King, Jr., who had been jailed in Atlanta following a sit-in in a department store. There is no evidence that Kennedy's decision—perhaps as critical as any of the campaign—was based on a comprehensive assessment of alternatives or possible consequences. Instead, according to Theodore H. White, the decision came about in this way:

The crisis was instantly recognized by all concerned with the Kennedy campaign. . . . [The] suggestion for meeting it [was made by] Harris Wofford. Wofford's idea was as simple as it was human—that the candidate telephone directly to Mrs. King in Georgia to express his concern. Desperately Wofford tried to reach his own chief, Sargent Shriver, head of the Civil Rights Section of the Kennedy campaign, so that Shriver might break through to the candidate barnstorming somewhere in the Middle West. Early [the next] morning, Wofford was able to locate Shriver . . . and Shriver enthusiastically agreed. Moving fast, Shriver reached the candidate [as he] was preparing to leave for a day of barnstorming in Michigan. The candidate's reaction to Wofford's suggestion of participation was impulsive, direct, and immediate. From his room at the Inn, without consulting anyone, he placed a long-distance telephone call to Mrs. Martin Luther King, assured her of his interest and concern in her suffering and, if necessary, his intervention. . . . The entire episode received only casual notice from the generality of American citizens in the heat of the last three weeks of the Presidential campaign. But in the Negro community the Kennedy intervention rang like a carillon.[11]

Congressional campaigns and election outcomes carry few surprises. Candidates win where they are expected to win and lose where they are

Television Advertising and the Voters

Candidates for major offices typically spend well over half of their budgets on television advertising. Is the money well spent? The results of a recent national survey by the Times Mirror suggest that it is—that TV ads have a significant impact on voter decisions. Here is what the voters had to say.

Statement	Completely agree	Mostly agree	Mostly disagree	Completely disagree	Don't know
I often don't become aware of political candidates until I see their advertising on television	17%	45%	28%	7%	3%
I get some sense of what a candidate is like through his or her TV commercials	9	49	30	8	4
I like to have a picture of a candidate in my mind when I go to vote for him or her	21	53	14	6	6

Which gives you a better idea of where a candidate stands on issues: news reports on TV or candidates' TV commercials?

News reports	74%
Candidates' TV commercials	17
Don't know	8

Which gives you a better idea of what a candidate is like personally: news reports on TV or candidates' TV commercials?

News reports	65%
Candidates' TV commercials	26
Don't know	9

SOURCE: *The People, the Press, and Politics 1990* (Washington, D.C.: Times Mirror Center for the People and the Press, 1990), 133.

NOTE: Percentages may not total to 100 because of rounding.

expected to lose. Incumbent House members who lose in their bids to retain office are almost as rare as some entries on the endangered species list. Senators have more reason to worry over what the voters will deal to them, but they, too, campaign from a position of strength. Congressional campaigns go as expected for two major reasons. One is that incumbents enjoy overwhelming advantages. Among other things, they have a public record to which they can point, resources that permit them to assist constituents with their problems, the franking privilege, generous travel allowances, a staff and offices, and steady access to campaign funds—especially from PACs. Voters are more familiar with them than with their challengers. By contrast, congressional challengers cannot bank on a large and attentive public audience. No matter how tirelessly they transmit their messages, much of what they say is lost on a public preoccupied with other things.

Second, members of Congress campaign year-round. Constituent problems are handled by their staffs, and members return home weekend after weekend. Everyone in the member's entourage knows that reelections are won in nonelection years:

> I have the feeling that the most effective campaigning is done when no election is near. During the interval between elections you have to establish every personal contact you can, and you accomplish this through your mail as much as you do it by means of anything else. At the end of each session I take all the letters which have been received on legislative matters and write each person telling him how the legislative proposal in which he was interested stands. Personally, I will speak on any subject. I am not nonpartisan, but I talk on everything whether it deals with politics or not. Generally I speak at nonpolitical meetings. I read 48 weekly newspapers and clip every one of them myself. Whenever there is a particularly interesting item about anyone, that person gets a note from me. . . . [You] cannot let the matter of election go until the last minute.[12]

> You can slip up on the blind side of people during an off-year and get in much more effective campaigning than you can when you are in the actual campaign.[13]

> The reason I get 93-percent victories is what I do back home. I stay highly visible. No grass grows under my feet. I show that I haven't forgotten from whence I came.[14]

Campaign issues are of two basic types: *position* and *valence*. Position issues "are specific issues such as raising tariffs (yea or nay) and cutting welfare entitlements (for or against) on which the rival parties or candidates reach out for the support of the electorate by taking different positions on policy questions that divide the electorate." Modern election campaigns, John J. Dilulio Jr. has argued, are dominated by valence issues—"issues on

Media-Driven Politics . . .

"Television has established itself as the prime medium of political communications. The most significant point to be made about television, as compared to printed media, is that it is personality dominated. It deals with political figures, not political institutions. . . . Political parties as such have almost no role in television's portrayal of the political drama."
—David S. Broder

"The media stand in a position today, especially in the nomination phase, where the old party bosses used to stand."
—John Sears

"In effect, Boss Tube has succeeded Boss Tweed of Tammany Hall, Boss Crump of Memphis, and the Daley machine in Chicago. Television brings politicians right into the living room and lets voters form their own impressions, rather than voters having to depend on what local party bosses, union leaders, church spokesmen, or business chiefs say. . . . [The] modern campaign is mass marketing at its most superficial. It puts a premium on the suggestive slogan, the glib answer, the symbolic backdrop. Television is its medium. Candidates must have razzle-dazzle. Boring is the fatal label. Programs and concepts that cannot be collapsed into a slogan or a thirty-second sound bite go largely unheard and unremembered, for what the modern campaign offers in length, it lacks in depth, like an endless weekend with no Monday morning."
—Hedrick Smith

which the voters distinguish parties and candidates not by their real or perceived differences on position issues but by the degree to which they are linked in the voters' minds with conditions, symbols, or goals that are almost universally approved of or disapproved of by the electorate, such as economic prosperity, public corruption, and resolute leadership."[15]

The development of positional issues is not necessarily of great importance in designing campaign strategy. For one thing, voters frequently are unable to identify the positions of the candidates, and this is particularly true

. . . in a Television Age

"The mark of a good day on the campaign trail is measured by the time devoted to the candidate's activities that gets on the air. A sound bite added to the picture is an extra elixir."

—Marvin Kalb

"Disdain for politicians as unprincipled power-seekers permeates the national media."

—S. Robert Lichter, Stanley
Rothman, and Linda S. Lichter

"This new relation, between image-conscious coverage and media-driven campaigns, raises with special urgency the deepest danger for politics in a television age. This is the danger of the loss of objectivity—not in the sense of bias, but in the literal sense of losing contact with the truth. It is the danger that the politicians and the press become caught up in a cycle that leaves the substance of politics behind, that takes appearance for reality, perception for fact, the artificial for the actual, the image for the event."

—Kiku Adatto

SOURCES: David S. Broder, "Of Presidents and Parties," *Wilson Quarterly 2* (Winter 1978): 109–110; Sears quoted in Albert R. Hunt, "The Media and Presidential Campaigns," in *Elections American Style,* ed. A. James Reichley (Washington, D.C.: Brookings Institution, 1987), 54; Hedrick Smith, *The Power Game: How Washington Works* (New York: Random House, 1988), 36, 693; Kalb quoted in Kiku Adatto, *Sound Bite Democracy: Network Evening News Presidential Campaign Coverage, 1968 and 1988* (Cambridge, Mass.: Barone Center on the Press, Politics and Public Policy, 1990), 2; S. Robert Lichter, Stanley Rothman, and Linda S. Lichter, *The Media Elite* (Bethesda, Md.: Adler and Adler, 1986), 115; and Adatto, *Sound Bite Democracy,* 6.

in congressional elections.[16] For another, although some voters are sensitive to the specific issues generated in a campaign, many others are preoccupied with the candidate's image, personality, and style. Candidates are often judged less by what they say than by how they say it, less by their achievements than by their personality. Voters' perceptions of a candidate's character are highly important—perhaps especially in presidential contests. Scandals in government typically have a major impact on the strategies of subsequent campaigns, serving to heighten the significance of the candidate's alleged personal virtues—particularly those of honesty and sincerity—and to diminish the significance of positional issues. "I don't think issues mean a great deal about whether you win or lose," observes a U.S. senator. "I think issues give you a chance to [demonstrate] your honesty and candor." [17] And along the same line, a Democratic media consultant contends: "I don't think inflation is an issue. Who's for it? . . . The real issue is which of the two candidates would best be able to deal with [it]." [18]

According to polls conducted by Voter News Service in 1996, voters supporting Bob Dole or Bill Clinton cited sharply different reasons for their choices. Those who supported Dole stressed the issues of taxes, foreign policy, and the deficit, and Clinton voters focused on Medicare and Social Security, the economy and jobs, and education. Evaluating the qualities of the candidates, voters who preferred Dole emphasized his honesty and trustworthiness, and those drawn to Clinton singled out his concern for "people like me" and his vision for the future (see Figure 4-1). [19]

Dramatic changes have taken place in the way television covers presidential campaigns. A study by Kiku Adatto found that the average "sound bite" (or interval of uninterrupted speech) for presidential candidates in 1968 was 42.3 seconds. Candidate statements of more than a minute's duration were uncommon. By 1988 the average sound bite had slipped to 9.8 seconds[20]—an impossibly brief period for the development of even the simplest argument. In an era of videopolitics, issue development is subordinated to staged events and to conveying messages through the presentation of striking images, such as the 1988 Republican ad on the "revolving door" furlough program of the state of Massachusetts. Adatto's analysis is particularly instructive:

> In the last twenty years, the politicians, assisted by a growing legion of media advisors, have become more sophisticated at producing pictures that will play on television. The networks, meanwhile, have been unable to resist the temptation to show the pictures. Vivid visuals make good television, and besides, the networks might argue, if the candidate goes to Disneyland [Bush] or rides in a tank [Dukakis], does not covering the campaign mean covering those events? Even as they film the media events and show them on the evening news, however, television journalists acknowledge the danger of falling prey to manipulation, of becoming accessories to the candidate's stagecraft. One way of distancing themselves from the scenes they show is to turn to theater criticism, to comment on the scenes as a performance made for television, to lay bare the artifice behind the images. The problem with theater criticism, or image-conscious coverage as a style of political reporting, is that it involves showing the potent visuals the campaigns contrive. Reporters become conduits for the very images they criticize.[21]

FIGURE 4-1   The Salience of Issues and Candidate Qualities for Clinton and Dole
Voters in the 1996 Presidential Election

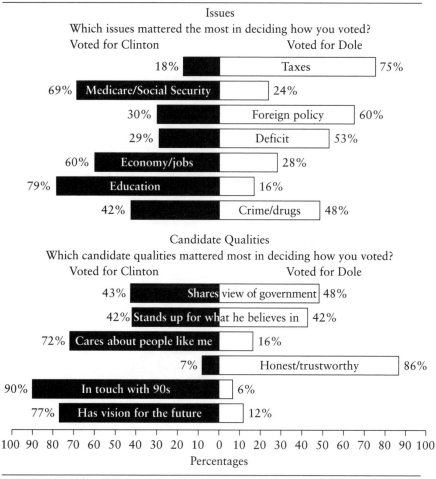

Issues
Which issues mattered the most in deciding how you voted?
Voted for Clinton   Voted for Dole

Candidate Qualities
Which candidate qualities mattered most in deciding how you voted?
Voted for Clinton   Voted for Dole

Percentages

SOURCE: Adapted from Voter Research and Surveys exit polls.

Campaign Money

Of all the requirements for successful campaigns, none may be more important than a strong infusion of money. Campaign costs have risen steadily
over the years. In 1952 expenditures for the nomination and election of public officials at all levels of government came to about $140 million. By 1968

The Public's Role in Financing Political Campaigns

Did you use the checkoff on your federal income tax return to make a political contribution this year?

Yes	12%
No	88

Did you give money to a political party during this election year?

Yes	6%
No	84
Don't know	10

Did you give money to an individual candidate running for public office?

Yes	5%
No	85
Don't know	10

Did you give any money to any other group that supported or opposed candidates?

Yes	5%
No	85
Don't know	10

SOURCE: The checkoff percentages for 1996 were provided by the Federal Election Commission. The other questions are drawn from the 1996 presidential election survey, National Election Study, Center for Political Studies, University of Michigan. The taxpayer checkoff was raised from $1 to $3 in 1993.

this figure had climbed to $300 million. Candidates and parties spent approximately $425 million in 1972, $540 million in 1976, $1.2 billion in 1980, $1.8 billion in 1984, $2.7 billion in 1988, $3.2 billion in 1992, and about $4 billion in 1996.[22]

Most of the cost of American elections is borne by private individuals and groups. In presidential elections, however, public financing is available. Under amendments adopted to the Federal Election Campaign Act (FECA) in 1974, candidates for the presidential nomination can qualify for matching public funds. Once the nominations have been settled, the candidates can elect to receive full federal funding in the general election campaign. Even so, private money dominates the financing of political campaigns at all levels of government.

The spiraling costs of running for office result from a number of factors. The steady increase in the general price level is one reason: inflation affects campaign costs as well as everything else. The growth in population and the enlargement of the electorate also make campaigning more expensive. The utilization of new techniques, such as computerized mailings, has proved costly. The substitution of presidential primaries for caucus-convention systems appears to have increased campaign expenditures. Considerable sums are spent by candidates in hiring political consultants to direct their campaigns. And the availability of private money in large quantities, particularly from the political action committees of interest groups,[23] encourages candidates to add to their campaign treasuries. Congressional incumbents believe that the best way to discourage challengers is to amass a large campaign fund well in advance of the next election. Thus it is common for members of Congress to solicit and accept PAC funds even when they have no serious competition. Some members use surplus funds to make contributions to the campaigns of colleagues.

Broadcast advertising in particular has driven up campaign costs. Television, critics contend, is the real culprit. David Broder has estimated that U.S. Senate candidates allocate 70 to 80 percent of their funds to paid television, turning them, as one senator put it, into "bag men for the TV operators."[24] Frank Greer, a Democratic media consultant, contends that 75 to 80 percent of the budgets in competitive campaigns is earmarked for television. Herbert E. Alexander, who believes that television costs in overall political spending are not as great as critics contend, observes that only about one-half of the candidates for the U.S. House of Representatives ever purchase television time. What everyone concedes is that the unit cost of television advertising in prime time has grown rapidly.[25]

Because of the restrictions placed on contributions to presidential campaigns, perhaps the best way to begin the analysis of money in national political campaigns is to examine the sources from which congressional candidates secure funds. Several features of the money hustle of the 1996 election (covering the two-year election cycle and including primary, runoff, and general elections) stand out. First, the contributions of individuals represent the major source of campaign money for congressional candidates. And because FECA limits individual contributions to $1,000 per election, these gifts arrive in relatively small sums. In 1996 private contributions made up 55 percent of the funds received by House candidates and 59 percent of the funds raised by Senate candidates. Second, PACs have also been a major source of money for congressional candidates. In the 1995–1996 election cycle, PACs contributed $201 million to congressional campaigns ($107 million to Republicans and $94 million to Democrats). PAC contributions amounted to 31 percent of receipts for all House races and 16 percent for all Senate races. Incumbents in particular depend on PAC money. In the House, Democratic incumbents received 49 percent of their receipts from PACs, and Republican incumbents received 39 percent. Although they are less dependent on interest groups, Senate incumbents nevertheless raised 24 percent of their funds from PACs.[26] Third, congressional campaign fund raising is, purely and simply, an incumbent-dominated system. Challengers do not fare nearly as well in the PAC sweepstakes (see Table 4-1).

Overall, 66 percent of all PAC funds in 1996 (both parties, both chambers) were given to incumbents,[27] 14 percent to challengers, and 20 percent to candidates for open seats. The average House incumbent received $295,000 from PACs, whereas the average challenger received $25,000. Fifty House candidates (thirty-four Republicans and sixteen Democrats) each accepted half a million dollars or more from PACs. Five House incumbents, including Speaker Newt Gingrich and minority floor leader Richard Gephardt, reported PAC gifts in excess of $1 million. Among Senate candidates, John Warner (R-Va.) led the way with PAC gifts of about $1.6 million, followed by Larry Pressler (R-S.D.), $1.5 million; Max Baucus (D-Mont.), $1.4 million; and Mitch McConnell (R-Ky.), $1.3 million. Thirty-nine Senate candidates each accepted more than half a million dollars from PACs.[28]

The overall growth of PAC contributions has been substantial (see Table 4-2). PACs contributed about four times as much money to House and Senate candidates in 1996 as they did in 1980. The numbers themselves are instructive: A total of $55 million was contributed in the 1980 election cycle and $201 million in the 1996 election cycle.

Political action committees target their gifts carefully, taking into consideration such key factors as incumbency, party, and legislative position. In 1996 labor PACs contributed $46.5 million to congressional candidates, with 93 percent given to Democrats. Corporate PACs gave $69.7 million to congressional candidates, with 72 percent given to Republicans.[29] Committee chairs and party leaders are major beneficiaries of interest group largesse. Committee membership is also taken into consideration. Members of the tax and commerce committees, for example, invariably receive more PAC money than members of the judiciary or foreign policy committees. The pattern of contributions is illustrated by these observations:

Selecting Congressional Candidates for Campaign Contributions: Factors in PAC Decisions

1. *Incumbency status.* The rule is simple: Reward your friends, based on past support, and recognize that incumbents are going to win anyway. Recently, about $5 out of every $6 contributed by political action committees (PACs) to congressional candidates has gone to incumbents.
2. *Ideological compatibility.* For distinctively liberal or distinctively conservative groups, political philosophy is sine qua non.
3. *Risk avoidance.* Steer clear of losers who will hurt the organization's batting average. Avoid alienating probable winners by not contributing to their opponents. Think twice about offering funds to candidates who are in crowded or difficult primaries.
4. *Networking.* Recognize viable contenders—candidates who are on the "right" lists, having been endorsed by other (key) PACs, or who have been targeted for support by the national parties.
5. *Reward pilgrims.* Give money to those challengers who make the pilgrimage to Washington (PAC City) to ask for it—if their policy stances are appropriate, if they have a credible campaign strategy, if they appear to have a reasonable chance of winning, if they have demonstrated they can raise money at home, and if they are not palpable nerds.

SOURCE: These propositions are fashioned from the observations of various PAC managers interviewed by Congressional Quarterly. See *Congressional Quarterly Weekly Report,* March 22, 1986, 655–659.

The main goal is to support our friends who have been with us most of the time. (An official of the UAW)

The prevailing attitude is that PAC money should be used to facilitate access to incumbents. (The director of governmental and political participation for the Chamber of Commerce of the United States)

We're inclined to support incumbents because we tend to go with those who support our industry. We are not out looking to find challengers. Our aim is not to change the tone of Congress. (A spokesperson for the Lockheed Good Government Program)

TABLE 4-1   The Sources of Funding for 1996 Congressional Candidates

	Individual contri- butions	PAC contri- butions	Candidate contri- butions	Candi- date loans	Other loans
House					
Democratic incumbents	52%	49%	*	*	*
Democratic challengers	56	24	1	18	*
Democratic candidates for open seats	52	21	4	22	*
Republican incumbents	60	39	*	*	*
Republican challengers	66	11	3	19	*
Republican candidates for open seats	59	20	5	16	*
Senate					
Democratic incumbents	80	14	0	6	*
Democratic challengers	55	7	28	10	0
Democratic candidates for open seats	67	20	2	12	0
Republican incumbents	65	33	*	2	0
Republican challengers	63	12	6	17	2
Republican candidates for open seats	51	15	2	32	*

SOURCE: Calculated from data in press release, Federal Election Commission, April 14, 1997.

NOTE: This analysis includes primary, runoff, and general election funds of all candidates running in the November 1996 general election.

* Less than one percent.

TABLE 4-2   The Contributions of Political Action Committees (PACs)
to Congressional Campaigns in Presidential Election Years:
1980 to 1996 (in millions of dollars)

	1980	1984	1988	1992	1996
Total PAC contributions	$55.2	$105.4	$147.9	$180.5	$201.4
All House campaigns	37.9	75.7	102.3	128.6	155.8
All Senate campaigns	17.3	29.7	45.6	51.9	45.6
PAC percentage of funds raised by					
All House candidates	26%	34%	37%	33%	31%
All Senate candidates	17	17	23	20	16

SOURCES: Data from press releases, Federal Election Commission, May 16, 1985; February 24, 1989; April 9, 1989; March 4, 1993; and April 14, 1997.

We're looking especially for members who serve on key committees, and people who help us on the floor. (A spokesperson for the Automobile and Truck Dealers Election Action Committee) [30]

Political action committees spread money around. Parties as well as candidates depend on them. In 1996 Democratic committees collected $19.2 million from PACs, and Republican committees garnered $13.8 million.[31] Putting these numbers in perspective, for every $1 that PACs gave to the party organizations, they gave $6 to congressional candidate organizations. PACs have been a significant factor in the weakening of American parties and in the emergence and consolidation of candidate-centered politics.[32]

In addition to making direct contributions to candidates, PACs are permitted to make unlimited *independent* expenditures for or against candidates, but they are prohibited from consulting candidates concerning these expenditures. In 1996 such independent expenditures by PACs totaled $11 million, with $7 million spent on behalf of candidates and $4 million spent against them.[33] Under the FECA, direct PAC contributions to any candidate in any election are limited to $5,000. Independent spending is a way to circumvent this restriction.

So popular are PACs that many members of Congress have created their own political action committees to raise and disburse campaign funds. The thrust of some member PACs is simply to help to reelect partisan or ideological allies. But for most member PACs the dominant purpose appears to be self-promotion. The most active congressional PACs are those created by members with aspirations for the presidency, the speakership, and a range of other positions, such as floor leader, whip, or committee chair. These leadership PACs distribute campaign funds to members (and occasionally to challengers) as a way of building good will and creating support. For presidential hopefuls in particular, having one's own PAC is invaluable in meeting the expenses of political travel necessary to capture public attention or to campaign for other congressional candidates. Probably the best known member PAC is North Carolina Republican senator Jesse Helms's National Congressional Club. Another well-known PAC is Sen. Edward F. Kennedy's Fund for a Democratic Majority. Of no particular surprise, most of the money contributed to member PACs comes from other PACs.[34]

The availability of PAC money makes life easier for incumbents. They and their aides understand the PAC network, know how to curry favor with PACs (or at least how to avoid their enmity), know how to solicit funds from them, and know how to respond to their initiatives. Members are largely comfortable in this world of organization money even though they resent the amount of time required to raise funds and worry over possible obligations to their benefactors. Nonetheless, access to PAC money is not the most important advantage of incumbents. Their main advantage is simply the opportunities and resources that are attached to holding congressional office: the franking privilege; a public record; name recognition; generous travel allowance; opportunities to make news; opportunities to take credit for "pork" brought into the constituency; and, perhaps most important of all, a large staff (many of whom are assigned to the district or state). "The Hill office," wrote David R. Mayhew, "is a vitally important political unit, part campaign management firm and part political machine." [35] The office is a political unit financed by the U.S. Treasury, and the contributions to incumbents are substantial. Michael Malbin estimates that House incumbents enjoy perquisites of office, supporting constituent contact, worth at least $1 million over the period of a two-year term ($400,000 for constituent-service staff; $400,000 for district office expenses, travel, phones, computers, and the like; and $250,000 for unsolicited mailings to constituents).[36] Hence the heavy support of political action committees is simply icing on the cake—double-rich.

Raising campaign money is a relentless pursuit for members of Congress and their aides. House and Senate rules permit each office to have at least one staff member assigned to receive campaign contributions. Additionally, many members hire professional fund raisers who advise them on the techniques for soliciting money (to ask for the "right" amount—not too much, not too little) and who travel around the country with them to court contributors. Increasingly, the money hunt has prompted members to seek funds from sources outside their home states. Fund-raising events at Washington watering holes occur night after night (cost of admission: usually $500 on the House side, $1,000 or more on the Senate side), attracting lobbyists and assorted contributors who know that gifts are acknowledged with the promise of access. Members solicit and accept out-of-state political money, first, because it is readily available and, second, because it is easier than asking their own constituents and perhaps offending them.[37]

The third most important source of campaign funds for congressional candidates is the political party. The party's role is limited, however, by the FECA, both in terms of how much money it is permitted to contribute directly to candidates and how much it can spend on their behalf. In making *direct* contributions to House candidates, national party committees—the national committee and the party's congressional campaign committee—are each limited to $5,000 per candidate per campaign. Candidates for the Senate can receive up to $17,500 in combined direct contributions from the national committee and the senatorial campaign committee in a calendar year. State and local committees also make limited contributions to congressional campaigns. Direct contributions by national party committees do not amount to much; Democratic national committees contributed $2.2 million to the party's congressional candidates in 1996, Republicans, $3.7 million.

Much more important are national party expenditures made on behalf of congressional candidates—so-called *coordinated* expenditures. Permitted only in the general election, coordinated expenditures are made by party committees alone, although the committees may consult with the candidates' organizations to decide how the money is to be spent. Based on state voting-age population, the amounts permitted are sizable for Senate campaigns in populous states. In California, for example, each party in 1996 could spend $1.4 million on behalf of each of its senatorial candidates; in New York, $840,000; in Texas, $823,000; in Pennsylvania, $566,000; and in some dozen relatively small states, $62,000. For House candidates in 1996, coordinated expenditures were limited to $31,000 (except in states with only one member, where the limit was $62,000).[38]

In addition, fortified by a Supreme Court ruling,[39] a state party committee can transfer its spending authority to the national committee, which effectively doubles the expenditures the national party can make on behalf of its candidates. These agency agreements have been a boon to the spending plans of the Republican party in particular.

Party support for congressional candidates is important.[40] In 1996 coordinated expenditures totaled more than $31 million for the Republican party and $23 million for the Democratic party.[41] Gary C. Jacobson estimates that national party committees can supply one fourth of the money necessary for a serious House campaign and, in some states, up to half of the funds necessary for a full-scale Senate campaign.[42] Nevertheless, the parties do not stack up particularly well in comparison with PACs. If the behavior of officeholders is influenced by campaign money, as Herbert E. Alexander

has observed, the parties do not have an especially strong claim for preference, given the contributions to legislators by individuals and PACs.[43]

Spending campaign money intelligently is problematic at the least. Candidates spend as heavily as they do because neither they nor their advisers
know which expenditures are likely to produce the greatest return in votes.
Lacking systematic information, they jump at every opportunity to contact
and persuade voters—and every opportunity costs money.

Political money does not lend itself to easy analysis. Tracing how it is
raised and how it is spent is far from simple. In a federal and fragmented system campaign money is collected and spent by many competing political ac-
tors and institutions. If there is fashion at all, it is helter-skelter. In addition,
the effects of money on elections, political behavior, and public policy are
not fully understood. One point about which there is substantial agreement,
however, is that campaign spending has grown dramatically in recent years.

Congressional campaigns provide a good example. They are expensive.
In 1978 House and Senate candidates collectively spent about $195 million.
In 1984 they spent about $374 million, and in 1988, about $459 million. In
1992 congressional campaign spending jumped by 52 percent, to $678 mil-
lion.[44] And in 1996 it grew to $765 million.[45]

Expenditures by winning congressional candidates have grown at a
rapid rate. Data on House and Senate spending by winning candidates from
1982 to 1996 are presented in Figure 4-2. Over this fourteen-year period,
expenditures by successful House candidates nearly tripled, and expenditures by winning Senate candidates doubled.

Spending is particularly heavy in the most competitive races, including those in which open seats are at stake. In the House elections of 1996,
for example, winning Republican challengers had median expenditures of
$1.2 million in defeating Democratic incumbents, whose median expendi-
tures were $700,000. The median expenditures for successful Democratic
challengers was $933,000, as contrasted with $1.1 million for losing Republican incumbents (see Table 4-3).

Several broad conclusions can be drawn concerning spending in House
campaigns. First, the most expensive races involve incumbents who think or
know they are in trouble with the voters. Campaigns costing in excess of
$1 million are common for anxious House incumbents. Of the fifty most ex-
pensive House campaigns in 1996, thirty-eight were run by incumbents;
each spent in excess of $1.2 million. Even incumbents who expect to win and
do win easily often have campaign expenditures of a half-million or more.
Second, with not many exceptions, incumbents outspend their challengers,
many of whom are severely underfinanced; numerous House challengers, in
fact, spend less than $50,000 on their campaigns. Third, challengers who
win or make a good showing generally are well financed. Fourth, spending

FIGURE 4-2   Total Spending by Winning Congressional Candidates:
1982 to 1996

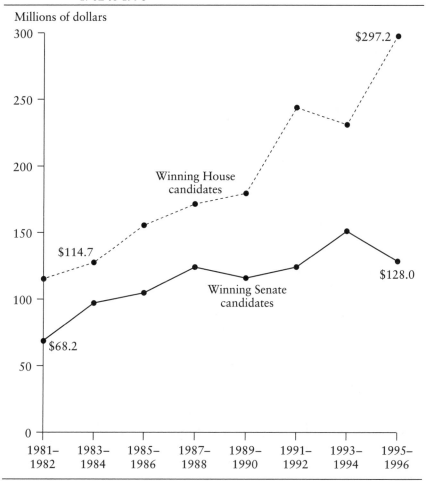

SOURCE: Press release, Federal Election Commission, April 14, 1997.

NOTE: Spending is for all campaigns, including primaries, runoffs, and general elections. An election cycle is for two years, the election year and the year preceding.

in campaigns for open seats is usually heavy, particularly in competitive districts. Fifth, the costs of some House campaigns border on the scandalous. Speaker Newt Gingrich spent $5.5 million in 1996 to defeat a Democratic challenger who spent $3.3 million. Minority leader Richard Gephardt spent $3.1 million to defeat a Republican challenger (59 percent to 39 percent) who spent only $62,000.

TABLE 4-3   Spending to Defeat Incumbents and to Win Open Seats and
Close Races, U.S. House Elections: 1996

No. of Districts		Median Expenditures		Median Expenditures
Winning challengers and losing incumbents				
3	Winning Republican challengers	$1,181,546	Losing Democratic incumbents	$708,788
17	Winning Democratic challengers	$933,425	Losing Republican incumbents	$1,144,540
Open seats				
26	Winning Republicans	$743,577	Losing Democrats	$526,735
22	Winning Democrats	$791,590	Losing Republicans	$453,510
Close races[a]				
37	Winning Republican incumbents	$927,715	Losing Democratic challengers	$544,875
19	Winning Democratic incumbents	$855,622	Losing Republican challengers	$506,793

SOURCE: Adapted from data in press release, Federal Election Commission, April 14, 1997.

[a] Winners received less than 55 percent of the vote.

In several Senate races in 1996, spending was out of the ordinary, though well short of record-setting. Mark Warren spent $11.6 million in a failed attempt to defeat incumbent John Warner (R-Va.), who spent $5.6 million. Sen. John Kerry (D-Mass.) spent $11 million in defeating Gov. William Weld, who spent $8 million. Altogether, twenty-one Senate candidates spent in excess of $4 million each on their campaigns.[46] The all-time record for expensive Senate campaigns is held by Michael Huffington, who spent nearly $30 million in 1994 in an unsuccessful attempt to defeat Dianne Feinstein (D-Calif.), who spent $14 million. Plainly, congressional campaign politics is not a poor person's game, at least not for candidates who want to be taken seriously.

Of all the issues in campaign finance, none provokes more controversy than the role of PACs, particularly in congressional campaigns. The national press often focuses on PAC gifts and on the members who rely on them heavily. Common Cause has prepared dozens of studies over the years that, in its view, point out the dangers of the PAC movement. More and more frequently, Congress itself becomes exercised over the "PAC problem"—the growing reliance of members on interest group money and the suspicion that these gifts undermine the independence of members. Are members' votes influenced by the PAC gifts they receive? On certain narrow economic issues, such as dairy price supports and cargo preference, a relationship between contributions and voting behavior has been found.[47] Nonetheless, influence is hard to establish: Does money follow votes or do votes follow money? Not surprisingly, members evaluate PAC money in sharply different ways, as the following observations show.

> It is fundamentally corrupting. At best, people say they are sympathetic to the people they are getting money from before they get it; at worst, they are selling votes. But you cannot prove cause and effect. I take the money from labor, and I have to think twice in voting against their interests. I shouldn't have to do that. (Former representative Richard L. Ottinger, D-N.Y.)

> There's a danger that we're putting ourselves on the auction block every election. It's now tough to hear the voices of the citizens in your district. Sometimes the only things you hear are the loud voices in the three-piece suits carrying a PAC check. (Former representative Leon E. Panetta, D-Calif.)

> PAC money is destroying the electoral process. (Former senator Barry Goldwater, R-Ariz.)

> I don't worry about being bought, because I'm not for sale. The truth is I am proud of the PACs and the people who support me. (Sen. Phil Gramm, R-Texas)

> If you're not able to fund your campaign and keep your responsibility to the people who send you here, you don't belong in office. (Rep. John D. Dingell, D-Mich.)

> PACs facilitate the political participation of hundreds of thousands of individuals who might not otherwise become involved in the election of an individual. (Sen. John W. Warner, R-Va.)[48]

Bills to curtail PAC influence in campaigns have been introduced frequently in Congress over the last decade. Among other things, these proposals have sought to place a cap on the total amount of PAC funds that congressional candidates can accept; cut the size of their contributions (usually from $5,000 to $3,000); limit their independent spending for or against candidates; and close a loophole in the law that permits them to receive individual contributions, bundle them together, and pass them along to candidates in the PAC's name but without falling under the limitations on spending. And a number of bills have been introduced under which PACs

The Money Chase
in the 1996 Congressional Elections:
PACs, Incumbents, and Challengers

Allocation of PAC Funds

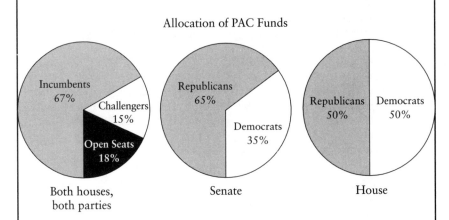

Of the $201 million given by PACs to congressional candidates in the 1995–1996 election cycle, 67 percent went to incumbents. (If open-seat candidates are excluded from the analysis, PACs gave 83 percent of their funds to incumbents and 17 percent to challengers.) For the first time in many years, PACs gave more money to Republicans ($107 million) than to Democrats ($94 million). Doubtless, the Republicans' control of both houses in the 104th Congress (1995–1996) contributed to their success in the PAC sweepstakes. Overall, PAC contributions to congressional candidates were up 11 percent over 1994.

SOURCE: Press release, Federal Election Commission, April 14, 1997.

would be banned altogether from making contributions to congressional campaigns.

Access to PAC funds represents a major advantage for incumbents over their challengers, and whether members will be willing to give it up remains to be seen. Yet if PAC contributions continue unabated, the intensity of this special interest issue will also grow. Whatever the reality of PAC influence on decision makers, PAC power is an issue made in heaven for good-government groups, reformers, certain insiders, and the media. At some point, probably sooner than later, members may feel compelled to impose restrictions on PAC contributions. Severe restrictions would likely be tested in the courts as a violation of the First Amendment's protection of free speech.

The Regulation of Campaign Finance

The public has long been restive over the role of money in American politics. Dissatisfaction focuses on three main complaints. The first is simply that campaign costs have risen to such an extent that candidates with limited resources are seriously disadvantaged in the electoral process. The doubt persists that some talented people never seek public office because they lack financial support or are unwilling to solicit funds from others because of the risk of incurring political indebtedness and of compromising their independence. Moreover, the high cost of elections may mean that the public hears only one side of the campaign, that of the candidate with access to large sums of money.

The second complaint is that the individuals, families, and groups that contribute lavishly to parties and candidates are suspected of buying influence and gaining preferments of some kind in return for the money they channel into campaigns. Whether this is true may not be as important as the fact that the public believes it to be true. In some measure, public suspicion about campaign financing contributes to public suspicion of government.

The third, as a result of the Watergate exposé, a heightened awareness exists of the potential for corruption and abuse when huge sums of money are collected and spent for political purposes.

To deal with a variety of maladies associated with the financing of federal political campaigns, Congress passed the Federal Election Campaign Act of 1971 (FECA), which has been discussed previously. This act, the first serious attempt since 1925 to reform campaign financing, is of unusual importance. Adopted prior to the Watergate incident, the act anticipated public financing of federal election campaigns by providing that taxpayers could earmark $1 on their personal income tax returns for use in the 1976 presidential election. Of at least equal importance, the act provided for rigorous disclosure requirements concerning campaign contributions, expenditures, and debts. Finally, a provision to stimulate private contributions to political campaigns was placed in the act. Under a tax-incentive system, taxpayers were permitted to deduct small campaign contributions from their tax obligations. In retrospect, the extraordinary dimensions of the 1972 presidential election scandal would not have been uncovered without the disclosure requirements for political contributions and expenditures contained in the law.

Crisis is often a spur to legislative action. Largely in response to Watergate, Congress in 1974 passed comprehensive amendments to the Federal Election Campaign Act. Designed to curtail the influence and abuse of money in campaign politics, these amendments placed tight restrictions on contributions, expenditures, disclosure, and reporting. Most important, the 1974 legislation provided for at least partial public financing of presidential primaries, elections, and nominating conventions. The constitutionality of the provisions relating to the presidential electoral process was promptly tested in the courts. In *Buckley v. Valeo,* decided in 1976, the Supreme Court held that the act's limitations on individual expenditures (either those of the candidate[49] or those of individuals spending independently on behalf of a candidate) were unconstitutional, because they interfered with the right of free speech under the First Amendment. Political money, in a sense, is political speech. The Court upheld the limitations on contributions to campaigns, the disclosure requirements, and the public-funding provisions for presidential primaries and elections. The main features of the nation's campaign finance law are included in Table 4-4.

The leading characteristic of the campaign finance law is its focus on the presidency. No provision is made for the public financing of campaigns for Congress. For those who believe that what is sauce for the goose is sauce for the gander, the observations of Senator Kennedy (D-Mass.) are especially appropriate:

> Abuses of campaign spending and private campaign financing do not stop at the other end of Pennsylvania Avenue. They dominate congressional elections as well. If the abuses are the same for the presidency and Congress, the reforms should also be the same. If public financing is good enough for presidential elections, it should also be good enough for Senate and House elections.[50]

Many members of Congress have become weary of the struggle to raise campaign funds:

> To raise $4 million means that for every single week for six years without exception a member of the Senate would have to figure out how to raise $15,000 in campaign contributions. (Former senator David L. Boren, D-Okla.)[51]

> The present system does not even allow the incumbents with new ideas to get them into place. We are too busy out engaging in the money chase. We cannot be here in the committees, we cannot be here on the floor doing our

TABLE 4-4   Major Provisions for the Regulation of Campaign Financing
in Federal Elections

Contribution Limits

- No individual may contribute more than $1,000 to any candidate or candidate committee per election. (Primary, runoff, and general elections are considered to be separate elections.)
- Individual contributions to a national party committee are limited to $20,000 per calendar year and to any other political committee to $5,000 per calendar year. (The total contributions by an individual to all federal candidates in one year cannot exceed $25,000.)
- A multicandidate committee (one with more than fifty contributors that makes contributions to five or more federal candidates) may contribute no more than $5,000 to any candidate or candidate committee per election, no more than $15,000 to the national committee of a political party, and no more than $5,000 to any other political committee per calendar year.
- The national committee and the congressional campaign committee may each contribute up to $5,000 to each House candidate, per election; the national committee, together with the senatorial campaign committee, may contribute up to a combined total of $17,500 to each Senate candidate for the entire campaign period (including a primary election).
- Political action committees formed by businesses, trade associations, or unions are limited to contributions of no more than $5,000 to any candidate in any election. No limits apply to their aggregate contributions.
- Banks, corporations, and labor unions are prohibited from making contributions from their treasuries to federal election campaigns. Government contractors and foreign nationals are similarly restricted. Contributions may not be supplied by one person but made in the name of another person. Contributions in cash are limited to $100.

Expenditure Limits

- Candidates are limited to an expenditure of $10 million each plus COLA (cost-of-living adjustment) in all presidential primaries. (In 1996 each candidate could spend up to $37 million in all presidential primaries.)
- Major party presidential candidates may spend no more than $20 million plus COLA in the general election (a total of $61.8 million each in 1996).
- Presidential and vice-presidential candidates who accept public funding may spend no more than $50,000 of personal funds in their campaigns.
- Each national party may spend up to two cents per voter on behalf of its presidential candidate.
- In addition to making contributions to candidates, the national committee, together with congressional and senatorial campaign committees, may make expenditures on behalf of House and Senate candidates. For each House member—in states with more than one district—the sum is $10,000 plus COLA. For each

(continued)

TABLE 4-4 *(continued)*

Expenditure Limits *(continued)*

> Senate candidate the sum is $20,000 plus COLA or two cents for each person in the state's voting-age population, whichever is greater. (Under the second formula, party committees could spend $1.4 million on behalf of a California Senate candidate in 1996.) State party committees may make expenditures on behalf of House and Senate candidates up to the same limits.

- As a result of the *Buckley v. Valeo* decision, there are no limits on how much House and Senate candidates may collect and spend in their campaigns (or on how much they may spend of their own or their family's money).
- Also in the wake of *Buckley v. Valeo,* there are no limits on the amount that individuals and groups may spend on behalf of any presidential or congressional candidate so long as the expenditures are independent—that is, not arranged or controlled by the candidate.
- As a result of the Supreme Court's 1996 decision in *Colorado Republican Federal Campaign Committee v. FEC,* political parties can now make unlimited *independent* expenditures on behalf of their candidates for federal office as long as these expenditures are not coordinated with the candidates or their campaigns. "Independent" expenditures, in other words, are entitled to First Amendment protection and are not to be treated as indirect campaign contributions subject to regulations.

Public Financing

- Major party candidates for the presidency qualify for full funding ($20 million plus COLA) prior to the campaign, the money to be drawn from the federal income tax dollar checkoff. In 1996 the Democratic and Republican nominees each received $61.8 million in campaign funds. Candidates may decline to participate in the public funding program and finance their campaigns through private contributions. Candidates who accept public funding may not accept private contributions.
- Minor party and independent candidates qualify for lesser sums, provided their candidates received at least 5 percent of the vote in the previous presidential election. New parties or parties that received less than 5 percent of the vote four years earlier qualify for public financing after the election, provided they drew 5 percent of the vote.
- Matching public funds up to $5 million (plus COLA) are available for presidential primary candidates, provided that they first raise $100,000 in private funds ($5,000 in contributions of no more than $250 in each of twenty states). Once that threshold is reached, the candidate receives matching funds up to $250 per contribution. No candidate is eligible for more than 25 percent of the total available funds. The maximum amount of matching funds available to any candidate in 1996 was $15.4 million.

- Presidential candidates who receive less than 10 percent of the vote in two consecutive presidential primaries become ineligible for additional campaign subsidies.
- Optional public funding of presidential nominating conventions is available for the major parties, with lesser amounts for minor parties.

Disclosure and Reporting

- Each federal candidate is required to establish a single, overarching campaign committee to report on all contributions and expenditures on behalf of the candidate.
- Frequent reports on contributions and expenditures are to be filed with the Federal Election Commission.

Enforcement

- Administration of the law is the responsibility of a six-member, bipartisan Federal Election Commission. The Commission is empowered to make rules and regulations, to receive campaign reports, to render advisory opinions, to conduct audits and investigations, to subpoena witnesses and information, and to seek civil injunctions through court action.

SOURCE: Federal Election Commission.

work. . . . We are kept so busy out there knocking on doors all over the country, seeking money, asking for money, begging for money, getting on our hands and knees for money, we do not have time to give thought to new ideas and to be putting them into creative legislation. (Sen. Robert C. Byrd, D-W.Va.)[52]

I have been introduced into 21st century campaigning and I don't like it. All of a sudden you have to hire a fundraiser, a media consultant, a press attaché, a mailing specialist. (Rep. Sidney R. Yates, D-Ill.)[53]

Today, for a modestly spirited [House] race, you have to raise a million dollars. That's ten thousand a week, two thousand dollars a day. I would think, "If I have not made arrangements to make two thousand dollars today, I'm behind." And I will have to raise four thousand dollars tomorrow. (Former representative Jim Chapman, D-Texas)[54]

Numerous attempts to overhaul the nation's election finance law have been made since the late 1970s, but thus far unsuccessfully. Reform proposals invariably have become entangled in partisan politics. On the whole, Democratic members have favored public financing of congressional campaigns and relatively strict limits on spending; Democrats are particularly united on the need to impose spending limits. Republicans believe that their chances are better under the present system of private financing.[55] They often deride public financing as "food stamps for politicians," and show little enthusiasm for spending limits.

The pressure to raise large sums of campaign money drives parties and candidates to cut corners and to engage in questionable (if not illegal) practices. Following the 1996 election, for example, it was discovered that the White House had been rewarding and beguiling Democratic party contributors by letting them spend a night in the Lincoln Bedroom, that numerous White House coffees had been held for prospective big donors (with confidential projections as to the size of their contributions), and that the vice president had placed various fund-raising telephone calls from the White House (in possible violation of a law that prohibits soliciting funds on federal property). Evidence of illegal foreign donations to the Democratic party from Indonesia and China also surfaced. Topping it off, the Democratic National Committee had to return a number of suspicious or illegal donations because their true source could not be established. Special access, money-hustling, favor-seeking, and buying influence were the central themes in story after story involving the White House's unusual efforts to raise millions of dollars in soft money to compete with the Republican party's highly successful money chase. Allegations that the Republican party may have benefited from foreign money were also made. For the most part, congressional campaign practices escaped media scrutiny except for the extended controversy over Speaker Newt Gingrich's use of tax-exempt foundation money to finance political programs.

Discontent over the parties' fund-raising practices derives not only from concern over sleazy behavior but from the perception that campaign finance laws are riddled with loopholes. Consider the matter of contribution limits. One of the major purposes of the FECA was to place sharp limits on the amount of money that could be given to federal campaigns by individuals and organizations (see Table 4-4). These restrictions are easily evaded, however. Wealthy individuals, corporations, and unions have found a way around them by making donations of "soft money" (money that cannot be used in connection with federal elections) to the political parties, not to the candidates. This opportunity emerged from a 1979 amendment under which parties were permitted to accept unlimited contributions for party-building activities, organizational overhead expenses, generic campaign activity, get-out-the-vote drives, and voter registration campaigns. Much easier to raise than hard money that is regulated by federal law and limited as to amount, soft money has become a dominant factor in campaigns. In the 1995–1996 election cycle, the Democrats collected $124 million in soft money, the Republicans $138 million—overall, about three times as much as garnered in the previous presidential election.

Growth in Soft Money
(In millions of dollars)

In 1979, Congress amended campaign finance law to encourage contributions to state and local political parties. New regulations by the Federal Election Commission in 1991 and a Supreme Court decision in 1996 have led to rapid growth in the amount of money received by national parties.

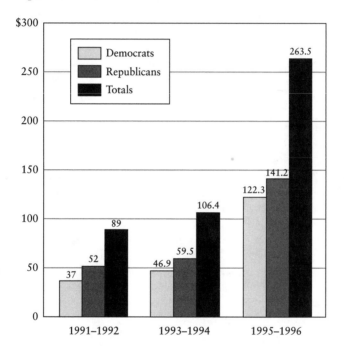

SOURCE: *Congressional Quarterly Weekly Report,* April 5, 1997, 773, based on data provided by the Center for Responsive Politics.

Soft money, relatively speaking, is easy money. As Ellen Miller of the Center for Responsive Politics observed, "The parties find it a lot easier to raise $100,000 in soft money with one call to a corporation than to try to collect $1,000 donations from individuals." [56]

Soft money found its way in huge quantities into the 1996 presidential race (presumably publicly financed) through issue advocacy advertisements that supposedly were independent of the candidates' campaigns. Issue ads showing images of the candidates are legal, the Supreme Court has ruled, as long as they stop short of using words such as "elect," "vote for," or "vote against"—even though an election message is clearly being conveyed. Issue ads accomplish virtually everything that a candidate's campaign ads can accomplish (except direct endorsement), and they are not subject to the limits on party spending for candidates. The courts regard them as a form of speech protected by the Constitution. What is more, the Supreme Court's 1996 ruling that political parties can spend unlimited sums on behalf of their candidates if their efforts are independent (that is, not coordinated with those of their candidates)[57] led to an explosion of spending on issue advocacy ads. The fine line between issue-oriented ads and electioneering ads, directly supporting or opposing federal candidates, was all but obliterated in the 1996 election. Solicitation of massive amounts of soft money, the new reliance on issue ads as a means of circumventing federal contribution limits, and party "independent" spending are tightly joined. They reflect the fact that the campaign finance law is out of date, porous, and, truthfully, in shambles.

Dozens of bills to reform campaign finance laws have been introduced in recent years, the best known of which is the McCain–Feingold bill [named for its sponsors, Sen. John McCain (R-Ariz.) and Russell D. Feingold (D-Wis.)]. Illustrative of current mainstream thinking about reform, McCain–Feingold (and complementary House versions) would ban soft money altogether, constrict PAC contributions, and provide incentives for candidates to adhere to voluntary spending limits. Senate spending limits would be based on each state's voting-age population, ranging from $1.5 million in a smaller state like Wyoming to $8.5 million in a large state like California. House spending limits would be set at $600,000. Candidates who voluntarily comply with these limits would be entitled to thirty minutes of free, prime broadcast time, discounts on additional broadcast time, and reduced postal rates. Moreover, if a candidate's opponent exceeded the spending limit, the complying candidate could accept larger individual contributions and exceed the limits as well.

Under the McCain–Feingold legislation, PAC contributions would be cut from $5,000 to $1,000 in primary and general elections, with the additional proviso that House candidates could not accept more than 20 percent of the spending limit from PACs and Senate candidates no more than 25 percent from this source. Another feature would provide that 60 percent of all contributions must come from home-state residents. Bundling of contributions would be outlawed. (A party committee can evade spending limits by getting donors to write checks directly to candidates; the party then bundles them together and delivers them. These contributions are not recorded as party receipts or expenditures. PACs do the same thing.) In addition, candidates in compliance with the spending limits would be permitted to exceed them if necessary to counter attack ads financed through independent expenditures.

Whatever the motives that underlie members' attitudes toward campaign finance reform, it is plain that this issue bears peculiarly on congressional careers. The temptation is strong for members to evaluate all proposals for reform in personal and political terms, favoring or opposing legislation in light of its probable impact on their electoral security and the welfare of their party. At the same time, members feel pressure to do something in view of the runaway costs of recent years and the heavy involvement of PACs in campaign spending.

Despite the partisan conflict that has smothered campaign finance legislation in recent years, as well as heightened House-Senate conflict over the issue, Congress is coming closer and closer to passing some type of reform bill. Campaign finance scandals, such as those of 1996, highlight the need for tighter regulations. Members feel the heat. What is more, members of both parties now profess the need to reduce out-of-state funding, to reign in soft-money contributions and spending, to diminish candidates' excessive reliance on PAC money, and to make the playing field at least somewhat more level for challengers. And there is broad support on both sides of the aisle for legislation that would cut the costs of television time for candidates and require broadcasters to make available for campaign messages the best time slots in their advertising schedules. Whatever changes ultimately are made, one should expect the legislation to contain provisions that benefit the members who adopted it.

At this point it is useful to take stock of what has happened since the adoption of the FECA and its subsequent amendments. Experience with the campaign finance law for two decades provides support for a number of observations concerning its impact on citizens, parties, candidates, and the political system: [58]

The campaign finance law and its amendments have encouraged citizen contributions to the parties and candidates.
As a result of the adoption of income tax checkoff provisions at federal and state levels, citizens' financial participation in campaigns has grown. In 1980, 29 percent of all taxpayers took advantage of the federal checkoff option, though by 1996 this participation had dropped to only 12 percent. The tax checkoff is a relatively low-cost activity, because it does not increase the individual's tax liability; its cumulative impact is nevertheless enormous in financing presidential preconvention and general election campaigns. [59] Al-

together, about $211 million in federal funds was distributed to presidential candidates in these election phases in 1996 (with another $25 million allocated for funding the parties' national conventions).[60] Citizens also make direct contributions. In 1992 about 14 percent of the public contributed money to a party, individual candidate, or political action committee.[61] Plainly, political parties no longer dominate the financing of campaigns.

The campaign finance law has aided the parties in some respects and weakened them in others.
Among the provisions of the Federal Election Campaign Act that benefit the parties are these: (1) individual contributors can give more money to the parties ($20,000) than they can to candidates ($1,000); (2) each national party can spend money on behalf of its presidential and congressional candidates (coordinated expenditures); (3) both national and state party committees can make direct contributions to House and Senate candidates; (4) public funds are available to defray the costs of presidential nominating conventions; and (5) under a 1979 amendment, state and local parties can spend unlimited sums on campaign materials, voter registration, and get-out-the-vote drives in presidential elections—so-called party-building activities.

Other features of the law, however, do not serve the party interest. The parties' impact on presidential elections has been diminished. The public funds made available in the nominating and election phases go directly to the candidates instead of to the parties; each major party candidate received $61.8 million in 1996. In this major feature, the law is plainly candidate-centered. Moreover, the parties are limited in the amounts they can contribute to their candidates and in the amounts they can spend on behalf of them. Many observers believe that the limits are too stringent, and some believe they should be abolished altogether. PACs and individuals can spend unlimited amounts on federal campaigns (opposing as well as supporting candidates) as long as these expenditures are made independently—that is, made without consulting the candidate or the candidate's organization. And, as noted, direct contributions by PACs to candidates for Congress have increased substantially in recent years. On the whole, the campaign finance law has increased the influence of nonparty groups in American politics. No one apparently planned for that to happen.

Spending in congressional and senatorial primaries and elections has increased dramatically.
The 1976 ruling of the Supreme Court in *Buckley v. Valeo* that restrictions on the personal and total expenditures of candidates for Congress were unconstitutional led to an explosion of spending. Winning candidates for the Senate in 1976 spent a total of $20 million; in 1996 they spent $128 million,

more than six times as much. Winning candidates for the House in 1976 spent a total of $38 million; in 1996 they spent $297 million, more than seven times as much. In 1996 forty Senate candidates spent more than $2.5 million on their campaigns; twenty-one spent more than $4 million. Fifty House candidates spent more than $1.3 million each.[62] As a result of the *Buckley* decision, it is not unusual today for a candidate to spend half a million dollars or more of personal funds in a campaign. A few spend much more than that. The sky is the limit. Whatever can be raised can be spent. The overall spending record belongs to California, where the two Senate candidates in 1994 spent a total of $44 million.

Interest group involvement in campaign funding is greater than in the past. The impact of interest groups is especially pronounced at the congressional level. In 1974 PACs made campaign contributions of about $12.5 million to congressional candidates. In 1996 their contributions totaled $201 million— more than sixteen times as much. Currently there are more than 4,000 PACs, about seven times as many as in 1974.

Although FECA places certain restrictions on the parties in raising and spending funds, the parties' role in campaigns is nevertheless growing in importance.
According to Federal Election Commission data, the three Republican national committees (national, senatorial, and congressional) spent $332 million in 1996, and the corresponding Democratic committees spent $163 million.[63] Although the Republican party is still more effective in overall fund raising, the gap between the parties has narrowed—to about two-to-one from what was five-to-one just a few years ago. Table 4-5 shows how much money the national parties allocated for congressional races in 1988, 1992, and 1996. The parties secure the great bulk of their contributions from individuals—77 percent for the Democrats and 87 percent for Republicans in 1996. Democratic committees received 9 percent of their funds from PACs, Republicans 3 percent.[64]

The direct influence of wealthy contributors on electoral politics has declined, at least at the national level.
The contributions of an individual to federal candidates are limited to $1,000 for each election and to a total of $25,000 in a calendar year. In reality, this is not a stringent limitation. Wealthy individuals can spend an unlimited amount of money to help elect a candidate if the money is spent *independently* of the candidate's campaign. Moreover, there are no limits on how much they can donate to the national parties in soft money, ostensibly to be used for get-out-the-vote drives and other party-building activities.

Public Subsidies in Presidential Elections: 1984–1996

Presidential elections have been publicly financed since 1976 under the terms of the Federal Election Campaign Act. Presidential candidates who agree to observe spending limits in primary and general elections are eligible for public funds. Candidates may also choose to finance their campaigns with private funds, as did Ross Perot in 1992 (but not in 1996). The data presented in the table below show the funds made available and the number of recipients in each election since 1984. Third-party and long-shot candidates find it relatively easy to qualify for matching funds in the primary/caucus season (simply by raising $5,000 in sums of $250 or less in each of twenty states). Unless more voters decide to support public financing by checking off $3 for the fund on their income tax returns, the fund may face a shortfall in the future.

	1984		1988		1992		1996	
	Amount	Recipients	Amount	Recipients	Amount	Recipients	Amount	Recipients
Prenomination period	$36.1	9D/1R/1C	$67.2	8D/6R/1NA	$41.8	7D/2R/1NA/1NL	$58.2	2D/8R/1NL
National conventions	16.2	1D/1R	18.4	1D/1R	22.0	1D/1R	25.8	1D/1R
General election	80.8	1D/1R	92.2	1D/1R	110.4	1D/1R	152.7	1D/1R 1RE
Total	$133.1		$177.8		$174.2		$236.7	

SOURCES: U.S. Congress, Library of Congress, Congressional Research Service, *Campaign Financing in Federal Elections: A Guide to the Law and Its Operation* (Washington, D.C.: Government Printing Office, 1989), 24; *Congressional Quarterly Weekly Report,* September 9, 1989, 2326–2329; and *Federal Election Commission Record,* February 1993, 2. Data for 1996 provided by Sharon Snyder of Federal Election Commission.

NOTE: D = Democrat, R = Republican, RE = Reform, NU = National Unity, C = Citizens, NA = New Alliance, NL = Natural Law. Dollar figures are in millions.

TABLE 4-5 Party Money Spent on Congressional Candidates
(in Millions of Dollars)

	1988	1992	1996
Democratic National Committee	$8.2	$11.4	$6.7
Republican National Committee	8.3	12.1	23.3
Democratic Senatorial Campaign Committee	6.6	12.1	10.3
National Republican Senatorial Committee	11.0	17.4	10.7
Democratic Congressional Campaign Committee	3.1	5.1	6.7
National Republican Congressional Committee	5.7	5.9	8.6

SOURCES: Calculated from data in press releases, Federal Election Commission, March 11, 1993, and March 19, 1997.

NOTE: The spending reflects contributions to congressional candidates, coordinated expenditures made on their behalf, and, in the case of the senatorial committees in 1996, independent expenditures. Coordinated expenditures are much more important than direct contributions in financing congressional campaigns.

Gifts by individuals of $100,000 or more to the Democratic and Republican National Committees are not at all uncommon. In addition, well-heeled individuals can contribute $5,000 to state parties (all fifty if they like), knowing that this money will help the overall ticket. Thus it is a myth that private money is excluded from the presidential campaign and that strict limitations govern contributions to federal campaigns. Only direct contributions to federal candidates are effectively limited.

The importance of raising large amounts of money in small sums has become apparent to all candidates, and particularly to those seeking the presidential nomination.
As provided by FECA, matching federal funds become available for presidential primary and caucus candidates who first raise $100,000 in small sums—by obtaining $5,000 in contributions of $250 or less in each of twenty states. Once a candidate has reached the $100,000 threshold, the government matches the first $250 of any gift. In the preconvention campaign of 1996, Democratic, Republican, and minor-party candidates received about $58 million in federal matching funds. One result of the new emphasis on small gifts is that firms that engage in direct-mail solicitations, working with computerized mailing lists, have assumed even greater importance in the fund-raising efforts of candidates. In fund raising, as in certain

other respects, the party organizations now face major competition from other quarters.

Opportunities for persons to engage in corrupt practices in the use of money in federal elections have been constricted to some extent.
The risks of detection are greater as a result of timely and comprehensive disclosure provisions, requirements for centralized accounting of contributions and expenditures, curbs on cash contributions, and the existence of a full-time agency—the Federal Election Commission—to administer the law and to investigate alleged infractions of it. Every major presidential candidate organization has numerous accountants and lawyers to analyze and monitor the candidate's financial activities. Bookkeeping has thus become a major feature and expense of campaigns for federal office, congressional as well as presidential. The knowledge that legal action by the Federal Election Commission will not be taken until well after the election doubtlessly tempts some candidates to play fast and loose with the rules on contributions and expenditures anyhow.

Although paying lip service to the finance law, both parties have nevertheless searched imaginatively for ways around its restrictions—and they have been successful.
As noted earlier, the finance law limits the amount of money that national party committees can give directly to candidates and the amount that party committees can spend on behalf of candidates—so-called coordinated expenditures. Actually, these restrictions are not taken seriously. Under regulations of the Federal Election Commission, a party is permitted to collect checks from donors that are earmarked for specific candidates, bundle them together, and pass them on to designated candidates. These sums do not count against FECA party limits. And bundling is only part of the problem. Other controversies have arisen concerning party solicitation of contributions from corporations to pay for a national television address by the president on the eve of the election, misuse of soft money (limited to party-building activities such as paying for campaign headquarters or get-out-the-vote drives) for the promotion of candidates, foreign contributions, groups' illegal coordination of election activities with candidates, expenditures on issue advertisements with an electioneering message, creative accounting to evade spending limits in primaries, and the explosion of PAC independent spending, effectively bypassing the limits on direct contributions to candidates. At a minimum, the parties and PACs are now skirting, if not violating, the law. New techniques for raising and allocating funds, combined with unprecedented spending, seem likely to place new pressures on Congress to revise the basic law.

Adoption of the Federal Election Campaign Act (and its 1974, 1976, and 1979 amendments) has not by any means solved all the problems of financing American elections.

Inequities, confusion, and uncertainties persist. Have campaigns become too costly? Some close observers argue that they are underfinanced.[65] Should congressional as well as presidential campaigns be publicly financed? Thus far, Congress has said no. And if public financing of these campaigns is adopted, should spending limits also be established? And what of interest groups, now spending with a vengeance and undoubtedly gaining improved access to policy makers and securing questionable preferments? Should new limits on direct and independent expenditures be imposed on PACs? How much regulation will the Supreme Court permit? And if tighter limits on PAC contributions are adopted, will PACs be encouraged to make even heavier independent expenditures? Is it realistic to think of passing new campaign finance legislation that makes elections more competitive by diminishing the advantages of incumbents over their challengers? As it stands, the massive advantages of office for incumbents, who are benefited additionally by one-sided PAC campaign support, ordinarily leave challengers with no more than an outside chance of winning, particularly in House elections. And in some years Senate challengers find their prospects equally bleak. Both law and practice have combined to build a comprehensive incumbent-protection system. Can campaign finance legislation be designed to strengthen the parties, and should this be a public policy goal? Should party committees be permitted to contribute larger sums to House and Senate candidates and to spend more on their behalf or on behalf of presidential candidates? Should the contribution limits for individuals (set at $1,000 in 1974) be raised? Should campaigns be financed exclusively by hard money? These are some of the questions that will inform debate on campaign finance and its reform. Answers to them are not easy to fashion. The consequences of change, moreover, are not easy to anticipate. Protecting the status quo is the best single safeguard against the unanticipated outcomes that invariably accompany change.[66]

The manner in which political campaigns are financed has long been a source of controversy. Devising acceptable public policy on the subject has proved to be difficult, as it usually is on complex questions. But the objectives of regulation have been clear: to increase public confidence in the political process by curbing the abusive uses of political money, to enhance the opportunities for citizens to participate in politics by running for public office, and to reduce the vulnerability of candidates and public officials to the importunings and pressures of major benefactors. The campaign finance law has contributed in varying measure to the achievement of these objectives. It has also created new problems, accentuated certain old ones, fostered uncertainties, confounded observers, fostered cynicism, conferred advantages on some politicians and disadvantages on others, and, arguably, done more to weaken the parties than to strengthen them.

Notes

1. Press release, Federal Election Commission, April 22, 1997.
2. For an analysis of the new style of campaigning, particularly in terms of the role of campaign management firms, see Robert Agranoff, *The New Style in Election Campaigns* (Boston: Holbrook Press, 1972).
3. Quoted by Joe McGinniss, *The Selling of the President* (New York: Trident Press/Simon and Schuster, 1968).
4. Barbara G. Salmore and Stephen A. Salmore, *Candidates, Parties, and Campaigns* (Washington, D.C.: CQ Press, 1989), 215–216.
5. David A. Leuthold, *Electioneering in a Democracy* (New York: Wiley, 1968), 3. Leuthold's study of congressional campaigns shows that "the problems of acquisition are more significant than the problems of using the resources. As a result, the decision on making an appeal for the labor vote, for example, will depend not only on the proportion of the constituency which is labor-oriented, but also on the success that the candidate has had in acquiring such resources as the support of labor leaders, the money and workers needed to send a mailing to labor union members, and information about issues important to labor people."
6. A study of women's and men's campaigns for the U.S. House of Representatives shows that they have more similarities than differences. The most important difference is that women are more likely than men to stress social issues, such as children's issues, poverty, and education. Kirsten la Cour Dabelko and Paul S. Herrnson, "Women's and Men's Campaigns for the U.S. House of Representatives," *Political Research Quarterly 50* (March 1997): 121–135.
7. V. O. Key, Jr., *Politics, Parties, and Pressure Groups* (New York: Crowell, 1964), 464.
8. For an interesting argument that negative campaigning is not necessarily bad campaigning, see William G. Mayer, "In Defense of Negative Campaigning," *Political Science Quarterly 111* (Fall 1996): 437–455.
9. Lewis A. Froman, Jr., "A Realistic Approach to Campaign Strategies and Tactics," in *The Electoral Process*, ed. M. Kent Jennings and L. Harmon Zeigler (Englewood Cliffs, N.J.: Prentice Hall, 1966), 7–8.
10. Stimson Bullitt, *To Be a Politician* (Garden City, N.Y.: Doubleday, 1961), 72–73.
11. From Theodore H. White, *The Making of the President, 1960* (New York: Atheneum, 1961), 322–323. For analysis of the major models of campaign decision making, see Karl A. Lamb and Paul A. Smith, *Campaign Decision-Making: The Presidential Election of 1964* (Belmont, Calif.: Wadsworth, 1968).
12. Charles L. Clapp, *The Congressman: His Work as He Sees It* (Washington, D.C.: Brookings Institution, 1963), 332.
13. Clapp, *The Congressman*, 331.

14. *Congressional Quarterly Weekly Report,* July 7, 1979, 1350.
15. John J. Dilulio Jr., "Valence Voters, Valence Victors," in *The Election of 1996,* ed. Michael Nelson (Washington, D.C.: CQ Press, 1997), 172.
16. Salmore and Salmore, *Candidates, Parties, and Campaigns,* 113.
17. "Campaign Consultants: Pushing Sincerity in 1974," *Congressional Quarterly Weekly Report,* May 4, 1974, 1105.
18. Salmore and Salmore, *Candidates, Parties, and Campaigns,* 113.
19. Voter News Service exit poll.
20. Kiku Adatto, *Sound Bite Democracy: Network Evening News Presidential Campaign Coverage, 1968 and 1988* (Cambridge, Mass.: Barone Center on the Press, Politics and Public Policy, 1990), 4.
21. Adatto, *Sound Bite Democracy,* 7.
22. See Herbert E. Alexander, *Financing the 1980 Election* (Washington, D.C.: CQ Press, 1983); William J. Crotty and Gary C. Jacobson, *American Parties in Decline* (Boston: Little, Brown, 1980), 816–823; and Frank J. Sorauf, *Money in American Elections* (Glenview, Ill.: Scott Foresman/Little, Brown, 1988), 186–221. The 1988, 1992, and 1996 estimates are those of Herbert E. Alexander.
23. The development of political action committees represents a major change in American electoral politics. See an article by Frank J. Sorauf that examines the organizational lives of PACs, the role of donors to PACs, and PAC accountability: "Who's in Charge? Accountability in Political Action Committees," *Political Science Quarterly* 99 (Winter 1984–1985): 591–614. Also see the studies of PAC goals, organization, and decision making by Theodore J. Eismeier and Philip H. Pollock III, "An Organizational Analysis of Political Action Committees," *Political Behavior* 7, no. 2 (1985): 192–216, and "Strategy and Choice in Congressional Elections: The Role of Political Action Committees," *American Journal of Political Science 30* (February 1986): 197–213. The authors distinguish three PAC roles: *accommodationist* (seek access in Congress through gifts to incumbents); *partisan* (basically financial auxiliaries of the major parties); and *adversary* (seek to defeat members whom they regard as hostile to their interests).
24. *Washington Post,* June 15, 1987.
25. See "Spend, Spend, Spend," in *National Journal,* June 16, 1990, 1450–1452.
26. Press release, Federal Election Commission, April 14, 1997.
27. Alan I. Abramowitz identifies two trends that help account for the extraordinary success of incumbents in House elections: first, the increasingly high cost of running competitive campaigns and second, the inability of challengers to raise substantial campaign money. See his article, "Incumbency, Campaign Spending, and the Decline of Competition in U.S. House Elections," *Journal of Politics 53* (February 1991): 34–56.
28. Press release, Federal Election Commission, April 14, 1997.
29. Press release, Federal Election Commission, April 14, 1997.
30. *Congressional Quarterly Weekly Report,* April 8, 1978, 850–851; and November 11, 1978, 3260–3262.
31. Press release, Federal Election Commission, March 19, 1997.
32. For an interesting study of the growth of candidate-centered politics in the United States, see Martin P. Wattenberg, *The Rise of Candidate-Centered Politics* (Cambridge, Mass.: Harvard University Press, 1991).
33. Press release, Federal Election Commission, April 22, 1997.

34. *Congressional Quarterly Weekly Report,* August 2, 1986, 1751–1754.
35. David R. Mayhew, *Congress: The Electoral Connection* (New Haven, Conn.: Yale University Press, 1974), 84.
36. *Wall Street Journal,* September 24, 1986.
37. See an interesting account, "Don't Look Homeward," in *National Journal,* June 16, 1990, 1458–1460.
38. *Federal Election Commission Record* (Washington, D.C.: Federal Election Commission, April 1996), 14–15.
39. *Federal Election Commission v. Democratic Senatorial Campaign Committee,* 454 U.S. 27 (1981).
40. For a study that finds that national party contributions to congressional candidates enhance their party loyalty, see Kevin M. Leyden and Stephen A. Borrelli, "Party Contributions and Party Unity: Can Loyalty Be Bought?" *Western Political Quarterly 43* (June 1990): 343–365.
41. Press release, Federal Election Commission, April 14, 1997.
42. Gary C. Jacobson, "Party Organization and Distribution of Campaign Resources: Republicans and Democrats in 1982," *Political Science Quarterly 100* (Winter 1985–1986): 611.
43. Herbert E. Alexander, "Political Parties and the Dollar," *Society 22* (January/February 1985): 49–58.
44. Press release, Federal Election Commission, March 4, 1993.
45. Press release, Federal Election Commission, April 14, 1997.
46. Press release, Federal Election Commission, April 14, 1997.
47. For studies of the relationship between PAC contributions and congressional floor votes, see John R. Wright, "PACs, Contributions, and Roll Calls: An Organizational Perspective," *American Political Science Review 79* (June 1985): 400–414; W. P. Welch, "Campaign Contributions and Voting: Milk Money and Dairy Price Supports," *Western Political Quarterly 35* (December 1982): 478–495; Henry W. Chappell, Jr., "Campaign Contributions and Voting on the Cargo Preference Bill: A Comparison of Simultaneous Models," *Public Choice 36,* no. 2 (1981): 302–312; James B. Kau and Paul H. Rubin, *Congressmen, Constituents, and Contributors* (Boston: Martinus Nijhoff, 1982); and Frank L. Davis, "Balancing the Perspective on PAC Contributions: In Search of an Impact on Roll Calls," *American Politics Quarterly 21* (April 1993): 205–222. A recent study by Jay K. Dow and James W. Endersby finds no connection between the campaign contributions received by California incumbent state legislators and their subsequent legislative behavior. "Campaign Contributions and Legislative Voting in the California Assembly," *American Politics Quarterly 22* (July 1994): 334–353.
48. These observations on PACs by members of Congress are drawn respectively from *Congressional Quarterly Weekly Report,* March 12, 1983, 504; *Time,* March 3, 1986; *Congressional Quarterly Weekly Report,* January 11, 1986, 99; December 7, 1985, 2568; March 12, 1983, 504; and *Washington Post,* December 5, 1985.
49. 424 U.S. 1 (1976). Struck down by the Court were provisions that limited the spending of personal funds by candidates ($35,000 for Senate candidates and $25,000 for House candidates) and those that limited total expenditures. Senate candidates were to be limited to total expenditures of no more than $100,000 or 8 cents per eligible voter (whichever is greater) in primaries, and $150,000 or 12 cents per voter (whichever is greater) in general elections. Fund-raising costs

of up to 20 percent of the spending limit could be added to these amounts. House candidates were to be limited to no more than $70,000 in primaries and $70,000 in general elections (plus fund-raising costs of up to 20 percent of the spending limit).

50. *Congressional Quarterly Weekly Report,* October 12, 1974, 2865.
51. U.S. Congress, Senate, *Congressional Record,* daily ed., 101st Cong., 1st sess., May 11, 1990, S6037.
52. U.S. Congress, Senate, *Congressional Record,* daily ed., 101st Cong., 1st sess., May 11, 1990, S6038.
53. *Congressional Quarterly Weekly Report,* June 30, 1990, 2023.
54. *Congressional Quarterly Weekly Report,* April 5, 1997, 774.
55. What campaign money buys for nonincumbents is voter recognition. See Gary C. Jacobson, "The Effects of Campaign Spending in Congressional Elections," *American Political Science Review* 72 (June 1978): 469–491; Jacobson, "Money in the 1980 and 1982 Congressional Elections," in *Money and Politics in the United States: Financing Elections in the 1980s,* ed. Michael J. Malbin (Washington, D.C.: American Enterprise Institute for Public Policy Research, 1984), 60–63; Jacobson, "The Effects of Campaign Spending in House Elections: New Evidence for Old Arguments," *American Journal of Political Science* 34 (May 1990): 334–362; and Donald P. Green and Jonathan S. Krasno, "Rebuttal to Jacobson's 'New Evidence for Old Arguments,'" *American Journal of Political Science* 34 (May 1990): 363–372. Also see Scott J. Thomas, "Do Incumbent Campaign Expenditures Matter?" *Journal of Politics* 51 (November 1989): 965–976. Thomas argues that incumbent expenditures do make a difference: "The principal effect of incumbent spending is to win back voters who would have voted for the incumbent in the absence of the receipt of challenger (negative) advertisements." Quotation on p. 973.
56. *New York Times,* September 8, 1996.
57. *Colorado Republican Federal Campaign Committee v. FEC,* 116 S. Ct. 2309 (1996).
58. For a discussion of some of these themes, see an insightful essay by F. Christopher Arterton, "Political Money and Party Strength," in *The Future of American Political Parties,* ed. Joel Fleishman (Englewood Cliffs, N.J.: Prentice Hall, 1982), especially 116–122.
59. See Ruth S. Jones and Warren E. Miller, "Financing Campaigns: Macro Level Innovation and Micro Level Response," *Western Political Quarterly* 38 (June 1985): 187–210; and Ruth S. Jones, "Campaign Contributions and Campaign Solicitations: 1980–1984" (Manuscript, Arizona State University, 1986). These studies rest on data drawn from the National Election Study.
60. These data were furnished by Sharon Snyder of the Federal Election Commission.
61. National Election Studies, Center for Political Studies, University of Michigan.
62. Press release, Federal Election Commission, April 14, 1997.
63. Press release, Federal Election Commission, April 14, 1997.
64. Press release, Federal Election Commission, March 19, 1997.
65. Alexander, "Political Parties and the Dollar," 49–58.
66. For insight into the reform question, see Michael J. Malbin, "Looking Back at the Future of Campaign Finance Reform: Interest Groups and American Elections," in *Money and Politics in the United States,* 232–270.

Chapter Five

Political Parties
and the Electorate

It is a nagging fact of American life that for a large proportion of the population politics carries no interest, registers no significance, and excites no demands. A vast array of evidence shows that the political role of the typical citizen is that of spectator, occasionally aroused by political events but more often inattentive to them. However tarnished this commonplace, it comes close to being the chief truth to be known about the political behavior of American citizens. Much less certain, however, is what this means. Whether it is necessary to have greatly interested and active citizens to have strong and responsible political institutions is by no means clear. No neat or simple formula exists for assessing public support for political institutions. Does the presence of a large nonvoting population reflect substantial disillusionment with the political system and its processes, or does it reflect a general satisfaction with the state of things? The answer is elusive.

Whatever the consequences of low or modest turnouts for the vitality of a democratic political system, it is obvious that some American citizens use their political resources far more than others. Their political involvement is reflected not only in the fact that they vote regularly but also in the fact that they participate in politics in various other ways—perhaps by attempting to persuade other voters to support their candidates or party, by making campaign contributions, or by devoting time and energy to political campaigns. The net result of differential rates of participation is that some citizens gain access to political decision makers and can influence their decisions, whereas other citizens are all but excluded from the political process.

An important element in understanding the political behavior of the active members of the American electorate is the political party. More than any other agency, the party provides cues for the voters and gives shape and meaning to elections. Some voters elude party labeling, preferring the role of the independent. Even though their importance cannot be minimized, especially in presidential elections, their consistent impact on politics is less than that of party members. The reason for this is partly a matter of numbers: About two out of three voters classify themselves as members of one or the other of the two major parties. Before examining the behavior of partisans and nonpartisans, however, it is appropriate to consider the broad characteristics of citizen participation in politics.

Turnout: The Diminished Electorate

Few facts about American political behavior stand out more sharply than the comparatively low level of citizen involvement in politics. And there are clear signs that popular participation is declining.

Atrophy of the Electorate

In presidential elections during the last quarter of the nineteenth century, turnout was regularly high; in the presidential election of 1876, for example, more than 85 percent of the eligible voters cast ballots (see Figure 5-1). Beginning around the turn of the century, however, a sharp decline in voting set in, reaching its nadir of 44 percent in 1920. A moderate increase in turnout occurred during the next several decades, with participation hovering around 60 percent during the 1950s and 1960s. But participation declined again in the 1970s, dropping to 54.3 percent in 1976 and to 53.2 percent in 1980—its lowest level since 1948. In the 1984 election between Ronald Reagan and Walter F. Mondale, turnout rose only fractionally, to 53.3 percent. In 1988 turnout declined further, with only 50.16 percent of the voting-age population casting ballots. In 1992 thirteen million more Americans voted than in 1988, resulting in a 55.9 percent turnout—the highest percentage since 1968. Ross Perot's populist and flamboyant campaign, the feeble state of the economy, and the pervasive demand for change combined to attract voters to the polls. It remained for 1996 to reflect the worst performance of American voters since 1924: Only 48.8 percent of the voting-age population turned out to decide the election between Bob Dole and Bill Clinton.

Although these data on American voting participation are far from impressive, they may conceal more of the problem than they uncover. The hard truth is that turnout is much lower in nonpresidential elections. In off-year congressional elections from 1950 to 1970, turnout percentages ranged

FIGURE 5-1 Percentage of Voting-Age Population Casting Votes for the Office of President: 1856 to 1996

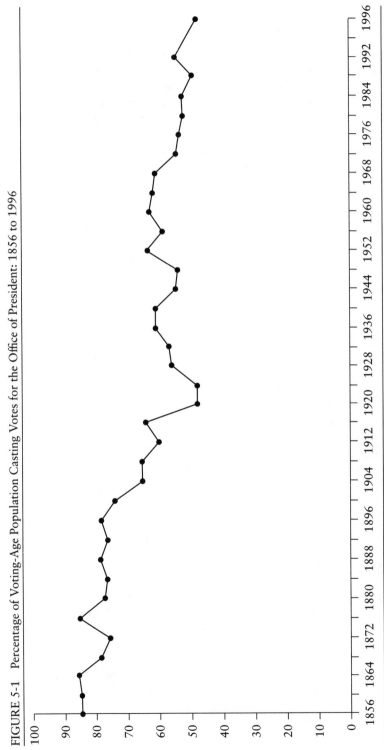

SOURCE: Developed from data in Paul Allen Beck, "The Electoral Cycle and Patterns of American Politics," *British Journal of Political Science* 9 (April 1979): 134 (as updated).

between 41 and 45 percent of the eligible voters. In the midterm election of 1974, turnout dropped to 36 percent; in 1978, it fell to 35.1 percent. In the midst of a marked economic slump in 1982, the turnout percentage rose to 37.7 percent. But it eased off to 33.4 percent in 1986. It rose slightly in 1990, to about 36 percent, and remained at that level in 1994. More than 60 percent of all eligible voters do not take the trouble to vote in off-year elections (see Figure 5-2).

Turnout in state and local elections is more of the same story of citizen indifference. An analysis of voting for the office of governor, for example, supports three main generalizations. First, the states differ sharply in their turnout patterns. As a rule, higher voter participation rates occur in midwestern, western (especially plains and mountain), and New England states, and lower turnout rates characterize most southern states. Second, those states that elect governors in presidential years (about one fifth of the total) nearly always have higher turnouts than those in which gubernatorial elections occur in off years. Third, notwithstanding major variations among the states, overall citizen performance is disappointing. The average turnout in off-year gubernatorial elections hovers around 40 percent, and in some southern states it fails to reach 30 percent.

The low point in participation is ordinarily plumbed in primary elections—a total primary vote of only 20 to 25 percent of the eligible electorate is not unusual. In certain southern states, however, participation in primary elections—often the real election in that region—is about as high as it is in general elections. Primary turnout is highest in states where primaries are open (and particularly high in blanket or nonpartisan primaries), where the parties are most competitive, where presidential primaries coincide with other primaries, and where higher educational levels are present among voters. There is some evidence that closeness of election stimulates turnout and that incumbency diminishes it. Each state has a different mix of these factors, thus contributing to variations in turnout rates.[1]

It is a major and uncomfortable fact of American political life that a great many citizens—comprising about half of the eligible electorate even in presidential years—are almost wholly detached from the political system and the processes through which its leadership is selected. What reasons help to account for the poor performance of twentieth century American electorates? In the case of southern states, limitations placed on black political participation shortly before the turn of the century drastically reduced turnout. A variety of legal abridgments and strategies, buttressed by social and economic sanctions of all kinds, effectively disfranchised all but the most persistent and resourceful black citizens. The ingenuity of southern white politicians during this era can scarcely be exaggerated. Poll taxes, literacy tests, understanding-the-Constitution tests, white primaries,[2] stringent

FIGURE 5-2 Voter Turnout in Off-Year Elections: 1946 to 1994

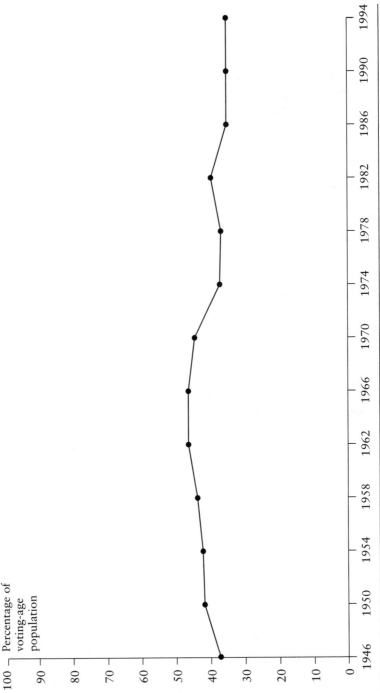

SOURCES: Norman J. Ornstein, Thomas E. Mann, and Michael J. Malbin, *Vital Statistics on Congress, 1993–1994* (Washington, D.C.: Congressional Quarterly, 1994), 48; *Congressional Quarterly Weekly Report*, April 15, 1995.

residence and registration requirements, and discriminatory registration administration—all were consciously employed by dominant elites to maintain a white electorate and thus to settle political questions within the white community.

Another prime reason for the sharp contraction of the active electorate stems from the advent of one-party politics throughout large sections of the country. Democratic domination of the South began shortly after the Civil War Reconstruction governments were terminated. Nevertheless, even in the 1880s, the Republican presidential vote was at least half of the Democratic vote in all but a few southern states. The election of 1896, one of the most decisive elections in American history, culminated in the virtual disappearance of the Republican party in the South and in a precipitate drop in Democratic strength in the North. E. E. Schattschneider's analysis of this election is instructive:

> The 1896 party cleavage resulted from the tremendous reaction of conservatives in both major parties to the Populist movement, a radical agrarian agitation that alarmed people of substance all over the country. . . . Southern conservatives reacted so strongly that they were willing to revive the tensions and animosities of the Civil War and the Reconstruction in order to set up a one-party sectional southern political monopoly in which nearly all Negroes and many poor whites were disfranchised. . . . The northern conservatives were so badly frightened by the [William Jennings] Bryan candidacy that they adopted drastic measures to alarm the country. As a matter of fact, the conservative reaction to Bryanism in the North was almost as spectacular as the conservative reaction to Populism in the South. As a result the Democratic party in large areas of the Northeast and Middle West was wiped out, or decimated, while the Republican party consolidated its supremacy in all of the most populous areas of the country. The resulting party lineup was one of the most sharply sectional political divisions in American history. . . . Both sections became more conservative because *one-party politics tends strongly to vest political power in the hands of the people who already have enormous power.* Moreover, in one-party areas (areas of extreme sectionalism) votes decline in value because the voters no longer have a valuable party alternative.[3]

The smothering effect of a noncompetitive environment on participation can be seen in election turnouts following the realignment of the 1890s. Consider this evidence: between 1884 and 1904, turnout in Virginia dropped 57 percent; in Mississippi, 51 percent; and in Louisiana, 50 percent. Part of the explanation for these drop-offs undoubtedly can be associated with the success of southern efforts to disfranchise blacks, but one-party politics also had a decisive impact on the electorate. In the first place, the drop in participation was too large to be accounted for merely by the disappearance of black votes. And, in the second place, the impact of the new sectionalism was not confined simply to the South. Despite their growing populations, some fourteen northern states had smaller turnouts in 1904 than they did in 1896.[4]

The lower rate of turnout in the South in the twentieth century is partially attributable to diminished competition between the parties. If the outcome of an election is predictable, voters have scant inducement to invest the time, energy, and other costs that voting requires. Changes in the turnout of southern voters, however, are under way. Today, elections in the South (especially presidential) are substantially more competitive than they were a generation ago, and voter turnout rates have been increasing, here and there dramatically. The elimination of legal barriers to registration and voting (such as the poll tax and the literacy test) has also contributed to the expansion of southern electorates. In presidential elections, voters in some southern states now participate at a level only marginally lower than voters in other parts of the country.

Still other reasons have been advanced for the decline in mass political involvement in this century. One concerns woman suffrage. Although women were given the vote in 1920, large numbers of them were indifferent to their new right and did not use it immediately. In subsequent decades, a significantly larger proportion of women entered the active electorate; today, their rate of participation is about the same as that of men.[5]

After 1971, the number of potential voters increased again when the voting age was lowered to eighteen. Younger voters have the lowest participation rate of any group in American society. It is not unusual for a mere third of those persons between eighteen and twenty-one to vote in presidential elections.

In the past, stringent registration laws served to keep many citizens away from the polls. During the latter part of the nineteenth century, when turnout was regularly between 75 and 85 percent of the eligible electorate, in many parts of the country voters were not required to register, or automatic registration was in effect. During the early twentieth century, registration laws became much more restrictive, making voting more difficult. Provisions were adopted, for example, requiring voters to register annually in person, purging voters' names from the registration rolls if they failed to vote within a particular period, and requiring that voters reside within a state at least a year (and sometimes two) before becoming eligible to register. In addition, poll taxes and literacy tests were used, particularly in the South, to disfranchise prospective voters. The effect of these legal barriers was to diminish turnout.

Major changes in the 1960s and 1970s, however, greatly relaxed registration laws. Poll taxes and literacy tests were eliminated. Periodic registration gave way virtually everywhere to permanent registration. As a result of an act passed by Congress in 1970, the residency requirement for federal elections is now limited to a maximum of thirty days before the election; moreover, for other elections, only a handful of states have closing dates earlier than thirty days. In about one-third of the states, registration is possible up to twenty days before the election. Minnesota, Maine, and Wisconsin permit voters to register and vote on election day; turnout rates in these states are now among the highest in the nation.[6] Finally, all states must now meet certain minimum national standards for absentee registration.[7]

Another effort to expand the ranks of voters occurred in 1993 when Democratic majorities in Congress, with the help of a handful of moderate Republicans in the Senate, adopted the National Voter Registration Act, known popularly as the "motor voter" law. Effective in 1995, the law provides that states must permit citizens eighteen years or older to register to vote when they apply for or renew a driver's license. It also requires states to permit registration by mail and to make available registration forms at state and federal agencies that administer programs dealing with public assistance, disability benefits, and armed forces recruitment. To secure several Republican votes, a provision to include unemployment benefit offices as registration sites was dropped from the bill.

Millions of new voters have been added to the rolls under this new federal statute. Its effects on turnout and election outcomes, however, have not yet been systematically investigated. Ease of registration does not necessarily translate into a significant increase in voting. But it should be noted that when motor-voter registration was introduced earlier in various states, beginning with Michigan in 1975, turnout levels did increase.[8] Whether motor-voter helps one party more than the other also remains to be investigated. Scattered newspaper accounts report that more than an ordinary number of independents have registered under the new system.

Reforms to increase turnout typically fall short of expectations. Staci L. Rhine wrote,

> All of the evidence suggests that most of the registration reforms have made small differences in turnout. Same-day registration, on one hand, is closely related to higher turnout, but that provision is not part of the new federal law. Mail registration, on the other hand, although part of the new law, does not seem likely to increase turnout. Motor-voter registration has recently had a positive impact on turnout [in certain states]. Its use nationally may increase turnout several percentage points, particularly if other state agencies offer registration.[9]

In the 1996 election there were perhaps 100 million nonvoters, including citizens who were of voting age but unregistered and persons who were registered but failed to vote.[10] Curtis Gans, director of the Committee for the

The People's Choice?

Most presidential winners have sought to portray their victories as mandates from the American people. But even landslide victors in the nationwide popular vote have been the choice of barely one third of the entire voting-age population.

The following chart compares the percentage of the popular vote that presidential winners since 1932 have received with the percentage of the entire voting-age population that their vote total represents. The latter percentage is based on voting-age population estimates updated each election year by the U.S. Bureau of the Census.

Year	Winner	Percentage of total popular vote	Percentage of voting-age population
1932	Roosevelt (D)	57.4	30.1
1936	Roosevelt (D)	60.8	34.6
1940	Roosevelt (D)	54.7	32.2
1944	Roosevelt (D)	53.4	29.9
1948	Truman (D)	49.6	25.3
1952	Eisenhower (R)	55.1	34.0
1956	Eisenhower (R)	57.4	34.1
1960	Kennedy (D)	49.7	31.2
1964	Johnson (D)	61.1	37.8
1968	Nixon (R)	43.4	26.4
1972	Nixon (R)	60.7	33.5
1976	Carter (D)	50.1	26.8
1980	Reagan (R)	50.7	26.7
1984	Reagan (R)	58.8	31.2
1988	Bush (R)	53.4	26.8
1992	Clinton (D)	43.0	23.8
1996	Clinton (D)	49.2	24.0

SOURCE: *Congressional Quarterly Weekly Report*, January 21, 1989, 137 (as updated).

NOTE: D = Democrat; R = Republican. The votes cast for third-party candidates are included in this analysis.

Study of the American Electorate, pointed out that there are two nonvoting problems. One is *low* voter turnout, which to some extent has been the result of registration barriers. The other is *declining* voter turnout. Although the country's voting laws have been liberalized in recent decades, these changes have had no major effect on turnout. The best explanation for declining participation is *declining motivation* to vote.[11]

Nonvoters offer a variety of reasons for their failure to vote. A growing number of people do not take the trouble to register—typically the explanation offered by at least one third of the nonvoters. People who change residence are required to sign up again, and many fail to do so. Because nearly one third of the nation now moves every two years, a recent study shows, change of residence has become a significant explanation for failure to vote.[12] Other people do not vote because they disapprove of the candidates—usually about 10 to 15 percent in Gallup surveys of nonvoters. And then there are those who are not interested in politics, those who find voting inconvenient, and those who have "no particular reason" for not voting.

California may or may not be a special case, but a 1990 poll by the *Los Angeles Times* found that the main reason people in that state fail to vote is that they are too busy doing other things to bother voting. This reason was given by an extraordinary 35 percent of the respondents. The next most frequent reason, cited by 8 percent, was a lack of interest in politics.[13]

A central explanation for nonvoting thus lies in the public's attitude toward politics and political institutions.[14] It seems likely, for example, that participation has declined because an increasing number of citizens care less which party or which candidate wins, because they believe that their votes will not make much difference, because they believe that public officials are not concerned about what voters think, because they think that politicians cannot be trusted, and because they believe public officials are unresponsive.[15] It also seems clear that the overall decline in the strength of voters' party identification has played a role in the decline of electoral participation.[16] Indifference, alienation,[17] declining party loyalty, and a generalized distrust of government combine to cut the turnout rate in elections. Frequent elections also discourage turnout, particularly among the peripheral electorate—those people who easily lapse into nonvoting unless party and campaign organizations make a special effort to turn them out.[18] For many citizens, "voting simply isn't worth the effort."[19]

Turnout in other industrialized democracies averages about 80 percent of the eligible electorate, vastly higher than the average turnout in American presidential elections. A study by G. Bingham Powell, Jr., using aggregate and comparative survey data, finds that voter participation in the United States is "severely inhibited" by institutional factors such as voluntary registration (as opposed to automatic registration common in other

Participation in Elections:
Comparing the United States with Twenty-seven Other Nations

Highest Turnout, Any National Election: 1968–1986
(in percentages)

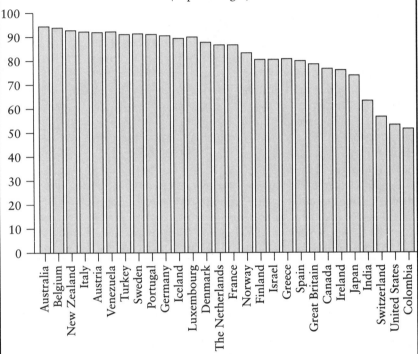

Why is turnout in elections in other nations so much higher than in the United States? One reason is that some nations, such as Australia and Belgium, have laws requiring citizens to vote. Another is that other nations commonly hold their elections on nonworkdays, a practice that encourages participation. A third major reason is that other countries automatically register all persons eligible to vote, instead of requiring the individual to take the initiative to register, as in the United States. Registration laws in the American states, on the whole, do little to facilitate voting. (The size of the electorate in all of these countries except the United States is the number of registered voters. In the United States it is the voting-age population as computed by the U.S. Bureau of the Census.)

SOURCE: Developed from data generated by the Congressional Research Service of the Library of Congress, November 1987.

nations), low levels of competition in many electoral districts, and weak linkages between parties and social groups (thus making the parties' task of voter mobilization more difficult). To approach the turnout levels of other democracies, Powell argues, the United States would need to adopt automatic registration laws and change the structure of party competition to mobilize lower-class voters.[20] Obviously, changing registration laws would be easier to accomplish than changing party character and party competition.[21]

The Regulation of Voting

As stipulated in the U.S. Constitution, states have control over suffrage. The basic reference to suffrage in the Constitution appears in Article I, Section 2, which provides that for elections to the House of Representatives "the electors [that is, voters] in each state shall have the qualifications requisite for electors of the most numerous branch of the state legislature." Until recently the major national intrusions involving suffrage came in the form of constitutional amendments. The Fifteenth Amendment (1870) forbade the states to deny citizens the right to vote on the grounds of race, and the Nineteenth Amendment (1920) provided that states could not deny citizens the ballot on account of gender. The Twenty-fourth Amendment (1964) outlawed poll taxes, and the Twenty-sixth Amendment (1971) lowered the voting age in all elections to eighteen.

In recent decades, the tradition of state control over suffrage has been significantly challenged by Congress through the passage of a series of civil rights acts (1957, 1960, 1964, and 1965). The acts of 1957 and 1960 were designed primarily to prevent discrimination against blacks seeking to register to vote. Individuals who were denied the right to register by local registrars could seek relief from the federal government through the attorney general and the federal court system. Where discriminatory practices affecting registration were found to exist, the court was empowered to appoint federal voting referees to enroll black voters. Although the overall impact of these early acts on black voting was marginal, due largely to the cumbersome procedural requirements involved in jury trials and in establishing patterns of discrimination, they were important for establishing the power of the federal government, through a legislative enactment, to intervene in state election systems.

Of much greater substantive significance have been the Civil Rights Act of 1964 and the Voting Rights Act of 1965. In its provisions concerning voting, the 1964 act made a sixth-grade education presumptive evidence of literacy and required that all literacy tests be administered in writing. In addition, registrars were required to administer registration procedures fairly and were forbidden to reject registration applications because of immaterial errors on registration forms.

With the support of strong majorities of both parties, Congress passed the Voting Rights Act of 1965. Under its terms, literacy tests or other voter qualification devices used for discriminatory purposes were suspended in any state or county in which fewer than 50 percent of the voting-age residents were registered to vote in November 1964 or fewer than 50 percent voted in the 1964 presidential election. Augmenting the federal government's power to supervise elections, the act called for the appointment of federal voting examiners with the authority to register persons who had been unable to register even though they met state requirements for voting. Finally, the act provided that if a state or local governmental unit decides to change its voting regulations, the U.S. attorney general or the U.S. District Court for the District of Columbia must first certify that the new rules will not serve the purposes of racial discrimination. In 1975 this act was extended for another seven years, with its coverage expanded to include "language minorities" (including Spanish-speaking populations, American Indians, Alaskan natives, and Asian Americans). The extension also placed a permanent ban on voter qualifying tests.

In its most important respects, the regulation of voting is today as much a matter of federal law as it is of state law. Had the civil rights movement in the 1950s and 1960s not taken place, such fundamental changes probably would not have occurred in the regulation of suffrage. What has been the impact of the role of the national government in protecting the right to vote? For black political participation, the results have been dramatic (see Table 5-1). In 1960 only 29 percent of the blacks of voting age were registered to vote in the eleven states of the South; in 1986, 61 percent. In Mississippi, nearly fourteen times as many blacks were registered to vote in 1986 as there had been in 1960. The vast majority of these new voters in Mississippi and elsewhere were enrolled following the passage of the Voting Rights Act of 1965. In 1986 voters in the rural Mississippi Delta (Second Congressional District) elected the state's first black representative since the military occupation, or Reconstruction, following the Civil War.

Widespread black political participation is now a reality throughout the South. To be sure, registration and voting will not solve all the problems of the black citizen. But political participation does give blacks much greater leverage in the political system. The number of black elected officials has increased dramatically in recent years, particularly in the South. And as a result of interpretations of the Voting Rights Act requiring states to offer minorities maximum opportunity to elect candidates of their choice, black and

TABLE 5-1   Percentage of Voting-Age Population Registered to Vote in
Eleven Southern States, by Race: 1960 and 1986

State	1960		1986	
	White	Black	White	Black
Alabama	63.6	13.7	77.5	68.9
Arkansas	60.9	38.0	67.2	57.9
Florida	69.3	39.4	66.9	58.2
Georgia	56.8	29.3	62.3	52.8
Louisiana	76.9	31.1	67.8	60.6
Mississippi	63.9	5.2	91.6	70.8
North Carolina	92.1	39.1	67.4	58.4
South Carolina	57.1	13.7	53.4	52.5
Tennessee	73.0	59.1	70.0	65.3
Texas	42.5	35.5	79.0	68.0
Virginia	46.1	23.1	60.3	56.2
Total	61.1	29.1	69.9	60.8

SOURCES: Developed from data in U.S. Bureau of the Census, *Statistical Abstract of the United States* (Washington, D.C.: U.S. Government Printing Office, 1989), 261. The data for 1960 are drawn from the 1986 edition of the *Statistical Abstract,* 257.

Hispanic representation in Congress increased substantially in the 1990s. Between 1990 and 1993, 52 congressional districts were formed with either black (32) or Hispanic (20) population majorities. Under these more favorable conditions, with districts drawn specifically to give minority voters more electoral influence, the number of African American House members increased from 26 to 39 in 1992, and to 41 in 1994, and the number of Hispanics from 13 in 1992 to 18 in 1994.

The constitutionality of "majority-minority" districts was soon challenged. In *Shaw v. Reno* (1993), the Supreme Court held that a state's electoral redistricting plan can be an unconstitutional racial gerrymander if it contains districts of a "bizarre" or "irrational" configuration, even though the plan's central purpose was to increase the representation of blacks.[22] In *Miller v. Johnson* (1995), decided by a 5 to 4 vote, the Court invalidated a Georgia congressional black majority district, saying that race cannot be a "predominant factor" in drawing district lines. Districts become questionable, the ruling held, when "race for its own sake" becomes "the legislature's dominant and controlling rationale in drawing its district lines."[23]

In two 5 to 4 decisions in 1996, *Shaw v. Hunt* and *Bush v. Vera,* citing the Fourteenth Amendment's equal protection guarantee, the Court invalidated one North Carolina congressional district and three in Texas as unconstitutional racial gerrymanders.[24] "Significant deviations from traditional districting principles," Justice Sandra Day O'Connor wrote in *Bush,* "such as the bizarre shape and noncompactness demonstrated by the districts here, cause constitutional harm insofar as they convey the message that political identity is, or should be, predominantly racial."[25]

Majority-minority districts are not objectionable in and of themselves. They trigger the "strict scrutiny" of the Court when traditional districting criteria—such as partisanship, compactness, or incumbency protection— are "subordinated to race."

Other districts that have been drawn to increase minority representation will come under the Court's review, doubtlessly leading to some reduction in the number of African American and Hispanic members of Congress and state legislatures. Plainly, these decisions will make it harder to elect minorities to legislative positions.

The southern electorates of today are vastly different from those of the 1950s. Whatever the future of southern politics, black voters and black politicians will play a more important role in political decision making than at any time since Reconstruction.

Forms of Political Participation

The act of voting is an appropriate point of departure for exploring the political involvement of American citizens, but it is not the only form of participation. A comprehensive survey of political participation in America by Sidney Verba and Norman H. Nie shows the range and dimensions of citizen activities in politics (see Table 5-2). Several findings should be emphasized. Perhaps of most importance, the only political activity in which a majority of American citizens participate is voting in presidential elections. Voting regularly in local elections follows as a rather distant second. The survey discloses that as political activity requires more time, initiative, and involvement of the citizen—working to solve a community problem, attempting to persuade others how to vote, working for a party or candidate, contributing to political campaigns—participation levels drop even lower.

The impression most deeply conveyed by the data is that a relatively small group of citizens performs most of the political activities of the nation. There is obviously much more than a germ of truth to this. Yet, to some extent, the data underrepresent the political activity of citizens, because those citizens who perform one political act are not necessarily the same as those who perform another act. Verba and Nie indicate that less than a third of their sample reported engaging in no political activities (other than voting).[26] Even so, this is a fairly large lump of the citizenry.

TABLE 5-2   A Profile of the Political Activity of American Citizens

Form of activity	Percentage of citizens
Report regularly voting in presidential elections	72
Report always voting in local elections	47
Acting in at least one organization involved in community problems	32
Have worked with others in trying to solve some community problems	30
Have attempted to persuade others to vote as they were	28
Have ever actively worked for a party or candidates during an election	26
Have ever contacted a local government official about some issue or problem	20
Have attended at least one political meeting or rally in last three years	19
Have ever contacted a state or national government official about some issue or problem	18
Have ever formed a group or organization to attempt to solve some local community problem	14
Have ever given money to a party or candidate during an election campaign	13
Presently a member of a political club or organization	8

SOURCE: Sidney Verba and Norman H. Nie, *Participation in America: Political Democracy and Social Equality* (New York: Harper and Row, 1972), 31.

The evidence indicates that people do not get involved randomly in politics. Instead, there is a hierarchy of political involvement (see Figure 5-3).[27] Individuals who are politically active engage in a wide variety of political acts. A major characteristic of their participation is that it tends to be cumulative. The active members of a political party, for example, are likely to be found soliciting political funds, contributing time and money to campaigns, attending meetings, and so on. Individuals who are minimally involved in politics typically take part only in limited activities such as those grouped near the base of the hierarchy. At the very bottom are those persons who stand on the outskirts of the political world, scarcely aware of the political forces that play on them or of the opportunities open to them to use their resources (including the vote) to gain political objectives.

Some portion of the explanation for the passivity of American citizens may lie with the parties and candidates themselves. They are not particularly active in clearing the way for popular participation. A recent Gallup survey found that only a small proportion of citizens are contacted by party or candidate organization workers in an effort to win their vote. During the 1992 election campaign only 12 percent of the public reported that they had been

FIGURE 5-3   Hierarchy of Political Involvement

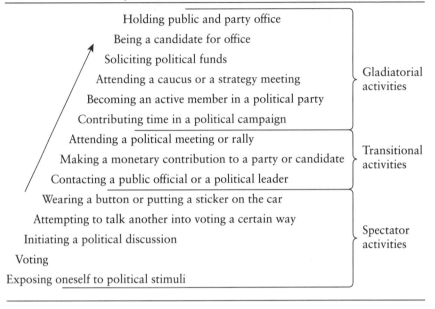

SOURCE: Lester W. Milbrath, *Political Participation* (Chicago: Rand McNally, 1965), 18.

contacted by someone from the Democratic party and only 10 percent by someone from the Republican party. The individuals most likely to come in contact with electioneering activities are those with high socioeconomic status—in particular, those with a college education, a professional or business background, and a high income. For most Americans the party organization, *qua* organization, is all but invisible.[28]

The Active and Passive Citizenry

Several social, demographic, and political variables are related to the act of voting. The data in Table 5-3 provide a profile of those citizens who are more likely to turn out at elections and those who are less likely to turn out. Some of the characteristics are closely related—for example, high income,[29] high occupational status, and college education. Nevertheless, the high rate of participation by citizens of higher socioeconomic status is not simply a function of status. The explanation lies in the civic orientations that are linked to upper-class status and environment. Upper-status citizens, for example, are more likely than citizens of lower status to belong to organizations and to

TABLE 5-3   A Profile of the More Active and Less Active Citizenry

More likely to vote	Less likely to vote
High income	Low income
High occupational status	Low occupational status
College education	Grade school or high school education
Middle-aged	Young and elderly
White	Black and Hispanic
Metropolitan area resident	Small-town resident
Northern state resident	Southern state resident
Resident in competitive party environment	Resident in noncompetitive party environment
Union member	Nonunion member
Homeowner	Renter
Married	Single, separated, divorced, widowed
Government employees	Private workers
Catholics and Jews	Protestants
Strong partisan	Independent

SOURCES: These findings were drawn from a large number of studies of the American electorate. For wide-ranging analyses, see Lester W. Milbrath, *Political Participation* (Chicago: Rand McNally, 1965); Raymond E. Wolfinger and Steven J. Rosenstone, *Who Votes?* (New Haven, Conn.: Yale University Press, 1980); and M. Margaret Conway, *Political Participation in the United States,* 2d ed. (Washington, D.C.: CQ Press, 1991).

participate in their activities, more likely to possess the resources and skills to be effective in politics, and more likely to be attentive to political problems and to feel efficacious in dealing with them.[30]

How much the factors that influence participation at the individual level can account for the differences among the states in voter turnout is not altogether clear. What is clear is that of all the sections of the country, the South ranks not only lowest in turnout but also lowest in terms of family income, levels of education, and other measures of economic well-being. Moreover, the legal structures (for example, election laws) in southern states typically do not encourage voting as much as those in northern states. The level of participation in southern states probably will increase as their sociodemographic characteristics change (for example, an improved economic position) or as their legal structures become more facilitative.

For all their interest, the distinctions drawn from the data presented in Table 5-3 cannot be taken at face value. The differences between voters and nonvoters are less apparent today than in the past. The participation rates of people who live in rural or urban areas are about the same today. Men and

Interest in Politics

Would you say you follow what's going on in government and public affairs most of the time, some of the time, only now and then, or hardly at all?

Most of the time	23%
Some of the time	40
Only now and then	26
Hardly at all	11

Would you say that you were very much interested, somewhat interested, or not much interested [in the 1996 campaign]?

Very much interested	32%
Somewhat interested	52
Not much interested	16

Ideology

We hear a lot of talk these days about liberals and conservatives. Here is a 7-point scale on which the political views that people hold are arranged from extremely liberal to extremely conservative. Where would you place yourself on this scale, or haven't you thought much about this?

Extremely liberal	2%
Liberal	8
Slightly liberal	9
Moderate, middle of road	23
Slightly conservative	13
Conservative	15
Extremely conservative	3
Don't know	2
Haven't thought much	25

. . . *toward Political Activity*

Political Efficacy

Sometimes politics and government seem so complicated that a person like me can't really understand what's going on.

Agree	71%
Disagree	29

Political Activity

During the campaign, did you talk to any people and try to show them why they should vote for or against one of the parties or candidates?

Yes	29%
No	71

Did you wear a campaign button, put a campaign sticker on your car, or place a sign in your window or in front of your house?

Yes	10%
No	90

Did you go to any political meetings, rallies, speeches, dinners, or things like that in support of a particular candidate?

Yes	6%
No	94

Did you do any work for one of the parties or candidates?

Yes	3%
No	97

Did you give money to a political party during this election year?

Yes	6%
No	94

SOURCE: These questions are drawn from the 1996 presidential election survey, National Election Study, Center for Political Studies, University of Michigan. The political efficacy data are for 1992.

Voters and Nonvoters

As Contrasted with Voters, Nonvoters
are more likely to

- describe voting as difficult
- be frustrated over lack of information about candidates
- find other things more important than voting (twice as many non-voters as voters would choose to receive overtime pay than to vote, and a great many would prefer to take advantage of a sale or to watch a new TV show than to vote)
- describe themselves as independents and liberals
- live in the South or West than in the Midwest or Northeast

are less likely to

- be integrated into their community through memberships in multiple organizations
- believe their vote counts
- believe that elections make a difference
- see important policy differences between the parties
- be contacted by various groups and organizations such as candidate organizations, political parties, unions, and issue groups
- be engaged in politics on a daily basis, such as following public affairs or discussing political issues
- be strong partisans
- see that government plays a positive role in their lives

but are no more or no less cynical about government.

SOURCE: The Mellman Group and Wirthlin Worldwide, *Analysis of A Survey on Nonvoting* (Washington, D.C.: The League of Women Voters, 1996) (as adapted).

women now vote at about the same rate. Turnout in the South is on the rise, whereas it is decreasing in the North. A noticeable decline in voting by middle-aged persons has occurred. What stands out most is that participation has declined along a broad demographic front. The lower turnout of Protestants is also deceptive. It is undoubtedly a result in part to the lower levels of participation of southern and rural voters, who happen to be largely Protestant. Finally, it should be stressed that the variables are not of equal

TABLE 5-4   Education and Voting Turnout in Presidential Elections

	Percentage voting			
Educational level	1980	1984	1988	1992
Grade school	58.6	58.0	41.7	54.8
High school	54.8	66.3	58.2	65.4
College	76.4	85.5	82.4	88.1

SOURCE: Adapted from M. Margaret Conway, *Political Participation in the United States,* 2d ed. (Washington, D.C.: CQ Press, 1991), 22 (updated). As Conway pointed out, individuals who are more highly educated are also more likely to overreport voting.

importance. The best indicators of voting participation are those that reflect socioeconomic status: education, income, and occupation. And of these, education is the most important (see Table 5-4).[31]

Scholars who study electoral behavior contend that education is the predominant influence on turnout. The importance of education is said to derive from the fact that education inculcates a sense of civic duty, that it increases political efficacy, that it enhances political awareness, and that it makes registration easier. Although there is good evidence to support each of these explanations, Robert A. Jackson found that education's impact on registration is especially important: "Advanced schooling cultivates skills and interests that make the hurdle of registration easier to overcome, which, in turn, elevates voting odds."[32]

Citizens who show enthusiasm for voting and who participate regularly in elections can be distinguished by their psychological makeup as well as by their social and economic backgrounds. The prospect that persons will vote is influenced by the intensity of their partisan preferences: the more substantial their commitments to a party, the stronger the probability that they will vote (see Table 5-5). Persons who have a strong partisan preference and who perceive the election as close are virtually certain to vote.[33] Voters are also more likely than nonvoters to perceive major differences between the parties' positions on public policy questions, such as Medicare, taxes, and the deficit.[34] Voters can also be distinguished by other indices of psychological involvement in political affairs. Survey research data show them to be more interested in campaigns and more concerned with election outcomes.[35] They are also more likely than nonvoters to possess a strong sense of political efficacy; that is, a disposition to see their own participation in politics as important and effective. Finally, in contrast to nonvoters, voters are more likely to accept the norm that voting is a civic obligation. In sum, the evidence suggests that psychological involvement—marked by interest in elec-

TABLE 5-5   Partisanship and Turnout in
the 1996 Presidential Election

Party identification	Percentage voting
Strong Democrat	86
Weak Democrat	69
Independent Democrat	70
Independent-Independent	55
Independent Republican	76
Weak Republican	80
Strong Republican	96

SOURCE: Center for Political Studies, University of Michigan.

NOTE: Actual turnout is lower than self-reported turnout.

tions, concern over their outcome, a sense of political efficacy, and a sense of citizen duty—increases the probability that a person will pay the costs in time and energy that voting requires.

The most interesting question concerning participation is the one for which empirical evidence is in shortest supply: Does who votes matter? Does it affect public policy outcomes? In all probability, yes. One bit of evidence is found in the research of Kim Quaile Hill and Jan E. Leighley, which found that where poor people have higher levels of turnout, welfare benefits are higher.[36] It is clear, moreover, "that individuals with high levels of socio-economic status, positive civic orientation, and appropriate political resources are more likely to participate than those without."[37] Hence, it is not much of a reach to believe that these advantaged elements have a much stronger claim than inactive citizens on the attention and dispositions of representatives.

Party Identification in the Electorate

Examining the distribution of party identification in the electorate from 1960 to 1996 is an interesting study in stability[38] and change (see Figure 5-4). Throughout most of this lengthy period, the proportion of persons identifying themselves as Democrats remained relatively stable.[39] In the usual survey from 1950 to 1992, between 40 and 48 percent of the respondents

FIGURE 5-4 The Distribution of Party Identification in the Electorate: 1960 to 1996

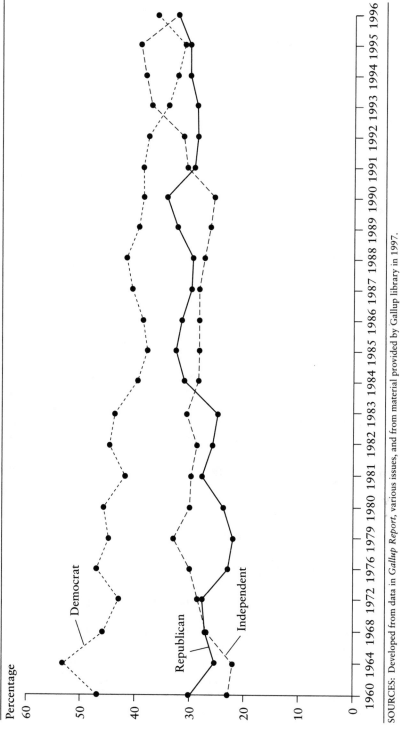

SOURCES: Developed from data in *Gallup Report*, various issues, and from material provided by Gallup library in 1997.

NOTE: Data for 1979 to 1996 are in one-year increments; this is not the case for the time span at the beginning of the figure.

TABLE 5-6   Party Identification, Selected Presidential Years:
1952 to 1996

Party identification	1952	1964	1980	1984	1988	1992	1996
Strong Democrat	22%	27%	18%	18%	17%	18%	19%
Weak Democrat	25	25	23	22	18	18	20
Independent Democrat	10	9	11	10	12	14	14
Independent-Independent	6	8	13	6	11	12	8
Independent Republican	7	6	10	13	13	12	11
Weak Republican	14	14	14	15	14	14	15
Strong Republican	14	11	9	14	14	11	13
Apolitical	3	1	2	2	1	1	1

SOURCE: Center for Political Studies, University of Michigan.

NOTE: Columns may not add to 100 because of rounding.

identified themselves as Democrats, with the remainder reflecting changing divisions between Republicans and independents.[40] At certain intervals during the 1960s and 1970s (but not in recent years), Democratic identifiers outnumbered Republican identifiers by a margin of two-to-one. (Data showing the intensity of party identification over time appear in Table 5-6.)

Of greater interest are the changes that have occurred in party identification, particularly of late. According to Gallup Polls, during the late 1970s only about 21 to 24 percent of the voters saw themselves as Republicans—the smallest proportion of Republican partisans since the first surveys were taken half a century ago. The election of Ronald Reagan was followed by a sharp increase in the number of Republican partisans, reaching 35 percent in early 1985 (to the Democrats' 37 percent), before settling back to 32 percent in 1986 (to the Democrats' 39 percent). In 1988, about the time of the election, the division between the parties was 42 to 30, with the Democrats still ahead. In 1992 Democratic identifiers led Republican identifiers by a margin of 38 percent to 29 percent. By 1996 voters professing to be Democrats outnumbered Republicans by a margin of only 36 percent to 32 percent.

An especially interesting change in partisan affiliation has occurred along racial lines. Since 1952 the commitment of black voters to the Democratic party has grown markedly. Current surveys disclose that about 70 percent of all blacks see themselves as Democrats, with independents outnumbering Republicans about two to one among the remainder. The overall growth in Republican identifiers in recent years is a result almost entirely of a shift of white voters, particularly in the South. As the data of Table 5-7

TABLE 5-7   Party Identification in the South,
by Race: 1996

Party identification	Black southerners	White southerners
Strong Democrat	43%	16%
Weak Democrat	23	19
Independent Democrat	13	11
Independent-Independent	11	8
Independent Republican	6	15
Weak Republican	2	17
Strong Republican	2	14

SOURCE: Center for Political Studies, University of Michigan.

show, white southern Republicans are not vastly outnumbered by white southern Democrats; black voters in the South, as in the North, identify overwhelmingly with the Democratic party.[41] Overall, the pattern of party identification in the South increasingly resembles that of the nation as a whole.

The party identification of members of religious groups has also undergone change. Jewish voters today are overwhelmingly identified with the Democratic party, but not to the same degree as in the 1970s. Catholic voters' identification has changed substantially. Catholics are much more likely to identify with the Republican party today than in the past; indeed, they are now split about evenly between the parties. But the most important shift has occurred among white Protestants, who constitute almost half of all voters in presidential elections. A clear majority now identifies with the Republican party. Among born-again Christians, the Republican party holds a huge advantage (see Table 5-8).

The most important change of all has been the growth in the number of persons who perceive themselves as independents.[42] In 1940 one out of five persons was classified as an independent; during the 1970s and 1980s the proportion was almost one in three. Current surveys show that independents ("leaners" and "pure") constitute between 32 and 38 percent of the electorate.[43] It is by no means an unusual survey that turns up more independents than either Democrats or Republicans. Many voters, moreover, change their party identification over a short period of time, thus contributing further to partisan instability.[44]

The evidence of recent elections confirms the proposition that independents hold the balance of power between the major parties. Republican pres-

TABLE 5-8   Party Identification, by Religion: 1978 and 1996

	1978		1996	
Religious group	D	R	D	R
Protestant	45	28	33	35
White evangelical Christian	—	—	25	42
Catholic	56	6	33	29
White Catholic	—	—	32	30
Jewish	64	10	56	15
Other	41	15	35	29
None	39	13	36	15

SOURCES: Data are drawn from surveys by the Gallup Organization as reported in *The Public Perspective* (October/November 1996): 28, and from a press release of The Pew Research Center for the People & The Press, August 7, 1996, 9.

NOTE: Data on party identification of born-again Christians and white Catholics unavailable for 1978.

idential candidates benefited from the support of independents in the 1980s, Democratic candidates from their support in the 1990s.

Declining partisanship can be detected throughout the electorate. The loyalty of older voters to the parties is not as firm as in the past. Of greater significance, many younger voters who entered the electorate as partisans have deserted their parties in favor of independence. But the most important factor in partisan dealignment has been the entry of new voters with low levels of partisanship. The new voters and the younger voters who have abandoned their partisan ties, one study shows, account for about 75 percent of the decline in partisanship in the electorate.[45] In sum, the broad picture is one of younger persons who are less partisan than their parents and hence more volatile in their voting behavior. As these younger voters succeed older ones, M. Kent Jennings and Gregory B. Markus observed, "the role of political parties in mass politics may be substantially redefined."[46]

The Significance of Party Identification

The distribution of underlying partisan loyalties in the electorate is an advantage for the Democratic party. Over most of the last four decades, the Democratic party has launched each national campaign (including that of 1992) with at least 60 percent of all partisans affiliated in one degree or another with it. When the party has received relatively strong support from those who identify themselves as Democrats and made a reasonably good showing among independents, it has won. The Republican party has faced a more formidable task. It has had to hold its own partisans, carry a major share of the independents, and attract a significant number of Democrats. One factor that has helped Republicans to win is that the turnout rate of Democratic partisans is always lower than that of Republicans.[47]

Despite its electoral disadvantage, the Republican party has done remarkably well in presidential elections, beginning with the election of Dwight D. Eisenhower in 1952. In 1956 one out of four Democrats and three out of four independents joined a united Republican party to reelect Eisenhower by a comfortable margin. Following the Kennedy and Johnson interlude, Republicans again captured the presidency with Richard Nixon's narrow victory in 1968 and his decisive reelection in 1972. The predictive value of party identification suffered again in the presidential elections of the 1980s when Reagan and Bush both won comfortably despite the Democrats' advantage in party identification. In a reversal of fortunes, Clinton won in 1992 and 1996 by running stronger among Democrats than Bush and Dole did among Republicans and by winning the independent vote. Nevertheless, the Republican party has won seven out of the last twelve presidential elections and five out of the last eight.

In three respects, party identification is less important today than it was several decades ago. First, fewer persons now choose to identify with a party. During the 1950s and early 1960s, nearly 80 percent of all persons classified themselves as either Democrats or Republicans. During the 1980s, the proportion hovered around 70 to 72 percent. In the 1990s it fell below 70 percent. Second, the proportion of strong partisans in the nation has declined, particularly in the Democratic party. Less than one third of all voters now profess to be strong, rain-or-shine partisans. And third, in a period of weakened party ties, the influence of party identification on voting is less pronounced, though it is by no means inconsequential.

Although party identification is less significant today in explaining voter decisions, it remains the best single explanation of voters' decisions on candidates.[48] Most voters support the candidates of the party with which they identify. In 1996, for example, 97 percent of white voters describing themselves as strong Democrats voted for Clinton, whereas only 4 percent of white strong Republicans did.[49] Ordinarily, in presidential elections, about 80 percent of party identifiers vote for their own party's candidate, and in congressional elections party-line voters make up 70 to 75 percent of the electorate (see Table 5-9 for evidence from the past two decades). First, Democratic victories in congressional elections year in and year out are due in no small degree to the party's superior position in party affiliation. Second, party loyalty is closely associated with political involvement. Strong partisans are more likely than weak partisans or independents to be inter-

The Voting Behavior of Independents . . .

	1964		1968		1972		1976	
	D	R	D	R	D	R	D	R
National vote	61%	39%	43%	43.4%	38%	62%	50%	48%
Independents	56	44	31	44	31	69	38	57

SOURCES: Developed from data in *Gallup Report,* November 1988, 6–7; for 1992, Voter Research and Surveys, as reported in *New York Times,* November 5, 1992.

The American public is composed of partisans, independents, and apoliticals. The number of independents has grown significantly in recent decades. All candidates and political analysts take them seriously today, and much more is known about their behavior.

Independents are a varied lot. They are not simply civic misfits who reside on the outskirts of politics, as they have sometimes been portrayed. Like other citizens, independents are both attentive and inattentive to politics, involved in elections and indifferent to them, well informed and uninformed, ideological and nonideological. There are "pure" independents, whose voting behavior is especially volatile, and "leaners," who tilt toward one party or the other and whose voting behavior resembles that of partisans. Typically, almost one third of the electorate classifies itself as independent, with leaners much more numerous than the pure variety. Whites are twice as likely to be independents as blacks.

Independents like winners, independents produce winners, or both. In eight of the nine presidential elections between 1964 and 1996, independents voted on the side of the winner and contributed substantially to these victories. But in 1976 independents voted decisively for Ford over Carter.

ested in political campaigns, to vote, and to express concern over election outcomes. Third, and most important, despite the overall decline in party identification, it continues to be salient for a great many voters (especially older ones), serving to orient them to candidates, issues, and political events and to simplify and order their political choices.[50]

Party Identification and National Election Outcomes

Traditionally, presidential elections have been classified in broad contour by examining the relationship between election outcomes and the pattern of

... in Presidential Elections: 1964 to 1996

1980		1984		1988		1992			1996		
D	R	D	R	D	R	D	R	Perot	D	R	Perot
41%	51%	41%	59%	46%	54%	43%	37%	19%	49%	41%	9%
29	55	33	67	43	57	38	32	30	43	37	16

NOTE: D = Democrat; R = Republican.

When the nation has favored a Republican candidate for president (and with no third party or independent candidates in the race), independents have voted for him emphatically—averaging about 7 percent more Republican than the national average (elections of 1956, 1972, 1980, 1984, and 1988). "Hidden" Republicans among self-identified independents are apparently more numerous than "hidden" Democrats. In the nine presidential elections between 1964 and 1996, independents favored the Democratic candidate only twice (1992 and 1996).

Independents are more likely than partisans to vote for a non-major party candidate. In 1968, 25 percent of all independents voted for George C. Wallace, presidential candidate of the American Independent party. In 1980, 14 percent of independents voted for the self-styled independent candidate John B. Anderson, a former Republican representative from Illinois who began his presidential quest in Republican presidential primaries. And in 1992, 30 percent of independents voted for Ross Perot, almost as many as voted for George Bush. Perot received 16 percent of the vote of independents in 1996.

party loyalties present in the electorate. Three basic types of elections have been identified: *maintaining, deviating,* and *realigning.*[51] A maintaining election is described as one in which the pattern of party attachments in the electorate fixes the outcome; the winning party owes its victory to the fact that more voters identify with it than with any other party. A deviating election, by contrast, is one in which existing party loyalties are temporarily displaced by short-term forces, enabling the minority (or second) party to win the presidency. In a realigning election the majority party in the electorate not only loses the election but also finds that many of its previous supporters have abandoned their loyalties and moved into the ranks of the other party.

TABLE 5-9   Party-Line Voting in Presidential and House Elections: 1972 to 1994

	Presidential elections			House elections		
Year	Party-line voters[a]	De-fectors[b]	Pure inde-pendents[c]	Party-line voters[a]	De-fectors[b]	Pure inde-pendents[c]
1972	67	25	8	75	17	8
1974				74	18	8
1976	74	15	11	72	19	9
1978				69	22	9
1980	70	22	8	69	23	8
1982				76	17	6
1984	81	12	7	70	23	7
1986				72	22	6
1988	81	12	7	74	20	7
1990				72	22	5
1992	68	24	9	70	22	8
1994				77	17	6

SOURCE: Norman J. Ornstein, Thomas E. Mann, and Michael J. Malbin, *Vital Statistics on Congress, 1995–1996* (Washington, D.C.: CQ Inc., 1996), 74 (as adapted).

NOTE: Figures are a percentage of all voters. Percentages may not add to 100 because of rounding.

[a]Party identifiers who vote for the candidate of their party.
[b]Party identifiers who vote for the candidate of the other party.
[c]The SRC/CPS National Election Surveys use a seven-point scale to define party identification, including three categories of independents—those who "lean" to one or the other party and those who are "pure" independents. The "leaners" are included here among the party-line voters. Party identification here means self-identification as determined by surveys.

So fundamental is the transformation of partisan affiliation that the second party becomes the majority party.

From a historical perspective, the most common form of presidential election has been that in which the party dominant in the electorate wins the presidency—that is, a maintaining election. The dynamics of a maintaining election are furnished by the majority party; the minority party loses because it has been unable to develop either issues or candidates sufficiently attractive to upset the prevailing pattern of party affiliation. Most of the Republican victories during the last half of the nineteenth century and the first quarter of the twentieth century would be classified as maintaining elections. Recent elections of this type occurred in 1948, 1960, 1964, 1976, 1992, and

Split-Ticket Voting and Split-Party Victories

Declining partisanship in the electorate is a paramount fact of contemporary American politics. Candidate organizations, rather than party organizations, now dominate most campaigns for office at all levels of government. Another result of the declining salience of party in the electorate has been an increase in split-ticket voting and split-party victories.

Year	Number of states electing governor and senator at same time	Number of states electing governor and senator of different parties	Percentage of split victories
1950	19	3	16
1952	20	6	30
1954	25	5	20
1970	23	11	48
1972	12	6	50
1974	26	11	42
1976	10	3	30
1978	24	10	42
1980	9	5	56
1982	22	6	27
1984	7	3	43
1986	26	11	42
1988	10	4	40
1990	25	14	56
1992	8	4	50
1994	23	11	48
1996	5	4	80

SOURCES: Data drawn from Richard M. Scammon, ed., *America Votes 1* (New York: Macmillan, 1956); and various issues of *Congressional Quarterly Weekly Report*.

Change and Continuity . . .

Ninety-two million individuals cast ballots in the 1988 presidential election, 104 million in 1992, and 96 million in 1996. Their voting decisions were influenced by their independent judgments, political party affiliation, and membership in various groups.

The most important factor in voter decisions is political party affiliation. Although the impact of party identification on voting behavior is clearly less significant today than it was several decades ago, it is nevertheless true that about two out of three Americans still hold attachments to the Democratic or Republican party. The great majority of these partisans vote in keeping with their identification. Party has declined but not disappeared in the voting calculus.

Group membership historically has also had a major effect on voting. Each party has been distinguished by group-based loyalties. The Republican party has carried special appeal for upper-income groups, whereas the Democratic party has appealed to the relatively disadvantaged in the process of assembling a coalition of minorities. Today, these loyalties are in flux. The accompanying graphs reflect the voting behavior of key groups in the Democratic and Republican coalitions over the past forty-four years. As a vote predictor, group membership, like party identification, is less reliable than in the past.

Social class does not explain much about voting behavior in the presidential elections of the current era. Voters from the ranks of the professions and business do not vote Republican much more than the national Republican average; manual workers are less committed to the Democratic party than they once were.

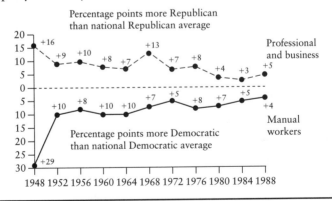

Percentage points more Republican than national Republican average

Professional and business

Percentage points more Democratic than national Democratic average

Manual workers

... in Voting Behavior

Nor does Catholic or Protestant religious affiliation. The voting behavior of Catholics and Protestants is becoming increasingly similar, with Catholics showing much less Democratic preference, and Protestants somewhat less Republican.

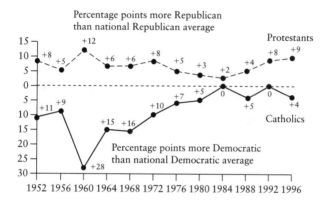

But blacks and Jews continue to have a distinct preference for Democratic presidential candidates.

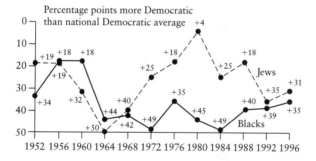

SOURCES: Calculated from data in *Gallup Report,* November 1988, 7; and *New York Times*/CBS News poll, as reported in *New York Times,* November 10, 1988. For social class vote in 1948, see Robert R. Alford, *Party and Society* (Chicago: Rand McNally, 1963), 352. Data on Jewish vote, for 1952–1968, drawn from Mark R. Levy and Michael S. Kramer, *The Ethnic Factor* (New York: Simon and Schuster, 1972), 103; for 1972–1980, Robert J. Huckshorn, *Political Parties in America* (Monterey, Calif.: Brooks/Cole, 1984), 214; for 1988, *New York Times*/CBS News poll; and for 1992 and 1996, Voter Research and Surveys.

NOTE: In 1980, 14 percent of the Jewish vote was cast for John B. Anderson.

1996. The 1976 election is of special interest. Following a period of party decline, party affiliation assumed much of its earlier importance, as a significantly larger proportion of party identifiers cast votes in agreement with their affiliations. As Warren E. Miller and Teresa E. Levitan observed, "the 1976 election was as much a party election as those elections from the 1950s or early 1960s in which party was acknowledged to be a major determinant of voters' decisions."[52]

Deviating elections are those in which the party that occupies minority status in terms of electoral preferences wins the presidential office. Although the Republicans held an electoral majority in the early twentieth century, Democrat Woodrow Wilson was twice elected president—in 1912, when the Republican party was split between Theodore Roosevelt and William Howard Taft, and in 1916, when Wilson's incumbency and the war issue were sufficient to give him a slight edge. More recent examples are the elections of 1952, 1956, 1968, 1972, 1980, and 1984. Similarly, Democrats were clearly ahead in party identification in 1988 when George Bush defeated Michael Dukakis by a margin of 54 to 46 percent. Despite the appeal of the minority party's presidential candidate, the coattail effect rarely has been strong enough to give the candidate's party control of Congress. Hence, deviating elections are likely to result in control of the presidency by one party and control of Congress by the other.

The familiar terrain of American politics is sharply changed as a result of realigning elections. Large numbers of voters move out of the majority party and into the minority party, switching not only their vote but their party allegiance. Major changes in public policy are likely to result.[53] The most recent examples of realigning elections are those of 1896 and 1932. In the former, a great many Democrats left their party following the financial panic of 1893, voted for William McKinley in 1896, and became part of the strong Republican majority that dominated the country until 1932. An even sharper upheaval in the electorate occurred in the election of 1932, when the normal Republican majority collapsed as a result of the Great Depression. Franklin D. Roosevelt was swept into office, and millions of Republicans shifted into the ranks of the Democratic party. And even more important, the new voters entering the electorate during the realignment era were predominantly Democratic.[54]

Based on party identification, the categories of elections currently are less useful in analyzing presidential elections than they are in analyzing congressional and subnational elections. In the first place, for many voters party identification has lost its saliency.[55] And second, voters' evaluations of presidential candidates have increasingly focused on personality characteristics rather than on parties or issues. Thus in judging presidential contenders, a study suggests, many people use broad categories, assessing candidates in terms of competence (political experience, ability, intelligence), integrity (honesty, sincerity, trustworthiness), reliability (dependability, productivity, decisiveness), charisma (leadership, dignity, ability to communicate and inspire), and personal features (age, health, smile, religion, and the like). By far the most important of these dimensions is competence, followed by integrity and reliability.[56] For voters who use the personality mode of organizing information about candidates, in the process of making assessments of them, party identification is obviously of slight significance.

Voting in presidential and other elections can also be examined in terms of prospective and retrospective perspectives. In prospective voting, voters consider the platforms, policy positions, and promises of the candidates and seek to assess which one is closest to their own view of what is important and what should be done. They then vote accordingly.[57] In retrospective voting, a less demanding form of evaluation, voters simply judge how well things have been going—how well the party or incumbent has done in the past—and vote accordingly. Incumbents (or the parties or both) are rewarded if they have been successful and punished if they have been unsuccessful. Thus Jimmy Carter was defeated in 1980 primarily because voters evaluated his performance as largely unsatisfactory.[58] Ronald Reagan was reelected in 1984 primarily because of positive retrospective evaluations of his administration. George Bush's election in 1988 undoubtedly owed a great deal to the voters' favorable assessment of the Reagan administration; according to an ABC News exit poll, 93 percent of the voters supporting Bush indicated that they "wanted to keep to the Reagan course."[59] And in his bid for reelection in 1992, Bush lost, in large part, because three out of four voters judged the economy to be in serious trouble. Satisfied with the status quo and with the incumbent's embrace of middle-of-the-road principles, the voters returned Bill Clinton to office in 1996, but to be on the safe side, gave him a Republican Congress. The evidence is persuasive that retrospective voting has played a major role in all recent elections.[60] Interestingly, partisanship is closely related to retrospective evaluations.[61]

The Voting Behavior of Social Groups

The role of social groups needs to be examined in explaining the behavior of the American electorate.[62] It has long been known that the voting behavior of individuals is influenced not only by their personal values[63] and predilections but also by their affiliations with social groups.[64]

The most important conclusion to be drawn from an examination of the relationships between social categories and voting behavior over several decades is that each party has enjoyed a set of relatively loyal followings within the electorate—at least until recently. In most elections since the New Deal, the Democratic party has received strong, sometimes overwhelming, support from the poor, members of the working class, union households, blacks, Catholics, Jews, voters with limited formal education, central-city voters, and younger voters. In contrast, the Republican party has received disproportionate support from the nonpoor, nonunion families, whites, Protestants, voters with college educations and professional and business backgrounds, white-collar workers, older voters, and voters from outside central cities. Additionally, in recent elections gender has become a more important factor, with women tilting toward the Democrats, men toward the Republicans. Overall, these party-group linkages have contributed something to the continuity and stability of the political system. (See Table 5-10 for group voting patterns since 1980.)

Yet voting patterns are not static. The Democrats' majority status in the electorate is less imposing now than in the past. Split-ticket voting is widespread. An extraordinary number of voters ignore elections altogether. And the Democrats' hold on the groups composing the New Deal coalition has eased.[65] In the presidential elections of the 1980s, blue-collar workers, younger voters, members of labor union families, and Catholics became more supportive of the Republican party. The shift of white southerners to the Republican party, which began earlier, has been pronounced.

The election of 1992 reversed the voting patterns of the 1980s. In a three-way race, Bill Clinton won a modest popular-vote victory by carrying states in every region; by doing especially well among blacks, Hispanics, Jews, union families, and lower income voters; and by receiving stronger support from Catholics, younger and older voters, women, and independents than had Walter Mondale or Michael Dukakis. He was comfortably reelected in 1996 by again doing well among these groups, and especially among women, Hispanics, Catholics, blacks, and union families.

The broad point of this analysis is that loyalties and group ties to the parties have become attenuated, particularly in presidential elections. Some longstanding religious, regional, and class differences between the parties have weakened or disappeared. Political affiliation for many voters is casual at best, and for some simply irrelevant. An electorate distinguished by deep-rooted group loyalties is a thing of the past. Whatever else may be said about the present condition, it clearly indicates party dealignment and electoral volatility.

What do these changes mean for the future of American politics and parties? Is the nation now in the process of a critical realignment that will culminate in the transformation of the party system, or is the present

TABLE 5-10   Vote by Groups in Presidential Elections: 1980 to 1996

	1980			1984		1988		1992			1996		
	D	R	Anderson	D	R	D	R	D	R	Perot	D	R	Perot
National	41%	51%	7%	41%	59%	46%	54%	43%	37%	19%	49%	41%	8%
Men	38	53	7	36	64	44	56	41	38	21	43	44	10
Women	44	49	6	45	55	48	52	46	37	17	54	38	7
White	36	56	7	34	66	41	59	39	41	20	43	46	9
Black	85	11	3	90	9	86	12	82	11	7	84	12	4
Hispanic	59	33	6	62	37	69	30	62	25	14	72	21	6
Under 30 years old	47	41	11	40	60	37	63	44	34	22	53	34	10
30–49 years old	38	52	8	40	60	45	55	43	35	17	48	41	9
Age 50 and over	41	54	4	41	59	49	51	46	37	11	48	42	8
White Protestant	31	63	6	27	72	32	66	33	46	21	36	53	10
Catholic	42	50	7	45	54	47	52	44	36	20	53	37	9
Jewish	45	39	15	67	31	64	35	78	12	10	78	16	3
White born-again Christian	33	63	3	22	78	18	81	23	61	15	26	65	8
Republicans	8	86	5	4	96	7	93	11	72	18	13	80	6
Democrats	69	26	4	79	21	85	15	78	10	13	84	10	5
Independents	29	55	14	33	67	43	57	39	31	30	43	35	17
East	43	47	9	46	54	51	49	47	35	18	55	34	9
Midwest	41	51	7	42	58	47	53	42	37	21	48	41	10
South	44	52	3	37	63	40	60	42	43	16	46	46	7
West	35	54	9	40	60	46	54	44	34	22	48	40	8
Members of labor union families	50	43	5	52	48	63	37	55	24	21	69	30	9

SOURCES: *Gallup Report*, November 1988, 6–7; *New York Times*, November 10, 1988; Voter Research and Surveys, as reported in *New York Times*, November 5, 1992; Voter News Service exit poll, as reported in *New York Times*, November 10, 1996.

condition merely a state of dealignment that might persist on a long-term basis (without leading to a new and durable partisan alignment)?[66]

That is a hard question to answer. But several general observations can be made. First, scholars themselves do not agree on the answer; nor do politicians. Second, it helps to remember that "we cannot be sure that realignment has occurred until after it has ended."[67] Third, the Republican party has shown that it stands a good chance of winning presidential elections, irrespective of its trailing position in party identification, and that control of Congress is also within its reach. Despite three impressive victories by Reagan and Bush in the 1980s, the Republican party never gained a "lock" on the presidency. And it is hard to imagine that the Democrats can do so either. No administration or party can elude responsibility for things that appear to go wrong at a time when many problems are intractable, if not insoluble, and when the media focus tirelessly on dislocations, perceived policy failures, and other bad news.

Probably the best guess about the electoral future, or at least its near future, calls for a continuation of the dealignment process—marked by loose ties between the public and the parties; voter ambivalence and suspicion; and voting behavior that reflects ticket-splitting,[68] a preference for incumbents in legislative elections, a vulnerability to populist and reformist pitches and pitch people, and an inclination to switch parties without giving it a second thought. Faithful to this pattern, voting decisions are likely to be heavily influenced by voter inferences concerning presidential candidates' qualities (resolute leadership, empathy, trustworthiness), beguiling valence issues, and voters' retrospective appraisals of the performance and success of presidents, administrations, and parties in promoting the nation's well-being and the well-being of key interests close to home. Nothing in this picture suggests the emergence of tidy and predictable politics.

Notes

1. Patrick J. Kenney, "Explaining Primary Turnout: The Senatorial Case," *Legislative Studies Quarterly 11* (February 1986): 65–73. Also see Malcolm E. Jewell, "Northern State Gubernatorial Primary Elections: Explaining Voter Turnout," *American Politics Quarterly 12* (January 1984): 101–116; and Malcolm E. Jewell and David M. Olson, *American State Political Parties and Elections* (Homewood, Ill.: Dorsey Press, 1982). Several studies deal with the question of whether election night forecasts decrease turnout: Raymond E. Wolfinger and Peter Linquiti, "Tuning In and Tuning Out," *Public Opinion 4* (February/March 1981): 56–60; John E. Jackson, "Election Night Reporting and Voter Turnout," *American Journal of Political Science 27* (November 1983): 615–635; and Michael X.

Delli Carpini, "Scooping the Voters?: The Consequences of the Networks' Early Call of the 1980 Presidential Race," *Journal of Politics* 46 (August 1984): 866–885.

2. The white primary in southern states resulted from the exclusion of blacks from membership in the Democratic party, which was held to be a private organization. Because the real election at this time in most southern states occurred in the Democratic primaries, blacks had little opportunity to make their influence felt. After many years of litigation, the Supreme Court in 1944 held that the white primary was in violation of the Fifteenth Amendment. The Court's position in *Smith v. Allwright* was that the primary is an integral part of the election process and that political parties are engaged in a public, not a private, function in holding primary elections. After the white primary was held unconstitutional, southern states turned to the development of literacy and understanding tests, along with discriminatory registration systems, to bar black access to the polls.

3. E. E. Schattschneider, *The Semisovereign People* (New York: Holt, Rinehart and Winston, 1975), 78–80.

4. Ibid., 84.

5. See a study of gender differences in voting behavior by Susan Welch and John Hibbing, "Financial Conditions, Gender, and Voting in American National Elections," *Journal of Politics* 54 (February 1992): 197–213. Welch and Hibbing found that men are more likely than women to cast egocentric economic votes (voting in terms of their own economic interests). By contrast, women are more likely than men to behave sociotropically—voting in terms of their perceptions of the nation's best interest rather than their own or their family's economic well-being.

6. Mark J. Fenster, "The Impact of Allowing Day of Registration Voting on Turnout in U.S. Elections from 1960 to 1992," *American Politics Quarterly* 22 (January 1994): 74–87. Fenster estimated that if all states permitted day-of-registration voting, turnout would increase by 5 percent.

7. Steven J. Rosenstone and Raymond E. Wolfinger, "The Effect of Registration Laws on Voter Turnout," *American Political Science Review* 72 (March 1978): especially 25–30. The most facilitative laws on closing dates, apart from North Dakota, which requires no registration, are those of Idaho and Vermont. Voters in these states may register as late as three days before the election. Maine provides for eight days and New Hampshire for nine.

8. Staci L. Rhine, "Registration Reform and Turnout Change in the American States," *American Politics Quarterly* 23 (October 1995): 409–426. Also see Staci L. Rhine, "An Analysis of the Impact of Registration Factors on Turnout in 1992," *Political Behavior* 18 (No. 2): 171–185, and Daniel P. Franklin and Eric B. Grier, "Effects of Motor Voter Legislation," *American Politics Quarterly* 25 (January 1997): 104–117.

9. Rhine, "Registration Reform and Turnout Change in the American States," 422.

10. See a study by Jonathan Nagler that found that persons with limited education are no more likely to be deterred from voting by restrictive registration laws than persons with substantial education: "The Effect of Registration Laws and Education on U.S. Voter Turnout," *American Political Science Review* 85 (December 1991): 1393–1405.

11. Curtis B. Gans, "A Rejoinder to Piven and Cloward," *PS* 23 (June 1990): 176–178.

12. Peverill Squire, Raymond E. Wolfinger, and David P. Glass, "Residential Mobil-

ity and Voter Turnout," *American Political Science Review 81* (March 1987): 45–65. The authors propose that change-of-address notices left with post offices be modified to permit movers to shift their voting address (as well as their mail) to their new residence. Using these forms, registration officials would automatically reregister the individual at the new address. With mobility no longer a factor in turnout, according to the authors' estimate, participation would increase by 9 percentage points.

13. *Pittsburgh Press,* July 9, 1990.
14. Recent research by Michael M. Gant and William Lyons, covering five presidential elections, shows that although voters are more likely than nonvoters to form preferences based on policy grounds, the two groups differ very little in their preferences for president. The failure to vote therefore does not affect policy outcomes. See their article, "Democratic Theory, Nonvoting, and Public Policy: The 1972–1988 Presidential Elections," *American Politics Quarterly 21* (April 1993): 185–204.
15. See Paul R. Abramson and John H. Aldrich, "The Decline of Electoral Participation in America," *American Political Science Review 76* (September 1982): 502–521.
16. Ibid., 504–510.
17. For a study that finds alienation to be a major factor in nonvoting, see Priscilla L. Southwell, "Alienation and Nonvoting in the United States: A Refined Operationalization," *Western Political Quarterly 38* (December 1985): 663–674.
18. On the relationship between frequent elections and turnout, see the research of Richard W. Boyd, "Decline of U.S. Voter Turnout: Structural Explanations," *American Politics Quarterly 9* (April 1981): 133–160; "Election Calendars and Voter Turnout," *American Politics Quarterly 14* (January–April 1986): 89–104; and "The Effects of Primaries and Statewide Races on Voter Turnout," *Journal of Politics 51* (August 1989): 730–739.
19. Richard A. Brody, "The Puzzle of Political Participation in America," in *The New American Political System,* ed. Anthony King (Washington, D.C.: American Enterprise Institute for Public Policy Research, 1978), 306.
20. G. Bingham Powell, Jr., "American Voter Turnout in Comparative Perspective," *American Political Science Review 80* (March 1986): 17–43.
21. Why do close elections increase turnout? One explanation is that ordinary citizens are more likely to participate in close elections because they believe their vote will make a difference. A second possibility is that turnout increases because the closeness of any election prompts elites (candidates and their financial supporters) to focus on getting voters to the polls (thus stimulating campaign expenditures). A recent study by Gary W. Cox and Michael C. Munger finds that closeness of elections affects behavior at both mass and elite levels. "Closeness, Expenditures, and Turnout in the 1982 U.S. Elections," *American Political Science Review 83* (March 1989): 217–231. Also see Kenneth D. Wald, "The Closeness-Turnout Hypothesis: A Reconsideration," *American Politics Quarterly 13* (July 1985): 273–296. Along the same line, Priscilla L. Southwell found that shifts in economic performance can have a mobilizing effect on turnout, particularly among less privileged individuals and groups. "Economic Salience and Differential Abstention in Presidential Elections," *American Politics Quarterly 24* (April 1996): 221–236.
22. *Shaw v. Reno,* 113 S. Ct. 2816 (1993).
23. *Miller v. Johnson,* 115 S. Ct. 2486 (1995).

24. *Shaw v. Hunt,* 116 S. Ct. 1894 (1996); *Bush v. Vera,* 116 S. Ct. 1941 (1996).
25. *Bush v. Vera,* 116 S. Ct. 1941 (1996).
26. The findings of these paragraphs are drawn from Sidney Verba and Norman H. Nie, *Participation in America: Political Democracy and Social Equality* (New York: Harper and Row, 1972), 25–43.
27. Lester W. Milbrath, *Political Participation* (Chicago: Rand McNally, 1965), 17–21. The holding that political participation involves a hierarchy of political acts—under which the citizen who performs a difficult political act, such as forming an organization to solve a local community problem, is virtually certain to perform less demanding acts—can be overstated. See Verba and Nie, *Participation in America,* especially Chapters 2 and 3. Their general position is that "the citizenry is not divided simply into more or less active citizens. Rather there are many types of activists engaging in different acts, with different motives, and different consequences." Quotation on p. 45.
28. For a study of political canvassing, see Peter W. Wielhouwer, "Strategic Canvassing by Political Parties, 1952–1990," *American Review of Politics 16* (Fall 1995): 213–238. A study of the various forms of voter contact and their relative effectiveness in influencing vote choice is available in Christopher Kenny and Michael McBurnett, "Up Close and Personal: Campaign Contact and Candidate Spending in U.S. House Elections," *Political Research Quarterly 50* (March 1997): 75–96.
29. Although the turnout of the highest income group exceeds that of the lowest income group by about 20 percentage points in the typical presidential election, there has been little change in socioeconomic class bias in the electorate since 1964. The only exception was in 1988 (Bush v. Dukakis), when class bias in turnout did increase. See Jan E. Leighley and Jonathan Nagler, "Socioeconomic Class Bias in Turnout, 1964–1988: The Voters Remain the Same," *American Political Science Review 86* (September 1992): 725–736.
30. See Verba and Nie, *Participation in America,* 133–137.
31. See Jan E. Leighley and Jonathan Nagler, "Individual and Systemic Influences on Turnout: Who Votes? 1984," *Journal of Politics 54* (August 1992): 718–740.
32. Robert A. Jackson, "Clarifying the Relationship between Education and Turnout," *American Politics Quarterly 23* (July 1995): 279–299.
33. In information-poor environments, such as House elections, voters tend to rely on prior beliefs concerning the closeness of elections in making their decisions on whether to vote. Stephen P. Nicholson and Ross A. Miller, "Prior Beliefs and Voter Turnout in the 1986 and 1988 Congressional Elections," *Political Research Quarterly 50* (March 1997): 199–213.
34. The Mellman Group and Wirthlin Worldwide, *Analysis of a Survey on Nonvoting* (Washington, D.C.: The League of Women Voters, 1996), 25.
35. See a study by David Moon that finds that voters with high levels of information are more likely to rely on issues in deciding how to vote than voters who have moderate or low levels of information. "What You Use Still Depends on What You Have: Information Effects in Presidential Elections, 1972–1988," *American Politics Quarterly 20* (October 1992): 427–441.
36. Kim Quaile Hill and Jan E. Leighley, "The Policy Consequences of Class Bias in State Electorates," *American Journal of Political Science 36* (May 1992): 351–365.
37. Jan E. Leighley, "Attitudes, Opportunities and Incentives: A Field Essay in Political Participation," *Political Research Quarterly 48* (March 1995): 181–209.

38. For interesting evidence on the stability of partisan balance in party identification, see Warren E. Miller, "Party Identification, Realignment, and Party Voting: Back to the Basics," *American Political Science Review 85* (June 1991): 557–568.

39. The aggregate stability of partisanship over the years masks the existence of considerable short-term, individual-level change in party identification that stems from economic influences, particularly inflation and unemployment, and variations in presidential popularity. See Herbert F. Weisberg and Charles E. Smith, Jr., "The Influence of the Economy on Party Identification in the Reagan Years," *Journal of Politics 53* (November 1991): 1077–1092.

40. For an analysis of the phenomenon of independence in the United States, the various categories of independence, and what it means to be an independent, see two articles by Jack Dennis, "Political Independence in America, Part I: On Being an Independent Partisan Supporter," and "Political Independence in America, Part II: Towards a Theory," in *British Journal of Political Science 18* (January 1988, April 1988): 77–110, 197–219.

41. For a study of the attitudinal and demographic variables linked to black political participation, see Katherine Tate, "Black Political Participation in the 1984 and 1988 Presidential Elections," *American Political Science Review 85* (December 1991): 1159–1176. Tate finds that black participation is volatile and closely related to the context of a particular election. Black office seeking does not necessarily produce heightened turnout among blacks.

42. For a view that strengthened partisanship within the electorate depends on convincing people that the two parties are different in policy orientations and that these differences affect peoples' well-being, see Patrick R. Cotter, "The Decline of Partisanship: A Test of Four Explanations," *American Politics Quarterly 13* (January 1985): 51–78.

43. A central reason for the high proportion of independents is that independence has been transmitted to offspring more efficiently than partisanship. See Franco Mattei and Richard G. Niemi, "Unrealized Partisans, Realized Independents, and the Intergenerational Transmission of Partisan Identification," *Journal of Politics 53* (February 1991): 161–174.

44. *The Public Perspective,* October/November 1996, 52–54.

45. Helmut Norpoth and Jerrold G. Rusk, "Partisan Dealignment in the American Electorate: Itemizing the Deductions since 1964," *American Political Science Review 76* (September 1982): 522–537.

46. M. Kent Jennings and Gregory B. Markus, "Partisan Orientations over the Long Haul: Results from the Three-Wave Political Socialization Panel Study," *American Political Science Review 78* (December 1984): 1000–1018 (quotation on p. 1016). See an analysis of young adults that suggests that they are active in adjusting their partisan affiliation to coincide with their views on preferred policies: Charles H. Franklin, "Issue Preferences, Socialization, and the Evolution of Party Identification," *American Journal of Political Science 28* (August 1984): 459–478.

47. A disposition to participate in elections is related to high interest, information, and involvement. The Democratic vote regularly suffers because citizens who might be expected to vote Democratic—those in the lower socioeconomic strata—are often not sufficiently interested or involved in the election to turn out on election day. See the persuasive evidence of Benjamin Radcliff that greater turnout increases the size of the Democratic vote. "This [turnout] effect is rea-

sonably pronounced. It is sufficient to alter the outcome of any but the most uncompetitive of recent presidential elections." "Turnout and the Democratic Vote," *American Politics Quarterly 22* (July 1994): 259–276.

48. For evidence on the significance of party identification for different offices over time, see Stephen D. Shaffer, "Voting in Four Elective Offices: A Comparative Analysis," *American Politics Quarterly 10* (January 1982): 5–30.

49. SRC/CPS National Election Survey, 1996.

50. Scholars differ over the relative stability of party identification. Some find considerable fluctuation, whereas others find little. Nevertheless, it is clear that a great many voters never change their party identification. When change does occur, it is usually reflected in the intensity of loyalty to party—moving, say, from strong Democrat to weak Democrat—rather than in a switch of parties. See Tom W. Rice and Tracey A. Hilton, "Partisanship over Time: A Comparison of United States Panel Data," *Political Research Quarterly 49* (March 1996): 191–201.

51. Angus Campbell, Philip E. Converse, Warren E. Miller, and Donald E. Stokes, *The American Voter* (New York: Wiley, 1960), 531–538.

52. Warren E. Miller and Teresa E. Levitan, *Leadership and Change: Presidential Elections from 1952 to 1976* (Cambridge, Mass.: Winthrop, 1976), 211.

53. The major effect of a realignment, David W. Brady argues, is the creation of a unified majority party in Congress that is capable of bringing about significant changes in public policy. See David W. Brady, "A Reevaluation of Realignments in American Politics: Evidence from the House of Representatives," *American Political Science Review 79* (March 1985): 28–49; David W. Brady and Joseph Stewart, Jr., "Congressional Party Realignment and Transformations of Public Policy in Three Realignment Eras," *American Journal of Political Science 26* (May 1982): 333–360; and Barbara Sinclair, "Party Realignment and the Transformation of the Political Agenda: The House of Representatives, 1925–1938," *American Political Science Review 71* (September 1977): 940–953.

54. James E. Campbell, "Sources of the New Deal Realignment: The Contributions of Conversion and Mobilization to Partisan Change," *Western Political Quarterly 38* (September 1985): 357–376.

55. It is interesting to find that partisan defectors (those who identify with one party but vote for the other party's presidential candidate) are much more likely to cast a negative or anticandidate vote than persons who vote in keeping with their party identification. See Michael M. Gant and Lee Sigelman, "Anti-Candidate Voting in Presidential Elections," *Polity 18* (Winter 1985): 329–339.

56. Arthur H. Miller, Martin P. Wattenberg, and Oksana Malanchuk, "Schematic Assessments of Presidential Candidates," *American Political Science Review 80* (June 1986): 521–540. Interestingly, college-educated voters place particular emphasis on these characteristics. Party competence evaluations are also important in explaining the congressional vote. See Albert D. Cover, "Party Competence Evaluations and Voting for Congress," *Western Political Quarterly 39* (June 1986): 304–312.

57. For interesting evidence that voters look to the future (prospective voting, independent of party affiliation) as well as to the past, see Brad Lockerbie, "Prospective Voting in Presidential Elections, 1956–1988," *American Politics Quarterly 20* (July 1992): 308–325; and Michael B. MacKuen, Robert S. Erikson, and James A. Stimson, "Peasants or Bankers? The American Electorate and the U.S. Economy," *American Political Science Review 86* (September 1992): 597–611.

58. President Carter's relations with Congress were also unsatisfactory. See Charles O. Jones, "Keeping Faith and Losing Congress: The Carter Experience in Washington," *Presidential Studies Quarterly 14* (Summer 1984): 437–445.
59. *Washington Post,* November 9, 1988.
60. Retrospective voting is also a significant factor in vote choice in presidential primaries. See Fred M. Monardi, "Primary Voters as Retrospective Voters," *American Politics Quarterly 22* (January 1994): 88–103.
61. See Morris P. Fiorina, *Retrospective Voting in American National Elections* (New Haven, Conn.: Yale University Press, 1981).
62. The significance of social groups in electoral choices has another dimension as well. How people feel about the groups they associate with the major parties affects how they evaluate the parties and their presidential candidates. Certain activist groups now commonly associated with the Democratic party—such as gays and lesbians, militant blacks, and feminists—have damaged the party's popular appeal, particularly among Republicans and independents. See Arthur H. Miller, Christopher Wlezien, and Anne Hildreth, "A Reference Group Theory of Partisan Coalitions," *Journal of Politics 53* (November 1991): 1134–1149.
63. For an analysis of the importance of friends and family in influencing voter decisions, see John G. Geer, "Voting and the Social Environment," *American Politics Quarterly 13* (January 1985): 3–27.
64. Studies of electoral behavior that bear too heavily on the group as the unit of analysis may do some injustice to individual voters, making them appear as objects to be managed by skillful propagandists or as victims of social determinants (for example, occupation, race, or education). Preoccupation with the gross characteristics of voters may lead the analyst to minimize the individual's awareness of and concern about issues. V. O. Key, Jr., has argued that "the electorate behaves about as rationally and responsibly as we should expect, given the clarity of the alternatives presented to it and the character of the information available to it." By and large, in Key's study, the American voter emerges as a rational and responsible person concerned about matters of public policy, governmental performance, and executive personality. See V. O. Key, Jr. (with Milton C. Cummings), *The Responsible Electorate* (New York: Vintage Books, 1966), 7. But see the evidence of Paul Goren that votes cast for the president are strongly influenced by emotional (gut-level) reactions as well as by cognition. "Gut-Level Emotions and the Presidential Vote," *American Politics Quarterly 25* (April 1997): 203–229.
65. As the ties between social groups (e.g., Catholics, Jews, industrial workers) and the Democratic party have become attenuated, ideology has become more important in shaping partisanship. Ideology cuts across traditional social group cleavages. See the work of Jeffrey Levine, Edward G. Carmines, and Robert Huckfeldt, "The Rise of Ideology in the Post-New Deal Party System, 1972–1992," *American Politics Quarterly 25* (January 1997): 19–34.
66. Harold W. Stanley and Richard G. Niemi find that changes in group support for the parties have been limited and slow to develop. In fact, much of the movement of voters has been from partisan to independent or from independent to partisan rather than from one party to the other. Although the New Deal coalition has become weaker, the Republican party has not yet been able to consolidate its support among groups that traditionally vote Democratic. "Partisanship and

Group Support, 1952–1988," *American Politics Quarterly 19* (April 1991): 189–210.

67. Paul A. Beck, "Realignment Begins: The Republican Surge in Florida," *American Politics Quarterly 10* (October 1982): 421–438. Quotation on p. 433.

68. The most important factor in ticket-splitting is strength of party identification: That is, the stronger a voter's party identification, the less likely he or she is to defect to vote for a candidate of the other party. A second important factor is the visibility of the candidate of the other party; the principal source of visibility is incumbency. See Paul Allen Beck, Lawrence Baum, Aage R. Clausen, and Charles E. Smith, Jr., "Patterns and Sources of Ticket Splitting in Subpresidential Voting," *American Political Science Review 86* (December 1992): 916–928.

Chapter Six

The Congressional Party
and the Formation of
Public Policy

The tasks that confront the American major party are formidably ambitious. From one perspective, the party is a wide-ranging electoral agency organized to make a credible bid for power. Here and there a party organization is so stunted and devitalized that it seldom can make an authentic effort to win office. Where it is not taken seriously, the party finds it difficult to develop and recruit candidates, to gain the attention of the media, and to attract financial contributors. Elections may go by default to the dominant party as the second party struggles merely to stay in business. But throughout most of the country the parties compete on fairly even terms—if not for certain offices or in certain districts, at least for some offices or in a state at large. Presidential elections are vigorously contested virtually everywhere. As electoral organizations, the parties recruit candidates, organize campaigns, develop issues, and mobilize voters. Typical voters get their best glimpse of the workings of party when they observe the "party in the electorate" during political campaigns.

From another perspective, the party is a collection of officeholders who share in some measure common values and policy orientations. In the broadest sense, its mission is to take hold of government, to identify national problems and priorities, and to work for their settlement or achievement. In a narrower sense, the task of the "party in the government" is to consolidate and fulfill promises made to the electorate during the campaign. How it is organized to do this and how it does it is the concern of this chapter. The focus is the party in Congress.

218

Congressional Elections

The two most important variables in the election of members of Congress are incumbency status and party affiliation.[1] Congressional incumbents have numerous advantages in elections. The offices and staffs of members are basic units in their campaign organizations. Voters are much more likely to recognize the name of the incumbent than that of the challenger. Some voters will have benefited from the many services that members regularly perform for their constituents. The franking privilege permits members to send mail to their constituents at government expense. And of major importance, incumbents ordinarily find it much easier than challengers to raise campaign funds, particularly from interest groups. It is not surprising then that incumbents are difficult to defeat. It is rare for less than 90 percent of all House incumbents seeking reelection to be successful; the last time this happened was in 1974. Often the reelection rate surpasses 95 percent. Although Senate incumbents usually face stronger competition, they also win with great regularity. In 1990, 97 percent of all Senate incumbents running for reelection were successful; in 1992, in the midst of a fierce national campaign against incumbents, 85 percent were still reelected. In 1996, 95 percent of Senate incumbents were returned for another term.

Party affiliation is also a key factor in congressional elections. In the typical state, some districts nearly always elect Democratic legislators and some districts nearly always elect Republican legislators. Some districts are so thoroughly dominated by one party that the second party has virtually no chance of winning. With few exceptions, for example, House districts in major cities are securely Democratic, irrespective of the incumbency factor. In other suburban, small-town, and rural districts Democratic candidates may face insurmountable odds in election after election.

Districts do not often switch from one party to the other. In no election from 1954 to 1992 did more than 13 percent of the 435 seats switch party control.[2] Often the percentage is much lower than that.

Incumbency and party combine to yield a great many one-sided elections, especially in the House. Districts are typically won by a vote of 60 percent or more. In 1996, 54 percent of all House elections were won by a 60 to 40 margin or better. In fact, both parties are accustomed to having a number of House races in which their candidates face no major party opposition.

The decline of party competition for congressional seats is one of the most conspicuous features of contemporary American politics. A number of possible explanations exist for this. One notion is that Democratic and Republican state legislators cooperate to protect each party's incumbents: They draw congressional district lines (along with their own) in such a way as to create as many safe districts as possible. Incumbents of both parties obviously prefer this solution when faced with redistricting. David R. Mayhew contends that incumbents have become more skillful in "advertising" their names, in "claiming credit" for federal governmental programs that benefit their districts, and in "position taking" on key issues of concern to their constituents. And they have large and talented staffs to help them cultivate their constituents.[3] Another study finds that information on the candidates is an important factor. If it is not available on both candidates, voters "are likely to vote for incumbents, whom they already like and may have voted for, faced with challengers they know little, if anything, about."[4] The success of incumbents also seems to be promoted by the relative weakness of congressional challengers.[5] Finally, it may be that competition has declined because voters now attach more importance to incumbency than to party affiliation in casting their ballots. Because the electoral parties are plainly weaker today than in the past, they are less capable of providing voting cues for the public.[6]

It is hard to say exactly how public policy is affected by the relatively stable membership of both houses of Congress. Conventional wisdom holds that opportunities for major policy change are limited by a membership that remains largely intact election after election.

Party Representation in Congress

Figures 6-1 and 6-2 show the representation of the parties in each house over the past half-century, from 1932 to 1996. The broad picture is one of Democratic dominance with but brief interludes of Republican control of one or both chambers. But party fortunes changed sharply in 1994. The Republicans gained an extraordinary fifty-four seats in the House and ten in the Senate, winning control of Congress for the first time since the mid-1950s. Although they lost eight House seats in the 1996 election, they gained two Senate seats. Party-switching by several Democratic House members reduced the Republicans' net loss of seats.

Several explanations for the new Republican success have been advanced by Gary Jacobson. First, the reallocation of House seats following the 1990 census rewarded those regions, such as the South and the West, that are favorable to the Republican party. Second, the creation of majority-minority districts had the effect of bunching African American voters into a few districts, while at the same time making the surrounding areas relatively more Republican. Third, the Republicans began to win seats that, given their characteristics, should have been Republican all along. Fourth, the

FIGURE 6-1 Democratic Strength in Senate Elections: 1932 to 1996

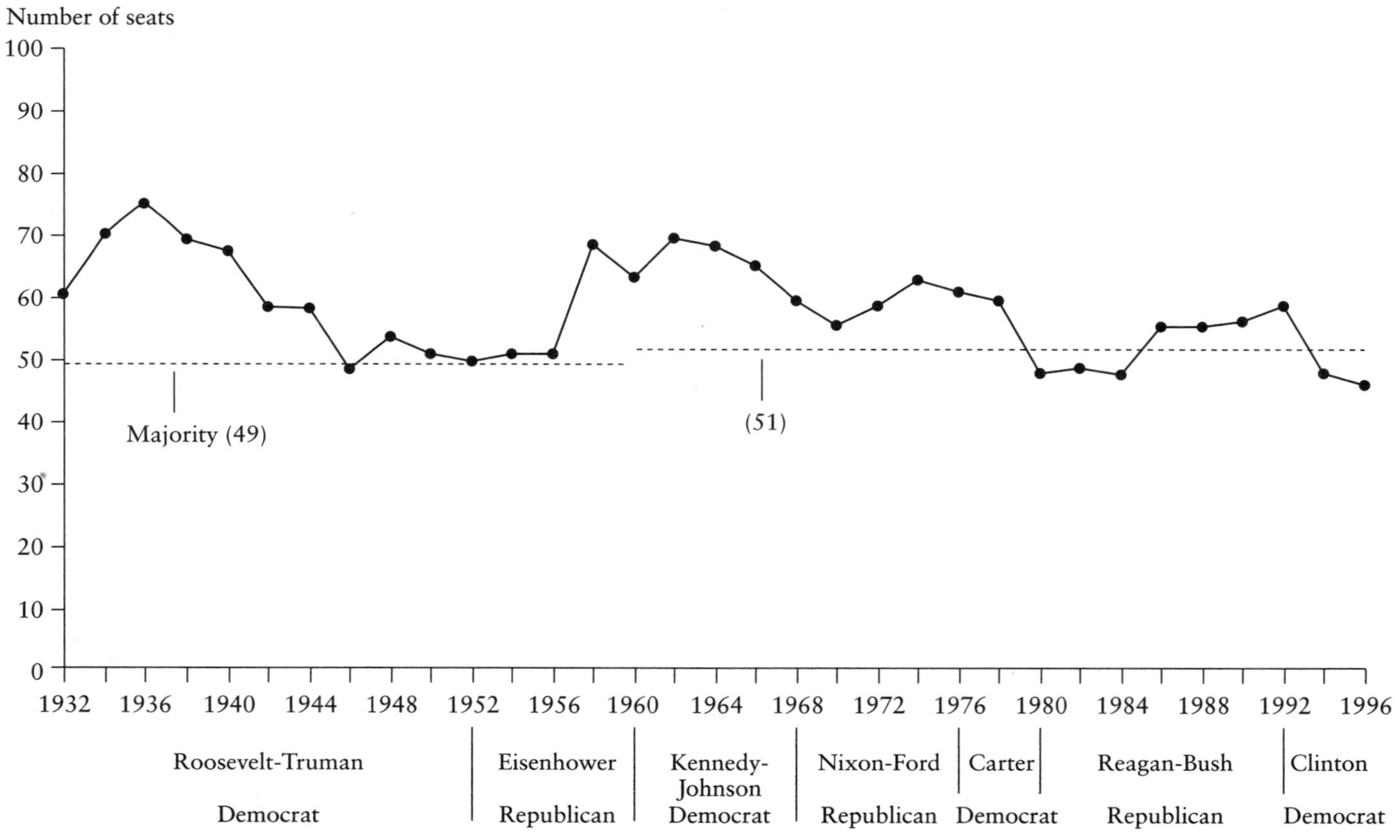

Number of seats

FIGURE 6-2 Democratic Strength in House Elections: 1932 to 1996

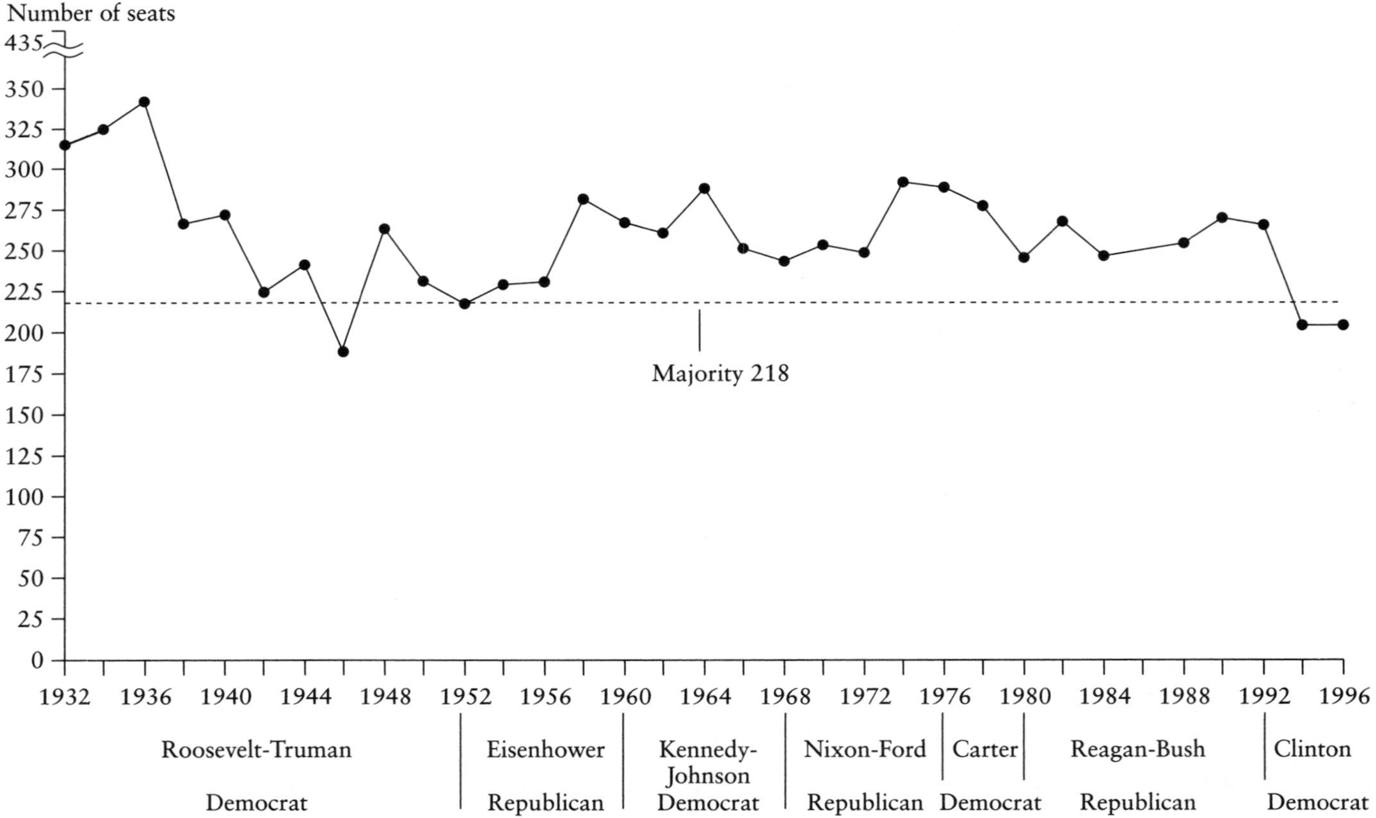

Democrats' minority status in Congress, stemming from the 1994 debacle, prompted a number of members to retire in 1996, thus giving the Republicans an opportunity to win open seats in districts disposed toward their party. Fifth, the Republicans' capture of Congress in 1994 upset the pattern of PAC contributions; Republican Senate candidates, for example, collected twice as much money from PACs in 1996 as their Democratic opponents. And sixth, another legacy of the Democrats' loss of majority control in 1994 was that it was more difficult for them to recruit quality candidates to challenge Republican incumbents in 1996. So fundamental are these developments, Jacobson contends, that the best opportunity for Democrats to recapture Congress will occur when voters become disillusioned with some future Republican administration.[7]

Party membership is a major factor not only in determining who is elected to Congress but also in influencing members' behavior once they have taken office. The fact that party cohesion collapses on certain issues that come before Congress does not alter the general proposition that party affiliation is a major explanation of voting behavior. Party cues are not taken lightly by most members. They recognize that there are advantages to going along with the leadership and voting in agreement with their party colleagues. An examination of party voting follows an analysis of congressional party organization.

Party Organization in Congress

Party Conferences

The central agency of each party in each chamber is the conference or caucus. All those elected to Congress automatically become members of their party's caucus. During the early twentieth century, and particularly during the Wilson administration, the House majority party caucus was exceptionally powerful. Following World War I, disillusionment with the caucus became manifest, and members came to question the right of the caucus to bind them to a course of action. The power of the caucus declined sharply in the 1920s, and soon its functions were limited to the selection of party leaders such as the Speaker of the House, the floor leaders, and the whips.

For all intents and purposes, the caucus was moribund for the next half century. In 1969, after years of somnolence, the Democratic caucus began to hold regular monthly meetings to examine proposals for reforming the House. In the early 1970s, the caucus made several modifications of the seniority system, the most important of which provided for secret ballots on nominees for committee chairs. A Steering and Policy Committee was cre-

Party Leaders and Committees . . .

House Democrats

Party Leaders

Speaker
majority leader
majority whip
caucus chair
caucus vice chair
chief deputy whip
deputy whips
at-large whips

Party Committees

Steering and Policy: assigns Democratic members to committees and helps to develop party policy. Speaker serves as chair, majority leader as vice chair.

Democratic Congressional Campaign Committee: provides campaign support for Democratic House candidates.

Personnel Committee: supervises the party's patronage positions.

House Republicans

Party Leaders

minority leader
minority whip
conference chair
conference vice chair
conference secretary
chief deputy whip
deputy whips

Party Committees

Policy: helps to develop Republican policy positions.

Committee on Committees: assigns Republican members to committees.

National Republican Congressional Committee: provides campaign support for Republican House candidates.

Personnel Committee: supervises the party's patronage positions.

ated by the caucus in 1973 to formulate legislative programs and to participate in the scheduling of legislation for floor consideration.

The power of the Democratic caucus was dramatically demonstrated at the opening of the Ninety-fourth Congress in 1975 when, among other things, the caucus voted to remove three committee chairs from their positions, transferred to the Steering and Policy Committee the power to make committee assignments from the Democratic members of the Ways and Means Committee, and made a number of changes involving nominations and subcommittee procedures. Included in these changes was a provision to

... in 105th Congress (1997–1998)

Senate Democrats

Party Leaders

president pro tempore
majority leader
majority whip
conference chair
conference secretary
chief deputy whip
deputy whips

Party Committees

Policy: helps to develop party policy and advises on the scheduling of legislation. Majority leader serves as chair.

Steering: assigns Democratic members to committees. Majority leader serves as chair.

Legislative Review Committee: analyzes legislative proposals and makes recommendations.

Democratic Senatorial Campaign Committee: provides campaign support for Democratic Senate candidates.

Senate Republicans

Party Leaders

minority leader
assistant minority
    leader
conference chair
conference secretary

Party Committees

Policy: helps to develop party policy and advises on the scheduling of legislation.

Committee on Committees: assigns Republican members to committees.

National Republican Senatorial Committee: provides campaign support for Republican Senate candidates.

empower the Speaker, subject to caucus approval, to nominate the Democratic members of the powerful Rules Committee. The key test in filling vacancies on this committee now appears to be the member's allegiance to the leaders. Major disciplinary action by the Democratic caucus occurred again at the start of the Ninety-eighth Congress (1983–1984). In an unusual action, the caucus voted to remove a Texas representative from the Budget Committee because in the previous Congress he had worked closely with the administration in the design of President Reagan's budget strategy.

The revitalization of the Democratic caucus has weakened the hold of the seniority system and strengthened the positions of party leaders. But to what extent can the caucus influence the behavior of party members on major policy proposals? Caucus power collides with the nagging reality of all legislative politics: The individual member's electoral security, and thus his or her primary interest, lies in the constituency. For many members of the House, the attractions of a cohesive party are not nearly so great as the attractions of independence, with all the opportunities it affords the legislator to concentrate on constituency interests and problems. Party leaders and committee leaders, moreover, usually take a dim view of caucus involvement in policy questions. As Speaker Thomas P. ("Tip") O'Neill, Jr. (D-Mass., 1977–1986), observed, "I don't like any of these [policy] matters coming from the caucus on a direct vote." A similar view was expressed by Richard Bolling (D-Mo.) during his long tenure in the House: "I think [members] would have an awful time if they tried [to set party policy in the caucus]. It's better left to the committee system." [8] The cards are stacked against centralized power in any form. The independence of today's members makes a return to the earlier days when "King Caucus" reigned over the House all but impossible.

The Speaker of the House

The most powerful party leader in Congress is the Speaker of the House. In the early twentieth century, the Speaker's powers were almost beyond limit, the House virtually his private domain. It is scarcely an exaggeration to say that legislation favored by the Speaker was adopted and that legislation opposed by him was defeated. The despotic rule of Speaker Joseph G. ("Uncle Joe") Cannon (R-Ill., 1903–1911) eventually proved his undoing. In 1910 Democrats and rebellious Republicans formed a coalition to challenge his leadership. After a struggle of many months, it succeeded in instituting a number of rules changes to curb the Speaker's powers. Cannon was removed from membership on the Rules Committee (which he had chaired), his power to appoint and remove members and chairs of the standing committees was eliminated, and his power to recognize (or not to recognize) members was limited. Although the "revolution of 1910–1911" fundamentally altered the formal powers of the Speaker, it did not render the office impotent. Since then, a succession of Speakers—men disposed to negotiate rather than to command—has helped to rebuild the powers of the office. What a Speaker like Joseph Cannon secured through autocratic rule, today's Speakers secure through persuasion and the astute exploitation of the bargaining advantages inherent in their positions.

Each Speaker leaves an imprint on the office. Changes in the times and in the character of politics also help to shape the speakership. Speaker Tip O'Neill once observed,

> Old Sam Rayburn [Speaker for seventeen years between 1940 and 1961] couldn't name 12 new members of Congress, and he was an institution that awed people. Only on the rarest of occasions could a Congressman get an appointment to see him. And when he called the Attorney General and said, "You be in my office at 3 in the afternoon," that Cabinet officer was there at 3 in the afternoon. Politics has changed. I have to deal in dialogue, in openness; if someone wants to see me, they see me. And of course they're highly independent now. You have to talk to people in the House, listen to them. The whole ethics question has changed. Years ago you'd think nothing of calling Internal Revenue and saying that this case has been kicking around for a couple of years, and it ought to be civil instead of criminal. You'd think nothing of calling a chairman of a committee and saying, "Put this project in, put this dam in." Well, you can't do that now.[9]

The Speaker's formal powers are wide ranging, though not especially significant in themselves. The Speaker is the presiding officer of the House and in this capacity announces the order of business, puts questions to a vote, refers bills to committees, rules on points of order, interprets the rules, recognizes members who desire the floor, and appoints members to select and conference committees. The Speaker also has the right to vote and enter floor debate. Ordinarily he exercises these rights only in the case of major, closely contested issues.

Although difficult to delineate with precision, the informal powers of the Speaker are far more impressive. As the foremost leader of his party in Congress, he is at the center of critical information and policy-making systems. No one is in a better position than the Speaker to obtain and disseminate information, to shape strategies, or to advance or frustrate the careers of members. Perhaps the principal tangible preferment the Speaker has at his disposal is the influence he can exert to secure favorable committee assignments for members of the majority party. The Speaker's good will is important to majority-party members anxious to move ahead in the House. The following analysis by Randall B. Ripley describes the structure of the Speaker's influence:

> His personal traits influence his ability to deal with members of his party. The one constant element is the importance of his showing trust in and respect for individual members of his party. A smile or nod of the head from the Speaker can bolster a member's ego and lead him to seek further evidences of favor. Being out of favor hurts the individual's pride, and may be noticed by his colleagues. Most Speakers have had an instinct for knowing their loyal followers on legislative matters. Others have either kept records

themselves or made frequent use of whip polls and official records to inform themselves about the relative loyalty of their members. Speakers have been able to convey critical information to members on a person-to-person basis, often with the help of the Parliamentarian. They have also encouraged their floor leaders and whip organizations to become collectors and purveyors of information on a larger scale. Particularly useful to a number of Speakers has been an informal gathering of intimates and friends of both parties to discuss the course of business in the House. Through such discussions, Speakers have been able to keep themselves informed of developments in the House and, at the same time, convey their desires to other members invited to attend.[10]

Another way of viewing the Speaker and other party officials is provided by Joseph Cooper and David W. Brady. Today's party leaders, they write, "function less as the commanders of a stable party majority and more as brokers trying to assemble particular majorities behind particular bills."[11] Similarly, David W. Rohde observes, "In their day, Speakers such as Reed or Cannon ordered and punished the members at will. But it is . . . inconceivable to think of this in the modern Congress. The members now tell the leaders what to do, and the leaders do it."[12]

The Floor Leaders

In addition to the Speaker of the House, the key figures in the congressional party organizations are the House and Senate floor leaders, who are chosen by party caucuses in their respective chambers. The floor leaders serve as the principal spokespersons for party positions and interests and as intermediaries in both intraparty and interparty negotiations. The floor leaders of the party that controls the presidency also serve as links between the president and his congressional party. Because floor leaders are obliged to play several roles at the same time—for example, representatives of both the congressional party and the president—it is not surprising that role conflicts develop. Serving the interests of their congressional party colleagues or perhaps those of their constituents is anything but a guarantee that they will be serving presidential interests.

Floor leaders have a potpourri of informal, middling powers. Their availability, however, does not ensure that they can lead their colleagues or strongly shape the legislative program. By and large, their influence is based on their willingness and talent to exploit these powers steadily and imaginatively in their relations with other members. They can, if they choose, (1) influence the allocation of committee assignments (not only rewarding individual members but also shaping the ideological makeup of the committees); (2) help members to advance legislation of particular interest to them; (3) assist members in securing larger appropriations for their committees or sub-committees; (4) play a major role in debate; (5) intercede with the president or executive agencies on behalf of members (perhaps to assist their efforts to secure a federal project in their state or district); (6) make important information available to members; (7) help members to secure campaign money from a congressional campaign committee or from the political action committee of an interest group; (8) campaign on behalf of individual members; and (9) focus the attention of the communications media on the contributions of members. Much of the influence of floor leaders, like that of the Speaker, is derived from informal powers, in particular from opportunities afforded them to advance or protect the careers of party colleagues. In solving problems for them and in making their positions more secure, floor leaders increase the prospects of gaining their support on critical questions. By the same token, floor leaders can in some measure hamper the careers of those members who continually refuse to go along with them. At the center of active floor leaders' powers is the capacity to manipulate rewards and punishments.

An important function and a major source of power for the majority floor leader, particularly in the Senate, is the scheduling of bills on the floor. (In the House, the Rules Committee dominates the agenda.) However pedestrian the scheduling function may sound, it is a surprisingly important source of power. The majority leader who fails to keep lines of communication clear, who misjudges the sentiments of members, who neglects to consolidate the majority by winning over undecided members or by propping up wavering members, or who picks the wrong time to call up a bill can easily go down to defeat. Prospective majorities are much more tenuous and much more easily upset than might be supposed. Support can be lost rapidly as a result of poor communications, missed opportunities for negotiation and compromise, and bad timing. The effective leader builds his or her power base by tending to the shop, by ordering priorities, by having a sense of detail that overlooks nothing, by taking account of the demands placed on members, by sensing the mood of congressional opinion (especially that of key members), and by exhibiting skill in splicing together the legislative elements necessary to fashion a majority.

The principal power of the floor leader is the power of persuasion. As a former Democratic leader of the Senate, Lyndon B. Johnson (D-Texas), once observed, "the only real power available to the leader is the power of persuasion. There is no patronage; no power to discipline; no authority to fire Senators like a President can fire his members of Cabinet." [13] Jim Wright (D-Texas), former Speaker and former majority leader in the House, expressed a similar view of the leader's role: "The majority leader is a conciliator, a mediator, a peacemaker. Even when patching together a tenuous majority he must respect the right of honest dissent, conscious of the limits of his claims upon others."[14] A former House majority leader, Richard A. Gephardt (D-Mo.), described his view of the office in this way: "We've had huge turnover in the last ten years and they are not the kind of people who came here to take orders. [Ours] will be a leadership that will be engaged in lots of meetings."[15] Another dimension of the position is suggested in these observations by a House Republican leader: "Everyone has a different idea as to how the leadership is to operate. I think that's perfectly healthy. But I think everybody also understands that you can't please everybody on everything. To please the majority, you have to keep from going too far to the left or to the right."[16]

To be persuasive, a leader must know the members well, know what they want and what they will settle for, what concessions they can make and what concessions they cannot make, given their constituencies. The critical importance of such information requires the leader to develop a reliable communications network within the party. But more than that, it requires good lines of communication into the other party to pick up support when elements of the majority party appear likely to wander off the reservation. Members prefer to support their leader and the party position rather than the opposing forces. The task of the leader is to find reasons for them to do so and conditions under which they can.

The development of a legislative program requires the majority leader to work closely with the key leaders in his or her party, particularly the chairs of the major committees. As Lyndon Johnson observed during his tenure as Senate majority leader, "You must understand why the committee took certain actions and why certain judgments were formed."[17] His successor, Mike Mansfield (D-Mont.), observed, "I'm not the leader, really. They don't do what I tell them. I do what they tell me. . . . The brains are in the committees."[18] The effective leader works with the resources available—in essence, the power of persuasion. Relations between the leader and the committee chairs are never characterized by a one-way flow of mandates. On the contrary, the leader must be acutely sensitive to the interests of the chairs, adept at recognizing their political problems, and flexible in negotiations with them. Bargaining is the key characteristic of the relationships between the majority leader and the committee chairs.

Party management in Congress has become increasingly difficult in recent years. Several reasons help to explain this situation. First, the adoption of "sunshine" rules in both houses has made Congress a much more open institution. For the most part, committee, subcommittee, and even party caucus meetings are now open to the public. Second, combined with the new visibility of congressional actions, the growing power of interest groups, stemming particularly from their campaign contributions, has made members more vulnerable to outside pressures and, at the same time, increasingly resistant to the influence of party leaders. Third, the weakening of the electoral parties has been accompanied by an extraordinary growth in candidate-centered campaigns. Members who are elected to Congress largely on their own efforts have less reason to concern themselves with party objectives, less reason to defer to the wishes of party leaders. Freewheeling independence has become the modus vivendi of many members of Congress. Finally, internal changes have contributed to the further decentralization of congressional power. Subcommittees have grown both in number and in independence. The influence of committee chairs has declined as that of subcommittee chairs has grown. In addition, both chambers now limit the number of committee and subcommittee chairs that a member may hold, the effect of which has been to spread leadership positions (and thus power) among more members. The presence of a large number of specialized policy caucuses may also have made it more difficult for the parties to integrate policy making. Singly and in combination, these changes have diminished the capacity of the parties to build majorities and to mobilize their members for concerted action.

A prominent New York Democrat, Emanuel Celler, who served fifty years in the House (nearly twenty-five years as chair of the Judiciary Committee), made these comments on the devolution of congressional power:

> When I was in Congress, we had strong chairmen. . . . They ruled the roost. . . . Then came along the so-called young Turks, insisting upon lessening the power of the chairmen. And you have all these youngsters clamoring for power and more power and more help, so that there's a tremendous proliferation of [staff] assistants to the subcommittees. And they are yammering and hollering for more and more power, which results in the combined efforts of Congress shouting and trying to make itself heard above the power of the president.[19]

The more individualistic Congress becomes, the more difficult it becomes for the party leadership to play a decisive role. As former Senate majority whip Alan Cranston (D-Calif.) observed, "A lot of leadership is just housekeeping now. Occasionally you have an opportunity to provide leadership, but not that often. The weapons to keep people in line just aren't there."[20]

The usual position of party leaders in Congress is explained by Barbara Sinclair in this way:

> Members of Congress are elected on their own: they build their own organizations, they raise their own money and, to a considerable extent, they manage to cultivate their constituencies to insulate themselves from national tides. Consequently, party leaders cannot influence whether members

attain their reelection, power or policy goals to the extent that the pre-1910 party leadership could. To be sure, current leaders do have resources that can be employed to influence their members, but, for most members, most of the time, what the leaders can do for them or to them is not critical for their goal attainment. Current leaders must rely upon persuasion-based strategies; they do not possess the resources necessary to command.[21]

What has been said thus far suggests that several important constraints shape the positions of the floor leaders. The leaders are not free to fashion their role as they might like to see it. The limited range of powers available to them, their personality, their relationship to the president, and their skills in bargaining—all affect in some measure the definition of their role. Moreover, no two leaders are likely to perceive their roles in exactly the same light. In addition, the nature of the floor leaders' position is strongly influenced by the nature of the legislative parties. Persistent cleavages within both parties make it necessary for leaders to play mediating roles. Leaders are middlemen in the sense that they are more or less steadily involved in negotiations with all major elements within their party, and also in terms of their voting record.[22] In the passage of much legislation the test is not so much the wisdom of the decision as it is its political feasibility. Leaders identified with an extreme group within their party would find it difficult to work out the kinds of compromises necessary to put together a majority. Leaders are, first and foremost, brokers. Candidates for leadership positions whose voting records place them on the ideological edges of their party ordinarily are less likely to be elected than those whose voting records fall within the central range of party opinion.

The Whips

Another unit in the party structure of Congress is the whip organization. Party whips are selected in each house by the floor leaders or by other party agencies. Many assistant whips are required in the House because of the large size of the body. On the Democratic side, for example, more than one quarter of all members are now in the whip organization, making it a "mini-caucus every week."[23] Working to enhance the efforts of the leadership, the whips carry on a number of important functions. They attempt to learn how members intend to vote on legislation; relay information from party leaders to individual members; work to ensure that a large number of "friendly" members will be present at the time of voting; and attempt to win the support of those party members who are in opposition, or likely to be in opposition, to the leadership. The influence of the Speaker and the majority leader supplements the pressure of the whips. As described by one chief staff assistant to the majority whip, whips apply "the heavy party loyalty shtick. Then it's more personalities than issues. There are some members who can only be gotten by the Speaker or the majority leader." [24]

The central importance of the whip organization is that it forms a communications link between the party leadership and rank-and-file members. The whips are charged with discovering why members are opposed to certain legislation and how that legislation might be changed to gain their support. The intelligence the whips supply sometimes spells the difference between victory and defeat on a major issue. On some issues no amount of activity on the part of the leadership can bring recalcitrant members into the fold. If the outlook for a bill is unpromising following a "whip check" of members' sentiments, the leadership will often postpone its floor consideration. Whip checks can thus protect the leadership from embarrassing losses.

Being in the whip system gives members access to information from the leadership and some small measure of status, as these comments by a deputy whip, Rep. Norman Mineta (D-Calif.), illustrate.

> Among my colleagues, I'm given some recognition for having some information, being connected. Like Ivy League eating clubs, . . . well, I'm part of the Speaker's eating club. . . . People say to me, "You're part of the leadership, what's going on?" And then I say, "Gee I don't know," and I go and find out. I think you're part of the inside track in asking questions.[25]

The Policy Committees

Few proposals for congressional reform have received as much attention as those designed to strengthen the role of political parties in the legislative process. The Joint Committee on the Organization of Congress recommended in its 1946 report that policy committees be created for the purpose of formulating the basic policies of the two parties. Although this provision was later stricken from the reorganization bill, the Senate independently created such committees in 1947. The House Republicans established a policy committee in 1949, though it did not become fully active for another decade.[26] Rounding out the list, the rejuvenated House Democratic caucus voted to establish a policy committee in 1973.

The high promise of the policy committees as agencies for enhancing party responsibility for legislative programs has never been realized. Neither party leaders nor rank-and-file members agree on the functions of the policy committees. The policy committees are so in name only. The policy committees in the Senate "have never been 'policy' bodies, in the sense of considering and investigating alternatives of public policy, and they have never put forth an overall congressional party program. The committees do not assume leadership in drawing up a general legislative program . . . and only rarely have the committees labeled their decisions as 'party policies.' " [27]

It is not surprising that the policy committees have been unable to function effectively as agencies for the development of overall party programs. An authoritative policy committee would constitute a major threat to the scattered and relatively independent centers of power within Congress. The seniority leaders who preside over the committee system would undoubtedly find their influence over legislation diminished if the policy committees were to assume a central role in defining party positions. The independence of the committee system would be affected adversely, and many individual members would suffer an erosion of power. If the policy committees had functioned as planned, a major reshuffling of power in Congress would have resulted. To those who hold the keys to congressional power, this is scarcely an appealing idea. However attractive the proposal for centralized committees empowered to speak for the parties in Congress, these committees are unlikely to emerge so long as the parties are decentralized and fragmented, composed of members who represent a wide variety of constituencies and ideological positions.

Although the lack of internal party agreement prevents the policy committees from functioning in a policy-shaping capacity, it does not render them useless. Both parties require forums for the discussion of issues and for the negotiation of compromises, and for these activities the policy committees are well designed. Moreover, the staffs of the committees have proved helpful for individual members seeking research assistance. Most important, the policy committees have served as a communications channel between the party leaders and their memberships.

The policy committees are an ambitious attempt to deal with the persistent problem of party disunity. If they have generally failed in this respect, they have nonetheless succeeded in others. As clearinghouses for the exchange of party information and as agencies for the reconciliation of at least some intraparty differences, they have made useful contributions.

Informal Party Groups and Specialized Congressional Caucuses

In addition to the formal party units in Congress, several informal party organizations meet more or less regularly to discuss legislation, strategy, and other questions of common interest. Among these organizations are the Democratic Study Group (DSG) (liberal), Conservative Democratic Forum, Blue Dog Democrats, United Democrats of Congress (conservative), Republican Study Committee (conservative), Wednesday Group (Republican, liberal), and Tuesday Lunch Bunch (Republican, moderate). Formed to promote the policy positions of a faction within the party, these groups are major sources of information for their members. They focus primarily on the congressional agenda, drafting and introducing legislation and amendments as well as seeking to attract the interest and support of other members and outside forces. Extending their reach, some of these groups have sought to influence the content of party platforms.

Informal party groups compete and cooperate with dozens of other specialized policy caucuses organized to advance particular interests. These relatively narrow-gauge groups are formed around geographic, economic, race, gender, and assorted concerns. Included in this far-flung policy network are such caucuses as the Steel Caucus, Coal Caucus, Textile Caucus, Travel and Tourism Caucus, Farm Crisis Caucus, Wine Caucus, Mushroom Caucus, Port Caucus, Human Rights Caucus, Black Caucus, Blue Collar Caucus, Hispanic Caucus, Sunbelt Caucus, Northeast-Midwest Congressional Coalition, Border Caucus, Congresswomen's Caucus, Rural Caucus, Suburban Caucus, Crime Caucus, Arts Caucus, and Drug Enforcement Caucus. Groups such as these have come to play a significant role in the policy process through problem identification, member mobilization, and coalition building. They are centers for information exchange.[28] At the same time, they reflect the fragmentation of power in Congress. Whether they enhance or inhibit the capacity of party leaders to control the policy-making process is an empirical question. But whatever the answer, it is not likely that these mechanisms of representation will disappear.

Factors Influencing the Success of Party Leaders

The cohesiveness of the parties in Congress can never be taken for granted. The independence of the committees and their chairs, the rudimentary powers of elected leaders, the importance of constituency pressures, the influence of political interest groups, and the disposition of members to respond to parochial impulses—all, at one time or another, contribute to the fragmentation of power in Congress and to the erosion of party unity. The member who ignores or is oblivious to leadership cues, or who builds a career as a party maverick, is far more common than might be supposed. In the end the leadership can do little to bring refractory members into line.

Research on the Democratic party in the House by Lewis A. Froman, Jr., and Randall B. Ripley identifies a number of conditions under which leadership influence on legislative decisions will be either promoted or inhibited.[29] First, leadership success is likely to be contingent on a high degree of agreement among the leaders themselves. Ordinarily the Speaker, majority leader, and whip will be firm supporters of their president's legislative program; frequently, however, other key leaders, such as committee chairs, will be allied with opponents. When unity among the leaders breaks down, prospects for success fall sharply. Second, leadership success in gathering the party together tends to be affected by the nature of the issue under consideration—specifically, whether it is procedural or substantive. On procedural issues (for example, election of the Speaker, adoption of rules, motions to adjourn), party cohesion is ordinarily much higher than on issues that involve substantive policy. Third, the efforts of party leaders are most likely to be successful on issues that do not have high visibility to the general public. When issues gain visibility conflicting pressures emerge, and the leaders must commit greater resources to keep party ranks intact. Fourth, the visibility of the action to be taken will have a bearing on the inclination of members to follow the leadership. Not all forms of voting are equally noticeable. Roll-call votes on final passage of measures are highly conspicuous—the member's "record" on a public question is firmly established at this point. On the one hand, voting with the leadership on the floor may seem to the member to pose too great a risk. On the other hand, supporting the leadership in committee or on a key amendment is less risky, because these actions are not as easily brought into public focus. Fifth, and perhaps most important, members are most likely to vote with their party when the issue at stake does not stir up opposition in their constituencies. Party leaders know full well that they cannot count on the support of members who feel that they are under the thumb of constituents on a particular issue—for example, some southern members on certain questions relating to civil rights. Finally, support for the leadership is likely to depend on the activity of the state delegations. Leadership victories are more likely when individual state delegations are not involved in bargaining with leaders over specific demands.

These conditions, then, constitute the background against which leaders try to mold their party into a unit. Party loyalty, it should be emphasized, is more than a veneer. By and large, members prefer to go along with their party colleagues. But they will not queue up in support of their leaders if the conditions appear wrong, or if it appears that more is to be lost than gained by following the leadership. Members guard their careers by taking frequent soundings within their constituencies and among their colleagues and by making careful calculations of the consequences that are likely to flow from their decisions.

National Party Agencies and the Congressional Parties

In theory, the supreme governing body of the party between one national convention and the next is the national committee, which is composed of representatives from each state. In the best of all worlds, from the perspective of those who believe in party unity and responsibility, close and continuing relationships would be maintained between the national committee of each party and fellow party members in Congress. Out of such associations, presumably, would come coherent party policies and a heightened sense of responsibility among members of Congress for developing a legislative program consistent with the promises of the party platform. The tone and mood that dominate relations between the national committees and the congressional parties, however, are as likely to be characterized by suspicion as by cooperation. Congressional leaders in particular are little disposed to follow the cues that emanate from the national committees or, for that matter, from any other national party agency.

Not only do national party leaders have a minimal impact on congressional decision making, but they are also largely excluded from the process of nominating congressional candidates. Although the National Republican Congressional Committee (NRCC) sometimes enters House primary fights, giving funds to the Republican candidate it prefers, the practice is not common. "We don't look for fights, which would do both us and [the candidates] damage," the NRCC campaign director said. "The thing we look for is whether a candidate has [local] support." The Democratic Congressional Campaign Committee does not make funds available to primary candidates.[30]

National party leaders seldom become involved in the congressional nominating process because state and local leaders are likely to resent it. Occasionally an intrepid president has sought to influence congressional nominations, as Franklin D. Roosevelt did in 1938. Disturbed by mounting opposition to his program in Congress, Roosevelt publicly endorsed the primary opponents of certain prominent anti-New Deal incumbent Democrats. As it turned out, nearly all of the lawmakers marked for defeat won easily, much to the chagrin of the president. Twelve years later President Harry S. Truman met the same fate when he endorsed a candidate in the Democratic senatorial primary in Missouri. The state party organization rallied to the other side, and the president lost. Although a few presidential "purges" have succeeded, most attempts have failed. The lesson seems evident: Congressional nominations are regarded as local matters, to be decided in terms of local preferences.

The national party is concerned with the election of members who are broadly sympathetic to its traditional policy orientations and its party platform. In counterpoise, local party organizations aim to guarantee their own survival as independent units. Occasional conflict between the two is predictable. The principal consequence of local control over congressional nominations is that all manner of men and women get elected to Congress. Those who find it easy to accept national party goals rub elbows with those who are almost wholly out of step with the national party. The failure of party unity in Congress is due as much as anything to the folkway that congressional nominations are local questions to be settled by local politicians and voters according to preferences they alone establish.

Do the Parties Differ on Public Policies?

Party affiliation is the cutting edge of congressional elections. Ordinarily few surprises occur on election day: Democratic candidates win where they are expected to win, and Republican candidates win where they are expected to win.[31] The public at large may continue to believe that each election poses an opportunity for the outs to replace the ins, but this happens infrequently. The chief threat to an incumbent legislator is a landslide presidential vote for the other party, one so great that congressional candidates on the winning presidential ticket are lifted into office on the presidential candidate's coat-tails. Even landslide votes, however, do not disturb the great majority of congressional races.

If party affiliation largely determines who goes to Congress, does it also significantly influence their behavior once in office? The answer for most legislators—for majorities within each party—is yes. Party affiliation is the most important single variable in predicting how members will respond to questions that come before them. Indeed, the key fact to be known about any member is the party to which he or she belongs—it influences the choice of friends, group memberships, relations with lobbies, relations with other members and the leadership, and, most important, policy orientations. Party loyalty does not govern the behavior of members; neither is it taken lightly.

The proportion of roll-call votes in Congress in which the parties are sharply opposed to each other is not particularly large. A study of selected congressional sessions between 1921 and 1967 shows that the number of "party votes" that occur in the House has declined markedly over the years. Between 1921 and 1948, about 17 percent of House roll-call votes were party votes—votes in which 90 percent of the voting membership of one party opposed 90 percent of the voting membership of the other party. In the usual House sessions since 1950, party votes have numbered between 6 and 10 percent of the total.[32] The "90 percent versus 90 percent" standard is a rigorous test of party voting. If the standard is relaxed to "50 percent versus 50 percent," the proportion of party votes rises sharply. Between 1992 and 1996, for example, about 60 to 65 percent of all roll-call votes in both houses found party majorities arrayed against each other; these votes occur more frequently now than at any time during the recent past. Partisan conflict is somewhat less common in the Senate than in the House.[33]

One reason why party voting is not greater is found in the behavior of the wings of each party. Responding to the interests of their constituents, eastern Republicans sometimes find that they have more in common with liberal northern Democrats than with the rest of their party, and some southern Democrats, for the same reason, join Republican majorities to pursue conservative objectives.

Although the level of party voting in Congress is not particularly high, it is higher at some times than at others. What factors appear to promote partisan cleavage? Examining a recent thirty-five-year period, Samuel C. Patterson and Gregory A. Caldeira found that party voting in the House increases significantly when external party conflict is high—in particular, during periods when sharp differences exist between the national parties on central issues of the economy, labor-management questions, and the distribution of wealth. Interparty conflict also escalates when the presidency and House are controlled by the same party. In the Senate, where party voting is less common, presidential leadership is the key factor; specifically, when the Senate majority is of the same party as the president, party voting increases. Surprisingly, in view of conventional interpretations, the election of many new members does not lead to markedly greater increases in partisan cleavages.[34]

Research on party voting in the House by Mary Alice Nye, covering nearly half a century (1946 to 1990), finds that the best explanation for changing levels of partisanship is the changing voting patterns of members who continue from one Congress to the next; that is, they vote differently in response to the events and circumstances ("period effects") of a particular session of Congress. Conversion takes place. Nye finds little evidence that changing party support is explained by generational change (e.g., newly elected members are more or less partisan than those they replaced) or by the life-cycle hypothesis that members tend to stray from their party as their tenure increases. The importance of period effects may reflect such factors as party leadership (particularly the role of the Speaker) and the party caucus.[35]

Important issues are often at stake when party lines do form. In general, Democrats have been much more likely than Republicans to support expanded health and welfare programs, legislation advantageous to labor and low-income groups, government regulation of business, higher taxes on the wealthy, the use of federal funds for family planning, reductions in the defense budget, federal assistance for cities, and a larger role for the federal government.

The Parties and Liberal-Labor Legislation

The current policy orientations of the parties in Congress are not distinctly different from those they have held over the past half century. The positions

FIGURE 6-3   House Support for Labor Legislation, by Party and Region, 104th Congress, First Session

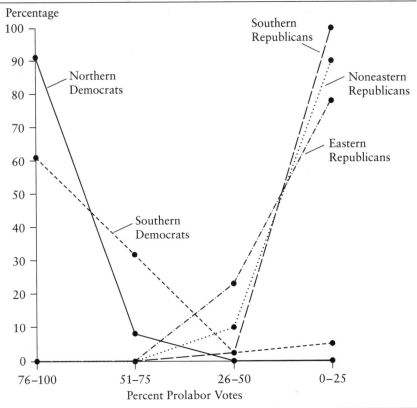

SOURCE: Developed from data in *AFL-CIO Report on the 1995 U.S. Congress* (Washington, D.C., 1996).

NOTE: House members are ranked by the percentage of votes they cast in accord with the positions of the AFL-CIO. The South is defined as the eleven states of the Confederacy plus Kentucky and Oklahoma. Noneastern Republicans are all northern members except those from eastern states.

of the parties (and the wings within them) on proposals of interest to the AFL-CIO in the 104th Congress are presented in Figures 6-3 and 6-4. A member voting in agreement with the AFL-CIO would have supported such measures as bargaining rights for transit workers, workplace safety and labor protection programs, affirmative action, and an increase in the minimum wage. And he or she would have opposed cuts in Medicare funding, reductions in entitlement spending, a cutback in education funding, an easing in the use of replacement workers, appropriations reductions for the Occupational Safety and Health Administration (OSHA) and the National Labor

FIGURE 6-4   Senate Support for Labor Legislation, by Party and Region,
104th Congress, First Session

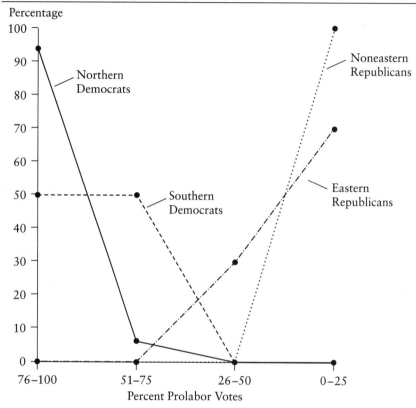

SOURCE: Developed from data in *AFL-CIO Report on the 1995 U.S. Congress* (Washington, D.C., 1996).

NOTE: Senate members are ranked by the percentage of votes they cast in accord with positions of the AFL-CIO. The South is defined as the eleven states of the Confederacy plus Kentucky and Oklahoma. The eastern states electing Republicans in this Congress were Delaware, Maine, New Hampshire, New York, Pennsylvania, Rhode Island, and Vermont.

Relations Board (NLRB), and a constitutional amendment to provide for a balanced budget.

Figures 6-3 and 6-4 show two broad patterns of congressional voting on issues of concern to organized labor. First, the parties are not altogether cohesive in voting on this legislation. Second, despite certain intraparty divisions, substantial differences between the parties are apparent. Without question, the parties view liberal labor legislation from different perspectives. Northern Democrats give overwhelming support to labor objectives.[36]

Although less united than northern Democrats, southern Democrats in both houses are clearly prolabor. Many southern Democrats, in fact, have voting records on labor legislation that are indistinguishable from those of their northern colleagues. Interestingly, southern Democrats and southern Republicans are poles apart on labor issues. Of all Republicans, those from the East are most likely to be sympathetic to labor initiatives.

Another way of looking at the policy orientations of the congressional parties is to examine the range of attitudes in the Senate during the first session of the 104th Congress on issues deemed important by the liberal-oriented Americans for Democratic Action (ADA) and the conservative-oriented American Conservative Union (ACU) (see Figure 6-5). Senators are located on the diagram according to the percentage of votes they cast in agreement with the positions of each political interest group. Sens. Barbara Boxer (D-Calif.), Paul Sarbanes (D-Md.), Carl Levin (D-Mich.), and Patrick Leahy (D-Vt.) emerge as the most liberal members of the upper house. At the conservative pole are such senators as Jesse Helms (R-N.C.), Phil Gramm (R-Tex.), Don Nickles (R-Okla.), and John Kyl (R-Ariz.).

The data in Figure 6-5 reinforce the conclusions reached earlier. Despite the party-in-disarray quality that appears in the Senate scattergram, significant differences separate the majorities of the two parties. Nearly all of the Republican senators are found on the right-hand side of the diagram, indicating their agreement with the ACU, whereas Democratic senators are on the left side, showing agreement with ADA policy objectives. Deviant behavior is largely confined to eastern Republicans.

Biparty Coalitions

Of all the problems that confront the legislative party, none is more persistent or difficult than that of maintaining party unity. Some members assiduously ignore the requests and entreaties of leaders; others cling tenaciously to constituency lines without pausing to consider the requirements of party; still others seek to tailor party measures to the specifications of those parochial interests to which they respond. The party is a repository for divergent claims and preferences. Getting it to act as a collectivity is no mean feat.

The disruption of party lines leads to the formation of biparty coalitions. The most durable biparty coalition in the history of Congress has been the so-called conservative coalition—an informal league of southern Democrats and northern Republicans. Data in Table 6-1 provide a statistical picture of the power held by the coalition from 1961 to 1996. In recent years the coalition has appeared on 11 to 12 percent of the roll-call votes held during a session—much less frequently than in the past. The coalition's success rate, however, continues to be impressive. In only two sessions since 1961 (the

FIGURE 6-5   Support for Positions Held by Americans for Democratic Action
(ADA) and by American Conservative Union (ACU) by Each
Senator, 104th Congress, First Session

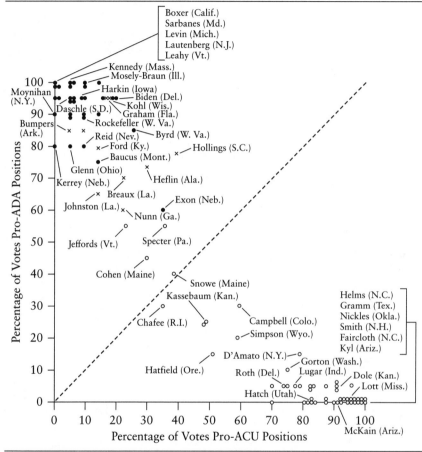

SOURCES: Developed from data appearing in *ADA Today,* March 1996 (Washington, D.C.) and American
Conservative Union, *1995 Rating of Congress* (Alexandria, Va., 1996).

NOTE: • = Northern Democrat; x = Southern Democrat; o = Republican

first two years of Johnson's Great Society, 1965 and 1966) did the coalition
win fewer than 50 percent of the roll calls on which it appeared. In twenty-
seven of the thirty-six sessions, the batting average of the coalition exceeded
60 percent. Recently the coalition has won nine out of every ten appearances.

Although the conservative coalition is not as powerful as in the past, it
is still a force to be reckoned with on certain kinds of issues. In 1996, for example, the coalition had fifty-one victories in the House and thirty-seven in

TABLE 6-1 The Conservative Coalition in Congress, Appearances and Victories: 1961 to 1996

Year	Percentage of roll calls in which the coalition appeared in Congress	Percentage of coalition victories		
		Congress	House	Senate
1961	28	55	74	48
1962	14	62	44	71
1963	17	50	67	44
1964	15	51	67	47
1965	24	33	25	39
1966	25	45	32	51
1967	20	63	73	54
1968	24	73	63	80
1969	27	68	71	67
1970	22	66	70	64
1971	30	83	79	86
1972	27	69	79	63
1973	23	61	67	54
1974	24	59	67	54
1975	28	50	52	48
1976	24	58	59	58
1977	26	68	60	74
1978	21	52	57	46
1979	20	70	73	65
1980	18	72	67	75

the Senate—involving such issues as space station funding, nuclear waste disposal, defense spending, the death penalty, Cuban trade policy, anti-terrorism policy, gay rights, welfare, UN commanders, abortion, immigration, gun control, and dolphin-safe tuna.[37]

Some portion of the explanation for the declining influence of the conservative coalition may be that Democratic party leadership, particularly in the more partisan House, has become more effective in bridging regional differences and diminishing intraparty conflict. Although there is some impressionistic evidence on this score, it is not the main reason for the changing behavior of southern Democrats, who have become more in tune with northern Democrats because the South itself has lost some of its distinctiveness.[38] Since passage of the Voting Rights Act of 1965, blacks have entered southern state electorates in great numbers, and their participation in turn

TABLE 6-1   *(continued)*

1981	21	92	88	95
1982	18	85	78	90
1983	15	77	71	89
1984	16	83	75	94
1985	14	89	84	93
1986	16	87	78	93
1987	8	93	88	100
1988	9	89	82	97
1989	11	87	80	95
1990	11	82	74	95
1991	11	91	86	95
1992	12	87	88	87
1993	9	94	98	90
1994	8	82	92	72
1995	11	98	100	95
1996	12	99	100	97

SOURCES: For recent scores, see *Congressional Quarterly Weekly Report*, December 30, 1989; January 6, 1990; December 22, 1990; December 28, 1991; December 19, 1992; December 18, 1993; December 31, 1994; January 27, 1996; and December 21, 1996.

NOTE: A "coalition roll call" is defined as any roll call on which the majority of voting southern Democrats and the majority of voting Republicans are opposed to the majority of voting northern Democrats. Congressional Quarterly groups these states in the southern wing of the Democratic party: Alabama, Arkansas, Florida, Georgia, Kentucky, Louisiana, Mississippi, North Carolina, Oklahoma, South Carolina, Tennessee, Texas, and Virginia. The other thirty-seven states are classified as northern in this analysis.

has driven Democratic incumbents and challengers to adopt more liberal positions on certain domestic policy questions. Black voters in southern Democratic primaries are now in a much better position to influence the behavior and policy stances of Democratic congressional candidates. The behavior of white voters also enters the calculus. Richard Fleisher writes, "In districts with large minority populations and white constituents [who] show a willingness to support progressive Democratic candidates, representatives in Congress respond with liberal voting and party support similar to that of northern Democrats."[39] In addition, economic development in the South has made that region resemble the North in many ways. The bottom line is simply that southern constituencies have changed, prompting southern politicians to change. The Democratic party is now more of a national party than at any time in its history.

Party "Loyalists" and "Irregulars" . . .

High party loyalty		High party loyalty	
Democratic senators	Votes cast with own party against majority of other party	Republican senators	Votes cast with own party against majority of other party
Akaka (Hawaii)	95%	Nickles (Okla.)	99%
Daschle (S.D.)	94	Inhofe (Okla.)	99
Boxer (Calif.)	94	Coverdell (Ga.)	98
Sarbanes (Md.)	94	Craig (Idaho)	98
Levin (Mich.)	94	Hutchison (Tex.)	98
Murray (Wash.)	94	Lott (Miss.)	97
Kennedy (Mass.)	93	Thurmond (S.C.)	97
Kerry (Mass.)	92	Ashcroft (Mo.)	97
Mikulski (Md.)	92	Burns (Mont.)	97
Wellstone (Minn.)	92	Kyl (Ariz.)	96
Harkin (Iowa)	91	Helms (N.C.)	96
Average Democratic senator	84	Average Republican senator	89

SOURCE: Adapted from data in *Congressional Quarterly Weekly Report,* December 21, 1996, 3463.

The President and the Congressional Party

Presidential power appears more awesome at a distance than it does at close range. Although the Constitution awards the president a number of formal powers—for example, the power to initiate treaties, to make certain appointments, and to veto legislation—his principal everyday power is simply the power to persuade. The president who opts for an active role in the legislative process, who attempts to persuade members of Congress to accept his leadership and his program, runs up against certain obstacles in the structure of American government. Foremost among these is the separation of powers. This arrangement of "separated institutions sharing powers" [40] not only divides the formal structure of government, thus creating independent centers of legislative and executive authority, but it also contributes to the fragmentation of the national parties. The perspectives of those elements of the party for whom the president speaks are not necessarily the same as

... in the Senate, 104th Congress, Second Session

Limited party loyalty		Limited party loyalty	
Democratic senators	Votes cast in opposition to own party majority	Republican senators	Votes cast in opposition to own party majority
Heflin (Ala.)	40%	Jeffords (Vt.)	41%
Nunn (Ga.)	37	Specter (Pa.)	36
Johnston (La.)	31	Chafee (R.I.)	36
Breaux (La.)	29	Hatfield (Ore.)	30
Baucus (Mont.)	27	Snowe (Maine)	28
Robb (Va.)	24	Cohen (Maine)	27
Lieberman (Conn.)	24	Campbell (Colo.)	16
Ford (Ky.)	21	Kassebaum (Kan.)	15
Exon (Neb.)	20	D'Amato (N.Y.)	13
Average Democratic senator	14	Average Republican senator	9

NOTE: Members are ranked according to their behavior on party unity votes, which are defined as those recorded votes that split the parties, with a majority of voting Democrats opposing a majority of voting Republicans. Failures to vote lower both party unity and opposition-to-party scores.

those for whom members of his congressional party speak. Policy that may suit one constituency may not suit another. Indeed, the chances are high that the presidential constituency and the constituencies of individual members of his party in Congress will differ in many important respects, thus making inevitable a certain amount of conflict between the branches.

Limits on Presidential Influence

The separation of powers is not the only constraint that faces the activist president who hopes to move Congress to adopt his program. The limited influence of party leaders on Congress, the insulation and independence of members that stem from the substantial staff and other office resources they enjoy,[41] the relative independence of committees and subcommittees, the difficulty of applying sanctions to wayward legislators, and the parochial cast in congressional perceptions of policy problems all converge to limit presidential influence. Moreover, electoral arrangements and electoral be-havior may make executive leadership difficult. Off-year elections are nearly always more damaging to the president's party than they are to the out party.[42] In off-year elections from 1926 to 1986, for example, the president's party gained seats in only one House election (1934) and in only three Sen-ate elections (1934, 1962, and 1970). Losses are often severe. The Demo-cratic party emerged from the 1966 election with forty-seven fewer seats in the House, and the Republican party lost forty-three House seats in the 1974 election. Following the first two years of the Reagan administration, the Re-publicans lost twenty-six seats in the House (while holding their margin in the Senate). In 1986 the Republicans lost eight seats in the Senate but only five in the House. In 1990, when many incumbents of both parties won by smaller margins than usual, Republicans suffered a loss of eight House seats and one Senate seat. In 1994 the Democratic party lost an extraordinary fifty-four seats in the House and ten in the Senate—the worst loss in any off-year election since 1946. Over the sixty-eight-year period from 1926 to 1994, the administration party had an average loss of thirty-one House seats in off-year elections. The president has every reason to fear the worst when these elections roll around; the next two years are certain to be more difficult.

Finally, the root of the president's legislative difficulties may lie with the voters themselves. The election that produces a president of one party may yield a Congress dominated by the other party or one with a different ideo-logical coloration. James Sundquist's analysis of John F. Kennedy's congres-sional miseries is informative:

> [It] is neither fair nor accurate to blame the failure of the Kennedy domes-tic program in the Eighty-seventh Congress primarily upon congressional organization or procedure—the power of the reformed House Rules Com-mittee, the seniority system, or any other of Congress' internal processes. The failure of Congress to enact the Kennedy program is chargeable, rather, to the simple fact that the voters who elected Kennedy did not send to Con-gress enough supporters of his program. His razor-thin popular majority was reflected in a Congress formally Democratic but actually narrowly bal-anced between activists and conservatives. If the machinery of both houses had been entirely controlled by supporters of the Kennedy program, that in itself would not have changed the convictions of the members so as to pro-duce a dependable administration majority. The machinery might have been used more effectively to coerce Democratic congressmen into voting in opposition to their convictions—but that is another matter.[43]

Conflict between the president and Congress is built into the system in the constitutional design of separation of powers and checks and balances. But there is more to it than that: Complex electoral politics also shape relations between the branches. Different coalitions form around offices. The coalition that elected Bill Clinton in 1996, for example, had a much different cast from the one that produced a Republican majority in the House of Representatives. A disproportionate number of Clinton voters were females (58 percent), African Americans/Hispanics (24 percent), white Catholics (32 percent), and people earning less than $50,000 annually (66 percent). The Republican House majority, by contrast, was elected by a coalition of males (53 percent), whites (92 percent), religious right (24 percent), and people earning more than $50,000 annually (44 percent). Additionally, the Clinton and Republican coalitions clashed on their views of the role of government: Sixty percent of the Clinton voters believed that government "should do more," and 73 percent of the voters who supported Republican House candidates believed that government "should do less." Optimism about life in the future also was reflected in the two coalitions: 75 percent of the Clinton voters held that life would be better contrasted with 60 percent of the Republican coalition who thought it would be worse.[44] With two different coalitions making claims on the executive and legislative branches, it would be altogether surprising if the relationships at key points were not contentious, conflictual, muddled, or reflective of some class concerns.

A measure of the legislative success enjoyed by presidents from 1953 to 1996 is presented in Figure 6-6. This analysis shows how frequently Congress voted in accordance with positions taken by each president during his administration. The highest rate of success of any of these eight presidents was achieved by Lyndon Johnson; in 1965 his position prevailed 93 percent of the time. The major reason for his success was undoubtedly that the Democratic party controlled both houses by such large margins that even the defections of southern members had minimal impact on outcomes. Ronald Reagan's 82 percent success rate in 1981 ranks third highest in the preceding thirty years. In the process of winning numerous legislative victories, Reagan received unusually strong support from Republican members in both houses, but especially in the Senate where his party held a majority. His overall party support scores were higher than those of any other president since 1953.[45] And, as expected, his support declined after the honeymoon period. During 1987 and 1988 Reagan's success rate slipped below 50 percent, a level lower than for any year of the Carter administration. It was more of the same for George Bush, whose success rate averaged only 51.8 percent over his term—the lowest score of any president since 1953.[46]

Overall, Bill Clinton was more successful in gaining congressional support for his proposals than his predecessor, Bush. During each of his first two years in office, when Democrats held a majority in both houses, he had an impressive 86 percent success score. But his third year in office, following the Republican takeover in the 1994 election, was a disaster. His legislative

FIGURE 6-6 Presidential Success on Legislative Votes: 1953 to 1996

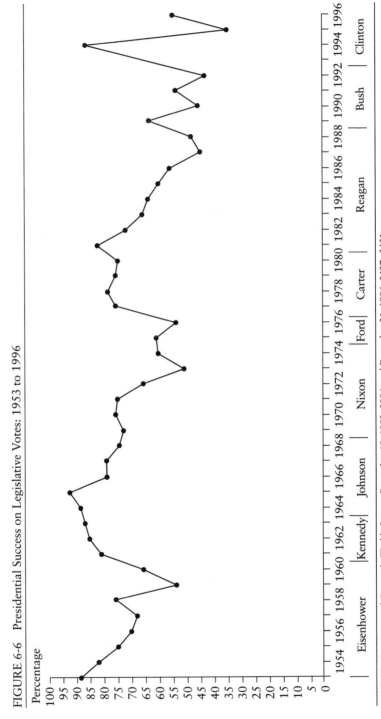

SOURCE: *Congressional Quarterly Weekly Report*, December 19, 1992, 3896; and December 21, 1996, 3427–3431.

success rate fell to 36 percent, the lowest score of any president since the *Congressional Quarterly* began its survey in 1953. In the last year of his first term, 1996, Clinton rebounded to 55 percent, winning a number of important concessions from a Republican majority weakened by the public's reaction to its role in shutting down the federal government in the winter of 1995–1996.

When the opposition party controls one or both houses of Congress, presidential influence is typically constrained. Republican presidents understand this better than anyone. The past five Republican presidents—Eisenhower, Nixon, Ford, Reagan, and Bush—were all confronted by this nagging reality. And of course Clinton's success rate fell dramatically when the Democrats became the minority party in the 104th Congress.

So many words have been written about the role of the president as chief legislator that it is easy to lose sight of the fact that members of Congress have power in their own right. Although in recent decades the initiative for generating legislation has shifted to the president, Congress remains one of the world's most powerful legislative bodies. A good many conditions are inimical to presidential domination of Congress. Congress may adopt what the president proposes but in the process may change the accent and scope. Sometimes it merely disposes of what he proposes. Nothing in the president's plans is inviolable. No certainty exists that Congress will share his perceptions or succumb to his influence. The careers of individual legislators are not tightly linked to the president's, except perhaps for those members from marginal districts, and even here the link is firm only when the president's popularity is high.[47] Indeed, some members of Congress have made their careers more secure through the visibility that comes from opposing the president and his program. Notwithstanding the worldwide trend toward executive supremacy, Congress remains a remarkably independent institution—a legislature almost as likely to resist executive initiatives as to embrace them.

The president and Congress get along as well as they do because of one element that the president and some members of Congress have in common: party affiliation. In substantial measure, party provides a frame of reference, an ideological underpinning, a rallying symbol, a structure for voting, and a language for testing and discussing ideas and policies. The member's constituency has never been the only valid criterion for assessing the wisdom of public policies. Legislators prefer to ride along with their party if it is at all possible, if the costs do not loom too large. Moreover, the president and his legislative leaders are not at liberty to strike out in any direction they feel may be immediately popular with the voters. They are constrained by party platforms, by previous policy commitments, by interest group involvement, and by the need to consult with party officials and members at all levels, particularly with those who compose the congressional wing. Consensus politics is the essence of party processes.

The President and Legislative Leaders

A study of majority party leadership in Congress indicates that the president and party leaders in Congress can structure their relations with one another in many ways. Typically, when the president and the majority leadership in Congress are of the same party and the president assumes the role of chief legislator, relations between the two branches have been characterized by cooperation. Within this pattern leaders tend to see themselves as lieutenants of the president, of necessity sensitive to his initiatives and responsible for his program. However, even though his party controls Congress, the president may decline to play a central role in the legislative process. In this situation, relations between the president and congressional leaders tend to be mixed and nonsupportive. Collegial rather than centralized leadership usually emerges as Congress generates its own legislative program instead of relying on presidential initiative. Finally, when the president and the majority in Congress (at least in one house) are of opposing parties (a so-called truncated majority), relations between the president and congressional leaders are often characterized by conflict and opposition. Leadership tends to be highly centralized, but legislative successes are usually few in number. "The leader of a truncated majority has great room for maneuver in the tactics of opposition and embarrassment on the domestic front, if his followers are willing to go along with him, but he must necessarily remain partially frustrated by his inability to accomplish much of his program domestically." [48]

David Truman has described the relationship between the president and the elective leaders of his congressional party as one of "functional interdependence." There are mutual advantages in this interdependence. The president needs information to make intelligent judgments, and the leaders can supply it. Moreover, they can offer him policy guidance. At the same time, the leaders can do their jobs better if bolstered by the initiatives and leverage of the president. They have no power to give orders. They can only bargain and negotiate, and their effectiveness in doing this, in notable measure, is tied to the president's prestige and political assets. [49] The nature of their jobs makes it important for the president's program to move through Congress. If the president wins, they win; if he loses, they lose. [50]

The Role of the Minority Party in Congress

A study by Charles O. Jones identifies a number of political conditions that individually and in combination help to shape the role the minority party plays in mobilizing congressional majorities and in shaping public policy. Some of these conditions originate outside Congress; others manifest themselves inside Congress. The principal external forces are the temper of the times (for example, the presence of a domestic or international crisis), the relative political strength of the minority party in the electorate, the degree of unity within the parties outside Congress, and the power of the president and his willingness to use the advantages inherent in his office. Conditions within Congress that affect minority party behavior are legislative procedures, the majority party's margin over the minority, the relative effectiveness of majority and minority party leadership, the time the party has been in a minority status (perhaps contributing to a minority party mentality), and the relative strength of the party in the other house.[51]

The important point to recognize about the behavior of the minority party is that the strategies open to it are determined not simply by the preferences of the leadership or the rank-and-file members, by idiosyncratic circumstances, or by opportunities thrust up from time to time. Rather, what it does is influenced to a significant extent by conditions of varying importance over which it has little or no control. By and large, the conditions most likely to affect the minority party's behavior and shape its strategies are, among the external group, party unity and presidential power, and among the internal group, the size of the margin and the effectiveness of party leaders in both parties. Although restrictive political conditions depress the range of alternatives available to the minority party, a resourceful minority leadership can occasionally overcome them, enabling the minority party to assume an aggressive, creative role in the legislative process. Among twentieth-century Congresses, however, this has been the exception, not the rule.[52]

The Party in Congress: Unfavorable Odds

It is as difficult to write about congressional parties without uncertainty as it is to pin a butterfly without first netting it. The party is hard to catch in a light that discloses all its qualities or its basic significance. Party is the organizing mechanism of Congress, and Congress could not do without it. It is hard to imagine how Congress could assemble itself for work, process the claims made on it, lend itself to majority coalition building, or be held accountable in any fashion without a wide range of party activities in its midst. Moreover, there are some sessions of Congress in which the only way to understand what Congress has done is to focus on the performance of the majority party. But that is only part of the story. In the critical area of policy formation, majority party control often slips away, to be replaced by enduring biparty alliances or coalitions of expediency. Party counts, but not predictably—hence the reason for the uncertainty in assessing the role of the congressional party.

Summary arguments may help to establish a perspective on the congressional parties. The indifferent success that sometimes characterizes party efforts in Congress is easy to explain. The odds are stacked against the party. In the first place, members of Congress are elected under a variety of conditions in a variety of constituencies: They are elected in environments where local party organizations are powerful and where they are weak; where populations are homogeneous and where they are heterogeneous; where competition is intense and where it is absent; where the level of voter education is high and where it is low; where income is high and where it is low; where one interest dominates and where many interests compete. The mix within congressional parties is a product of the mix within the nation's constituencies. It could scarcely be otherwise. The net result of diversity is that the men and women who make their way to Congress see the world in different ways, stress different values, and pursue different objectives. A vast amount of disagreement inevitably lurks behind each party's label.

In the second place, the salient fact in the life of legislators is their career. If they fail to protect it, no one else will. Representatives and senators know that their party can do very little to enhance their security in office and, conversely, very little to threaten it. As a member of Congress put it, "If we depended on the party organization to get elected, none of us would be here." [53] Members are on their own. Whether they are reelected or not depends more on the decisions they make than on those their party makes, more on how they cultivate their constituency than on how their party cultivates the nation, more on the credit they are able to claim for desirable governmental action than on the credit the party is able to claim,[54] more on the electoral coalition they put together or from which they are able to benefit than on the electoral coalition of their party. Although sweeping electoral tides may carry members out of office from time to time, individual members cannot do much about such movements. Hence, typical members concentrate on immediate problems. They take their constituency as it is; if they monitor and defend its interests carefully, they stand a good chance of having a long career in Congress, no matter what fate deals to their party.

The growing importance of party campaign expenditures on behalf of congressional candidates (so-called coordinated expenditures) may ultimately increase the members' dependence on the party and, accordingly, be reflected in their voting behavior in Congress. But there is little evidence now that members vote one way or another in response to party pressures linked to financial aid in campaigns. Parties are in business to win elections, and each prefers the election of its own mavericks to the election of loyal members of the opposition. The ability of members to attract interest-group contributions, moreover, gives them additional political space in which to maneuver, free from party controls. What those groups extract from the members is another question.

In the third place, party efforts are confounded by the fragmentation of power within Congress. Those who chair major committees and subcommittees are as likely to have keys to congressional power as are the elected party leaders. Committees go their separate ways, sometimes in harmony with the party leadership and sometimes not. Powerful committees are sometimes under the control of party elements that are out of step with the party's leadership in Congress and with national party goals. No power to command rests with the party leadership, and there is not a great deal it can do to bring into line those members who steadily defy the party and oppose its objectives. Two former members of the House comment on the problems that confront party leaders:

> In order for the Speaker to twist arms he has to have power, and we haven't recovered from the revolt against Uncle Joe Cannon which stripped power from a dictatorial Speaker nearly 65 years ago. (James O'Hara, D-Mich.)

> We Democrats are all under one tent. In any other country we'd be five splinter parties. Years ago we had patronage. [Now] the Speaker doesn't have any goodies to hand out. The President can promise judgeships, public works and fly [members] around in the airplanes. There's nothing like having the White House.[55] (Thomas P. ["Tip"] O'Neill, Jr., former Speaker of the House)

In addition, the party caucuses and the policy committees have never in any real sense functioned as policy-shaping agencies. "Parties" within parties, such as the House Democratic Study Group, bear witness to the lack of party agreement on public policy. Numerous specialized caucuses (steel, coal, textiles, cotton, sunbelt, New England, and the like) also contribute to the decentralization of power in Congress.

In the fourth place, the intricacies of the legislative process make it difficult for the parties to function smoothly and effectively. For the party to maintain firm control, it must create majorities at a number of stages in the legislative process: first in the standing committee, then on the floor, and last in the conference committee. In the House a majority will also be needed in the Rules Committee. Failure to achieve a majority at any stage is likely to mean the loss of legislation. Even those bills that pass through the obstacle course may be so sharply changed as to be scarcely recognizable by their sponsors. In contrast, the opponents of legislation have only one requirement: to splice together a majority at one stage in the decision-making process. Breaking the party leadership at some point in the chain may not require great resources or much imagination. For these reasons, the adoption of a new public policy is immeasurably more difficult than the preservation of an old one. All the advantages, it seems, rest with those legislators bent on preserving existing arrangements.

In the fifth place, the congressional party functions as it does because, by and large, it is a microcosm of the party in the electorate, beset by the same internal conflicts. The American political party is an extraordinary collection of diverse, conflicting interests and individuals brought together for the specific purpose of winning office. The coalition carefully put together to make a bid for power comes under heavy stress once the election is over and candidates have become officeholders. Differences ignored or minimized during the campaign soon come to the surface. Party claims become only one input among many the members consider in shaping their positions on policy questions. Not surprisingly, national party objectives may be disregarded as members sort out their own priorities and take account of those interests, including those of the local party organization, whose support may be essential to reelection.

The astonishing fact about the congressional parties is that they perform as well as they do. One reason for this is the phenomenon of party loyalty—typical members are more comfortable when they vote in league with their party colleagues than when they oppose them. Another reason is that most members within each party represent constituencies that are broadly comparable in makeup; in "voting their district" they are likely to be in harmony with the general thrust of their party. A third reason is found in the informal powers of the elected leaders. Members who respond to their leadership may be given assistance in advancing their pet legislation, awarded with an appointment to a prestigious committee, or armed with important information. There are advantages to getting along with the leadership. Lastly, presidential leadership seems to serve as a unifying force for the president's party in Congress. Members may not go along with the president gladly, but many of them do go along, and even those who do not give his requests more than a second thought.

Notes

1. For an analysis of the literature on congressional elections, see Peverill Squire, "Candidates, Money, and Voters—Assessing the State of Congressional Elections Research," *Political Research Quarterly* 48 (December 1995): 891–917.
2. Norman J. Ornstein, Thomas E. Mann, and Michael J. Malbin, *Vital Statistics*

on Congress, 1989–1990 (Washington, D.C.: Congressional Quarterly, 1990), 42, 52.

3. David R. Mayhew, *Congress: The Electoral Connection* (New Haven, Conn.: Yale University Press, 1974), especially 49–77. For a sampling of other studies that bear on the decline of competitive seats, see John C. McAdams and John R. Johannes, "Constituency Attentiveness in the House: 1977–1982," *Journal of Politics 47* (November 1985): 1108–1139; Glenn R. Parker and Suzanne L. Parker, "Correlates and Effects of Attention to District by U.S. House Members," *Legislative Studies Quarterly 10* (May 1985): 223–242; Albert D. Cover, "The Electoral Impact of Franked Congressional Mail," *Polity 17* (Summer 1985): 649–663; and Melissa P. Collie, "Incumbency, Electoral Safety, and Turnover in the House of Representatives, 1952–1976," *American Political Science Review 75* (March 1981): 119–131.

4. Lyn Ragsdale, "Incumbent Popularity, Challenger Invisibility, and Congressional Voters," *Legislative Studies Quarterly 6* (May 1981): 215. When accused of corruption, House incumbents and challengers are likely to be defeated 25 percent of the time, according to a study by Susan Welch and John R. Hibbing, "The Effects of Charges of Corruption on Voting Behavior in Congressional Elections, 1982–1990," *Journal of Politics 59* (February 1997): 226–239. Corruption allegations, in fact, play a significant role in congressional turnover.

5. See Gary C. Jacobson, "The Effects of Campaign Spending in Congressional Elections," *American Political Science Review 72* (June 1978): 469–491.

6. See Warren Lee Kostroski, "Party and Incumbency in Postwar Senate Elections," *American Political Science Review 67* (December 1973): 1213–1234; and Donald A. Gross and James C. Garrand, "The Vanishing Marginals, 1824–1980," *Journal of Politics 46* (February 1984): 224–237.

7. Gary C. Jacobson, "The Congressional Elections of 1996," in *1996 Elections: Toward a Republican Reign, Extension of Remarks,* ed. Burdett A. Loomis (January 1997): 2–4, 14.

8. *Congressional Quarterly Weekly Report,* April 15, 1978, 875–876.

9. *New York Times,* April 5, 1977. In discussing President Carter's many difficulties with Congress, Speaker O'Neill observed, "Maybe the President ought to go the route I go. I just come into a congressman's office and get down on bended knees." *U.S. News and World Report,* June 11, 1979, 17.

10. Randall B. Ripley, *Party Leaders in the House of Representatives* (Washington, D.C.: Brookings Institution, 1967), 23–24.

11. Joseph Cooper and David W. Brady, "Institutional Context and Leadership Style: The House from Cannon to Rayburn," *American Political Science Review 75* (June 1981): 417.

12. *Congressional Quarterly Weekly Report,* December 30, 1989, 3550.

13. "Leadership: An Interview with Senate Leader Lyndon Johnson," *U.S. News and World Report,* June 27, 1960, 88. See also Ralph K. Huitt, "Democratic Party Leadership in the Senate," *American Political Science Review 55* (June 1961): 333–344.

14. *Congressional Quarterly Weekly Report,* December 11, 1976, 3293.

15. *Congressional Quarterly Weekly Report,* June 10, 1989, 1377.

16. *Congressional Quarterly Weekly Report,* July 7, 1979, 1345.

17. "Leadership," 90.

18. *New York Times,* July 17, 1961, 11.
19. *Pittsburgh Press,* September 23, 1978.
20. *Congressional Quarterly Weekly Report,* September 4, 1982, 2181.
21. Barbara Sinclair, "Leadership Strategies in the Modern Congress," in *Congressional Politics,* ed. Christopher J. Deering (Chicago: Dorsey Press, 1989), 136.
22. Concerning the mediating role of the floor leader, see these studies: David B. Truman, *The Congressional Party* (New York: Wiley, 1959), 106–116 and 205–208; Barbara Hinckley, "Congressional Leadership Selection and Support: A Comparative Analysis," *Journal of Politics* 32 (May 1970): 268–287; and William E. Sullivan, "Criteria for Selecting Party Leadership in Congress," *American Politics Quarterly* 3 (January 1975): 25–44.
23. Burdett A. Loomis, *The New American Politician: Ambition, Entrepreneurship, and the Changing Face of Political Life* (New York: Basic Books, 1988), 175.
24. *Congressional Quarterly Weekly Report,* May 27, 1978, 1304.
25. Quoted in Loomis, *The New American Politician,* 177.
26. For a detailed study of this committee, see Charles O. Jones, *Party and Policy-Making: The House Republican Policy Committee* (New Brunswick, N.J.: Rutgers University Press, 1964).
27. Hugh A. Bone, "An Introduction to the Senate Policy Committees," *American Political Science Review* 50 (June 1956): 352. Also see Robert L. Peabody, *Leadership in Congress* (Boston: Little Brown, 1976), 337–338.
28. Among the studies to consult on this subject are Susan Webb Hammond, "Congressional Caucuses in the 104th Congress," in *Congress Reconsidered,* ed. Lawrence C. Dodd and Bruce I. Oppenheimer (Washington, D.C.: CQ Press, 1997): 274–292; Susan Webb Hammond, Daniel P. Mulhollan, and Arthur G. Stevens, Jr., "Informal Congressional Caucuses and Agenda Setting," *Western Political Quarterly* 38 (December 1985): 583–605; Arthur G. Stevens, Jr., Daniel P. Mulhollan, and Paul S. Rundquist, "U.S. Congressional Structure and Representation: The Role of Informal Groups," *Legislative Studies Quarterly* 6 (August 1981): 415–437; Burdett A. Loomis, "Congressional Caucuses and the Politics of Representation," in *Congress Reconsidered,* 2d ed., ed. Lawrence C. Dodd and Bruce I. Oppenheimer (Washington, D.C.: CQ Press, 1981), 204–220; Arthur G. Stevens, Jr., Arthur H. Miller, and Thomas E. Mann, "Mobilization of Liberal Strength in the House, 1955–1970: The Democratic Study Group," *American Political Science Review* 68 (June 1974): 667–681; and Kenneth Kofmehl, "The Institutionalization of a Voting Bloc," *Western Political Quarterly* 17 (June 1964): 256–272. Of related interest, see Barbara Sinclair, "State Party Delegations in the U.S. House of Representatives: A Comparative Study of Group Cohesion," *Journal of Politics* 34 (February 1972): 199–222; Richard Born, "Cue-Taking within State Party Delegations in the U.S. House of Representatives," *Journal of Politics* 38 (February 1976): 71–94; and Jeffrey E. Cohen and David C. Nice, "Changing Party Loyalty of State Delegations to the U.S. House of Representatives, 1953–1976," *Western Political Quarterly* 36 (June 1983): 312–325.
29. See Lewis A. Froman, Jr., and Randall B. Ripley, "Conditions for Party Leadership: The Case of the House Democrats," *American Political Science Review* 59 (March 1965): 52–63.
30. *Congressional Quarterly Weekly Report,* November 1, 1980, 3235.
31. Robert A. Bernstein finds an interesting association between House members' ideological deviation and support for their reelection. At the primary stage,

Democratic incumbents lose support for being too conservative, and Republicans, for being too liberal. In general elections, by contrast, Democratic incumbents lose support for being more liberal than their constituents prefer, whereas Republicans hurt themselves by being more conservative than their constituencies prefer. The net impact, in general elections, is that deviation (Democratic incumbents to the right of their constituencies' preferences, Republican incumbents to the left) tends to help reelection prospects. "Limited Ideological Accountability in House Races: The Conditioning Effect of Party," *American Politics Quarterly 20* (April 1992): 192–204.

32. See Edward V. Schneier's revised version of a classic study by Julius Turner, *Party and Constituency Pressures on Congress* (Baltimore, Md.: Johns Hopkins Press, 1970), especially Chapters 2 and 3, from which certain data in this paragraph were drawn. Also see *Congressional Quarterly Weekly Report,* January 16, 1988, 103.

33. *Congressional Quarterly Weekly Report,* December 21, 1996, 3462.

34. Samuel C. Patterson and Gregory A. Caldeira, "Party Voting in the United States Congress," *British Journal of Political Science 18* (January 1988): 111–131. The authors employ the "majority versus majority" concept of a party vote.

35. Mary Alice Nye, "Party Support in the House of Representatives: Generational Replacement, Seniority, or Member Conversion," *American Politics Quarterly 22* (April 1994): 175–189.

36. See an interesting study of the strong relationship between organized labor and congressional Democrats by Taylor E. Dark, "Organized Labor and the Congressional Democrats: Reconsidering the 1980s," *Political Science Quarterly 111* (Spring 1996): 83–104.

37. *Congressional Quarterly Weekly Report,* December 21, 1996, 3467.

38. For a study of the "northernization" of southern Democratic politics, see Stanley P. Berard, "Constituent Attitudes and Congressional Parties: Southern Democrats in the U.S. House, 1973–1992" (Ph.D. dissertation, University of Pittsburgh, 1994).

39. Richard Fleisher, "Explaining the Change in Roll-Call Behavior of Southern Democrats," *Journal of Politics 55* (May 1993): 327–341.

40. Richard E. Neustadt, *Presidential Power: The Politics of Leadership* (New York: Wiley, 1960), 33.

41. See a particularly instructive discussion of the insulation of members from party and committee controls in Loomis, *The New American Politician,* Chapter 6.

42. See a study by Jeffrey E. Cohen, Michael A. Krassa, and John A. Hamman that finds that, contrary to conventional wisdom, presidential campaigning in midterm Senate elections helps candidates in close races, particularly through the mobilization of voters: "The Impact of Presidential Campaigning on Midterm U.S. Senate Elections," *American Political Science Review 85* (March 1991): 165–178.

43. James Sundquist, *Politics and Policy: The Eisenhower, Kennedy, and Johnson Years* (Washington, D.C.: Brookings Institution, 1968), 478–479.

44. See an assortment of data on the parties' coalitions in the *Washington Post,* November 7, 1996.

45. *Congressional Quarterly Weekly Report,* January 2, 1982, 20–21.

46. *Congressional Quarterly Weekly Report,* December 19, 1992, 3841–3842.

47. There is additional evidence that a member's support for the president's policy proposals is influenced by how well the president ran in his or her district. In

essence, the stronger the president runs in the member's district, the more policy support he will receive from that member. Presidential elections thus do more than select winners; they help to shape support patterns in Congress for presidential initiatives. See George C. Edwards III, "Presidential Electoral Performance as a Source of Presidential Power," *American Journal of Political Science* 22 (February 1978): 152–168. For a recent study that finds that the president's coattails significantly help his party's Senate candidates (covering the years 1972–1988), see James E. Campbell and Joe A. Sumners, "Presidential Coattails in Senate Elections," *American Political Science Review 84* (June 1990): 513–524.

48. From Randall B. Ripley, *Majority Party Leadership in Congress* (Boston: Little, Brown, 1969), 175.

49. One little-appreciated way that presidents influence members of Congress is to time their announcements of federal projects that benefit members to coincide with presidential and congressional elections. John A. Hamman and Jeffrey E. Cohen, "Reelection and Congressional Support: Presidential Motives in Distributive Politics," *American Politics Quarterly 25* (January 1997): 56–74.

50. See Truman, *The Congressional Party,* especially 279–319. *The Congressional Party* is required reading for an understanding of the role of party in the contemporary Congress. Its central conclusions continue to ring true. To examine congressional parties from other perspectives, see these studies: Keith T. Poole and R. Steven Daniels, "Ideology, Party, and Voting in the U.S. Congress, 1959–1980," *American Political Science Review 79* (June 1985): 373–399; Sara Brandes Crook and John R. Hibbing, "Congressional Reform and Party Discipline: The Effects of Changes in the Seniority System on Party Loyalty in the U.S. House of Representatives," *British Journal of Political Science 15* (April 1985): 207–226; Ross K. Baker, "Party and Institutional Sanctions in the U.S. House: The Case of Congressman Gramm," *Legislative Studies Quarterly 10* (August 1985): 315–337; David W. Brady, "A Reevaluation of Realignments in American Politics: Evidence from the House of Representatives," *American Political Science Review 79* (March 1985): 28–49; Burdett A. Loomis, "Congressional Careers and Party Leadership in the Contemporary House of Representatives," *American Journal of Political Science 28* (February 1984): 180–202; David W. Brady and Barbara Sinclair, "Building Majorities for Policy Changes in the House of Representatives," *Journal of Politics 46* (November 1984): 1033–1060; Donald A. Gross, "Changing Patterns of Voting Agreement among Senatorial Leadership: 1947–1976," *Western Political Quarterly 37* (March 1984): 120–142; Jeffrey E. Cohen and David C. Nice, "Changing Party Loyalty of State Delegations to the U.S. House of Representatives, 1953–1976," *Western Political Quarterly 36* (June 1983): 312–325; Charles S. Bullock III and David W. Brady, "Party, Constituency, and Roll-Call Voting in the U.S. Senate," *Legislative Studies Quarterly 8* (February 1983): 29–43; Thomas H. Hammond and Jane M. Fraser, "Baselines for Evaluating Explanations of Coalition Behavior in Congress," *Journal of Politics 45* (August 1983): 635–656; Robert G. Brookshire and Dean F. Duncan III, "Congressional Career Patterns and Party Systems," *Legislative Studies Quarterly 8* (February 1983): 65–78; Richard A. Champagne, "Conditions for Realignment in the U.S. Senate, or What Makes the Steamroller Start?" *Legislative Studies Quarterly 8* (May 1983): 231–249; William R. Shaffer, "Party and Ideology in the U.S. House of Representatives," *Western Political Quarterly 35* (March 1982): 92–106; Thomas E. Cavanagh,

"The Dispersion of Authority in the House of Representatives," *Political Science Quarterly* 97 (Winter 1982–1983): 623–637; Walter J. Stone, "Electoral Change and Policy Representation in Congress," *British Journal of Political Science* 12 (January 1982): 95–115; and Patricia A. Hurley, "Predicting Policy Change in the House," *British Journal of Political Science* 12 (July 1982): 375–384.

51. Charles O. Jones, *The Minority Party in Congress* (Boston: Little, Brown, 1970), especially 9–24.

52. This study by Charles O. Jones identifies eight strategies open to the minority party in the overall task of building majorities in Congress: support of the majority party by contributing votes and possibly leadership, inconsequential opposition, withdrawal, cooperation, innovation, consequential partisan opposition, consequential constructive opposition, and participation (this strategy representing a situation in which the minority party controls the White House and thus is required to participate in constructing majorities). Strategies may vary within a single session of Congress and from one stage of the legislative process to the next. Jones, *The Minority Party in Congress,* 19–24 and Chapters 4–8.

53. Charles L. Clapp, *The Congressman: His Work as He Sees It* (Washington, D.C.: Brookings Institution, 1963), 30–31.

54. For an analysis of the "credit claiming" activities of members, see Mayhew, *Congress: The Electoral Connection,* 52–61. The basic assumption of this remarkable little book is that reelection to Congress is the singular goal of members, and the relentless pursuit of it steadily influences not only their behavior but also the structure and functioning of the institution itself.

55. *Washington Post,* June 17, 1975, 12.

Chapter Seven

The American Party System: Problems and Perspectives

Extolling the virtues of the American party system is something of an anomaly in popular commentary and scholarship. A few scholars have found merit in the party system, particularly in its contributions to unifying the nation, fostering political stability, reconciling social conflict, aggregating interests, and institutionalizing popular control of government. But the broad thrust in evaluations of this basic political institution has been heavily critical. American parties, various authors contend, are too much alike in their programs to afford voters a meaningful choice, are dominated by special interests, are unable to deal imaginatively with public problems, are beset by a confusion of purposes, are ineffective because of their internal divisions, are short on discipline and cohesion, are insufficiently responsive to popular claims and aspirations, and are deficient as instruments for assuming and achieving responsibility in government.

The Doctrine of Responsible Parties

The major ground for popular distress over the parties may be simply that most people are in some measure suspicious of politicians and their organizations. The criticism of scholars, meanwhile, has focused mainly on the lack of party responsibility in government. The most comprehensive statement on behalf of the doctrine of party responsibility is found in a report of the Committee on Political Parties of the American Political Science Association (APSA), *Toward a More Responsible Two-Party System*, published in 1950. The report, a classic document in political science, argues that what is required is a party system that is "democratic, responsible, and effective." In the words of the committee:

> Party responsibility means the responsibility of both parties to the general public, as enforced in elections. Party responsibility to the public, enforced in elections, implies that there be more than one party, for the public can hold a party responsible only if it has a choice. . . . When the parties lack the capacity to define their actions in terms of policies, they turn irresponsible because the electoral choice between the parties becomes devoid of meaning. . . . An effective party system requires, first, that the parties are able to bring forth programs to which they commit themselves and, second, that the parties possess sufficient internal cohesion to carry out these programs.[1]

Two major presumptions underlie the doctrine of responsible parties. The first is that the essence of democracy is to be found in popular control over government rather than in popular participation in the immediate tasks of government. A nation such as the United States is far too large and its government much too complex for most citizens to become steadily involved in its decision-making processes. But this fact does not rule out popular control over government. The direction of government can be controlled by the people only as long as they are consulted on public matters and possess the power to replace one set of rulers with another set, the "opposition." The party, in this view, becomes the instrument through which the public— or more precisely, a majority of the public—can decide who will run the government and for what purposes. Government by responsible parties is thus an expression of majority rule.

The second tenet in this theory holds that popular control over government requires that the public be given a choice between competing, unified parties capable of assuming collective responsibility to the public for the actions of government. A responsible party system would make three contributions. One, it "would enable the people to choose effectively a general program, a general direction for government to take, as embodied in a set of leaders committed to that program." Two, it would help to "energize and activate" public opinion. Three, it would increase the prospects for popular control by substituting the collective responsibility of an organized group, the party, for the individual responsibility assumed, more or less adequately, by individual officeholders.[2]

The responsible parties model proposed by the Committee on Political Parties is worth examining because it presents a sharp contrast to the contemporary party system. Disciplined and programmatic parties, offering clearer choices to voters, would replace the loose and inchoate institutions to which Americans are accustomed. The committee's report deals with national party organization, party platforms, congressional party organization, intraparty democracy, and nominations and elections.

National Party Organization

The national party organizations envisaged by the committee would be much different from those existing today. The national convention, for example, would be composed of not more than five hundred or six hundred members, more than half of whom would be elected by party voters. Ex officio members drawn from the ranks of the national committee, state party chairs, and congressional leaders, along with certain prominent party leaders outside the party organizations, would make up the balance of the convention membership. Instead of meeting every four years, the convention would assemble regularly at least once every two years and perhaps in special meetings. Reduced in size, more representative of the actual strength of the party in individual states, and meeting more frequently and for longer periods, the new convention would gain effectiveness as a deliberative body for the development of party policy and as a more representative assembly for reconciling the interests of various elements within the party.

The most far-reaching proposal for restructuring national party organization involves the creation of a party council of perhaps fifty members, composed of representatives from such units as the national committee, the congressional parties, the state committees, and the party's governors. Meeting regularly and often, the party council would examine problems of party management, prepare a preliminary draft of the party platform for submission to the national convention, interpret the platform adopted by the convention, screen and recommend candidates for congressional offices, consider possible presidential candidates, and advise such appropriate party organs as the national convention or national committee "with respect to conspicuous departures from general party decisions by state or local party organizations." Empowered in this fashion, the party council would represent a firm break with familiar and conventional arrangements that contribute to the dispersion of party authority and the elusiveness of party policy. The essence of the council's task would be to blend the interests of national, congressional, and state organizations to foster the development of an authentic national party, one capable of fashioning and implementing coherent strategies and policies.

Party Platforms

Party platforms, the report holds, are deficient on a number of counts. At times the platform "may be intentionally written in an ambiguous manner so as to attract voters of any persuasion and to offend as few voters as possible." State party platforms frequently espouse principles and policies in conflict with those of the national party. Congressional candidates and members of Congress may feel little obligation to support platform planks. No agency exists to interpret and apply the platform in the years between conventions. There is substantial confusion and difference of opinion over the binding quality of a platform—that is, whether party candidates are bound to observe the commitments presumably made in the adoption of the platform.

To put new life back into the party platform, the report recommends that it should be written every two years to take account of developing issues and to link it to congressional campaigns in off-year elections; that it should "emphasize general party principles and national issues" that "should be regarded as binding commitments on all candidates and officeholders of the party, national, state and local"; that state and local platforms "should be expected to conform to the national platform on matters of general party principle or on national policies"; and that the party council should take an active role in the platform-making process, both in preparing tentative drafts of the document in advance of the convention and in interpreting and applying the platform between conventions. In sum, the report argues that present party platforms and the processes through which they are formulated and implemented are inimical to the development of strong and responsible parties.

Congressional Party Organization

One of the most vexing problems in the effort to develop more responsible parties has been the performance of the congressional parties. The proliferation of leadership committees in Congress, the weakness of the caucus (or conference), the independence of congressional committees, and the seniority system have combined to limit possibilities for the parties to develop consistent and coherent legislative records. To tighten up congressional party organization would require a number of changes. First, each party in both the Senate and the House should consolidate its various leadership groups (for example, policy committees, committees on committees, House Rules Committee) into a single leadership group; its functions would be to manage legislative party affairs, submit policy proposals to the membership, draw up slates of committee assignments, and assume responsibility for scheduling legislation.

Second, more frequent meetings should be held by the party caucuses, their decisions to be binding on legislation involving the party's principles and programs. Moreover, members of Congress who ignore a caucus decision "should not expect to receive the same consideration in the assignment of committee posts or in the apportionment of patronage as those who have been loyal to party principles."

Third, the seniority system should be made to work in harmony with the party's responsibility for a legislative program. The report states,

> The problem is not one of abolishing seniority and then finding an alternative. It is one of mobilizing the power through which the party leadership can successfully use the seniority principle rather than have the seniority principle dominate Congress. . . . Advancement within a committee on the basis of seniority makes sense, other things being equal. But it is not playing the game fairly for party members who oppose the commitments in their party's platform to rely on seniority to carry them into committee chairmanships. Party leaders have compelling reason to prevent such a member from becoming chairman—and they are entirely free so to exert their influence.

Fourth, the assignment of members of Congress to committees should be a responsibility of the party leadership committees. "Personal competence and party loyalty should be valued more highly than seniority in assigning members to such major committees as those dealing with fiscal policy and foreign affairs." At the same time, the party caucus should review committee assignments at intervals of no more than two years. A greater measure of party control over committee assignments is essential if the party is to assume responsibility for a legislative program.

Fifth, party leaders should take over the function of scheduling legislation for floor consideration. In particular, the power of the House Rules Committee over legislative scheduling should be vested in the party leadership committee. If the party cannot control the flow of legislation to the floor and shape the agenda, there is little chance that it can control legislative output, which is the essence of responsible party performance in Congress.

Intraparty Democracy

The achievement of a system of responsible parties demands more than the good intentions of the public and of party leaders. It requires widespread and meaningful political participation by grassroots members of the party, democratic party processes, and an accountable leadership. According to the report:

> Capacity for internal agreement, democratically arrived at, is a critical test for a party. It is a critical test because when there is no such capacity, there is no capacity for positive action, and hence the party becomes a hollow pretense. It is a test which can be met only if the party machinery affords

the membership an opportunity to set the course of the party and to control those who speak for it. The test can be met fully only where the membership accepts responsibility for creative participation in shaping the party's program.

The task of developing an active party membership capable of creative participation in the affairs of the party is not easy. Organizational changes at both the summit and the base of the party hierarchy are required. "A national convention, broadly and directly representative of the rank and file of the party and meeting at least biennially, is essential to promote a sense of identity with the party throughout the membership as well as to settle internal differences fairly, harmoniously, and democratically." Similarly, at the grassroots level, local party groups need to be developed that will meet frequently to generate and discuss ideas concerning national issues and the national party program. The emergence and development of local, issue-oriented party groups can be facilitated by national party agencies engaged in education and publicity and willing to undertake the function of disseminating information and research findings.

A new concept of party membership is required—one that emphasizes "allegiance to a common program" rather than mere support of party candidates in elections. Its development might take this form:

> The existence of a national program, drafted at frequent intervals by a party convention both broadly representative and enjoying prestige, should make a great difference. It would prompt those who identify themselves as Republicans and Democrats to think in terms of support of that program, rather than in terms of personalities, patronage, and local matters. . . . Once machinery is established which gives the party member and his representative a share in framing the party's objectives, once there are safeguards against internal dictation by a few in positions of influence, members and representatives will feel readier to assume an obligation to support the program. Membership defined in these terms does not ask for mindless discipline enforced from above. It generates the self-discipline which stems from free identification with aims one helps to define.

Nominations and Elections

The report's recommendations for changing nomination and election procedures fit comfortably within its overall political formula for strengthening the American party system. It endorses the direct primary—"a useful weapon in the arsenal of intraparty democracy"—while expressing preference for the closed rather than the open version. The open primary is incompatible with the idea of a responsible party system, because permitting voters to shift from one party to the other between primaries subverts the concept of membership as the foundation of party organization. Preprimary meetings of party committees should be held for the purpose of proposing and endorsing candidates in primary elections. Delegates to the national conventions should be selected by the direct vote of party members instead of by state conventions. Local party groups should meet prior to the convention to discuss potential candidates and platform planks.

Three major changes should be made in the election system. First, the electoral college should be changed to give "all sections of the country a real voice in electing the president and the vice-president" and to help develop a two-party system in areas now dominated by one party. Second, the term of members of the House of Representatives should be extended from two to four years, with coinciding election of House members and the president. If this constitutional change were made, prospects would be improved for harmonizing executive and legislative power through the party. Third, the report recommends a variety of changes in the regulation of campaign finance, the most important of which calls for a measure of public financing of election campaigns.

The Promise of Responsible Parties

In the broadest sense, the publication of *Toward a More Responsible Two-Party System* was an outgrowth of increased uneasiness among many political scientists over the performance of the nation's party system and the vitality of American government. Specifically, the report sought to deal with a problem that is central to the overall political system: the weakness of political parties as instruments for governing in a democratic and responsible fashion. The report is not a study in political feasibility. It does not offer a blueprint depicting where the best opportunities lie for making changes in the party system. What it does offer is a set of wide-ranging prescriptions consonant with a particular model of political organization. If the model sketched by the committee were to come into existence, the American party system would bear only modest resemblance to that which has survived for well over a century. The key characteristics of the new parties would be the national quality of their organization, a much greater degree of centralization of party power, a tendency for party claims to assume primacy over individual constituency claims in public policy formation, heightened visibility of the congressional parties and their leadership and of the president as party leader, and a greater concern over party unity and discipline.

To its credit, the report was not accompanied by the usual somnolence that settles over prescriptive efforts of this kind. Nor, however, did queues of reformers form in the streets, in the universities, or elsewhere to push for its implementation. What occurred instead was that the report gave substantial impetus to the study of American political parties and helped to foster a concern for reform that, in one respect or another, continues to the present.

The goal of advocates of party responsibility is to place the parties at the creative center of policy making in the United States. That is what party responsibility is all about. Voters would choose between two disciplined and cohesive parties, each distinguished by relatively clear and consistent programs and policy orientations. Responsibility would be enforced through elections. Parties would be retained in power or removed from power depending on their performance and the attractiveness of their programs. Collective responsibility for the conduct of government would displace the individual responsibility of officeholders. Such are the key characteristics of the model party system.

How well responsible parties would mesh with the American political system is another matter.[3] Critics have contended that disciplined parties might contribute to an erosion of consensus, to heightened conflict between social classes, to the formation of splinter parties (and perhaps to a full-blown multiple-party system), and to the breakdown of federalism. Moreover, the voting behavior and attitudes of the American people would have to change markedly to accommodate the model of centralized parties, because many voters are more oriented to candidates than they are to parties or issues. The indifference of the public to the idea of programmatic parties would appear to be a major obstacle to rationalizing the party system along the lines of the responsible parties model.

Responsible Parties and Party Reform

The reform wave of the past three decades has produced a number of organizational and procedural changes in the American party system and in Congress. Perhaps as much by accident as by design, a surprising number of these changes are largely or fully compatible with the recommendations of the APSA report.

Intraparty Democracy

Consider the steps that have been taken to foster intraparty democracy. No feature of the reform movement of the Democratic party, beginning with the guidelines of the Commission on Party Structure and Delegate Selection (the McGovern–Fraser Commission), stands out more sharply than the commitment to make the party internally democratic and more responsive to its grassroots elements.

Commenting on the overall process by which delegates were selected to the 1968 convention, the McGovern–Fraser Commission[4] observed that "meaningful participation of Democratic voters in the choice of their presidential nominee was often difficult or costly, sometimes completely illusory, and, in not a few instances, impossible." For example, the commission found that (1) in nearly half the states, rules governing the selection process were either nonexistent or inadequate, "leaving the entire process to the discretion of a handful of party leaders"; (2) more than one-third of the convention delegates had, in effect, been chosen prior to 1968—well before all the possible presidential candidates were known and before President Johnson had withdrawn from the race; (3) "the imposition of the unit rule from the first to the final stage of the nominating process, the enforcement of binding instructions on delegates, and favorite-son candidacies were all devices used to force Democrats to vote against their stated presidential preferences"; (4) in primary, convention, and committee delegate selection systems, "majorities used their numerical superiority to deny delegate representation to the supporters of minority presidential candidates"; (5) procedural irregularities, such as secret caucuses, closed slate making, and proxy voting, were common in party conventions from the precinct to the state level; (6) the costs of participating in the delegate selection process, such as filing fees for entering primaries, were often excessive; and (7) certain population groups—in particular blacks, women, and youth—were substantially underrepresented among the delegates.

To eliminate these practices and conditions, the commission adopted a series of guidelines to regulate the selection of delegates for future conventions. Designed to permit all Democratic voters a "full, meaningful, and timely" opportunity to take part in the presidential nominating process, the guidelines set forth an extensive array of reforms to be implemented by state parties.

The initial step required of state Democratic parties was the adoption of a comprehensive set of rules governing the delegate selection process to which all rank-and-file Democrats would have access. Not only were these rules to make clear how all party members could participate in the process but they were also to be designed to facilitate their "maximum participation." In addition, certain procedural safeguards were specified. Proxy voting and the use of the unit rule were outlawed. Party committee meetings held for the purpose of selecting convention delegates were required to establish a quorum of no fewer than 40 percent of the members. Mandatory assessments of convention delegates were prohibited. Adequate public notice of all party meetings called to consider delegate selection was required, as were rules to provide for uniform times and dates of meetings.

The commission enjoined state parties to seek a broad base of support.

Standards eliminating all forms of discrimination against minority group members in the delegate selection process were required. To overcome the effects of past discrimination, moreover, each state was expected to include in its delegation blacks, women, and young people in numbers roughly proportionate to their presence in the state population.

A number of specific requirements for delegate selection were adopted by the commission. For example, delegates must be selected in a "timely manner" (within the calendar year in which the convention is held), alternates must be selected in the same manner as delegates, delegates must be apportioned within the state on the basis of a formula that gives equal weight to population and to Democratic strength, and at least 75 percent of the delegates must be selected at the congressional district level or lower (in states using the convention system). The number of delegates to be selected by a party state committee was limited to 10 percent of the total delegation.

One of the most remarkable aspects of this unprecedented action by the national party was the response of the state parties. They accepted the guidelines, altered or abandoned a variety of age-old practices and state laws, and selected their delegations through procedures more open than anyone thought possible. And with "maximum participation" in mind, they produced a convention whose composition—with its emphasis on demographic representation—was vastly different from any previous one.[5] Whether for good or ill, the Democratic party had by 1972 accepted the main tenets of intraparty democracy.[6]

No evidence exists, however, that party democratization has contributed to the development of a more responsible party system. Indeed, the reverse is probably true: The greater the degree of intraparty democracy, the harder it is to develop a coherent program of party policy.[7]

Strengthening the Congressional Parties

Reform, like conflict, is contagious. Essentially the same forces that produced major changes in the electoral structure of the Democratic party have produced major changes in the Democratic congressional party, particularly in the House. The thrust of these changes is in line with the theory of responsible parties. Advocates of this theory have sought not so much to promote the formation of a new party structure in Congress as to breathe new life into existing party structures and procedures. The changes have been impressive. Long dormant, the Democratic caucus became a more influential force in the House, particularly in controlling committee assignments and in shaping rules and procedures. At the opening of the Ninety-fourth Congress (1975–1976), the caucus removed three committee chairs from their positions, increased party control over the committee assignment process, brought the Rules Committee more firmly under the leadership of the Speaker, and established a requirement that the chairs of the appropriations subcommittees be ratified by the caucus. These were not stylized or marginal alterations. They should be seen for what they were: as systematically conceived efforts to reshape the power structure of Congress by diminishing the influence of senior leaders (who had often been out of step with a majority of the party) and augmenting the power of the party caucus and the leadership. There were other demonstrations of caucus power in the 1980s. At the outset of the Ninety-eighth Congress (1983–1984), the Democratic caucus voted to remove a southern party member from the Budget Committee because he had played a key role in fashioning President Reagan's budget strategy in the preceding Congress. Although party disciplinary action is not often taken, it can occur if the provocation is severe.

Similar developments have occurred in the Republican party. Supported by a cohesive party in the 104th Congress (1995–1996), Speaker Newt Gingrich ignored seniority in the selection of several committee chairs, named new members to the party's committee on committees (thus centralizing party control over assignments), directed an overhaul of the committee system that cut committee staffs and eliminated three standing committees, altered a variety of House procedures, and moved a "Contract with America" policy agenda through the House in the first one hundred days of the session. This interlude of responsible party government fell victim to the hubris of Republican leaders who shut down the government while trying to force President Clinton to accept their 1995 budget. With much of the public blaming their party for the debacle, and made anxious by an approaching election, many House Republicans abandoned the Speaker, sought accommodation with the president on a variety of policy fronts, forgot about the "contract," and focused on constituency business. As inevitable as anything in American legislative politics, leader-centered party government gave way to individual member preferences, including self-preservation.

Organization, Platforms, Nominations, and Elections

A potpourri of other recent reforms was anticipated by the APSA report on responsible parties. Among them were the reassertion of the national convention's authority over the national committee, the selection of convention delegates by direct vote of the rank and file, the allocation of national committee members on the basis of the actual strength of the party within the areas they represent, the use of closed primaries for the selection of convention delegates, the public financing of presidential elections, and the provision for holding a national party conference between national conventions.[8]

In sum, many of the reforms that have been introduced in the party structure and in Congress are consistent with recommendations carried in *Toward a More Responsible Two-Party System.* They touch far more than the outer edges of the party and congressional systems. Nevertheless, there is no reason to suppose that responsible party government is around the corner—that these reforms will somehow result in the institutionalization of a durable, highly centralized, and disciplined party system. Traditional moorings throughout the political environment make change of this magnitude all but impossible. And the current trends in American politics have done more to disable the parties than to strengthen them.

Trends in American Politics

Office holding in the United States is dominated by the two major parties. The vast majority of aspirants for public office carry on their campaigns under the banner of one or the other of the two major parties. The most important fact to be known about the candidates in a great many electoral jurisdictions throughout the country is the party to which they belong, so decisive is party affiliation for election outcomes. Virtually everywhere, save in nonpartisan environments, the trappings of party—symbols, sponsorship, slogans, buttons, and literature—are in evidence. The parties and their candidates collect money, spend money, and incur campaign deficits on a scale that dwarfs their budgets of a generation ago. Party bureaucracies are larger than in the past. More than two out of three citizens continue to see themselves as Democrats or Republicans, however imperfectly they may comprehend their party's program or the performance of their party's representatives. Party-based voting decisions are common in numerous jurisdictions. These signs of party vitality are largely misleading. Major problems confront the party system. Moreover, many of the key trends in contemporary politics are essentially antiparty in thrust.

The Loss of Power by Electoral Party Organizations

At virtually every point in the recruitment and election of public officials, the party organizations have suffered an erosion of power. The reasons are many and varied. At the top of the list, perhaps, is the direct primary. "He who can make the nominations is the owner of the party," E. E. Schattschneider wrote some years ago, and there is no reason to doubt his observation.[9] Given that nonendorsed candidates may defeat party nominees in primaries, one may wonder whether, in some elections and in some jurisdictions, anyone except the candidates really owns the parties. The party label has lost significance as candidates of all political colorations, with all variety of relationships to the organization, earn the right to wear it by capturing primary elections. Most important, a party that cannot control its nominations finds it difficult to achieve unity once it has won office and is faced with the implementation of its platform. Candidates who defeat the organization may see little reason to subscribe to party tenets, defend party interests, or follow party leaders. Not only does the primary contribute to the fragmentation of party unity in office but it also divides the party at large.

> Primaries often pit party leaders against party leaders, party voters against party voters, often opening deep and unhealing party wounds. They also dissipate party financial and personal resources. Party leadership usually finds that it has no choice but to take sides in a primary battle, the alternative being the possible triumph of the weaker candidate.[10]

The weakening of the parties is nowhere more apparent than in the domain of presidential campaign politics. The spread of presidential primaries and the opening up of caucuses introduced a participatory system that undermined the role of party leaders and organizations in the presidential nominating process. Candidates for the nomination touch bases with party leaders as much out of courtesy as out of need, and although leaders' endorsements may help, they are surely not critical. The introduction of public funding for presidential campaigns reduced the party's fund-raising role for the nation's highest office. And many believe that the typical national convention is a party conclave in name only. As Byron Shafer has observed, the Democratic reforms "restricted, and often removed, the regular party from the mechanics of presidential selection."[11] Additionally, in the election of the president, the linkage between party and outcome has no more than modest importance, if that.

Still other reasons may be adduced for the atrophy of the party's role in the electoral process. The great urban machines of a generation ago have practically disappeared. Employing an intricate system of rewards and incentives, the machines dominated the political process—controlling access to power, political careers, and, most important, votes. Their decline, for a number of reasons, has been accompanied by growing independence within the electorate and among politicians.

Electoral party organization is not particularly important in the political lives of today's self-reliant candidates. Some members of Congress, for example, have created their own political action committees (PACs) for electoral purposes. Virtually all of them not only campaign continuously, using all the resources of their office, but also have their own campaign operations (including staff aides assigned to the district) and reelection treasuries. John McCartney quotes a field representative of a California member of Congress:

I'm never through campaigning—except for one evening every two years. Election night there's no campaign. We have a victory party, I drink a lot of champagne, and I go home and go to bed. Next morning I begin campaigning all over again.[12]

Ambitious, issue-oriented, and media-conscious, the "new model" members of Congress exploit their office resources to the hilt in gaining publicity, advertising their names, and strengthening their reelection base. Some years before he became Speaker, Thomas S. Foley (D-Wash.) commented on the new style politician in Congress: "At worst, these guys say in effect, 'It doesn't matter. I am my own party,' [and] they emphasize their personal qualities." [13]

Finally, the easing of the party grip on the processes by which a person is recruited and elected to office is explained by a miscellany of reasons: the decline in the volume of patronage due to extension of the merit system, the decline in the attractiveness of patronage jobs, a better-educated electorate, the mobility of voters, the awesome costs of campaigns, the requirement for technical skills in the use of the mass media and in other innovative forms of campaigning, the emergence of the celebrity candidate, and the inability of the parties to capture the imagination and esteem of the voters.

The classic functions of party involve recruitment, nomination, and campaigning.[14] Today's parties are unable to dominate any of these activities, and often their impact is negligible. American politics in the media age is thoroughly candidate-centered. For most offices, major and minor, most of the time, candidates are on their own in making the decisions that count. No party organization or leadership tells them when to run, how to run, what to believe, what to say, or (once in office) how to vote. Candidates may tolerate party nudging on some matters while they welcome party money, technical assistance, and services. And they receive them, especially on the Republican side, where a well-developed national system is in place for raising funds and providing services to candidates and state party organizations. But it is unmistakably the candidates who decide what to make of their party membership and party connections—both in and out of government. And no one, including party leaders and party committees, can do much about it. In jurisdictions where American parties have more than ordinary importance, they are essentially facilitators, helping candidates who wear their label to do better what generally they would do in any case.

The Decline of Partisanship

One of the far-reaching changes in American politics during the modern era has been the decline of partisanship in the electorate. For many voters, party no longer carries much weight. Indeed, one third of all voters currently describe themselves as independents. Southerners have become decidedly more Republican and more independent than they were two or three decades ago. To be sure, not all voters who perceive themselves as independents actually behave as independents; some are undercover partisans who stay with the same party in most or all elections. Nonetheless, as the proportion of self-styled independents rises, problems mount for the maintenance of a vigorous party system. Independents in particular are attracted to third party or independent presidential candidates; in 1992, 30 percent of all independents voted for Ross Perot, greatly exceeding his national average of 18.9 percent. In 1996 independents gave Perot 16 percent of their vote, about twice his national average. The parties have been weakened all along the line, from the recruitment of candidates, through elections, to office holding. And the electoral prospects for the parties have become harder to forecast. To put it another way, voter independence is to party vitality what coalitional legislative voting is to party responsibility—a relationship of conspicuous incompatibility.

Every recent election attests to the "departisanization" of the electorate. In the 1986 House elections, a mere 8.4 percent of all voters said that the candidate's party was the most important factor in influencing their voting choice. The most important consideration was the candidate's character and experience, according to 41 percent of the sample. For 23 percent, state and local issues loomed most important. And of unusual interest, in this *national* election, only 20 percent reported basing their decision on *national issues*.[15] The stark fact is that personality factors and parochialism often dominate American elections.

The prevalence of ticket-splitting is further evidence of party decomposition. About two out of three people now cast split ballots in presidential elections, and in elections for local offices the proportion is even larger.[16] This behavior is not surprising because an overwhelming majority of the public believes that "the best rule in voting is to pick the best candidate, regardless of party label."[17] Ticket-splitting has major ramifications for the control of government, as can be seen in an examination of the vote for presidential and congressional candidates within congressional districts. Table 7-1 includes data on the number and percentage of congressional districts with split election results—districts won by the presidential candidate of one party and by the congressional candidate of the other party—from 1920 to 1996. The data depict a significant increase in split elections for these offices. A high point was reached in 1972, when 44 percent of all House districts split their results, due largely to the voters' rejection of George McGovern, the Democratic presidential nominee. The proportion of split results was almost as high in 1984 as voters everywhere voted for Ronald Reagan and Democratic House candidates. More split election outcomes occurred in the

TABLE 7-1   Congressional Districts with Split Election Results: Districts Carried by a Presidential Candidate of One Major Party and by a House Candidate of Other Major Party: 1920 to 1996

Year and party of the winning presidential candidate	Number of districts	Number of districts with split results	Percentage
1920 R	344	11	3.2
1924 R	356	42	11.8
1928 R	359	68	18.9
1932 D	355	50	14.1
1936 D	361	51	14.1
1940 D	362	53	14.6
1944 D	367	41	11.2
1948 D	422	90	21.3
1952 R	435	84	19.3
1956 R	435	130	29.9
1960 D	437	114	26.1
1964 D	435	145	33.3
1968 R	435	141	32.4
1972 R	435	193	44.4
1976 D	435	124	28.5
1980 R	435	141	32.4
1984 R	435	191	43.9
1988 R	435	148	34.0
1992 D	435	101	23.2
1996 D	435	111	25.5
Total	8,148	2,029	24.9

SOURCE: Milton C. Cummings, Jr., *Congressmen and the Electorate* (New York: Free Press, 1966), 32 (as updated).

NOTE: R = Republican; D = Democrat. Presidential returns for some congressional districts were not available between 1920 and 1948.

eight elections between 1968 and 1996 than in the twelve elections between 1920 and 1964. Party now provides less structure to voting, in the sense of shaping the choices of voters, than in the past.[18]

The data of Table 7-2 reflect two major features of contemporary American politics: massive split-ticket voting, on the one hand, and candidate-centered elections, on the other hand. Of the 279 congressional districts carried by Clinton in 1996, 91 were won by Republican House candidates. In

TABLE 7-2 Election Outcomes in Voting for President and House
Members in 1996: Party Unity and Party Splits
in 435 Congressional Districts

Winning candidates	Number of districts	Percentage
Dole and Republican House candidate	136	31
Dole and Democratic House candidate	19	5
Clinton and Democratic House candidate	188	43
Clinton and Republican House candidate	91	21

SOURCE: *Congressional Quarterly Weekly Report*, April 12, 1997, 859–862.

NOTE: An independent, Bernard Sanders of Vermont, was also reelected to the House.

another 19 districts, voters preferred a combination of Bob Dole and a Democratic House candidate.

Evidence that the party linkage between voters and government has atrophied can also be found in the contrast between presidential votes in the nineteenth and twentieth centuries. In the sixteen presidential elections from 1836 to 1896, only the election of 1872 was of landslide dimensions—that is, an election in which the winning candidate received 55 percent or more of the two-party vote. By contrast, eleven of twenty-five presidential elections from 1900 through 1996 were decided by landslide margins. Party switching from one election to the next has become increasingly common, and the party-oriented voter of the past century has been displaced by the volatile, candidate-oriented voter of this one. Consider the past several decades. Democrats by the millions deserted their party's presidential nominee in 1952, Adlai E. Stevenson, to vote for Republican Dwight D. Eisenhower. Similarly, Republicans in droves cast their ballots for Lyndon B. Johnson in 1964 instead of for Barry Goldwater, thus contributing substantially to the landslide Democratic vote. Even more massive switches occurred in 1968 and 1972. In the latter election, one third of all Democrats voted for the Republican presidential nominee, Richard Nixon. Even in 1976, an election in which party affiliation again surfaced, nearly one out of five Democratic identifiers voted for the GOP presidential candidate. A major reason for Ronald Reagan's victory in 1980 was that fully one fourth of all Democrats voted for him, and his support among Democrats was almost as great in 1984. Fifteen percent of all Democrats voted for George Bush in 1988. In 1992, in a three-way race, 29 percent of all Republicans and 24 percent of all Democrats failed to vote for their party's nominee. In another three-way race in 1996, 19 percent of all Republicans and 15 percent of all Democrats defected from their parties.

Departisanization of the electorate contributes significantly to the insularity of politics and elections. John R. Petrocik and Dwaine Marvick describe this nexus:

> State and local candidates find their fate almost unrelated to the success of the national ticket. With the decline in party loyalty among voters and the development of skills and resources that increase the individuality of any given candidate, only a notoriously weak national ticket seems able to influence congressional, state legislative, or city council elections.[19]

The Weakening of Group Attachments to the Democratic Party in Presidential Elections

Since Harry S. Truman's election in 1948, the Democratic party has won five of twelve presidential elections—in 1960 (Kennedy), 1964 (Johnson), 1976 (Carter), 1992 (Clinton), and 1996 (Clinton). Among the explanations for the party's modest success, two stand out. One is that Democratic presidential candidates have been rejected by independents. Between 1952 and 1988, the Democratic presidential candidate gained a majority of the independent vote only in 1964, a landslide Democratic year. Sixty-seven percent of independents voted for Reagan in 1984 and 57 percent for Bush in 1988.

But a more important reason is that the Democratic coalition, which began to take shape during the presidency of Franklin D. Roosevelt, has lost much of its potency. During its heydey, Democratic candidates became accustomed to receiving strong support from Catholics, southerners, blue-collar (especially union) workers, ethnic minorities, big-city dwellers, blacks, and young voters. The Reagan revolution in the 1980s altered the alignment of groups. The changes among Catholics, white southerners, and younger voters were particularly striking. In 1960 and 1964 about three out of four Catholics voted for John F. Kennedy and Lyndon Johnson. Support among Catholics for Jimmy Carter was also relatively high. But in all three elections of the 1980s, a majority of Catholic voters supported the Republican candidate. Younger voters also were drawn to the Republican candidates in the 1980s. Most decisive of all was the behavior of southern whites, once a mainstay of the Democratic coalition. They abandoned the Democratic party in droves. Only 28 percent voted for Walter Mondale in 1984 and only 33 percent for Michael Dukakis in 1988. Defections from the Democratic party became the norm.

The groups that remained staunchly Democratic in the 1980s were few. Heading the list was the black community. The black vote for Mondale and

Dukakis was about 90 percent. Also, about two out of three Jews, Hispanics, and unemployed persons voted for the Democratic candidates in 1984 and 1988.[20]

Republican support surged in the 1980s. Ronald Reagan received 72 percent of the vote of white Protestants in 1984, and George Bush received 66 percent in 1988. Bush gained an extraordinary 81 percent of the vote of born-again Christians; Reagan received 78 percent. In 1988 white Protestants and born-again Christians made up more than half of the voting public. Additionally, about two out of three upper-income voters ($50,000 and up) supported the Republican candidates in 1984 and 1988.[21]

The erosion of the Democratic coalition in the 1970s and 1980s, however, did not presage an endless stream of Republican victories. Despite his foreign policy successes and the nation's dramatic victory in the Gulf War, Bush's bid for reelection in 1992 was doomed by seemingly intractable problems of the domestic economy and the media's relentless dissemination of economic bad news. Convinced of the need for change, nearly two out of three voters opted for Bill Clinton or Ross Perot in the election.

For purposes of this analysis, the most interesting feature of Clinton's 1992 vote is how minimally it reflected the classic Democratic coalition. His support among Catholics was no better than his national average. His support among whites (87 percent of the electorate) was well under his national average, and among southern whites (24 percent of the electorate) he fared poorly. More than two out of three southern whites voted for Bush or Perot. Blue-collar workers gave Clinton a comfortable margin, but nothing like their support of Kennedy in 1960 (60 percent) or Johnson in 1964 (71 percent). Only among blacks (8 percent of the electorate), Jews (4 percent), and Hispanics (3 percent) did Clinton receive unusually strong backing.[22] Their votes were important in Clinton's victory, but he won because Republican identifiers in great number abandoned their party, because women voted for him in convincing numbers, and because independents (nearly 30 percent of the electorate) preferred him to Bush and Perot.

In broad lines, voting patterns in 1996 resembled those of 1992. In defeating Bob Dole, Bill Clinton reconstructed, to some extent, the old Democratic coalition, but without the South, which is now the most Republican section of the country. As he had in 1992, Clinton ran well among African Americans, Jews, Hispanics, persons of low income, persons of both limited education and postgraduate education, and women. Among larger groups, his most impressive gains were reflected in the vote of unmarried women (53 percent in 1992, 62 percent in 1996), Hispanics (61 percent, 72 percent), union households (55 percent, 60 percent), Catholics (44 percent, 53 percent), voters age 18 to 29 (43 percent, 52 percent), liberals (68 percent, 78 percent), and moderates (47 percent, 57 percent).[23] No evidence exists to suggest that Clinton's 1996 electoral support presages the reestablishment of the "classic" Democratic coalition. Party attachments are much less stable today. Moreover, the African American, Catholic, Jewish, and younger vote are less Democratic now than they were in the 1960s and earlier. And the union vote, strongly Democratic in 1996, is generally less cohesive and predictable. The reality is that Democratic candidates and strategists now have to be satisfied with less—that is, with simply "doing well," not "cleaning up," among traditional party following.

Whether a new, durable, and somewhat different Democratic coalition can be assembled for 2000 and beyond will depend on a number of factors, including how well the Clinton administration addresses nagging problems, how effectively Clinton balances the interests of liberals and moderates/conservatives in his party, how well he tends to the concerns of alienated voters, how wisely Republicans use their congressional majority, and how prospective candidates in both parties position themselves.

The Growth of Racial Polarization in Voting

Historically, the great divide in racial voting occurred in the 1960s, beginning with a massive shift by blacks in 1964 and continuing with a sizable shift by whites in 1968. In broad outline, this is what happened: Under the leadership of President Johnson, a bipartisan majority in Congress passed the Civil Rights Act of 1964, the most significant civil rights legislation since Reconstruction. The Republican National Convention shortly chose as its presidential nominee Barry Goldwater, a militant conservative, an exponent of states' rights, and one of the main opponents of the 1964 act. With the lines clearly drawn, blacks voted overwhelmingly (94 percent) for Johnson in November (see Table 7-3). Of the six states carried by Goldwater, five were in the Deep South, where his states' rights/civil rights stance undoubtedly was attractive to white voters. Following Johnson's landslide victory, a top-heavy Democratic Congress passed an even more important civil rights bill: the Voting Rights Act of 1965. This landmark legislation paved the way for blacks to enter fully into the nation's political life.

By 1968, as a result of movement by white voters, black–white voting divisions intensified; 85 percent of blacks but only 38 percent of whites voted Democratic. With a southerner, Jimmy Carter, at the head of the ticket in 1976, more whites (but less than a majority) voted Democratic than in either of the previous two elections. But this election was merely a blip—a modest exception to a profound trend. Today there are no signs that racial cleavages are ebbing, and the current split is quite sharp. In 1988 roughly more than eight out of ten blacks voted for Michael Dukakis, and six out of ten whites voted for George Bush. In a three-way race in 1992, more than

TABLE 7-3 Growing Racial Polarization in Voting in Presidential Elections

	1956	1960	1964	1968	1972	1976	1980	1984	1988	1992	1996
Percentage of electorate voting Democratic	42	50	61	43	38	50	41	41	46	43	49
Percentage of whites voting Democratic	41	49	59	38	32	46	36	34	41	40	43
Percentage of blacks voting Democratic	61	68	94	85	87	85	86	87	82	82	84
Racial differential: percentage-point difference between black and white Democratic vote	20	19	35	47	55	39	50	53	41	42	41

SOURCES: Developed from data in *Gallup Report*, November 1988, 6–7; *Gallup Poll Monthly*, November 1992, 9; 1996 national exit poll of Voter News Service.

eight out of ten blacks voted for Bill Clinton, and six out of ten whites voted for George Bush or Ross Perot. It was the same story in 1996, when more than eight out of ten African Americans voted for Clinton, and 55 percent of whites chose Bob Dole or Ross Perot. The division of the races along party lines, grounded in economic and social policies as well as civil rights, is one of the outstanding facts of contemporary American politics.[24]

The Escalation of Interest-group Activity

The growth in the number and influence of interest groups is one of the key developments in American politics in recent years. Members of Congress have become acutely sensitive to the power of lobbies. To quote former senator Abraham Ribicoff (D-Conn.): "Lobbying has reached a new dimension and is more effective than ever in history. It has become a big computerized operation in which the Congress and the public are being bombarded by single-issue groups."[25]

The increasing influence of interest groups has contributed to the weakening of the parties. Parties and interest groups compete for the same political space. When legislators are more concerned with satisfying interest-group claims than with supporting party positions and leaders, the vitality of legislative party organizations is sapped. When party lines collapse, collective responsibility for decisions is diminished. Increasingly, individual members are on their own, crowded and pressured by groups intent on getting their way. Rep. David R. Obey (D-Wis.) said, "It's a lot more difficult to say no to anybody because so many people have well-oiled mimeograph machines."[26] Or, in the grimly blunt words of Sen. Edward M. Kennedy (D-Mass.): "We have the best Congress money can buy. Congress is awash in contributions from special interests that expect something in return."[27]

For the past two decades the main controversy over interest groups has centered on their gifts to candidates for office. Recent contributions, unquestionably, have been sizable. PAC gifts to House and Senate candidates in 1988, for example, totaled $148 million. In the midst of a substantial increase in spending by congressional candidates in 1996, PAC contributions reached $201 million. PAC money accounted for 31 percent of the receipts for all House candidates and 16 percent for all Senate candidates; as usual, incumbents claimed the lion's share (66 percent) of it.[28] Surveys find that a large portion of the public now perceives campaign financing to be a corrupt system—one in which legislators are "bought and sold" and forced to compromise their independence to satisfy interest-group claims. Although the evidence of such favoritism is skimpy, the issue is likely to remain hot until Congress addresses the problem in major campaign-reform legislation. The chances that Congress will act to combat some of the worst abuses of campaign financing are perhaps better now than at any time in recent years—but still far from a certainty. Even if Congress decides to do something about questionable and unsavory campaign-finance practices, the "reforms" are likely to be viewed skeptically by many observers. Changes in public law affecting campaigns and elections are rarely neutral in their impact on candidates and parties.

Another dimension of the interest-group problem is that of single-issue groups.[29] Their issue is *the* issue; their position is the one on which legislators are to be judged. The compromises that occur naturally to practical politicians seldom carry much weight with the leaders of single-issue groups; members are either for or against gun control, abortion, tax reductions, equal rights, nuclear power, environmental safeguards, prayer in the public schools, or any of a number of other issues including certain foreign policies for which there are active domestic constituencies. Insistent groups gather on each side of each of these troublesome questions. Legislators do not find it easy to hide from such groups, especially because decision-making processes have opened up as a result of the reform wave of the 1970s.

Weakened parties provide slim protection for the harassed legislator in a free-for-all system. Middle-of-the-road politicians find themselves in trouble. Public service itself becomes increasingly frustrating in a politics of tiptoe and tightrope. Shortly before he was defeated for reelection in 1978, a northern Democratic senator observed,

> The single-interest constituencies have just about destroyed politics as I knew it. They've made it miserable to be in office—or to run for office—and left me feeling it's hardly worth the struggle to survive.[30]

The "special cause" quality of much of contemporary politics is also reflected in these comments by a leading official in Minnesota's Democratic-Farmer-Labor party:

> Frankly, there are very few of us in the party leadership now whose primary goal is the election of candidates committed to a broad liberal agenda. Most of the people in control are there to advance their own special causes. From the time we spend on it, you would think the most important problem in the world is whether there should be speedboats on six lakes in northern Minnesota.[31]

The arrival of narrow-issue politics has changed the American political landscape. Pragmatic politics has been diminished and compromise has declined as a way of doing business. In forming their positions on certain inflammatory, high-principle issues, members see a reduced margin for error. A wrong vote can cost them electoral support and produce new challenges to their reelection. And not in a few cases members believe they are

TABLE 7-4   Popular Trust in Government: 1972 to 1996

Question: How much of the time do you think you can trust the government in Washington to do what is right—just about always, most of the time, or only some of the time?

Response	1972	1974	1978	1980	1984	1988	1992	1996
Always	5%	3%	3%	2%	4%	4%	3%	3%
Most of the time	48	34	27	23	40	37	26	26
Some or none of the time	45	62	68	73	54	58	70	69
Don't know	2	1	2	2	2	1	1	2

SOURCE: National Election Studies, Center for Political Studies, University of Michigan.

faced with a no-win vote—where a vote on either side of a controversial, high-visibility issue appears likely to damage their electoral security.

The Public's Declining Confidence in Political Institutions

The confidence of the American public in its social and political institutions is substantially lower today than it was two or three decades ago. Nevertheless, it is not as low as it was in 1980.

Popular disillusionment concerning politics and political institutions did not emerge as a result of Watergate. The trend began earlier (see Table 7-4). The disclosures of criminal activities by White House officials, and Nixon's role in the coverup, merely accentuated it.

No simple explanation exists for the decline of trust in government. Many factors have been at work, probably the most important of which centers on public dissatisfaction with policy outcomes—including urban unrest and riots in the 1960s, the Vietnam War, and the government's inability to solve certain social and economic problems. In addition, the media's steady preoccupation with negative news, such as policies that go awry, and with skewering politicians, especially the president, have played a crucial, if unintended, role in the public's growing disenchantment with Washington and politics in general.

Whatever the explanation, many voters have a cynical view of government. Nearly eight out of ten people now believe, for example, that "government is pretty much run by a few big interests looking out for themselves." More than half of those surveyed agree that "public officials don't care much what people like me think" (Figure 7-1).

Interestingly, a 1996 survey finds almost no difference between voters

FIGURE 7-1   Evidence of Public Alienation from Government

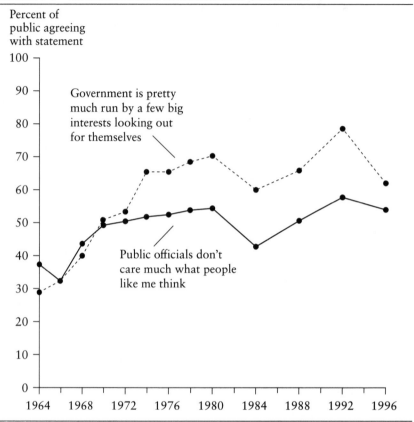

SOURCE: Data drawn from National Election Studies, Center for Political Studies, University of Michigan.

and nonvoters in the level of their mistrust of government. Neither has a benign view of Washington, and both are cynical about "the people running government."[32] Contrary to conventional wisdom, alienation appears to have no impact on turnout.

Declining trust in government has affected the party system. Though the evidence is elusive, the loosening of ties to party, the influx and successes of celebrity candidates, the preponderance of candidate-centered campaigns, the popular fascination with antiestablishment candidates, the apparent success of negative campaigns, and the preoccupation with party reform probably all bear a relationship to the depletion of popular good will toward government and to the generalized skepticism concerning political institutions.

Nothing about this condition of declining trust is immutable. Changes in political leadership, reorientations in governmental policies leading to amelioration or resolution of nagging problems, successful new policy ventures, and the more complete fulfillment of popular expectations could strengthen trust in government.

The Growing Importance of Professional Campaign Management Firms and the Media in Politics

American party organizations no longer dominate the process of winning political support for the candidates who run under their labels. The role of party organizations in campaigns has declined as professional management firms, pollsters, and media specialists—stirred by the prospects of new accounts and greater profits—have arrived on the political scene. Indeed, so important have they become in political campaigns, especially for major offices, that it often appears as if the party has been reduced to the role of spectator. To be sure, the parties continue to raise and spend money, to staff their headquarters with salaried personnel and volunteers, and to seek to turn out the vote on election day. What they do matters, but much less so than in the past.

The center of major political campaigns now lies in the decisions and activities of individual candidates and in their use of consultants, campaign management firms, and the mass media—not in the party organizations or in the decisions of party leaders. Modern political campaigning calls for resources and skills that the parties can furnish only in part (more so on the Republican than Democratic side). Public opinion surveys are needed to pinpoint important issues, to locate sources of support and opposition, and to learn how voters appraise the qualities of the candidate. Electronic data processing is useful in the analysis of voting behavior and for the simulation of campaign decisions. For a fee, candidates with sufficient financial resources can avail themselves of specialists of all kinds: in public relations, advertising, fund raising, communications, and financial counseling. They can hire experts in film making, speech writing, speech coaching, voter registration, direct-mail letter campaigns, computer information services, time buying (for radio and television), voter analysis, get-out-the-vote drives, campaign strategy, and "spinning" (interpreting) events and voter behavior. Fewer and fewer things are left to chance or to the vicissitudes of party administration. What a candidate hears, says, does, wears, and even thinks bears the heavy imprint of the specialist in campaign management.

Campaign consulting is a growth industry. Consultants whose candidates upset a favored opponent or win an overwhelming victory are celebrated by politicians and the media alike. They are hot commodities, and candidates vie to purchase their services. The right consultant appears to be the key to victory.

A seemingly endless variety of services are made available to candidates by management firms. The Campaign Communications Institute of America (CCI) has an arrangement under which a candidate low on cash can charge services on the American Express card. A glimpse of other services CCI provides may be gained from this account:

> Under a middleman arrangement with some 35 manufacturing and service firms, [CCI] has produced a swollen bag of personalized vote-getting tricks. There are the routine items—bumper stickers, buttons, litter bags, matchbooks, posters, and flags. But there is also a $19.95 tape-playing machine that enables the candidate to carry his inspirational messages into the homes of voters over the telephone. There are Hertz rental cars equipped with bullhorn sound systems. And there is a $39.95 portable projector that flashes slogans, pictures, and platforms on anything from a living-room wall to the side of an office building. "Our job," the board chairman of CCI has said, "is to enable the low-budget candidate to get the most votes for his bucks."

> For well-heeled candidates, CCI will also arrange mass telephone campaigns at a cent and a half a call, state-wide voter polls (sample prices: $4,000 for Vermont, $9,000 for New York) and direct campaigns through Western Union Services or New York's big Reuben H. Donnelly Corporation. . . . "Whenever and wherever people elect people, we'll be there," says the CCI board chairman. "That's our market." [33]

The coming of age of the mass media, technocracy, and the techniques of mass persuasion has had a marked impact on the political system.[34] The new politics is dominated by image makers and technical experts—organizations and persons who know what people want in their candidates and how to give it to them. Consider these views and prognoses for an issueless pseudopolitics:

> It is not surprising . . . that politicians and advertising men should have discovered one another. And, once they recognized that the citizen did not so much vote for a candidate as make a psychological purchase of him, not surprising that they began to work together. . . . Advertising agencies have tried openly to sell Presidents since 1952. When Dwight Eisenhower ran for reelection in 1956, the agency of Batton, Barton, Durstine and Osborn, which had been on a retainer throughout his first four years, accepted his campaign as a regular account. Leonard Hall, national Republican chairman, said: "You sell your candidates and your programs the way a business sells its products." [35]

> Day-by-day campaign reports spin on through regular newscasts and special reports. The candidates make their progress through engineered crowds, taking part in manufactured pseudo events, thrusting and parrying charges, projecting as much as they can, with the help of makeup and technology,

the qualities of youth, experience, sincerity, popularity, alertness, wisdom, and vigor. And television follows them, hungry for material that is new and sensational. The new campaign strategists also generate films that are like syrupy documentaries: special profiles of candidates, homey, bathed in soft light, resonant with stirring music, creating personality images such as few mortals could emulate.[36]

In all countries the party system has folded like the organization chart. Policies and issues are useless for election purposes, since they are too specialized and hot. The shaping of a candidate's integral image has taken the place of discussing conflicting points of view.[37]

[Party] organizations find themselves increasingly dependent on management and consultant personnel, pollsters, and image-makers. The professional campaigners, instead of being the handmaidens of our major political parties, are independent factors in American elections. Parties turn to professional technicians for advice on how to restructure their organizations, for information about their clienteles, for fund-raising, and for recruiting new members. Candidates, winning nominations in primaries with the aid of professional campaigners rather than that of political parties, are increasingly independent of partisan controls. The old politics does not rest well beside the new technology.[38]

If we get the visual that we want, it doesn't matter as much what words the networks use in commenting on it.[39]

If you're not on television, you don't exist.[40]

No matter what happens, the national political parties of the future will no longer be the same as in the past. Television has made the voter's home the campaign amphitheater, and opinion surveys have made it his polling booth. From this perspective, he has little regard for or need of a political party, at least as we have known it, to show him how to release the lever on Election Day.[41]

The Increasing Nationalization of Politics

So unobtrusively has the change come about that a great many American citizens are unaware of the extent to which sectional political alignments have been replaced by a national political alignment. The Republican vote in the South in the 1952 presidential election was, it turns out, more than a straw in the wind. Eisenhower carried four southern states, narrowly lost several others, made the Republican party respectable for many southern voters, and, most important, laid the foundation for the development of a viable Republican party throughout the South.

From the latter part of the nineteenth century until recently, the main obstacle to the nationalization of politics was the strength of the Democratic

TABLE 7-5   Republican Percentage of the Statewide Major-Party Vote
for the U.S. House of Representatives, Selected Years,
Southern States

State	Republican statewide percentage							
	1950	1952	1968	1978	1984	1988	1992	1996
Alabama	0.7	5.4	30.8	42.9	27.3	37.4	38.5	54.3
Arkansas	0.0	14.3	53.0	66.1	21.0	41.7	40.4	56.3
Florida	9.6	25.9	42.8	41.7	48.9	44.4	52.7	52.8
Georgia	0.0	0.0	20.5	32.6	28.3	33.3	45.1	56.8
Louisiana	0.0	8.7	18.8	50.0	*a*	*a*	*a*	*a*
Mississippi	0.0	2.5	7.5	36.9	38.5	33.6	28.9	54.2
North Carolina	30.0	32.2	45.4	35.9	47.6	44.2	48.3	51.6
South Carolina	0.0	2.0	32.8	37.6	48.4	44.4	53.5	66.5
Tennessee	30.3	29.8	51.1	47.3	44.8	38.9	45.5	50.8
Texas	9.5	1.3	28.1	40.6	42.3	40.3	48.8	56.2
Virginia	24.9	31.0	46.4	50.2	55.8	57.3	49.8	48.1

SOURCES: Developed from data in *The 1968 Elections* (Washington, D.C.: Republican National Committee, 1969), 115–116; and *Congressional Quarterly Weekly Report*, November 9, 1974, 3084–3091; November 11, 1978, 3283–3291; April 13, 1985, 689–695; November 8, 1986, 2864–2870; May 6, 1989, 1074–1080; April 17, 1993, 973–980; November 9, 1996, 3250–3257.

*a*In Louisiana, House candidates run on a nonpartisan ballot in the September primary. If no candidate receives a majority in the district, the top two (irrespective of party) face each other in November. Candidates who receive a majority in the primary are considered to be elected.

party in the South. Presidential, congressional, state, and local offices were won, as a matter of course, by the Democrats. No longer is this the case. Republicans now dominate presidential elections in the South. In the three elections of the 1980s, for example, among southern states only Georgia (in 1980) voted for the Democratic presidential candidate (Jimmy Carter, former governor of Georgia). In 1992 the Republicans won eight southern states (Alabama, Florida, Mississippi, North Carolina, Oklahoma, South Carolina, Texas, and Virginia) even though the Democrats offered an all-southern ticket in Bill Clinton (Arkansas) and Al Gore (Tennessee). In 1996 Clinton and Gore won only five southern states (Arkansas, Florida, Kentucky, Louisiana, and Tennessee).

Republican gains in southern congressional elections have been particularly impressive (see Table 7-5). The Republican statewide percentage of the vote for representative has grown more or less steadily since the 1950s. More than one third of all House members elected in the South from 1984 through 1996 were Republicans. Vigorous two-party competition occurs even in the states of the Deep South (Alabama, Georgia, Louisiana, Mississippi, and South Carolina). In the 1950s, by contrast, the Republican party rarely even nominated candidates for the House of Representatives in these states. And throughout the South Republican candidates for the Senate now compete with great success; following the 1996 election, for example, 69 percent of southern Senate seats were held by Republicans. A strong breeze of Republicanism has been coursing through southern electorates (see Table 7-6).

The movement from parochial to national politics has not been limited to the South. No matter what its history of party allegiance and voting, no state is wholly secure from incursions by the minority party. The vote in presidential elections[42] now tends to be distributed more or less evenly throughout the country; fewer and fewer states register overwhelming victories for one or the other of the major parties. One-party political systems dwindle. "It is probably safe to say that in national and state-wide politics we are in the time of the most intense, evenly-spaced, two-party competitiveness of the last 100 years."[43]

The sources for the growing nationalization of American politics are both numerous and varied. Social changes, rather than conscious party efforts to extend their spheres of influence, have provided the principal thrust for the new shape given to American party politics. Among the most important of these has been the emergence and extraordinary development of the mass media in political communications. Through the electronic media, national political figures can be created virtually overnight, national issues can be carried to the most remote and inaccessible community, and new styles and trends can become a matter of common knowledge in a matter of days or weeks. Insulation, old loyalties, and established patterns are difficult to maintain intact in the face of contemporary political communications. Consider these observations by Harvey Wheeler:

> Eisenhower was himself a newcomer to party politics. . . . He was heavily financed. He employed expensive and sophisticated mass media experts. "Madison Avenue" techniques were devised to project a predesigned "image." A new kind of electoral coalition was formed, composed largely of urban, white-collar people dissociated from the grass roots traditions of the agrarian past. His campaign cut across traditional party lines to orient itself about the personality of the candidate rather than the machine or the party. The new coalition of voter groups was socially and geographically mobile. The new politics required image manipulators rather than ballot box stuffers. The new organizations were ad hoc affairs created overnight by national cadres of advance men. The presidential primary overshadowed

TABLE 7-6   Republican Party Performance in Southern States: 1948 to 1996

	1948	1952	1984	1988	1992	1996
Presidential elections						
Percentage of two-party popular vote	36	49	63	59	43[b]	46[b]
Percentage of white popular vote	[a]	[a]	72	67	48	56
States won	0	5	13	13	8	8
Electoral votes won	0	65	155	155	116	96
Percentage of electoral votes	0	45	100	100	71	62
Congressional elections						
Percentage of House seats held following election	3	8	36	34	37	60
Percentage of Senate seats held following election	0	4	46	35	42	69
Gubernatorial elections						
Percentage of governorships held following election	0	0	15	46	23	69
State legislative elections						
Percentage of chambers controlled following election	0	0	0	0	0	23
Percentage of lower house seats held following election	5	6	24	27	30	39
Percentage of upper house seats held following election	4	5	19	23	30	40
Party identification						
Percentage Republican overall	[a]	[a]	36	34	34	35
Percentage of white southerners						
Strong Republicans	[a]	4	11	14	11	14
Weak Republicans	[a]	7	13	12	15	17
Independent Republicans	[a]	3	15	15	15	15

SOURCES: The data are drawn from a variety of sources, including *Congressional Quarterly Weekly Report, Statistical Abstract of the United States,* and *Gallup Opinion Index.* The data on the party identification of white southerners are from the Center for Political Studies, University of Michigan, some of which are reported in Raymond E. Wolfinger and Michael G. Hagen, "Republican Prospects: Southern Comfort," *Public Opinion 8* (October/November 1985): 9. Also see *Public Opinion 12* (January/February 1989): 34.

[a] Not available.
[b] This number is the Republican percentage of the three-candidate race in the South (including Perot). The South is defined as the states of the Confederacy plus Kentucky and Oklahoma.

the party convention. This was to be the wave of the future. Television truly nationalized campaign communications and undermined the federal structure of the old machines. Party politics gave way to personality politics.[44]

For all their importance to the changes under way, the electronic media have not by themselves transformed the face of American politics. Changes in technology, the diversification of the economic bases of the states, the growth of an affluent society, the higher educational attainments of voters, the mobility of the population, the migration of black citizens to the North, the enfranchisement of black citizens in the South, the illumination of massive nationwide problems, the growth of vast urban conglomerations, and the assimilation of immigrant groups have all contributed to the erosion of internal barriers and parochialism and, consequently, to the strengthening of national political patterns. Whatever the complete explanation for this phenomenon, one thing is clear: The forces for the nationalization of politics are far more powerful than the forces for localism and sectionalism. A changing party system is the inevitable result.

A Continuation of Party Competition Based on Meaningful Policy Differences between the Parties

The American parties are often criticized for being Tweedledum and Tweedledee—for being so similar that even attentive voters can miss the alternatives they present. This criticism has limited merit. Consider, first of all, the ideology and policy attitudes of Democratic and Republican elites—in this case, delegates to the 1996 party conventions (see Figure 7-2). Sixty-six percent of the Republican delegates described themselves as conservatives, as contrasted with a mere 5 percent of the Democratic delegates. At the other ideological pole, the differences are also striking: Liberals made up 43 percent of the Democratic delegates but were not to be found among the Republican delegates. Neither party elite, it should be emphasized, accurately reflected the ideological position of average party members: Democratic delegates were more liberal than the average registered Democrat, whereas Republican delegates were more conservative than the average registered Republican.[45]

Differences in ideological perception and in political philosophy translate into differences in public policy views and differences on the proper role of government. Democratic delegates to the 1996 party convention, for example, were much more likely then their Republican counterparts to agree with these propositions: that affirmative action programs should be continued, that government should do more to regulate the environment and safety practices of business and to do more to solve the nation's problems, that a

FIGURE 7-2 The Ideology of Democratic and Republican National Convention Delegates, 1996, Contrasted with the Ideology of Rank-and-File Democrats and Republicans

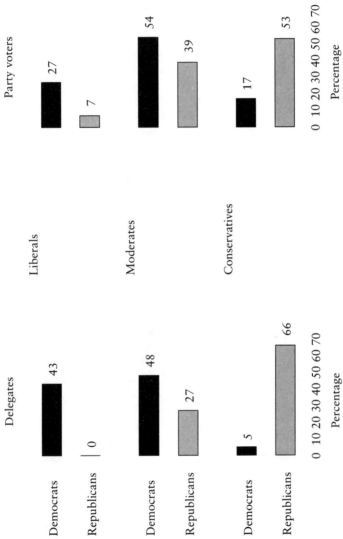

SOURCE: Adapted from *New York Times*/CBS News poll, published in the *New York Times*, August 26, 1996. A *Washington Post* survey of Democratic delegates found them to be somewhat less liberal than shown here; *Washington Post*, August 25, 1996.

NOTE: Ideological positions are based on self-classification. Party voters are self-identified Democrats and Republicans. Percentages may not add up to 100 because some respondents were unclassified.

nationwide ban on assault weapons should be instituted, and that laws to protect racial minorities are necessary. In addition, Democratic delegates were much more likely to be prochoice than Republican delegates, whereas Republican delegates were much more likely to believe that organized prayer should be permitted in public schools. The differences between the activists of the two parties are important and unmistakable; one set is clearly liberal, the other is clearly conservative.[46]

Party conflict in Congress also occurs along liberal–conservative lines. Over the years most Democratic members have supported labor-endorsed legislation, measures to provide for government regulation of business, social welfare bills of great variety, civil rights legislation, federal aid to education, and limitations on defense expenditures. By contrast, Republican members have generally favored business over labor, social welfare programs of more modest proportions, private action rather than government involvement, state rather than federal responsibility for domestic programs, the interests of higher-income groups over those of lower-income groups, and a greater emphasis on national defense. When viewing the economy, party members typically focus on different problems: Republicans are more concerned about inflation, Democrats more concerned about unemployment.[47]

Interest groups understand the relation between parties and policies as well as anyone and appreciate the genuine policy differences that separate the two parties in Congress. One way of supporting this proposition is to consult the ratings given members by prominent liberal and conservative groups. The data of Table 7-7 depict how four prominent organizations—two liberal and two conservative—scored House and Senate members in the 104th Congress (1995–1996). The distinctions are sharp. The average Democrat was ten to fifteen times as likely as the average Republican to vote in line with the positions of the Americans for Democratic Action or the AFL-CIO. In contrast, the average Republican was three to five times as likely as the average Democrat to share the policy stances of the Chamber of Commerce or the American Conservative Union. Those who believe that there is not "a dime's worth of difference" between the parties have not paid much attention to the preferences of the parties' congressional members on contemporary issues involving labor, business, social welfare, civil rights, and a variety of contentious social issues such as abortion and the death penalty.

The important point to recognize is that the parties' weaknesses—particularly apparent in the electoral process—have not clouded the ideological differences between their leaders. Meaningful differences separate the parties in Congress (or at least majorities of the two parties). Even larger differences divide the parties' national convention delegates. Quite plainly, Democratic

TABLE 7-7   Interest Group Ratings: Members' Agreement with Policy
Positions of Four Major Organizations, by Party,
104th Congress, First Session (in Percentages)

	Members' average score in agreement with group	
	House	Senate
Americans for Democratic Action		
Democrats	83	89
Republicans	7	8
AFL-CIO		
Democrats	91	92
Republicans	6	5
U.S. Chamber of Commerce		
Democrats	31	38
Republicans	94	93
American Conservative Union		
Democrats	17	9
Republicans	83	80

SOURCES: *ADA Today,* March 1996 (Washington, D.C.); *AFL-CIO Report on the 1995 U.S. Congress* (Washington, D.C., 1996); U.S. Chamber of Commerce, *1995 How They Voted* (Washington, D.C., 1996); American Conservative Union, *1995 Rating of Congress* (Alexandria, Va., 1996).

and Republican party elites do not evaluate public problems in the same light. Nor are they attracted to the same solutions.

Differences between the parties can also be examined from the perspective of the public. The survey data in Table 7-8 show the internal differences within the electoral parties as well as the broad differences between them. Obviously, neither party is monolithic, in the sense that its members share a common set of beliefs. On certain social issues, such as prayer in the public schools and abortions, certain Democratic and Republican subgroups share the same political space—one broadly defined in this Times Mirror study as intolerance for particular personal freedoms. Nevertheless, differences between the voters of the two parties appear to be more important. In their attitudes toward social justice, most Democratic partisans are easily distinguished from most Republican partisans. Democrats are aligned on the side of egalitarianism, social spending, the disadvantaged, and racial equality.

TABLE 7-8 Party in the Electorate: The Views of Democratic and Republican Voters on Major Social and Economic Issues

Position	Democratic groups				Republican groups	
	'60s Democrats	New Dealers	Passive poor	Partisan poor	Enterprisers	Moralists
Favor constitutional amendment to permit prayer in public schools	52%	83%	83%	81%	69%	88%
Favor mandatory drug testing for government employees	39	78	77	69	58	80
Favor changing laws to make it more difficult for a woman to get an abortion	26	54	47	38	40	60
Favor increased spending on programs that assist minorities	50	39	57	60	12	21
Favor death penalty	53	79	78	66	78	85
Favor cutbacks in defense and military spending	69	49	58	57	31	31
Favor increased spending on:						
programs for the homeless	77	73	82	83	38	62
programs for the unemployed	40	49	62	68	11	30
improving the nation's health care	76	80	85	84	42	68
improving the nation's public schools	80	70	77	77	56	65
aid to farmers	62	69	72	70	29	60
social security	62	76	81	85	29	57
programs for the elderly	79	84	84	87	44	71

SOURCE: Developed from data in *The People, the Press and Politics* (Los Angeles: Times Mirror, 1987), *passim.*

NOTE: '60s Democrats: well-educated, upper-middle class, tolerant on personal freedom issues, mainstream Democrats, committed to social justice. New Dealers: aging, traditional Democrats, blue collar, union members, less tolerant on personal freedom issues, moderate income. Passive poor: aging, poor, less well-educated, uncritical, disproportionately southern, committed to social justice. Partisan poor: firmly Democratic, very low income, poorly educated, urban, disproportionately black, concerned with social justice issues. Enterprisers: affluent, well educated, white, suburban, probusiness, antigovernment, tolerant on personal freedom issues. Moralists: middle-aged, middle income, white, disproportionately southern, suburban, small cities and rural areas, regular church-goers, anticommunist, prodefense.

They are much more likely than Republicans to favor increased spending on programs that assist minorities, the homeless, the unemployed, and the elderly. Republican voters tend to be dubious of big government, fiscally conservative, probusiness, anticommunist, and in favor of high defense spending. Divisions within Republican clusters are less serious than those found on the Democratic side. The profound point is that the policy views of the parties' adherents differ from one another in significant respects. Put another way, the parties do stand for something in the minds of many voters.

The public's images of the parties are more sharply developed than commonly supposed. A comprehensive study of likely voters by Donald C. Baumer and Howard J. Gold, covering the period 1976 to 1992, finds that roughly two thirds of the voters can articulate the dominant images of the parties. The Democratic party is viewed "as the party of inclusion and government spending" and the Republicans are viewed as "allies of the wealthy and opponents of government spending and intervention." Democrats are pictured by voters as "pro-common and working people," "pro-poor and needy people," "spenders," and "liberals." Republicans emerge as "pro-big business, rich, and upper-class" as well as "conservative."[48]

Still other evidence points to the public's sensitivity concerning party differences. Survey data presented in Table 7-9 shows the public's perceptions of the ideologies of the parties. Whatever else may be said, the public is not "clueless." Some of the fine points doubtlessly are missed by the general public, but the fact is that most voters are essentially accurate in their appraisals of the Democratic party as liberal, the Republican party as conservative. This perception of liberal–conservative differences between the parties is a classic distinction in American politics.[49] It is salient for many voters, helping them to organize political information, interpret political conflict, and evaluate candidates.[50]

An Era of Party and Governmental Reform

Ordinarily, changes in American politics do not come easily. No democratic political system anywhere rivals the American system for the number of opportunities to prevent or delay the resolution of public problems or the adoption of new forms and practices. American politics is slow politics. Nonetheless, in the current era many large-scale reforms have found their way into the party structure, into Congress, and into public policies that shape and regulate the political process. In the main, these changes took shape and were adopted during a time in which the political system was in substantial disarray. In the midst of an unpopular war, challenged on all sides, President Johnson withdrew from the presidential election campaign of 1968. Robert F. Kennedy was assassinated. The 1968 Democratic con-

TABLE 7-9   The Public's Perception of the Ideologies of the Parties
during the 1996 Presidential Campaign

Question: We hear a lot of talk these days about liberals and conservatives. Here
is a 7-point scale on which the political views that people might hold are arranged
from extremely liberal to extremely conservative. Where would you place the
Democratic party on this scale? The Republican party?

	Democratic	Republican
Extremely liberal	8%	2%
Liberal	28	4
Slightly liberal	24	7
Middle of road	17	14
Slightly conservative	9	22
Conservative	6	37
Extremely conservative	3	9
Don't know	5	5

SOURCE: National Election Study, Center for Political Studies, University of Michigan.

vention, meeting in Chicago, was an ordeal of rancor, tumult, and rioting.
And then came the Watergate affair—an assault on the political process itself. Public alienation from the political system, which had been building
for years, reached a high point. The stage was set for reform. Those who
brought it about owed their success to their ability to seize on these unusual
and transitory circumstances to develop new ways of carrying on political
business.

From almost any perspective, the changes were remarkable. More reforms were adopted between 1968 and 1974 than at any time since the early
nineteenth century.[51] The power of national party agencies to set standards
for state party participation in national nominating conventions was established—and the Supreme Court added its imprimatur to this development.
The first national party charter was adopted by the Democrats. At the state
level, presidential primary laws were adopted to broaden political participation, and caucus-convention systems were opened up—thus contributing
to the democratization of the nominating process. Nor was Congress im-
mune to change. The seniority system was modified by providing for secret
caucus ballots on nominees for committee chairs, thus increasing the re-
sponsiveness of these leaders to fellow party members. Committee power itself was dispersed as subcommittees and their chairs won new measures of
authority. The filibuster rule was revised, making it easier for a Senate ma-

jority to assert itself. The party caucus took on new roles and new vigor. To reduce the influence of private money and big contributors in political campaigns, the Federal Election Campaign Act was adopted, with its provision for public financing of presidential campaigns. In sum, numerous new choices and opportunities were presented to politicians and public alike.

For the most part, the party reforms of the modern period were designed to democratize political institutions and processes. Concretely, reformers set out to reduce the power of elites (that is, party leaders or "bosses") and to augment the power of ordinary citizens. And they were successful, at least on the surface. But as Nelson W. Polsby has shown, the reforms led to numerous other, unanticipated consequences, particularly on the Democratic side: State party organizations were weakened; party elites lost influence to media elites; candidate organizations came to dominate the presidential selection process; presidential candidates were encouraged to develop factionalist strategies (in seeking to differentiate their candidacies) rather than to build broad coalitions; and the national convention fell under the sway of candidate enthusiasts and interest-group delegates as its role in the presidential nominating process shifted from candidate selection to candidate ratification.[52] These changes are truly momentous.

In evaluating the party reforms, it is easy to lose sight of their relationship to the strength of American parties. As David B. Truman observed recently, the McGovern–Fraser Commission reforms "could not have been accomplished over the opposition of alert and vigorous state parties. The commission staff exploited the limitations and weaknesses of the state parties; they did not cause them."[53] The reforms, in other words, weakened an institution already in more than a little trouble.

Party reform is thus not the same as party strengthening. A more open political process, for example, does not necessarily contribute to the increased participation of the general public, to a heightening of political trust, or to popular acceptance of the parties. A demographically representative national convention, a central objective of the Democratic reforms, has not led to the selection of candidates who can best represent the party, unify it, or be elected. The public financing of presidential election campaigns has not by any means solved the problem of money in politics, as the spiraling costs of elections and the growing power of PACs show. Changes in party-committee relations in Congress have not altered congressional behavior in significant ways—Congress remains an institution whose members have an unusually low tolerance for hierarchy in any form. The adoption of a national party charter has not diminished the prevailing federalism of American politics or reduced the autonomy of state and local parties on most matters that count.[54]

The reform of the party system must therefore be taken with a grain of salt—for a reason obvious to anyone who began reading this book in advance of this page. American parties are to an important extent the dependent variable in the scheme of politics, more the products of their environment than the architects of it. The only governmental system the parties have known is Madisonian, marked by division of power and made to order for weak parties. Federalism, the separation of powers, and all manner of structural arrangements and election laws (for example, the direct primary, candidate-oriented campaign regulations, nonconcurrent terms for executive and legislature, nonpartisan elections, and staggered elections) militate against the development of strong parties. And by diminishing party control over the presidential nominating process, the reforms weakened the only national institution fully empowered to represent the party's constituent elements. The massive use of television for political campaigns, the increasing power of special-interest groups, and the arrival of public relations, media, survey, computer, and fund-raising experts also have contributed heavily to the current candidate-centered system that stresses personality over party and, frequently, style over substance. And for an American public that has never had much enthusiasm for parties, their current desuetude is not likely to be cause for popular concern.

A Growing Effort to Professionalize and Strengthen Party Organization

In this era of overall party decline, there is one bright spot: the increasing strength of parties in organizational terms. Evidence of professionalization and organizational strength is varied. It appears, for example, in the significant growth of permanent and professional party staffs at both national and state committee levels. The national committee's functions have been broadened and diversified, as the committee has shifted from an exclusive preoccupation with presidential matters. The Republican National Committee (RNC) has become heavily involved in a range of party-building activities that include serious efforts to promote party fortunes in state and local election campaigns. Operating budgets for the national committees have grown markedly. The capacity of the national parties to raise funds, particularly in direct-mail campaigns, has improved dramatically—in this respect, the Republican party again led the way, but the Democrats have been gaining ground. On the Democratic side, national party authority has been substantially enlarged through the development of rules for state party participation in national nominating conventions. Although the Democratic party has increased the legal authority of its national organization, the new importance of the national Republican apparatus has stemmed from successful fund raising that permits it to offer extensive services to state party organizations and candidates.[55]

The strength of state party organizations, a recent study finds, is partly a function of the party-building activities of the national party organization, leading to greater national-state party integration. The organizational strength of state parties appears in the form of services to candidates, staff size and complexity, newsletters and other communications, voter mobilization programs, public opinion polling, candidate recruitment, issue leadership, and money contributions to candidates. Many Republican state party organizations score high on these indicators. Virtually without exception, Democratic state organizations are substantially weaker than their Republican counterparts. Nonetheless, the weaker Democratic National Committee (DNC) seems to have had more success than the stronger RNC in adding to the capabilities of its state party organizations, perhaps because any addition of resources renders a weak organization more effective. For the most part, national–state party integration (or influence) is a one-way street, because most state parties rank low in the degree to which they are involved in (and thus influence) national committee affairs.[56]

The parties are becoming more professional. At the national level, their financial strength never has been greater. Staff development has been impressive. Through their staffs, the parties have become sophisticated in the use of modern campaign technologies that involve computers, electronic mail, television, marketing, advertising, survey research, data processing, and direct-mail solicitations. And of considerable interest, influence generally flows from the national level downward, a distinctly different pattern from the state-dominated party structure of the past.[57]

Intriguing to consider is whether the structural changes and other developments have arrested the parties' downward slide and strengthened their capacity to function as parties. Are they better able to discharge the traditional party functions of recruitment, nomination, campaign, and control of government? Specifically, how strong is party performance today in grooming and recruiting candidates, controlling nominations, managing campaign resources (money, manpower, expertise), electing candidates and controlling a range of offices simultaneously, mobilizing voters, stimulating competition, maintaining effective coalitions and inhibiting factional conflict, illuminating issues and fashioning policy alternatives, representing and integrating group interests, making public policy, enforcing discipline, providing public instruction, winning public acceptance and loyalty, and providing voters with a means for keeping government accountable? Exactly what a resurgence of the parties would consist of is hard to say, but it would seem to require them to conduct these activities, or at least most of them, reasonably well. National fund raising and provision of services aside, the reality is that the parties are unable to do most of these things any better than in the past. And in certain key respects the parties seem to be doing substantially worse.

In the old-fashioned sense of party organization as a network of individuals that does grassroots party work, as Byron Shafer observes, the parties are in "precipitous decline."[58] Unquestionably, the party-in-the-electorate has never been weaker.[59] Partisanship is at low ebb. Candidates and incumbents dominate the electoral system. Party coalitions, the quintessence of American parties, have atrophied. Control over nominations, the sine qua non of strong parties as E. E. Schattschneider and others have argued, is thin and insubstantial at all levels.[60] (In an ecumenical spirit, but only 5 to 4, the Supreme Court in 1986 opened the door for independents to vote in party primaries, if the parties approve.)[61] Split-election outcomes and divided government are the norm in nation and state. Party control over government continues to be uneven and unpredictable, and programmatic responsibility, which is occasionally impressive, is typically elusive and erratic. The influence of the media and interest groups in key phases of politics has probably never been greater. Indeed, in the presidential selection process, the media have simply supplanted the parties. The overall condition of American parties thus leaves a great deal to be desired. All things considered, and despite their heightened professionalism and enhanced bureaucratization, the parties are in about the same shape as observers have long known them—which is to say that, at best, they are no more than moderately successful in some of the things they do.

The Prospects

The American party system has been shaped more by custom and environment than by intent. Indeed, in broad contour, the parties of today resemble closely those of previous generations. For as long as can be remembered, the major parties have been loose and disorderly coalitions, heavily decentralized, lacking in unity and discipline, preoccupied with winning office, and no more than erratically responsible for the conduct of government and the formation of public policy. There is, of course, another side to them. They have performed at least as well as the parties of other democratic nations—and perhaps far better. Democratic politics requires the maintenance of a predictable legal system; institutionalized arrangements for popular control of government and the mobilization of majorities; methods and arenas for the illumination, crystallization, and reconciliation of conflict; and means for endowing both leaders and policies with legitimacy. To each of these requirements the parties have contributed steadily and often in major ways.[62]

A truism of American politics is that it is invariably difficult to cut free from familiar institutions. Old practices die hard. Conventional arrangements hang on and on. Change arrives incrementally and unnoticed. Most Americans are habituated to weak parties, and the parties themselves are accustomed to the environment in which they function. It would seem that prospects for the development of a system of responsible parties are thin at best. But the matter deserves a closer look.

On most counts the parties have lost ground in recent years. The electoral party organizations have been weakened. Their control over the nominating process, once a virtual monopoly, has gradually slipped away. Primary battles for major offices appear to occur more and more frequently. Increasingly, candidates use the party label "in the same spirit that ships sail under Liberian registry—a flag of convenience, and no more."[63] More voters have come to regard themselves as independents than ever before—occasionally independents are more numerous than Democrats or Republicans. The power of local party leaders probably never has been less than it is today. The media, public relations consultants, campaign management firms, and political action committees are now as much a part of campaigns as the party organizations—at least when important offices are at stake. So-called independent candidates seem to be more numerous and more successful than in the past. Popular dissatisfaction with the parties was so widespread in 1992 that Texas billionaire Ross Perot, running as an independent, won nearly one fifth of the presidential vote in a folksy and quirky campaign reduced essentially to peppery sound bites on the nation's ills. If nothing else, the Perot vote was a wake-up call for both major parties. His poor showing in 1996 may have put them back to sleep.

The sum of these developments is that American parties compete within the political process but do not dominate it. In some jurisdictions they are all but invisible. A great deal of contemporary politics lies outside the parties and beyond their control. Most troubling of all is that many voters profess deep skepticism of parties, politicians, and government.

The weakness of the parties makes the prospects dim for the development of a full-blown responsible party system. Too many obstacles—constitutional, political, and otherwise—stand in the way. But this is not to say that responsible party performance in government is unattainable. The way in which parties govern is not dependent on the strength and vitality of the electoral party organizations or on the way in which men and women are elected to office. The party-in-the-government, it is worth remembering, is both different from the party-in-the-electorate and largely independent of it.

The essence of a responsible party system is not to be found in party

What Would "Strong" Parties Look Like?

In the electorate:

1. Public perception of parties as legitimate and fair
2. Party electioneering, broad electoral appeal, and well-established "mainstream" constituencies
3. Sufficient power to limit fragmentation by keeping the nomination stage from becoming a free-for-all among numerous candidates
4. Sufficient resources (for example, money, manpower, expertise) to perform their functions adequately

In the government:

5. Power associated with responsibility: the capacity to govern through distinctive cooperation and cohesion among fellow partisans in the policy process

In electorate and government:

6. The presence of sufficient rewards and incentives to induce support and secure compliance among activists and officeholders
7. Capacity to limit disaffection and conflict among groups that compose the party coalition
8. Capacity to adapt in response to changes in the political environment

Do the parties meet these broad requirements? The answer is "hardly at all" in the case of 1, 2, 3, and 6 and "moderately at best" in the case of 4, 5, 7, and 8.

SOURCE: This is a modest adaptation of a list of attributes developed in David E. Price, *Bringing Back the Parties* (Washington, D.C.: CQ Press, 1984), 123.

councils, closed primaries, demographically representative national conventions, off-year party conventions, government financing of elections, or intraparty democracy. Instead, the key idea is party responsibility for a program of public policy. Such responsibility requires, in the first place, a strong measure of internal cohesion within the party-in-the-government in order to adopt its program and, in the second place, an electorate sufficiently sensitive to party accomplishments and failures that it can hold the parties accountable for their records, particularly in the case of the party in power. At times, neither requirement can be met to any degree. Nevertheless, occasionally American political institutions function in a manner largely consonant with the party responsibility model.

A responsible party system at the national level demands a particular kind of Congress—one in which power is centralized rather than dispersed. Over long stretches of time, Congress has not been organized to permit the parties, *qua* parties, to govern. The seniority system, the independence of committees and their chairs, the filibuster, the weaknesses present in elected party positions and agencies, and the unrepresentativeness of Congress itself have made it difficult for party majorities to assert themselves and to act in the name of the party. These barriers to party majority building have been notably diminished in recent years.

Every so often the congressional party comes fully alive. Consider the first session of the Eighty-ninth Congress (1965)—"the most dramatic illustration in a generation of the capacity of the president and the Congress to work together on important issues of public policy":

> In part a mopping up operation on an agenda fashioned at least in spirit by the New Deal, the work of the 89th Congress cut new paths through the frontier of qualitative issues: a beautification bill, a bill to create federal support for the arts and humanities, vast increases in federal aid to education. . . . [The] policy leadership and the legislative skill of President Johnson found a ready and supportive response from a strengthened partisan leadership and a substantial, presidentially oriented Democratic majority in both houses. A decade of incremental structural changes in the locus of power in both houses eased the President's task of consent-building and of legislative implementation. Yet Congress was far from being just a rubber stamp. On some issues the President met resounding defeat. On many issues, presidential recommendations were modified by excisions or additions—reflecting the power of particular committee chairmen, group interests, and bureaucratic pressures at odds with presidential perspectives.

> [The lessons of the Eighty-ninth Congress] proved that vigorous presidential leadership and sizable partisan majorities in both houses of the same partisan persuasion as the President could act in reasonable consonance, and with dispatch, in fashioning creative answers to major problems. The nation's voters could pin responsibility upon a national party for the legislative output. If that partisan majority erred in judgment, it could at least be held accountable in ensuing congressional and presidential elections.[64]

Party responsibility came to the fore again in the Ninety-seventh Congress (1981–1982). President Reagan was the beneficiary of the highest party support scores received by any president over the past three decades. His legislative proposals received unusually strong support in Congress. During the first session of the Ninety-seventh Congress, Senate Republicans voted in agreement with the president 80 percent of the time and House Republicans 68 percent of the time.[65] At session end, Republicans could reasonably claim that their party had moved the nation in a new direction. The major elements of their program consisted of major budget cuts, sizable reductions in individual and business taxes, the largest peacetime defense appropriation in the nation's history, a significant cutback in federal regulations, and a moderate reordering of federal–state relations that gave the states greater discretion in the use of funds provided through federal aid. Consonant with the party responsibility model, the performance of the Reagan administration was the overriding issue in the off-year election of 1982, in which Republicans lost twenty-six seats in the House while holding Democrats to a standoff in Senate races. In sum, presidential leadership, in concert with Republican congressional leaders and bolstered by party imagination and discipline, characterized the Ninety-seventh Congress (especially the first session) almost as much as it had the Eighty-ninth. From the perspective of the president, these were halcyon days, but they passed by quickly. Conflict between the branches intensified, the president's legislative successes declined, and legislative assertiveness during the latter stages of the Reagan administration, and particularly during the One-hundredth Congress (1987–1988), became manifest.

Government by party was conspicuously absent during the Bush administration. For one thing, the president's domestic agenda was limited. And second, both houses of Congress were controlled by the Democrats. Conflict between the parties increased in both houses over the course of Bush's term, reaching a near-record level during his last year in office; the president's success rate in Congress in 1992 was the lowest of any president in forty years. Few administration bills were passed, confrontations were frequent, and the president vetoed a number of major Democratic bills involving taxes, family planning, crime, campaign finance, fetal tissue research, cable TV, and trade with China. Low public opinion ratings further undermined the president's position. Toward the end of the Bush administration, "gridlock" vied with "morass" to become the most fashionable term to describe the state of Washington politics.

Control of the presidency and both houses of Congress by the Democrats in 1993 provided the first opportunity for authentic majority-party policy leadership in more than a decade. But getting the Democratic party to hang together did not come easily. President Clinton's major initiatives in his first year, including his deficit-reduction plan, were threatened by liberal–conservative conflict within his own party as well as by the concerted opposition of Republicans in both houses. One after another Clinton administration bill became a hostage to intraparty bargaining and deal-cutting for member, local, bloc, and regional advantages. Conflict between the parties was also at unusually high levels during the first three years of the

The Missing Link in the Party Responsibility Model: An Informed, Attentive Public

Do you happen to know which party had the most members in the House of Representatives in Washington before the election?

> Findings: 41 percent didn't know or selected the wrong party (Republican).

Do you happen to know which party had the most members in the U.S. Senate before the election?

> Findings: 46 percent didn't know or selected the wrong party (Republican).

Would you say that you have generally agreed with the way [your congressional representative] has voted on bills, agreed and disagreed about equally, generally disagreed, or haven't you paid much attention to this?

Agreed	17%
Agreed and disagreed about equally	13
Disagreed	3
Haven't paid much attention	67

SOURCE: These questions are drawn from the 1988 presidential election survey, National Election Study, Center for Political Studies, University of Michigan.

Clinton administration, and particularly in 1995, following the Republicans' off-year capture of both houses of Congress. More than 70 percent of all recorded floor votes were *party votes*—votes in which a majority of one party voted against a majority of the other party.[66] With the Democrats holding the presidency and the Republicans in control of Congress, little was accomplished. The government itself was shut down on two occasions, and the Republicans got most of the blame for the debacles. As the 1996 election approached and apprehension increased, both parties muted their partisanship, adopted more centrist positions, and cooperated to pass a number of major bills ranging from welfare to the minimum wage. The response of the voters to the bipartisan mood was to reelect Clinton by a comfortable margin (but short of a majority) and to return a (narrowed) Republican majority to Congress. (Many citizens simply stayed home, and turnout fell below 50 percent of the voting-age population.) Whether another spell of divided government in Clinton's second term would lead to confrontation and stalemate or renewed interparty cooperation and bipartisan deal making was anyone's guess. The reality is that when parties cannot bridge the gap between the branches, Washington politics becomes particularly unpredictable.

No one should expect party-oriented Congresses to be strung together, one following another. The conditions must be right: A partisan majority in general ideological agreement (or an effective majority, such as the Republican-led conservative coalition in the House during the Ninety-seventh Congress) and a vigorous president are essential. A long or innovative policy agenda may also be required. In any case, the point not to be missed is that, under the right circumstances, the deadlocks in American politics can be broken and the political system can function vigorously and with a high degree of cooperation between the branches of government. Party responsibility can thrive even if unrecognized and unlabeled. The evidence of these Congresses suggests that the first requirement for government by responsible parties—a fairly high degree of internal party agreement on policy—can, at least occasionally, be met.

The second requirement—an electorate attuned to party performance in government—is a different matter. This is the point at which the system of responsible parties tends to break down.

> What the public knows about the legislative records of the parties and of individual congressional candidates is a principal reason for the departure of American practice from an idealized conception of party government. . . . The electorate sees very little altogether of what goes on in the national legislature. Few judgments of legislative performance are associated with the parties, and much of the public is unaware even of which party has control of Congress. . . . Many of those who have commented on the lack of party discipline in Congress have assumed that the Congressman votes against his party because he is forced to by the demands of one of several hundred constituencies of a superlatively heterogeneous nation. In some cases, the Representative may subvert the proposals of his party because his constituency demands it. But a more reasonable interpretation over a broader range of issues is that the Congressman fails to see these proposals as part of a program on which the party—and he himself—will be judged at the polls, because he knows the constituency isn't looking.[67]

Experiments with forms of party responsibility, like fashion, will perhaps always possess a probationary quality—tried, neglected, forgotten, and rediscovered. The tone and mood of such a system will appear on occasion, but without the public's either anticipating it or recognizing it when it arrives. More generally, however, the party system is likely to resemble, at least in broad lines, the model to which Americans are adjusted and inured:

the parties situated precariously atop the political process, threatened and thwarted by a variety of competitors, unable to control their own nominations or to elect "their" nominees, active in fits and starts and often in hiding, beset by factional rifts, shunned or dismissed by countless voters (including many new ones), frustrated by the growing independence of voters, and moderately irresponsible. From the vantage point of both outsiders and insiders, the party system ordinarily will appear, to the extent that it registers at all, in disarray. And indeed it is in disarray—more so than at any time in the last century—but not to a point that either promises or ensures its enfeeblement and disintegration.

Notes

1. All of the proposals for reforming the party system cited in this section, along with quoted material, are drawn from the report of the Committee on Political Parties of the American Political Science Association, *Toward a More Responsible Two-Party System* (New York: Holt, Rinehart and Winston, 1950). The longer quotations appear on these pages of the report: 1, 2, 22 (definition of party responsibility), 61–62 (seniority), 66 (intraparty democracy), and 69–70 (party membership).
2. For a comprehensive development of the themes of this and the preceding paragraph, see Austin Ranney, *The Doctrine of Responsible Party Government* (Urbana: University of Illinois Press, 1954), 10–16.
3. There are a number of excellent analyses of party responsibility. See Austin Ranney, "Toward a More Responsible Two-Party System: A Commentary," *American Political Science Review* 45 (June 1951): 488–499; T. William Goodman, "How Much Political Party Centralization Do We Want?" *Journal of Politics* 13 (November 1951): 536–561; Evron M. Kirkpatrick, "Toward a More Responsible Two-Party System: Political Science, Policy Science, or Pseudo-Science?" *American Political Science Review* 65 (December 1971): 965–990; Gerald M. Pomper, "From Confusion to Clarity: Issues and American Voters, 1956–1968," *American Political Science Review* 66 (June 1972): 415–428; Michael Margolis, "From Confusion to Confusion: Issues and the American Voter (1956–1972)," *American Political Science Review* 71 (March 1977): 31–43; and David S. Broder, "The Case for Responsible Party Government," in *Parties and Elections in an Anti-Party Age,* ed. Jeff Fishel (Bloomington: Indiana University Press, 1978), 22–32.
4. The recommendations of the commission are found in *Mandate for Reform* (Washington, D.C.: Commission on Party Structure and Delegate Selection, Democratic National Committee, 1970).
5. The price of these reforms was high. Delegates of the new-enthusiast variety were far more numerous than party professionals. Moreover, the ideological cast of the delegates was markedly different—that is, much more liberal—from that of the general run of Democrats. And fewer delegates belonging to labor unions were present than is ordinarily the case. In some respects the new rules produced a most unrepresentative convention. The candidate it nominated, George Mc-

Govern, was overwhelmingly defeated in the election—a result in part to the defection of party moderates and conservatives. Ironically, though it was expected that the quota system for blacks, women, and youth would increase support among these groups in the election, nothing of the sort occurred. Blacks and youths supported the 1972 Democratic presidential candidate in about the same proportion as they did the 1968 candidate. Support among women voters declined notably. See Austin Ranney, *Curing the Mischiefs of Faction: Party Reform in America* (Berkeley: University of California Press, 1975), 153–156, 206–208.

6. To achieve a system of responsible parties, according to *Toward a More Responsible Two-Party System,* "The internal processes of the parties must be democratic, the party members must have an opportunity to participate in intraparty business, and the leaders must be accountable to the party." Committee on Political Parties of the American Political Science Association, *Toward a More Responsible Two-Party System,* 23.

7. See the analysis by Kenneth Janda, "Primrose Paths to Political Reform: 'Reforming' versus Strengthening American Parties," in *Paths to Political Reform,* ed. William J. Crotty (Lexington, Mass.: Heath, 1980), especially 319–327.

8. In addition, though tangential to this account, certain major recommendations of the report have been met through action by the federal government. A number of barriers to voting were eliminated as a result of the passage of the Voting Rights Act of 1965 and the adoption of the Twenty-sixth Amendment to the Constitution in 1971.

9. E. E. Schattschneider, *Party Government* (New York: Holt, Rinehart and Winston, 1942), 64.

10. Frank J. Sorauf, *Political Parties in the American System* (Boston: Little, Brown, 1964), 102.

11. Byron E. Shafer, *Quiet Revolution: The Struggle for the Democratic Party and the Shaping of Post-Reform Politics* (New York: Russell Sage Foundation, 1983), 529.

12. This quotation appears in Burdett A. Loomis, *The New American Politician: Ambition, Entrepreneurship, and the Changing Face of Political Life* (New York: Basic Books, 1988), 187.

13. Quoted by Loomis, *The New American Politician,* 10.

14. David B. Truman, "Party Reform, Party Atrophy, and Constitutional Change: Some Reflections," *Political Science Quarterly* 99 (Winter 1984–1985): 167.

15. These data are derived from a *New York Times*/CBS News poll, as reported in the *New York Times,* October 7, 1986.

16. See the *Public Perspective* (Roper Center), October/November 1996, 51 and Martin P. Wattenberg, *The Decline of American Political Parties, 1952–1994* (Cambridge, Mass.: Harvard University Press, 1996), 20.

17. See Jack Dennis, "Public Support for the Party System, 1964–1984" (Paper delivered at the annual meeting of the American Political Science Association, Washington, D.C., August 28–31, 1986), 19; and Wattenberg, *The Decline of American Political Parties,* 22.

18. See an analysis that finds ideology supplanting party as the primary structuring agent in presidential elections: George Rabinowitz, Paul-Henri Gurian, and Stuart Elaine Macdonald, "The Structure of Presidential Elections and the Process of Realignment, 1944 to 1980," *American Journal of Political Science* 28 (November 1984): 611–635.

19. John R. Petrocik and Dwaine Marvick, "Explaining Party Elite Transformation: Institutional Changes and Insurgent Politics," *Western Political Quarterly 36* (September 1983): 350.
20. See the exit interview data assembled by the *New York Times*/CBS News poll, as reported in the *New York Times,* November 10, 1988; and the ABC exit poll, as reported in the *Washington Post,* November 9, 1988.
21. *New York Times,* November 10, 1988.
22. *New York Times,* November 5, 1992.
23. Voter News Service 1996 exit poll.
24. For analysis of the voting patterns of blacks and whites, as well as other groups, see Harold W. Stanley and Richard G. Niemi, "Partisanship and Group Support, 1952–1988," *American Politics Quarterly 19* (April 1991): 189–210; Harold W. Stanley, William T. Bianco, and Richard G. Niemi, "Partisanship and Group Support over Time: A Multivariate Analysis," *American Political Science Review 80* (September 1986): 970–976; and Edward G. Carmines and James A. Stimson, "Racial Issues and the Structure of Mass Belief Systems," *Journal of Politics 44* (February 1982): 2–20.
25. *Time,* August 7, 1978, 15.
26. *Time,* January 29, 1979, 12.
27. *U.S. News and World Report,* January 29, 1979, 24.
28. Press release, Federal Election Commission, April 14, 1997.
29. See a discussion of single-issue and ideological PACs in William J. Crotty and Gary C. Jacobson, *American Parties in Decline* (Boston: Little, Brown, 1980), 117–155.
30. *Washington Post,* September 13, 1978. The comment was made by Sen. Wendell R. Anderson (D-Minn.) to columnist David S. Broder.
31. *Washington Post,* September 13, 1978.
32. The Mellman Group and Wirthlin Worldwide, *Analysis of A Survey on Nonvoting* (Washington, D.C.: The League of Women Voters, 1996).
33. *Newsweek,* April 29, 1968, 76. For a classic study of the public relations person in politics, see Stanley Kelley, Jr., *Professional Public Relations and Political Power* (Baltimore, Md.: Johns Hopkins Press, 1956).
34. See an analysis by Benjamin Ginsberg, "Money and Power: The New Political Economy of American Elections," in *The Political Economy,* ed. Thomas Ferguson and Joel Rogers (Armonk, N.Y.: M. E. Sharpe, 1984), 163–179.
35. Joe McGinniss, *The Selling of the President* (New York: Trident Press/Simon and Schuster, 1968), 27.
36. Robert MacNeil, *The People Machine: The Influence of Television on American Politics* (New York: Harper and Row, 1968), xvii.
37. Marshall McLuhan, as quoted by McGinniss, *The Selling of the President,* 28.
38. Dan Nimmo, *The Political Persuaders: The Techniques of Modern Election Campaigns* (Englewood Cliffs, N.J.: Prentice Hall, 1970), 197.
39. Comment by a Bush adviser quoted in *Time,* November 14, 1988, 66.
40. An unnamed gubernatorial candidate quoted by Barbara G. Salmore and Stephen A. Salmore, *Candidates, Parties, and Campaigns* (Washington, D.C.: CQ Press, 1989), 139.
41. Harold Mendelsohn and Irving Crespi, *Polls, Television, and the New Politics* (Scranton, Pa.: Chandler, 1970), 310–311.
42. The evidence of a recent study by Laura L. Vertz, John P. Frendreis, and James L. Gibson suggests that some offices are much more influenced by national forces

than others. They find that presidential elections have become nationalized and that congressional races remain localized. "[If] factors such as the *national* media are irrelevant to a race, as is usually the case with congressional elections, then the electorate responds to the more constituency-related, localized forces." "Nationalization of the Electorate in the United States," *American Political Science Review 81* (September 1987): 961–966 (quotation on p. 965).

43. Frank J. Sorauf, *Party Politics in America* (Boston: Little, Brown, 1980), 48.

44. Harvey Wheeler, "The End of the Two Party System," *Saturday Review*, November 2, 1968, 20.

45. These data on the 1992 national convention delegates are drawn from *Washington Post/*ABC News surveys; see issues of the *Post* dated July 12, 1992, and August 16, 1992.

46. See a study of party-switching among county-level activists in the 1988 presidential campaign by John A. Clark, John M. Bruce, John H. Kessel, and William G. Jacoby, "I'd Rather Switch than Fight: Lifelong Democrats and Converts to Republicanism among Campaign Activists," *American Journal of Political Science 35* (August 1991): 577–597. This study of elite realignment found that one third of the Republican leaders and one tenth of the Democratic leaders once considered themselves as members of the opposite party. Sharp policy differences distinguished the two groups of leaders. For interesting evidence that party leaders at the county level, in presidential elections, tend to be "true believers" (firmly committed to the enactment of certain policies), see John M. Bruce, John A. Clark, and John H. Kessel, "Advocacy Politics in Presidential Parties," *American Political Science Review 85* (December 1991): 1089–1105.

47. Concerning this point, see Edward R. Tufte, *Political Control of the Economy* (Princeton, N.J.: Princeton University Press, 1978), especially Chapter 4. See a study of presidential elections from 1948 through 1984 that finds that the *state of the economy* is an even better predictor of election outcomes than the *candidates' popularity* (or the voters' relative liking of them). Robert S. Erickson, "Economic Conditions and the Presidential Vote," *American Political Science Review 83* (June 1989): 567–573.

48. Donald C. Baumer and Howard J. Gold, "Party Images and the American Electorate," *American Politics Quarterly 23* (January 1995): 33–61.

49. For good evidence that Republican party activists in the South are substantially more conservative than their Democratic counterparts, see Harold D. Clarke, Frank B. Feigert, and Marianne C. Stewart, "Different Contents, Similar Packages: The Domestic Political Beliefs of Southern Local Party Activists," *Political Research Quarterly 48* (March 1995): 151–167.

50. Ronald B. Rapoport finds that popular and unpopular presidential candidates have a significant impact on voters' assessments of the parties. Parties find it hard to recover from the mistake of nominating an unpopular candidate. "Partisan Change in a Candidate-Centered Era," *Journal of Politics 59* (February 1997): 185–199.

51. Ranney, *Curing the Mischiefs of Faction*, 3.

52. For an elaboration of these themes, see Nelson W. Polsby, *Consequences of Party Reform* (Oxford, England: Oxford University Press, 1983), especially Chapter 2.

53. Truman, "Party Reform, Party Atrophy, and Constitutional Change: Some Reflections," 169.

54. Apart from its provisions concerning intraparty democracy, the Democratic party charter boasts very little that is new. The midterm party convention that

adopted the charter in 1974 rejected numerous provisions designed to centralize the party and to alter its federal character, including a dues-paying membership, a mandatory national party conference every other year, an independent national chairman elected for a four-year term (to reduce the presidential nominee's influence over the chairman), an elaborate regional party organization, and a strong national party executive committee. Few changes were made in the major organs of the party: the national convention, the national committee, and the office of the national chair. The vast majority of the compromises reached both prior to and during the convention were struck on the side of those who wanted to preserve a party system notable for its decentralization. See an interesting account of the convention's issues involving centralization versus decentralization by David S. Broder, *Washington Post,* December 1, 1974.

55. Cornelius P. Cotter and John F. Bibby, "Institutional Development of Parties and the Thesis of Party Decline," *Political Science Quarterly 95* (Spring 1980): 1–27. For a close analysis of the services made available to congressional candidates by national party committees, especially those of the Republican party, see Paul S. Herrnson, "Do Parties Make a Difference? The Role of Party Organizations in Congressional Elections," *Journal of Politics 48* (August 1986): 589–615.

56. Robert J. Huckshorn, James L. Gibson, Cornelius P. Cotter, and John F. Bibby, "Party Integration and Party Organizational Strength," *Journal of Politics 48* (November 1986): 976–991.

57. For the development of these and cognate themes that point to a political rebirth of the American party system, see Xandra Kayden and Eddie Mahe, Jr., *The Party Goes On: The Persistence of the Two-Party System in the United States* (New York: Basic Books, 1985). And also of interest, see Xandra Kayden, "The New Professionalism of the Oldest Party," *Public Opinion 8* (June/July 1985): 42–44, 49.

58. Byron E. Shafer, "The Democratic Party Salvation Industry," *Public Opinion 8* (June/July 1985): 47. And see the analysis of Michael Margolis and Raymond E. Owen, "From Organization to Personalism: A Note on the Transmogrification of the Local Political Party," *Polity 18* (Winter 1985): 313–328. For a finding that local parties have not become less active and less organized in the current era, see James L. Gibson, Cornelius P. Cotter, John F. Bibby, and Robert J. Huckshorn, "Whither the Local Parties?: A Cross-Sectional and Longitudinal Analysis of the Strength of Party Organizations," *American Journal of Political Science 29* (February 1985): 139–160. In addition, see Barbara C. Burrell, "Local Political Party Committees, Task Performance and Organizational Vitality," *Western Political Quarterly 39* (March 1986): 48–66.

59. No study documents and explains this better than Wattenberg, *The Decline of American Political Parties.*

60. E. E. Schattschneider, *Party Government,* 64 ff.

61. *Tashjian v. Republican Party of Connecticut,* 107 S. Ct. 544 (1986). Political scientists are divided on the *Tashjian* case. See an analysis by Leon D. Epstein, "Will American Political Parties Be Privatized?" *Journal of Law & Politics 5* (Winter 1989): 239–274.

62. To explore the literature that defends the American party system, see in particular Herbert Agar, *The Price of Union* (Boston: Houghton Mifflin, 1950); Pendleton Herring, *The Politics of Democracy* (New York: Norton, 1940); Arthur N. Holcombe, *Our More Perfect Union* (Cambridge, Mass.: Harvard University Press, 1950); and Edward C. Banfield, "In Defense of the American Party Sys-

315 The American Party System: Problems and Perspectives

tem," in *Political Parties, U.S.A.,* ed. Robert A. Goldwin (Chicago: Rand Mc-Nally, 1964), 21–39.

63. *Time,* November 20, 1978, 42.

64. Stephen K. Bailey, *Congress in the Seventies* (New York: St. Martin's Press, 1970), 102–103. Among the other major accomplishments of the first session of the Eighty-ninth Congress were the passage of bills to provide for medical care for the aged under Social Security, aid to depressed areas, the protection of voting rights, federal scholarships, the Teacher Corps, immigration reform, and a variety of programs to launch the War on Poverty.

65. *Congressional Quarterly Weekly Report,* January 2, 1982, 20–21.

66. *Congressional Quarterly Weekly Report,* Decemeber 21, 1996, 3432.

67. Donald E. Stokes and Warren E. Miller, "Party Government and the Saliency of Congress," in *Elections and the Political Order,* ed. Angus Campbell (New York: Wiley, 1966), 209–211.

Index